JUDGMENT DAY 2000!

How the Coming Worldwide Computer Crash Will Radically Change Your Life.

By

Richard D. Wiles

Treasure House

An Imprint of

Destiny Image® Publishers, Inc.

P.O. Box 310

Shippensburg, PA 17257-0310

*"For where your treasure is,
there will your heart be also."* Matthew 6:21

ISBN 1-56043-334-5

For Worldwide Distribution
Printed in the U.S.A.
This book and all other Destiny Image, Revival Press,
and Treasure House books are available
at Christian bookstores and distributors worldwide.
For a U.S. bookstore nearest you, call **1-800-722-6774.**
For more information on foreign distributors, call **717-532-3040.**
Or reach us on the Internet: **http://www.reapernet.com**

*Dedicated to
my wife, Susan,
and my daughter
and son, Karissa
and Jeremy.
Everything I do
is for you.*

*Acknowledgements*_____

I am deeply grateful to those brave, outspoken leaders who have been warning us for years about the dangers of Y2K. This book is written for the general public's understanding of a complex global problem. Without the diligent research and thoughtful analysis of many individuals in various fields of expertise, I would not have been able to compile and assimilate such a volume of research in so little time. As citizens, we owe these leaders a debt of gratitude for their foresight and persistence, in spite of being ignored or even ridiculed by society.

Research for this book has come from numerous sources. Those who deserve special recognition for their Y2K leadership include Dr. Gary North, Dr. Edward Yardeni, Ed Yourdon, Peter de Jager, Rick Cowles, Capers Jones, the Gartner Group, Cory Hamasaki, CBN's 700 Club, and Roleigh Martin.

A special thanks to my wife, Susan, who has endured piles of research in our home for months, and my "absence" during the writing of the manuscript. Also, my son and daughter, Jeremy and Karissa, for their assistance in helping to keep me organized.

Recognition should also be given to J. David Ford Associates in Hurst, TX, for their outstanding graphic design for the book cover, and for round-the-clock dedication in preparing the manuscript for printing.

Likewise, "thanks" to Destiny Image Publishers for boldly moving this book from a concept to finished product in a very short time.

Finally, my gratitude to Dr. Paul F. Crouch for graciously granting my request for a leave of absence from my position at Trinity Broadcasting Network to complete the manuscript. Without the time, it never would have been completed.

Table of Contents_____

Preface

This is not an End of the World book. There are no predictions about the return of Jesus Christ on January 1, 2000, or any other date. It is, however, a somber warning. I firmly believe the world is headed toward a global economic and technological meltdown. Instead of predicting the Rapture of the Church in the Year 2000, the book's premise is that divine chastisement of the nations is coming soon. For many years, Christians have declared, almost to the point of becoming a Charismatic cliché, that God will "shake everything that can be shaken." Well, the shaking is about to start. Soon, events will get out of control. Even the world's powerful leaders will tremble at the sudden and violent instability of the world's affairs. Everybody's life will be changed. Nobody will escape the ramifications of what is about to unfurl. You can, however, be protected. For those who have been marked by the Blood of Jesus Christ, there will be divine protection and provision. While this book deals with many facets of everyday life - such as the financial system, medical care, and government services - I have purposely avoided recommending strategies for personal survival through the coming storm. There are no instructions to buy a machine gun, move to Alaska, and build a bomb shelter. The most important step you can take is to prepare your heart and mind to be right with God. First, get your spiritual house in order. Then, be still - and God, himself, will instruct you in whatever necessary steps you should take to prepare for the days ahead. His instructions will be personal and unique to each family. He will instruct some people to move away, while others will be told to stay in their present location. Some will be told to sell off personal assets. Others will be instructed to change careers soon. Listen to the voice of the Holy Spirit. He will instruct you in all your ways. Time is quickly running out. If your life is not right with God, now is the time to stop sinning. The days ahead will be violent, turbulent, and frightening to those who do not have his mark. The safest place to be in the Year 2000 is as far under God's protective wings as you can get.

"Now I say that each believer should confess his sins to God when he is aware of them, while there is time to be forgiven. Judgment will not touch him if he does.

You are my hiding place from every storm of life; you even keep me from getting into trouble! You surround me with songs of victory. I will instruct you, says the Lord, and guide you along the best pathway for your life. I will advise you and watch your progress....Many sorrows come to the wicked, but abiding love surrounds those who trust in the Lord. So rejoice in him, all those who are his, and shout for joy, all those who try to obey him."

Psalms 32: 6-11

Introduction _____

New Year's Day 2000: The Worldwide Hangover

"The world will be at ease - banquets and parties and weddings - just as it was in Noah's time before the sudden coming of the flood; people wouldn't believe what was going to happen until the flood actually arrived and took them all away. So shall my coming be."

> *Jesus Christ*
> *Matthew 24: 38-39*
> *The Living Bible*

"December 31, 1999, will be a wild night," predicts Philip Bogdonoff, vice president of the Millennium Institute, a nonprofit group located just outside Washington, D.C.(1)

A wild night, indeed!

New Year's Eve 1999 will be the biggest party night ever in the history of the world.

The dawn of the Third Millennium will be celebrated around the globe by hundreds of millions of Earth's inhabitants. "One World. One Day. One Party," proclaims the headline in the Moscow News.(2) "It is clear that mankind is determined to throw one big party at the turn of the millennium - unprecedented in world history!," the Russian newspaper reported.

And what a party it will be!

For true jet setters, the party will last all night - in the air! Some of the world's elite will party all night aboard a super sonic Concorde jet chasing the dawn from time zone to time zone around the world. Other members of the world's rich and famous club will celebrate the New Millennium twice. First stop will be New Zealand's Chatham Islands where Britain's Royal Geographic Society has ruled the Third Millennium's first daylight will pass over the International Dateline. As New Zealand's twilight fades, these hearty globe trotting revelers will be whisked away by jet to Las Vegas, Nevada, where another rowdy New Year's Eve celebration will just be swinging into high gear.

Luxurious cruise ships will sail into the new millennium dawn too. The Silverseas cruise lines is offering discriminating world class travelers the opportunity to cross the International Dateline at midnight on New Year's Eve. The firm's two ships - the Silver Cloud and the Silver Wind

– are rated among the finest cruise ships in the world. And what a bargain! The lowest grade cabin is available at only $30,195 per person! The Grande Suite can be reserved for a mere $62,095. The price isn't so bad when you consider that both ships cross the International Dateline at midnight – meaning that you get two New Year's Eve parties for the price of one!

New York City, no amaturer when it comes to throwing a New Year's Eve bash, will hold its greatest party ever in Times Square. Knowing that the world's attention will be riveted on this momentous moment in mankind's history, New York City plans to party continuously for 24 hours. Celebrating Times Square's heritage as the Crossroads of the World, the city will salute the arrival of the Millennium in each of the world's 24 time zones. Beginning at 7 a.m. (EST) when the New Millennium breaks forth in the Fiji Islands, the city will celebrate the diverse cultures of nations in each of the world's time zones. Giant television screens will be placed in Times Square broadcasting images from parties from around the globe. Simultaneously, New York City's birthday bash will be televised around the world.

From continent to continent, small-town mayors and big-time prime ministers are busily preparing party plans for their once-in-a-lifetime opportunity to participate in the Millennial Madness. Great Britain's Tony Blair has no rivals when it comes to extravagance. The UK's new prime minister is leading the way to erect the Millennium Dome. Mr. Blair's $1.2 billion complex will occupy a 181-acre site on a peninsula on the Thames River. Although his government doesn't yet know what will go inside the Dome, there'll be plenty of room. At twice the size of the Georgia Dome in Atlanta, the Millennial Dome will hold up to 15,000 people.

"Millennia Parties" will unite most of the world's population on December 31, 1999. In Iceland, villagers will light bonfires. In Sri Lanka, citizens of Colombo will dance the night away at a gigantic beach party on the shores of the Indian Ocean. An adventurous group called the Millennium's First Sail Organization plans to usher in the next 1,000 years by bringing 2,000 boats to the International Dateline for a New Year's Eve "bluewater happening." Meanwhile, at the Vatican, the Pope will usher in the third millennium of Christianity with religious services that are expected to draw millions of pilgrims to Rome during the year 2000. Even tiny nations such as the Kingdom of Tonga and the Republic of Kiribati are pitching themselves to tourists as "the place to be" when the New Millennium arrives.

From quaint villages in the Swiss Alps, to the intersection of Hollywood and Vine in Los Angeles, together, the human race will herald the dawn of a New Age. An age of peace, prosperity, and world unity. A time to celebrate. This Mardi Gras mentality will move from New Zealand's Gisborne, advertised in travel publications as the first city in the world to see the millennial sun, to the bawdy bars of New Orleans' French Quarters. Around the planet, the night's revelry, drinking, eating, and lovemaking will have no equal in history. People will party like there's no tomorrow.

While the crowds flood into city streets around the world for the night's festivities, however, another group of people will be quietly making their exit.

Their exodus actually will begin days before Friday night, December 31, 1999. Only the most dedicated and hopeful will hold on to the very end. With all the hustle and bustle of the holiday season providing a convenient distraction from neighbors and coworkers, these people will pack their belongings into van lines and rented trucks. Some will just jam clothing and cherished personal belongings into the trunk and back seat of their automobile.

Bewildered wives will frantically question their suddenly panicked husbands. "What's wrong with you?," they'll cry out to their mates. "I've never seen you act like this before! Where are we going?"

Consider the plight of one such couple – Brad and Lisa.

At age 34, Brad has done well for himself. Hired four years ago as the IT manager for a fast-growing start-up biotech firm. Two years later, the company became a subsidiary of a Fortune 500 pharmaceutical firm. Brad moved quickly up the corporate ladder. Last year, he was named Chief Information Officer earning a comfortable $105,000 per year. Married with two children, Brad was looking forward to living the lifestyle he dreamed about as a boy.

His wife, Lisa, is a stunningly attractive 90's woman. Lisa has a blossoming career as an account executive at a prominent advertising agency in the city. Having just turned 31, Lisa enjoys the perks of her high-energy position. Meetings at top corporate headquarters. Luncheons with movers and shakers. Parties with the city's social elite. Her $62,000 base salary pales in comparison to her husband's paycheck, but Lisa's $46,000 bonus last year put her in the top five producers in the ad agency.

With their combined incomes, Brad and Lisa live in a very upscale condominium several blocks from the heart of the city. So many thirty-something yuppies live in the exclusive neighborhood. Sidewalk cafes, charming boutiques, and bountifully stocked bookstores line the streets near their condo. Definitely the "in" place to live.

As CIO, Brad has been working 60-hour weeks since the summer of 1998. The "Millennial Mess" – that's all Lisa knew was the culprit for seizing so many of her husband's hours away from her and the children. The last four months have been almost unbearable. Brad has worked countless hours. Sometimes spending the night at the office. Often irritable and exhausted, Brad has been under enormous pressure.

Despite Lisa's pleas to slow down, Brad only assured her, "I will, honey. After January 1. Until then, I've got to work. Please understand."

Clearly, Brad loves his job. He's the type of devoted manager that companies love to find. At a young age, however, Brad is showing signs of fatigue.

He hasn't been home for three days. Lisa is worried about Brad's health. His father had a heart attack at age 39. She wishes he would relax. The eve of the Third Millennium and he's still at work! With so many invitations to Millennia Parties all over the city, Lisa had planned to party all night! Now, she knew if Brad ever came home, he would be physically and mentally exhausted.

Of all the New Year's Eve parties, it was the city's official Third Millennium Birthday Bash that Lisa really wanted to attend. Through the forward-looking leadership of the mayor, the city spent over $42 million to stage one of the nation's grandest parties. The mayor mobilized the city's business and civic leaders to spend three years planning this once-in-a-lifetime extravaganza. A political supporter of the mayor, Lisa wanted to show her appreciation by being present for the gigantic outdoor event, held just 10 blocks from their condo. Tonight would be the crowning achievement of the mayor's legacy. Even the President of the United States was scheduled to address the crowd by satellite over six huge video screens erected in the City Square.

Finally, at 9:20 p.m., Lisa heard Brad unlocking the door. Deep furrows lined his forehead. A three-day beard covered his face. Dark circles surrounded his eyes. Her husband looked awful. Lisa met him at the door and kissed him. "I was so worried about you. You look terrible! You must be exhausted," Lisa consoled her husband.

"Pack our suitcases," Brad instructed her.

"What?," asked Lisa with apparent surprise. A cute grin shined on her face for a moment. Perhaps, she thought, Brad had secret plans, after all, for the New Year's Eve millennial celebration. "Where are we going at this hour?," Lisa asked.

"Just pack all our suitcases. As many clothes as you can pack. The children's clothes too. Hurry! We don't have much time!," Brad exclaimed.

The look in Brad's eyes told Lisa he didn't have plans for a secret trip to an exotic place to usher in the Third Millennium. This look was deeply troubling.

"Brad, what's wrong? Are you in trouble?," Lisa inquired with her green eyes fixed squarely on Brad.

"We're all in trouble! Lisa, just pack the suitcases! Now!," Brad shouted.

"Brad, I want an explanation!," Lisa retorted. "What is wrong with you tonight?"

Brad sighed and looked out their 22nd story window at the city lights below. At a distance, he could see the glow of the city's glorious celebration. He could see the streaming masses of citizens gathering in the city square. "This isn't happening," he mumbled. "This just can't be happening."

Lisa gently touched his shoulder. "What can't be happening?"

He sighed again. "They don't know what's coming tomorrow. Look at them! They're dancing and singing in the streets. What fools! Its over!"

"Brad, you're not making sense! What on earth are you talking about? Honey, I'm worried about you. You've been working too many hours for too many months," Lisa exclaimed.

"Lisa, look at me. Look in my eyes. What I'm about to tell you is the truth," Brad stated. "The computers will crash. In every city! In every nation! They're going down tonight!"

"Computers crash!," Lisa said with total shock. "You said the IT experts would fix the software bug. You said good old American ingenuity would solve the problem. Now you're saying computers around the world will crash tonight! Brad, I'm sorry. I don't understand."

"I thought we would solve it," Brad replied. "All of us in information technology have worked countless hours for the last two years. We gave it our best shot. But we just ran out of time. There's nothing more we can do. It is almost 10 p.m. It's over."

Sensing her mounting fear, Brad put his arms around his wife and held her tight. "We're going to make it. We'll start over."

"Start over?," Lisa asked with a puzzled look.

"We're leaving this city now. While we still have a chance," Brad whispered in her ear.

Lisa broke out in tears. "Brad, you're scaring me. Stop it! Stop it!"

"I can't deal with this, Brad. This isn't happening!," Lisa sobbed.

"Trust me," her husband replied. "Just trust me!"

"There's no time to argue! We've got to get out of this city now!," Brad emphatically declared.

"Why? Why won't you tell me what's going on?," Lisa asked with a frightened look.

"Because it's going down. The whole stinking system is going down!"

Seeing genuine fear in her husbands' eyes for the first time in their marriage, Lisa demanded to know the truth. "What's going down? I want to know the truth!"

Knowing that the nightmare was about to become real, Brad began to explain to his wife what he has known for a year - but didn't want to discuss. As professionals, Brad and his IT team did their best. From the time their employer discovered the problem in 1997, they worked long, hard hours to prevent the unthinkable from happening.

Now, it's too late. It's over. There just isn't any time left. All Brad can do is think of his family's safety and security first.

"The electric supply system! The water and sewage system! The city's airport! The banks! My employer! Your job! It's all going down tonight!," shouted Brad with exhaustion.

"We tried. We all tried. But the politicians ignored it. The big company executives couldn't face the truth. The public didn't care. Now, it doesn't matter. There's no time left to fix the computers!"

Lisa reminded Brad of his many assurances over the last year that the millennial bug would be conquered.

"Yes, honey, I told you that. I honestly believed it. I just believed that somehow, some way, we would find a solution to this crisis. Honey, I love you so much. I hated to frighten you, and make you worry. I just kept hoping all of us working around the world so hard would be able to salvage this mess, but we failed!

Then Brad shocked Lisa with his next disclosure. "Three months ago, I bought a small house in the country. A house with five acres. Just in case."

"Land? A house? Where?," Lisa demanded to know.

"About a hundred miles from here. Northwest of the city. You and the kids will be safe there. Out in the country. Away from the gangs and hoodlums. We'll wait it out. At least we'll have food and water," Brad assured his wife.

"Where did you get money to buy a house and five acres?," Lisa wanted to know.

Brad looked out the window again. "My retirement fund," he mumbled in a soft voice.

"Brad, you didn't! Tell me you didn't spend your retirement savings!," Lisa shouted.

"Yes, Lisa, I did," Brad replied. "Do you remember last August when I pulled our savings out of those high risk mutual funds," Brad asked his wife. "I told you I had a feeling that the stock market would drop in September. And it did. I just knew stock prices were going to fall. Serious investors see the handwriting on the wall. We're headed for a big cliff. If I hadn't pulled our money out in August, we would have lost a hundred thousand dollars," Brad reminded Lisa.

"But Brad, you said you were going to reinvest the money through our bank into a safe account until you thought the market was safe again," Lisa replied.

"I know. I said that. But, deep down, I knew we'd lose our money," Brad confessed. "Instead, I held onto the cash and quietly purchased the property in the country."

"Please don't cry. There's no time to waste. It's 11:00 p.m. We must get out of this city now. Start packing!

Without saying another word, Lisa went to the closet and brought out the suitcases. With tears streaming down her cheeks, she hurriedly packed their essential clothing.

Outside, the festive sounds of merriment and music, raucous laughter, and exploding fireworks filled the night air. What a party in the city's square. It seemed so surreal.

As Brad, Lisa, and their two children scurried to both of their automobiles to make a quick escape, they heard the roaring sound of helicopter blades swirling in the nighttime sky. Peering above the apartment buildings, Brad noticed the black helicopters hovering above his head.

"Look, Daddy!," his eight-year-old son shouts. "Soldiers!"

Brad suddenly stopped shoving suitcases in the trunk of Lisa's Toyota Camry. "Lisa, look at this!," he said as he pointed his finger toward the almost invisible black helicopters.

Dangling from the helicopters' tether lines, paratroopers scurried down to the street level.

"Brad, what's going on? Is this part of the New Year's Eve celebration?," Lisa asked. "Why are soldiers landing in our city?"

"Lisa, believe me. They're not here to celebrate New Year's Eve. Those are Delta Force paratroopers. The Army's elite fighting force. They've been in a two-year training program learning how to fight in urban warfare," Brad explained.

"Oh no!" Lisa cried out. "This can't be happening!"

"Quick! Get in the car! Our time is short. There's no time to lose!," Brad commanded. "Just stay close to my car and follow me to the interstate highway."

As they drove away, they could hear the mayor's voice reverberating off the tall buildings around their neighborhood. With great pride, the mayor proclaimed to the burgeoning mass of revelers, "This is the greatest event in the history of our city! We are making history tonight! As your mayor, I wanted to give you an experience you'll remember the rest of your life."

Thanks, Mr. Mayor.

They will.

1 Tower of Babel I: Technology's First Colossal Collapse

"Pride goes before destruction, and an haughty spirit before a fall."

Proverbs 16:18

The First Tower of Babel

It was the world's first massive technological failure. In the infancy of mankind's earthly dominion, early technology suffered a humiliating setback.

Mankind's first explosion of knowledge came generations after the Great Flood as told in Genesis.

Following the Great Flood, which destroyed all life except the inhabitants of Noah's Ark, the hearts of many men simmered with a slow burning rage against this unseen God who ruled over them from Heaven high above their heads.

Somehow, some way, mankind would overthrow this tyrannical heavenly ruler. If man was created in God's image, then surely men were gods too! Yes, mankind would find a way to discard the need for this God. Man himself would someday rule the earth as God.

Mankind would unite! Linked together, men would scale the skies and enter the very throne of this heavenly king.

Noah's Descendants Birth the World's First King

The descendants of Noah's three sons – Shem, Ham, and Japheth – repopulated the earth in the years following the worldwide judgment God brought upon mankind.

Noah's grandsons had become the inhabitants of luscious islands. Noah's grandson was Cush. A son of Cush was a skillful, daring hunter named Nimrod, known as a "slayer of men." Nimrod became, according to the Genesis account, "the first potentate on earth." An ambitious empire builder, Nimrod's kingdom controlled large areas of southern Mesopotamia. The beginning and heart of his kingdom was Babel.

There, in the plain of Shinar, was the capital of the Babylonian Empire, located on the Euphrates River. Called "the gate of God," Babel was originally known as Babylon. The city prospered from its strategic location. As the center of the overland trade route, Babylon connected the Persian Gulf and the Mediterranean sea. In ancient times, Babylon was the center of that period's "global economy."

According to legend, it was King Nimrod's driving ambition for wealth, fame, and power that inspired his people to construct a tower to reach heaven. Babylon's location brought wealth to the city's rapidly growing population through trade and commerce. The city's "movers and shakers" began talking about their dreams to build Babylon into a great city. They envisioned a temple-tower reaching to the skies. Such an edifice would be a proud monument to their booming economy, expanding knowledge, and technological achievements.

Babylon's business and civic leaders believed that such a magnificent temple-tower would unite the city's population. With grandiose vision and bravado, the city's powerful leaders launched the most massive public works project the world had ever known. "And they said, Go to, let us build us a city and a tower, whose top may reach unto heaven; and let us make us a name..." the Bible records in Genesis 11:4. Apparently, the city fathers also had an eye on building a lucrative tourist trade too!

Unfortunately, their monumental building project, however, suffered a disastrous setback. It appears they forgot to obtain the necessary building permit. The Bible says the Lord himself came down to the city to perform an on-site inspection of the ambitious project. "And the Lord came down to see the city and the tower, which the children of men builded." (Genesis 11:5)

What God saw wasn't encouraging. The Lord said, "Behold, the people is one, and they have all one language; and this they begin to do: and now nothing will be restrained from them, which they have imagined to do." (Genesis 11:6)

Jehovah realized the human race was just beginning to exploit their linguistic and political unity. With one mind and one language, no technological achievement would be beyond their reach. God knew that His creation, if left unchecked, would amass enormous power, even arrogantly challenging the Lord's sovereign rule. Mankind's unity was propelling technological achievements, causing many to question why they need a God at all. Mankind's unity had to be shattered.

"Go to, let us go down, and there confound their language, that they may not understand one another's speech. (Genesis 11: 7)

God knew the key to smashing mankind's audacious plans to become "little gods" would be to confuse their language. If they could not understand each other, they could not complete their pride-driven aspirations to build a one-world empire centered in Babylon.

Destroying their method of communication was the key to rebuking mankind's arrogance and pride. With no way to talk to each other, God ended in one swift act the threatening growth of their combined knowledge and technology.

"So, the Lord scattered them abroad from thence upon the face of all the earth: and they left off to build the city." (Genesis 11:8)

From that day, the city would be known as Babel, which means "confusion." "Because the Lord did there confound the language of all the earth: and from thence did the Lord scatter them abroad upon the face of all the earth." (Genesis 11: 9)

Mankind's Early Quest for Unity

An interesting Scripture regarding the days after the Great Flood is found in the preceding chapter. In the genealogy of the generations following Noah, the Bible speaks of the lands settled by the sons and grandsons of Noah. Each nation had its own separate language. "By these were the isles of the Gentiles divided in their lands; every one after his tongue, after their families, in their nations." (Genesis 10: 5)

Yet, the next chapter states that "the whole earth was of one language, and of one speech." (Genesis 11:1) Something happened over the years. Something that provoked God to take drastic action upon the earth again to keep mankind from going too far.

God flooded the earth with 40 days of rain because he "saw that the wickedness of man was great in the earth, and that every imagination of the thoughts of his heart was only evil continually." (Genesis 6:5). Saying that his spirit would not always strive with man, God gave the human race 120 years to clean up their act.

During that time, God instructed Noah to build the ark. Only Noah and his immediate family survived the Great Flood because God found Noah to be righteous.

Certainly, for many generations after the flood, families passed down to the next generation the stories of their ancestor, Noah. Families also told their children about Noah's ancestors – Adam and Eve. They recounted how God expelled Adam and Eve from the Garden in Eden. The storytellers told the young ones how Adam and Eve wanted for nothing in the garden, how everything was provided in overwhelming abundance. Adam's sin, however, cost him everything. He was expelled from the garden and forced to work by the sweat of his brow.

As the passage of time grew longer, and boys became men, many harbored deep resentment at their cruel fate in life. "Never again!" they determined in their hearts and minds. "Never will we suffer the fate of our forefathers by a god we can not see or touch." Civilization must never again be destroyed. Mankind had dominion over the whole earth. And mankind would someday rule as a god!

This heavenly God had gone too far. First, God expelled mankind from the Garden in Eden. Adam, their forefather, was robbed of the bountiful abundance of gold, fruits and vegetables. For centuries, men were forced to toil under the blazing sun in a harsh, unyielding environment just to obtain the food to survive. Not satisfied, these men declared, this God drowned the whole human race, save one family!

"Enough is enough!," they proclaimed throughout all tribal nations.

Through the ages following the Great Flood, the hearts of more men grew cold toward God. Pride, arrogance, and rebellion to God's righteousness filled their thoughts and molded their attitudes.

A movement began to unite the human race. Many generations passed by. A spirit, however, infested the hearts and minds of mankind. "We can live without this god!," they reasoned. "If we were created in His image, then we are gods too! No longer will we bow before his throne!"

Over time, a universal language spread worldwide. It became the politically correct language of the age. Mankind, the masses were told, was moving into a New Age of peace, prosperity and knowledge. People clinging to the old parochial languages belonged to the "old order." An exciting new day of science, technology, global trade, and adventure was about to dawn.

In the Garden, God had failed to keep mankind from eating from the Tree of Knowledge of Good and Evil. God was always trying to hold man back, in their eyes, from his destiny to rule.

Knowledge was power! Of course! That's why God forbade Adam and Eve from eating the tree's fruit. More knowledge meant more power!

Yes! Mankind would unite! Men would pool their combined knowledge and skills. Together, they would build a tower reaching into the heavens! Men would climb the tower and enter into God's realm as an equal. A New World order would be created that has no need for a Heavenly God. Man's new system would bring the human race the peace, wealth, and power that mankind deserved since his expulsion from the Garden.

Nothing could stop mankind! Nothing!

Except God.

God Regrets Creating Mankind

God had already concluded that creating mankind was a mistake. The wickedness, violence, greed, and pride that was rampant on earth during Noah's time grieved him. God saw that the direction in men's lives was always toward evil.

His heart was broken. God said he was sorry he had made them.

"And God saw that the wickedness of man was great in the earth, and that every imagination of the thoughts of his heart was only evil continually. And it repented the Lord that he had made man on the earth, and it grieved him at his heart." (Genesis 6: 5-6)

For that reason, God sent a devastating flood upon the entire earth. Only Noah and his family were spared from God's wrath.

After the flood, God made a covenant with Noah. Never again would he destroy the human race with a flood.

It was long after the flood, however, that man returned to their old ways. Once again, mankind dreamed of escaping from under the authority and dominion of Almighty God. Violence, murder, thievery, greed, and lust ruled men's hearts once more.

God had promised Noah he wouldn't destroy mankind with another flood. So, when the Lord observed King Nimrod's followers gathering huge stockpiles of bricks, He listened to their conversations. Amazed at mankind's resourcefulness and determination, God purposed in his heart to bring destruction to the plans of these Babylonians.

Essentially, God said to the other members of the Trinity, "Mankind has developed an universal language. Now each tribe can talk with all the other tribes. There are no communications barriers. Because they are all interconnected, mankind's knowledge is growing rapidly. Their pride and arrogance is growing too. They want to be gods! Lets go down to earth and throw a glitch into their communications system. Let's isolate each tribe so their collective power is diminished. The result will be mass confusion around the world."

This was mankind's first attempt at creating a one-world system.

Who Will Rebuild Nimrod's One-World System?

Mankind would not quit. The dream would not die within the hearts of kings and rulers. Through the ages, tyrants and despots came to Babylon seeking to rebuild the great city. The spirit of Nimrod was burning in their hearts.

Babel, the ancient city founded by Nimrod, would become the great city called Babylon. Empires would rise and fall within her massive walls. Dynasties would rule far away lands from the palaces of Babylon. Some kings even dreamed of rebuilding the great Tower of Babel, but all failed.

By 2200 BC, the city was known as "the gate of god." The city was the place of the temple of the god called Marduk. Worshipped by the Babylonians, Marduk was believed to be a star that was captured by the sun. Apparently a comet, Babylonian astronomers predicted that Marduk would appear every 3,600 years. Today, New Age believers are anticipating the return of Marduck to earth when the Third Millennium arrives.

Today, all that remains of the great empire called Babylon are the ancient ruins located 56 miles south of Baghdad in modern Iraq. Modern day archaeologists first excavated the ruins of Babylon just before the start of World War I. They discovered in the city's center the sacred temple of Babylon's god, Marduk. Just to the north, the archaeologists found the Etemenanki – a seven-storied edifice considered to be the original site of the Tower of Babel. Excavators also found the Hanging Gardens, one of the Seven Wonders of the World, built by King Nebuchadnezzar II for his wife. Close to the gardens, the excavators found the Processional Way – the route followed by religious and political leaders for the New Year's Day celebrations.

Yes, the spirit of Babylon lives today. Somewhere in this world, there is a charismatic world leader with the same steely look as was in the eyes of King Nimrod.

Someday, the world will be one mind again. One language. One system. A global village. And men will be able to do anything they imagine in their hearts. And finally, they will throw off the shackles of Almighty God.

Someday, Babylon will rise again.

2 Tower of Babel II: It All Came Crashing Down

"The computer has been a blessing; if we don't act quickly, however, it could become the curse of this age."

Honorable Patrick Moynihan — United States Senator
State of New York
Letter of Warning to President Bill Clinton
July 31, 1996

Nobody saw it coming.

Engineers said it would, most likely, never happen. The possibility so remote, no back-up system existed.

Without warning, the system crashed.

From coast to coast, millions of people were rudely reminded how dependent they had become on modern technology.

Doctors were stranded at hospitals, lest they leave and the medical staff have no way to contact them in a life-threatening emergency. Patients desperately waiting for organ transplants never ventured away from their telephone.

Motorists paying for gas with credit cards at 5,400 Chevron service stations actually had to walk into the station and give the attendant their credit cards. Lovers couldn't confirm midday rendezvous. Drug dealers had to find another way to transact dope deals. High-powered executives lost crucial tips on pending business deals. Airlines delayed flights because important weather data was unavailable.

The broadcasting media was hit hard too. CNN's Airport Channel went dark. So did the Gospel Television Network. Some television and radio stations were knocked off the air too. Without pictures, meteorologists couldn't make long-term weather forecasts.

For millions of people, it meant going back to old ways of communication. People actually had to talk to each other. Operators took messages. Secretaries sent important data by Fax. Couriers carried walkie-talkies and listened closely over the roar of bus engines and honking taxi cabs to the crackling voices giving directions. Office workers scrambled to track down their fast-moving sales force. Fax machines were humming. Even hospitals unpacked their antiquated wire-based pagers, and blew the dust off the hospital's old fashion loud speakers.

What happened?

At 6:13 p.m. EST on Tuesday, May 19, 1998, PanAmSat's Galaxy IV satellite suffered a computer failure.

On that spring evening, 90% of America's 45 million pagers went silent. Not a beep to be heard. Nowhere. Nada.

All this commotion because a computer on a $250 million satellite sent it rolling in space.

Eight of the nation's 10 biggest paging companies depend on Galaxy IV. Because certain satellites offer "eyes" with the best view of the nation, whole industries are clustered on the same satellites. Therefore, when trouble strikes, it wipes out more than one major company.

PanAmSat's officials, which is 81% owned by Hughes Electronics Corp., a GM subsidiary, had no immediate explanation for the satellite's sudden repositioning in space. They ruled out sabotage or that the satellite collided with another object.

The impact of this computer failure was dramatic. John Bletic, chief executive of PageMart Wireless, Inc., a paging company based in Dallas, underscored the severity of the failure to the nation's modern communications system. "The engineers would tell you this could never occur," Mr. Bletic was quoted in the Washington Post as saying. "For the first time in 35 years, pagers were silent – since the beginning of time, as far as the paging industry is concerned." (1)

A Nation Dependent on Technology

The communications chaos caused by a computer in an orbiting satellite clearly demonstrated our society's vulnerability to technology. The satellite snafu also illustrated our dependency on instant communications.

Except for hospitals, police, and rescue personnel, the loss of pagers is hardly a life-threatening crisis. An irritating inconvenience, but not something that will bring the nation to its knees.

Suppose, however, a massive computer failure crashed a vitally important component of our daily lives. Like the banking system.

Imagine a meltdown in our increasingly technology-dependent banking system. A meltdown that severely limits the electronic transfer of money in our nation. Now that 80% of all banking is electronic, such a failure would be devastating to our economy. Banks would be unable to electronically transfer hundreds of millions of dollars between other banks. Checks would take days, even weeks, to clear since they would have to be processed manually. People with direct deposit paychecks would be left without funds. ATM machines would not function. Credit cards would be invalid. College students waiting on dad to wire more money would be left standing in the cold at the local Western Union office.

Remote chance of happening, you say?

Consider the technical disaster that struck AT&T's national data network on April 13, 1998, less than six weeks prior to the collapse of the nation's 45 million pagers.

Just before 3 p.m. EST, the giant telephone company's frame-relay data network crashed. A frame-relay network – named for the method it uses to handle high-speed data – transports data in short, frequent bursts.

Data networks are used by numerous businesses to exchange large amounts of information, such as credit card transactions. Banks use frame-relay networks to communicate with ATM machines. Retailers confirm credit card transactions with these networks. Grocery chains use the networks to keep track of sales at individual stores. Airlines confirm flight reservations over the telephone with customers by using frame-relay networks.

AT&T is the nation's biggest supplier of data-network services to American businesses. Frame-relay data networks are a $1Billion a year industry. AT&T controls about 40% of the market.

The computer snafu that crippled AT&T's high-speed data network was triggered when two East Coast data switches, which direct data traffic on the network, failed. The problem intensified when the two malfunctioning switches "contaminated" the rest of AT&T's high-speed network, creating a domino effect. Like a Texas tornado, the virus moved swiftly from the East Coast to the West Coast, upsetting normal business transactions in thousands of communities.

The impact was felt immediately. AT&T's customer support telephone lines were overwhelmed with calls from desperate business managers wanting answers.

For Shelly Nash, senior vice president for data networking at Wells Fargo Bank, the message on her pager sounded the alarm.(2)

"MAJOR NETWORK OUTAGE. AT&T FRAME RELAY FAILURE. 1,023 SITES ARE DOWN."

The message was shocking. The San Francisco Bank had experienced network failures before, usually 45 to 50 sites at a time. A thousand sites was inconceivable. In all, Wells Fargo Bank lost communication with over 1,023 automatic teller machines, and left 600 branch offices out of touch with the bank's central computers.

Other major businesses were hit too.

Forth Worth-based American Airlines cut off orders for tickets at midnight Tuesday because the backlog of unverified credit cards was getting too big to handle. At 895 locations of Albertsons Food and Drug Stores, grocery clerks could not verify checks, debit cards, and credit cards. Millions of Visa and MasterCard users could not use their credit cards. British Airways reported "massive delays" at ticket offices in 10 major city airports. More than half of Wal-Mart's 2,359 stores lost their electronic inventory and credit card verification systems. Toyota Motor Manufacturing North America lost contact with its assembly plants in the United States and the home office in Japan. TCI, the giant Denver-based cable television firm, estimated the company lost $5 million on Monday afternoon and evening as customers were unable to order pay-per-view movies or pay their cable bills in over 500 offices. Even operations at the American Red Cross, which distributes half the nation's blood supply, were substantially slowed.

For AT&T, the impact of the network failure was the equivalent of a fatal crash of a major airline's flight.

The giant telephone company was so embarrassed by the shutdown of its network that AT&T hand-delivered personal messages from the company's chairman, C. Michael Armstrong. Mr. Armstrong, who had only been on board as chairman for six months, spent most of the night at the office working with technicians to solve the problem. An obviously humbled chief executive, Mr. Armstrong told reporters at a morning press conference, "Frankly, these outages let our customers down, and I want to apologize to every one of them."

Fortunately for AT&T, Mr. Armstrong's leadership during the crisis won applause from Wall Street investors. Within 24 hours, AT&T had the network back up. Mr. Armstrong pledged to not bill commercial customers until the company identified and fixed the problem.

Tremors Before the Quake

For technophiles, two major computer-generated crashes within a month must be unnerving. Such widespread technology failures are an ominous sign that we have become a technology-dependent society.

Increasing numbers of experts are beginning to worry.

Howard Anderson, managing director for the Yankee Group, a technology research firm based in New England, is one of those experts who are starting to raise serious questions about how dependent on vast computer networks that our nation's economy has become.

"This sort of thing is going to happen infrequently, but more and more in the future," Mr. Anderson was quoted in the New York Times following AT&T's crash. "And it makes you realize how vital to the lifeblood of the economy these complex computer networks have become." (3)

In the case of the pagers that crashed, all eight major paging companies were clustered on the same satellite, a practice common in other industries. For banks and retailers caught off guard by AT&T's data network failure, the danger was not having a back-up system in case of an emergency.

"Putting all your eggs in one basket is a recipe for disaster," says Jeffrey Kagan, a telecommunications consultant in Atlanta, Ga. "Like a tornado, these outages don't occur often, but when they do, they can be devastating." (4)

Viewed separately, neither of the two computer-generated crashes would be cause for alarm. When viewed together, they are unsettling.

Like California tremors before the quake, these technology melt-downs are disturbing warnings that the BIG ONE is near. These warnings are merely previews of coming attractions for the Year 2000.

The high-tech earthquake will register a 7.O on the Richter scale of world calamities. The global impact of this event will be unparalleled in mankind's history.

Like the Tower of Babel in ancient days, modern man is about to witness an unprecedented global collapse of his monument to the intelligence, pride, and arrogance of the human race at the turn of the next millennium. A pride and arrogance that exults science, technology, and economic greed above God's Kingdom.

Just as God came down and brought confusion on mankind's ability to communicate, so shall God bring worldwide confusion to our day's high-tech, globally networked communications system.

Suddenly, our inter-connected web of computers across the planet will be unable to communicate with each other.

For the same reasons, too, that brought judgment on Nimrod's empire.

The Spirit of Nimrod Lives Today

The spirit of Nimrod is alive and well in the hearts and minds of many rulers, princes, news commentators, political pundits, programmers, scientists, academic eggheads, and CEOs today. Mankind must be free, they proclaim from their lofty perches in modern-day Babylonian society, from the constraints and shackles of an Almighty God. By linking together – individuals, governments, businesses, nations – we can become ONE MIND. ONE PEOPLE. ONE WORLD.

Together, we can do anything.

Clone human beings. Genetically engineer new plants. Harvest living organs from test-tube human fetuses to be transplanted in waiting patients. Produce deadly biological weapons that can wipe out entire nations.

We are the human race! Nothing is impossible to us now! Our gods of science and technology has liberated the human race!

As in Nimrod's day, knowledge is exploding. Through computers, the world speaks ONE LANGUAGE!

The Third Millennium will belong to mankind.

More importantly, for the first time in mankind's existence, the world is moving quickly to discard the "old world" ways of religion and morality. "Who needs God?," they publicly sneer in classrooms, news reports, television sitcoms, rock music, and scientific conventions.

Finally, mankind will be free from God's influence and antiquated moral codes.

His name is name is publicly trashed by foul-mouthed comedians and radio deejays.   Like a poisonous toxic waste, educrats have practically eradicated any mention of Biblical morality from public institutions. Anybody identifying himself or herself as a Christian Believer is promptly labeled a lunatic, a nut case.

Sexual behavior that was, at one time, considered shameful, now is openly embraced in the media. The nation's morals have slid so far into the gutter that one TV talk show proudly presents men who boast of their sexual relationships with horses and dogs. Even worse, corporations are glad to sponsor such filthy programs.

Millions of babies are aborted each year; even their innocent brains sucked out during partial birth abortions. Perverts molest thousands of children.

Murder, violence, and crime fill our streets.

Television entertainment has degenerated to people cursing and hitting each other before a live audience.

Children hide in schoolyards with high-powered rifles, randomly murdering other children and teachers for fun.

January 1, 2000: The Storm That Will Shake the World

God is preparing to pay his children another visit. He dealt with this Tower of Babel stuff before. He knows how to deal with it again.

Make it impossible to communicate and bring confusion upon the earth.

That will put puny little man in his place again. Until that rebellious "Nimrod spirit" rises again in the human race.

There's a storm coming. A storm of unprecedented magnitude. The ferocity of its savage winds will spare no nation. Every nation will drink from God's cup of wrath.

When the winds subside, the political, military, and economic landscape of the world will be radically and permanently altered.

In the aftermath of this storm, some nations will lie in ruins. Their cities will smolder.

Other nations will emerge as superpowers.

New global empires will arise. Corporate states, transcending borders.

Up from the ashes will arise the New World Order. The Roman Empire will awaken from its millennial slumber.

The world is racing toward the day. The clock is ticking. The remaining days are quickly fleeing as sands in the hourglass.

It is a date that cannot be altered.

On New Year's Eve, December 31, 1999, the human race will unite in a global celebration of the Third Millennium. The world will rock with parties, music, laughter, booze, drugs, sex, and unbridled lasciviousness.

Ten! Nine! Eight! Seven!.....The jubilant crowds will shout in unison in villages and cities, counting down the final seconds of the Twentieth Century.

When the clock strikes midnight, an uninvited guest will crash mankind's worldwide millennial party.

God.

The Almighty himself will conduct a high-intensity stress test of modern man's high-tech, stressed-out society. "Let's see if all of man's little toys keep working!"

From time zone to time zone, His presence at the party will be made known.

Like a slow burning incendiary device, God will unleash a time bomb into mankind's global computer network. The detonation will eventually bring the world financial system to its knees. It will begin slowly, however, barely detected. Experts in each country, however, will closely monitor the impact and path of its destruction.

At first, news of its arrival will be kept from the public. Hardly anybody will be aware of the menace lurking in the computers. People will be too busy partying to notice what's happening around them. There will be isolated failures, here and there.

With gathering momentum, keeping the spreading virus contained will become impossible. With frightening speed, the virus will spread the contamination quickly to other systems.

God will ignite a fuse sending the destroying virus racing through a complex labyrinth of mainframe computers, telephone wires, high-speed data networks, routers, switches, frame-relay networks, satellite transponders, PCs, and hidden microprocessor chips. With each new hour, the stealth weapon will gather force as it cascades from mainframe to mainframe, PC to PC, network to network, city to city, state to state, nation to nation.

The Week America Stands Still

Life will be different on the first day of 2000. Inhabitants of the New Millennium will be greeted with a brave, New World.

Things that were taken for granted will suddenly be no more.

During the first days of 2000, the impact will vary from city to city, and from nation to nation. The possible disruptions will range from minor inconveniences to major catastrophes.

The following list illustrates some of the technologies that will be affected unless the world discovers the "silver bullet" miracle solution in the few months remaining before January 1, 2000:

Mainframe computers
Personal computers
Government computer system (i.e. Social Security, IRS, etc.)
Military weapon systems
Nuclear power generators
Electrical utilities
Telephone systems

Elevators
Credit Cards
ATM machines
Traffic lights
Airports
Aircraft navigation
Hospital medical equipment
Air cooling and heating systems
Electronic security gates in prisons
Bank vaults
Manufacturing equipment
Municipal water pumping stations
Food processing plants
Railroad traffic control systems
Emergency dispatch systems
Navigational systems
Cargo ships
Alarm systems

The first month of 2000 will profoundly change the face of this world. Like falling dominoes, a series of major events, systems' failures, and calamities will overpower the world's high and mighty.

The following fictional chronology offers a possible scenario of the first four weeks of the new millennium.

FRIDAY, December 31, 1999

11:59:00 p.m. New York City: Since 7 a.m., hundreds of thousands of celebrants have filled Times Square for the Big Apple's greatest party ever held, despite the below-normal winter temperature of 19 degrees. With 24 large-screen television sets positioned throughout the square, revelers have been celebrating the arrival of the new millennium with people around the world in each time zone. Although many of the TV screens have gone dark, as successive time zones have passed into the 21st Century, people in the streets have been oblivious to the loss of signals. They assume its part of the plan to "count down" the arrival of the Third Millennium in the Eastern Time zone. Finally, the moment arrives. "Five!...Four!...Three!...Two!....One!...the crowd shouts in joyful unison. "Happy New Year!," the masses roar through the canyons of Manhattan's streets. Across the nation, millions watch on TVs in living rooms, bars, nightclubs, police stations, fire houses, and hospital waiting rooms.

SATURDAY, January 1, 2000

12:01:12 a.m. An air traffic controller at New York City's John F. Kennedy Airport, who was assured by Federal Aviation Administration officials that JFK's mission-critical systems were Year 2000 compliant, gives permission to Flight 1520 to land on Runway 8W. Seconds later, the air traffic control center's radar equipment is shut down. The date-dependent computer system that initiates the automatic cooling pumps malfunctions when it can not read the correct date and time. Responding to the crisis, air traffic controllers are forced to monitor aircraft by altitude and time.

12:01:15 a.m. At a small fossil fuel electric utility plant 100 miles northwest of New York City, date-sensitive microprocessors, the building blocks of the power industry, suddenly shut down the generators that provide electricity for 300,000 households. A blackout hits the surrounding suburban communities. Because the city belongs to a regional pool that buys and sells power to dozens of New York State utilities, a sudden and dramatic surge is produced in the interconnected power grid for emergency electrical power to be sent to the affected city. Unbeknown to managers, who are watching the Times Square celebration and toasting the New Year, embedded microprocessors in a vital transformer in Queens starts sending error messages through the transmission lines to other stations. Meanwhile, back at the main ConEd plant, the control console had rebooted at midnight. The computers, however, rebooted as the date being January 1, 1980. The Programmable Logic Controls (PLC) interprets this erroneous data as a gross control failure. Suddenly, the feedwater regulating valves are closed, and the boiler trip logic is initiated. The main generating plant for New York City is tripped.

12:01:20 a.m. As the crowds roar with laughter and song in Times Square, without warning, the power system for New York City goes out. Darkness suddenly engulfs Manhattan. An eerie silence falls upon the hushed throngs of revelers.

12:01: 48 a.m. Flight 1520, an inbound flight from Las Vegas chartered by a travel agency specializing in Millennial parties, is descending at JFK Airport toward Runway 8W. Suddenly, while just 1,000 feet from the runway, all airport lights go out - including the control tower. A panic-stricken pilot lands the DC-9 in total darkness. He loses control of the aircraft while careening wildly down the invisible runway and crashes. Most of the flight's 150 passengers are killed.

12:02:10 a.m. Police announce on loud speakers that a power blackout has occurred. They assure the crowd that ConEd is working on the problem and will have the lights back on soon. People are admonished to remain calm and in their place.

12:02:30 a.m. Drunk participants in Time Square become unruly. Shouting, cursing, and shoving sends a chill in the hearts and minds of thousands eagerly waiting in the streets for power to be restored. Police move in with batons and begin arresting out-of-control gang members.

12:03:11 a.m. New York City's blackout sends a ripple effect cascading through the East Coast power grid. Malfunctioning computer systems in 18 utilities in New Jersey, Delaware, Eastern Pennsylvania, Maryland, and the District of Columbia send faulty data throughout the power grid.

12:05:02 a.m.   Much of the East Coast, from Boston, MA to Richmond, VA, goes dark as a massive power failure shuts down power generating facilities.

12:06:25 a.m.   Television viewers in the Central, Mountain, and Pacific time zones are told that the East Coast has experienced a major power outage.   From Ohio to California, people become concerned about the way the New Millennium is starting.   Millions of people, however, are unaware of the East Coast problems as they shout and sing at countless "Millennia" parties throughout the nation.

12:22:00 a.m.   A 34-year-old entrepreneur in Atlanta, GA, is entertaining eight of his top clients and spouses at an exclusive restaurant, at a premium price for the once-in-a-lifetime celebration.   The waiter returns to his table with his American Express card and whispers in his ear. "What do you mean, my card is expired!," the young businessman asks the waiter.   "We can accept your bank's debit card, sir, if you please," offers the discreet waiter.   Moments later, the waiter returns, looking slightly uncomfortable.   "Sir, the bank refuses to honor your debit card. It says you have insufficient funds in your account.   Would you like to speak with the manager about how you will pay this tab?"

12:29:10 a.m.   New York City Mayor Guillani declares a state of emergency.   Riot police are dispatched to all parts of the city as panic-stricken people struggle to find a way to escape the mayhem that has erupted in Times Square and spread to other parts of the city.

2:15 a.m.   A 73-year-old patient in a Cleveland, Ohio, hospital clings to his life following a mild heart attack earlier in the day.   The hospital's intravenous infusion pumps, controlled by embedded microchips, shuts down when it mistakenly believes it has not been recalibrated for 100 years.   The malfunction sends a deadly dose of medication into the veins of the seriously ill patient.   The man dies of cardiac arrest.

4:27 a.m.   A 58-year-old night watchman in a small rural bank in Eastern Tennessee discovers that the bank's vaults are wide open. Staring at the huge sums of cash stored in the vault, the man decides to take an early retirement.   He loads over $400,000 into the trunk of his car and heads south.

SUNDAY, January 2, 2000
6:00 a.m.   Following a day of looting, riots, fires, electrical outages, and other troubles, top national advisors to the President gather in the Cabinet meeting room.   The Vice President, the nation's high-tech politician, quietly stands by the window and looks at the darkened streets of Washington, D.C.   He mumbles something about the New

Hampshire primary. While the sirens of emergency vehicles are heard streaming down the Capitol's streets, the White House is operating on an emergency power supply.

As the meeting begins, FBI, CIA, military, and national security advisors brief the President. The President looks glum, as though the life of the party has evaporated. This isn't politics, or campaigning. It is a real national crisis.

Electrical power is still out in most of the East Coast. The West Coast, from Portland to San Diego, is dark too. Two of the nation's largest long-distance carriers are down.

Governors in 19 states are reporting widespread looting in major urban areas. National guard troops have been dispatched to settle the disturbances in 49 cities.

The temperature in Washington, D.C. at 6:00 a.m. is 12 degrees Fahrenheit   Millions of people throughout the East Coast are without heat.

8:00 a.m. Under a presidential directive, the FAA orders all commercial airlines to cancel all flights for 24 hours until airports and government agencies can reboot their mission-critical computer systems. Furthermore, the electrical blackouts make it impossible for airports to function normally. Chaos ensues in terminals around the nation as angry holiday passengers learn they are stranded indefinitely.

9:00 a.m. The Joint Chiefs of Staff meet in top secrecy with the President, the Secretary of Defense, and the National Security Advisor. The military's top brass can not guarantee that the nation's high-tech national defense system will operate in the event of a nuclear attack. Furthermore, cyber terrorists and hackers have launched an infowar attack by jamming the Pentagon's computers. Military leaders fear that terrorist may seek to send erroneous data to Russia or China making it appear that the U.S. has launched a nuclear strike.

9:30 a.m. The governor of Texas sends riot-equipped national guardsmen to a high-tech maximum-security prison in west Texas after learning the computer-controlled security system suddenly unlocked hundreds of cells.

11:00 a.m Miami's mayor responds to the pleas of the fire chief and assembles a quick-response team to the city's high-rise retirement condominiums. Elevators in 42 high-rise apartment buildings, controlled by embedded microchips, will not operate. Thousands of senior citizens are trapped inside their condos, with only the stairs as a means of escape.

4:00 p.m. The chairman of the Federal Reserve Board advises the President and the Secretary of the Treasury of almost certain panic in the nation's financial system when banks open on Tuesday morning following the January 3 holiday. The Fed chairman urges drastic actions to safeguard the banking system.

5:00 p.m. The Chairman of the Security and Exchange Commission advises the President that the nation's top investment firms are recommending that Wall Street not open on Tuesday morning. Weather forecasters tell the President that temperatures will drop to below zero after sunset.

8:00 p.m. The President goes on national television, radio, and Internet to speak to a troubled nation on the second day of the Third Millennium. Because of widespread power outages, many families listen to the President's speech on battery-powered radios. The President says the troubles are temporary, and will soon be fixed. Everybody needs to remain calm. Authorities are working to restore law and order. Curfews have been declared in 68 cities. Officials assure him that electrical power will be back within 24 hours. He's asking employers to extend the New Year's holiday by remaining closed on Tuesday. By presidential mandate, he orders banks and the stock market be closed on Tuesday to give financial service companies time to test their computers.

10:00 p.m. The Federal Reserve Chairman and Secretary of the Treasury meet in an emergency session with the President and Vice President. Reports coming in from Japan tell of widespread financial panic. Japan's shaky economy, barely surviving the Asian crisis, is teetering on collapse. The Russia economy has collapsed and the Red Communists have regained control of the Kremlin. The Fed Chairman says the collapse of the Japanese economy could set off a worldwide depression in light of the current economic conditions following the Year 2000 meltdown.

MONDAY, January 3, 2000
6:00 a.m. The President is advised that the Japanese stock market has crashed. Panic-stricken investors are withdrawing investments from stocks, mutual funds, and banks. Angry Japanese housewives are surrounding every bank in Japan, demanding their meager savings.

1:00 p.m. At a nationally televised news conference, the President announces that electrical power has been restored in half of the affected cities. He warns that more blackouts may occur, but the public should remain confident that the government will fix the problems. America's best computer professionals are working on the problems. The President says he is deeply "troubled" by the deteriorating economic conditions in Asia –especially Japan. Therefore, in order to allow "reason to rule" in the nation's financial affairs, he announces that, effective at 1:00 p.m. EST, all banks and the stock exchanges will be closed until Monday, January 10, 2000.

1:10 p.m. Angry crowds form at banks throughout the nation as word spreads that the President has declared a one-week bank holiday. People demand the right to get their money out of the banks. Police are overwhelmed by unruly mobs of average citizens who are outraged by the President's actions.

6:30 p.m. Nightly news reports on television stations around the nation describe the mounting tension and apprehension in the nation over the Year 2000 crisis. TV stations give airtime to local pastors to speak to the public, imploring them to remain calm.

TUESDAY, January 4, 2000
7:00 a.m. UAW members returning to work at a GM plant in Pontiac, Michigan are sent home after learning the factory's high-tech computerized robots will not operate. Another 1,100 employees at a Charlotte, NC, plant are sent home because the computerized security system will not allow the factory's doors to open.
9:00 a.m. The Speaker of the House and the Senate President meet with the President to discuss the national crisis. The President asks for the Congress to be called back into session immediately. Congressional leaders agree, but say most members of Congress are still in their home states following the holidays. It will be days until many members can make it to Washington because all air travel is canceled. The President orders the military to transport congressional members to the nation's capitol.
10:22 a.m. Thirty-six workers were killed in a fiery blast at a petro-chemical plant in New Jersey. The explosion occurred when embedded chips inside the high-tech plant's infrastructure failed to turn on the cooling system. Fireman battle the blaze for 10 hours. Four thousand residents of nearby communities are evacuated because of toxic fumes.
1:00 p.m. The President sends U.S. Army troops to rescue stranded passengers at airports throughout the nation. The FAA says it can not, for safety reasons, lift the ban on commercial flights.
3:00 p.m. The President listens to economic advisors about Europe's quickly crumbling economy. The new European Monetary Union is in disarray. Banks throughout the EMU are closed. Angry peasants in France, Italy, and Belgium say they will not use the new Euro dollar.

WEDNESDAY, January 5, 2000
8:00 a.m. Grocery store managers in major urban areas brace for another day of hoarding. Warehouses are dangerously low on food inventories. Fresh produce is in short supply in most large city grocery stores. Stores employ armed security guards to patrol the aisles and guard check-out counters. Aggravating the tension is the abundance of make-shift signs in stores declaring, "No Checks! No Credit Cards! CASH ONLY!" People complain that the banks are still closed and they are unable to access their funds. Fights break out in numerous grocery stores as desperate parents demand to buy food.
10:30 a.m. At an emergency meeting of the Cabinet, the President is briefed by Cabinet secretaries on the status of each government

agency's computer systems. The FAA glumly admits that three-fourths of the air traffic control computers are down. The Director of the Central Intelligence Agency reported that communications have been lost with many CIA agents around the globe. Secretary of Defense reveals that most of the Pentagon's systems are down, with military programmers working around the clock to repair. Director is very concerned for the lives and safety of Americans abroad. Health and Human Services also report widespread systems failure. Social Security Administration says most of its systems are still operating, but the Treasury Department, which actually issues Social Security checks, is in state of disarray. Serious systems failures are also plaguing Veterans Affairs and the Interior. Medicare has totally crashed.

The President is advised that the nation is in a state of emergency. Advisors recommend instituting a national military draft of all available computer programmers under the age of 70. Plan calls for military to allocate programmers to government agencies and businesses that are crucial to the nation's survival. Commerce secretary says a draft would totally cripple American businesses and the economy by robbing them of IT professionals that are critically needed to restore computer systems. The Chairman of the Joint Chiefs of Staff bluntly tell the president that the Pentagon has no way to defend the nation, except by infantry troops.

FRIDAY, January 7, 2000
9:00 a.m. Shocked employees in numerous businesses learn their company's payroll records have been lost. Paychecks will not be issued. Emergency vouchers of $200 will be handwritten. Furthermore, other employees who have direct deposit paychecks realized they have no access to their earnings as long as the bank holidays remain in effect. No word yet from the White House on whether banks and the stock market will open on Monday.

5:00 p.m. The first work week of the Year 2000 comes to a close as angry, frustrated, and disillusioned employees fight their way through incredible traffic jams. For a week, traffic signals in most cities have not operated. Air traffic is still curtailed. Amtrak trains are still running, but seriously delayed because of major logistical foul-ups by railroad freight lines. Many companies warn employees that layoffs could be forthcoming if vendors don't get needed parts and supplies to their plants by mid-week.

Get the picture?

It doesn't take much to see how everyday American life will change radically.

"OK," you say. "I can handle that for a few days. Even a week. No big deal."

You're right. You can handle the inconvenience (including no TV) for a day, even a week.

What about 10 days? Two weeks?

What if electricity, water, sewage, and telephone service is down for a month? Don't forget about the banks, credit unions, and brokerages. What if the banks close for weeks because of a panic run by the public for their savings and investments?

What about your family's food supply? There's only a 72-hour supply of food in any city's grocery stores and warehouses.

Are you prepared - physically, emotionally, and financially - to cope with the crisis?

Get ready.

The New Year's Party has just begun!

The Tower of Babel is coming down!

3 Two Missing Digits: What's The Big Deal?

"We're concerned about the potential disruption of power grids, telecommunications, and banking services…"

> *Sherry Burns — United States Central Intelligence Agency*
> *Commenting on her report about the Year 2000 crisis*
> *to the CIA's Chief Information Officer John Daley*
> *May 5, 1998*

We're headed for a terrific train wreck on the Information Super Highway.

It will be the most expensive global catastrophe in the history of the world

Known as Y2K, the Year 2000 computer crisis has the potential to disrupt the flow of information around the world. Unlike other major catastrophes, such as hurricanes and floods, which happen one at a time in one location, this event will be universal and simultaneous.

No amount of wishful, Pollyanna thinking will make it go away. January 1, 2000 is a non-negotiable deadline. It is a fixed deadline that will show no mercy. Computer systems that have not been fixed before January 1, 2000, simply *will not work.*

When the clock strikes midnight on Friday night, December 31, 1999, mankind's Tower of Babel will begin to self-destruct. First, colossal mainframe computers, the workhorses of government agencies and major corporations, will either completely shut down, or spit out erroneous information. Contaminated data will rapidly spread to other systems – including systems that were "fixed" in time. Second, millions of older desktop PCs - especially those built before 1997 - will share a similar fate as the mainframes. Third, potentially hundreds of millions of embedded microprocessors, found in everything from consumer products to the military's smart weapons of mass destruction, will shut down (or activate) the devices and systems they automatically control.

Because computers now interconnect every facet of modern day living, no area of society will be spared from the consequences of this fast approaching deadline. "This is not just an information technology challenge," stated Harris Miller, president of the Information Technology Association of America before a Congressional committee on May 7, 1998. The Year 2000 crisis, said Mr. Miller, "is a fundamental challenge to the ability of organizations throughout the world to continue to function." (1)

The potential for serious social and financial upheavals around the world is real. In his Congressional testimony, Mr. Harris stated, "And it is a challenge which could have tremendous negative consequences for economies and governments throughout the world if it is not met."

How worried is the president of the nation's leading information technology (IT) trade association? "Let me go on record publicly with what those in the know are thinking and saying privately," said Mr. Harris. "We are very worried."

Malfunctioning VCRs, microwave ovens, video games, and garage door openers will be only minor inconveniences. It is the loss of electrical power, public drinking water, and telephone service that will present much more serious trouble. Disruptions to the banking system threaten our very economic system. A meltdown in our national defense systems will expose the United States to the frightening risks of a devastating nuclear attack. The possible consequences of our failure as a society to deal with Y2K are extremely serious.

What is the source of this looming global crisis? How did we get in this mess? How can we solve it before it's too late?

Computers 101: A Crash Course (No pun intended!)

The first computer was not made by Radio Shack.

A German named Wilheim Schikard made it.

The German scientist invented the first computing device in 1623. The crude machine used 11 complete and 6 incomplete sprocketed wheels that could add. The machine could also multiply and divide with the aid of logarithm tables.

Mr. Schikard's invention was an oddity that found no practical use in his day and time. Perhaps sales of Mr. Schikard's machine would have been better had there been a Radio Shack in 1623!

Nineteen years later, the next big leap in computer technology came with the invention by Blaise Pascal, a French mathematician and physicist. Pascal's machine added and subtracted, automatically carrying and borrowing digits from column to column. Total sales of the unit: 50.

The next major advancement in early computer technology didn't come until the early 19th century. The public reaction to French inventor Joseph-Marie Jacquard's invention of the loom was not what the inventor expected. Angry weavers who feared for their livelihoods ran Monsieur Jacquard out of town by the loom's labor reduction savings. The loom used punched cards to program patterns that were produced as woven fabrics by the loom. Total sales: 30,000.

In 1820 Charles Babbage tried to make a difference. The British mathematician designed the Difference Engine. After further analysis, he later designed the Analytical Engine. Neither design was ever successfully built. Despite his failure, Babbage's work laid the foundation for modern computers. The key designs of Babbage's plans, such as the use of punched cards as a primitive memory, are found in many computers today.

The Age of Computers took a giant leap in the late 19th century. In 1890, the task of collecting and analyzing the data from the census became so great that the United States government contracted with Herman Hollerith, an American inventor and engineer, to build a machine to handle the gargantuan project. Hollerith invented a machine – the "tabulator" – that allowed census takers to record data by punching holes in a card. These cards, which were approximately the size of a dollar bill, were tabulated by Hollerith's mechanical device that read the holes punched in each card. Mechanical adding machines were used to tabulate the results.

The use of Hollerith's "tabulator" was the dawn of data processing. The machine had a profound impact on the government's census process. The computational time for the U.S. census was increased three to four times over traditional hand counts. In 1896, Hollerith founded the Tabulating Machine Company, later to become the Computing-Tabulating-Recording Company. After further acquisitions of smaller companies, the company became International Business Machines, known today as IBM.

The next advancement in computer technology came from a British mathematician who proposed the concept of a machine that could process equations without human direction. The theoretical precursor of today's modern computer was the Turing machine, invented by Alan Turing. Turing's machine resembled a typewriter that used symbols for math.

Under the leadership of Thomas Watson, IBM became an industrial giant as the leading producer of time clocks. In the 1930's, IBM built the Mark I calculating machine, developed by American mathematician Howard Aiken. Aiken's first prototype replaced mechanical components with electromagnetic components. The Mark I was used during World War II to perform calculations for the U.S. Navy. Later, Aiken pioneered the use of vacuum tubes and solid state resistors, which manipulated the binary numbers.

Computer technology made a substantial leap when John von Neumann, a Hungarian-American mathematician, developed the first electronic computer to use a program stored entirely within its memory. Von Neuman's computer was used in the 1940s to solve problems in hydrodynamics, mathematics, economics, and meteorology.

It was the ENIAC (Electrical Numerical Integrator and Computer) that ushered in the modern age of computers. Completed in 1945, the ENIAC, built at the Moore School of Engineering at the University of Pennsylvania in Philadelphia by John Mauchly and J. Presper Eckert, was the world's first all-electronic computer. As large as a small house, the ENIAC weighed 60,000 pounds, and contained more than 18,000 vacuum tubes. The computer had to be reprogrammed each week, and required a team of six technicians to replace 2,000 vacuum tubes each month.

The Remington Rand Corporation purchased the R&D company started by Mauchly and Eckert in the 1940s. Remington Rand introduced the UNIVAC in 1950. The Universal Automatic Computer was the first electronic programmable computer for data processing. The first UNIVAC was sold to the U.S. Census Bureau in 1951. The UNIVAC gained national attention in 1952 when ABC used the computer during a live television broadcast to predict the outcome of the presidential election. In 1954, General Electric became the first private company to own a computer. Other major corporations such as Du Pont quickly followed GE's leadership, followed by US Steel and Metropolitan Life Insurance Company. By 1957, there were 46 UNIVACs in use.

These large "mainframe" computers became the backbone of corporate America's data processing departments. In the early days of data processing, the various departments of a corporation, such as sales and customer support, would send all of its data to the data processing department, where data processing clerks would enter the information into the company's sole computer. Today, mainframe computers control businesses, large manufacturing and industrial operations, and are extensively used in scientific research.

The technological advancements at Bell Telephone Laboratories in 1948 had a major influence on the fledgling computer industry. The development of the transistor replaced the expensive vacuum tubes. IBM produced its first mass-produced computer – the IBM 701 – in 1953. Over 1800 units of the IBM 650 were sold. By the late 1960s, the individual transistors had been replace by integrated circuits, tiny transistors arranged on a silicone chip. Further advancements in integrated circuits led to the development of the microprocessor by the 1970s.

The growth of mainframe computer applications in business, military, and academic environments was accelerated by the development of programming languages in the 1950s and 1960s. COBOL (Common Business Oriented Language) and FORTRAN (Formula Translation) allowed extremely efficient programs to be developed for data processing applications. **Both languages are still used today.** Programming languages contain the series of commands that tell the computer what to do. Most languages are encoded in binary numbers (1s and 2s). Languages, which use numbers, are easier to understand by the computer than languages that use other commands since the computer must first translate the commands into numbers.

IBM, known as Big Blue, dominated the mainframe computer business throughout the 1960s and 1970s. The continued technological breakthroughs in microprocessors led to the development of the Personal Computer. With advent of cheaper and smaller integrated circuits, the first PC was sold by Instrumentation Telemetry Systems. The Altair 8800 soon followed it in 1975. The Altair 8800, which appeared on the front cover of _Popular Electronics_ magazine in 1975, had to be built from a kit. The early unit inspired many entrepreneurs, such as Steven Jobs and Stephen Wozniak who launched Apple Computer from their garage, to launch companies to produce new versions of the PC and accompanying software.

IBM viewed the PCs as a threat to the mainframe computer, which accounted for over 70% of the company's profits. IBM, however, did not act. IBM's protection of the mainframe business gave an opening to companies such as Hewlett-Packard, Data General, and Digital Equipment Corporation to help satisfy the public's demand for these smaller, cheaper, and easy-to-use computers. Finally, in 1981, IBM introduced the company's first PC. Despite the technological innovations of the IBM PC, the company lost market share as "IBM clones" flooded the market.

Since the early 1980s, rapid technological advancements have doubled the computing power of PCs every 18 months. PCs have become smaller, faster, have a larger memory, and are more powerful. Improvements in PC technology and falling prices have made the personal computer a commonly accepted appliance in many homes. Over 40% of U.S. households owned a PC by the end of 1997.

Today, computers are the heartbeat of most businesses: Mainframes, workstations, PCs, laptops, networks such as LAN (local area network) and WAN (wide area network), the World Wide Web, and the Internet. Moreover, the globalization of the world economy has compelled each nation's vast collection of computers to be intricately linked to each other through the World Wide Web and the Internet.

The most influential factor in the rapid growth of PCs is the advancement in microprocessor technology. Microprocessors are the heart of a PC. They are the electronic circuits that function as the central processing unit (CPU) of the computer. Today's most sophisticated microprocessors contain approximately 10 million transistors, and up to 50 million transistors by the year 2000.

Electronics firms extensively use microprocessors in a wide variety of applications. They are found in VCRs, video games, mobile telephones, Fax machines, automobiles, jet aircraft, nuclear missiles, electric utilities, and factory machines. Nearly four billion microprocessors were produced in 1995. Most chips are **embedded inside appliances, equipment, or machines.**

Early Origins of the Y2K Crisis

At the core of this science fiction horror story is a simple, innocent looking culprit. A shared programming flaw consisting of two missing digits.

Remember, computers talk in the language of numbers – 1s and 2s.

The genesis of this digital dilemma began in the 1950s with the use of punch cards. According to economist Edward Deak in testimony before a U.S. Senate committee, many shortcuts were employed by early programmers to save space. "In the early days of mechanical and later electronic tabulation and analysis, these cards contained the tabulation programs and raw data. They are 80 characters wide, severely limiting the amount of information that can be stored on a single card." (2)

As explained by Mr. Deak, one of the shortcuts employed by those early programmers was the "truncation of annual dates to the last two digits." In other words, the first two digits of the date were deleted. Therefore, 1958 was entered as simply "58."

With improvements in technology, punch card-based systems were transferred to magnetic tapes and disks. Old habits, however, remained the same. Throughout the 1960s and into the 1970s, programmers brought the two-digit methodology into the next era of the computer age. Therefore, the use of two digits to represent years has become, over nearly 40 years of rapidly developing technology, a programming habit.

In the early days of the computer revolution, young programmers just out of college saw no urgency in rectifying a practice that had been used for years. Think about it. A 30-year-old programmer in 1965 saw the Year 2000 as a space-age time in the distant future – 35 years away! "There's plenty of time to fix the problem," they assured each other. "Besides, nobody will be using our programs in the Twenty-first Century anyway!," they confidently proclaimed. "People will be living on the moon by 2000!," they imagined.

Of course, nobody foresaw that computer programs developed in the 1950s, '60s, and 70s – such as COBOL, FORTRAN, and BASIC - would still be running in 2000 on those early mainframe computers. Forty years of layering flawed data fields on top of flawed data fields built the foundation for today's monumental information technology crisis. Little by little, date by date, program by program, layer by layer, the tiny problem has multiplied into a planetary predicament.

The layering effect is similar to arsenic poisoning, says Capers Jones, chairman of Software Productivity Research Inc. in Burlington, MA. "...It is well known that poisons such as arsenic accumulate slowly in the body. Tiny does, each harmless in itself, can slowly accumulate until the victim perishes. In some ways, the Year 2000 software problem resembles the slow accumulation of arsenic. For many years, software applications have been built with two-digit field year dates. Year by year, these two-digit fields have been accumulating in software packages all over the world." (3)

Like a silent killer virus, this simple programming flaw has been copied so many times by software and microchip designers that almost all of the world's computers are infected.

If Geeks Are So Smart, Why Did They Let This Happen?

Nobody planned for this mess to develop. Like all other serious problems, programmers assumed "they" (those mysterious, invisible people who do all kinds of unpleasant things we don't want to be bothered with) would eventually take care of the situation.

Well, "they" didn't do it.

Now, we must.

Looking back with hindsight, programmers now recognize several important factors that contributed to the present situation.

- Memory Space Limitations

In the very early days of computing, memory space was a rare and premium commodity. We have palm-held computers today with much mormemory than the largest mainframe computers had in the early days. Literally, every little "bit" counted in those days. Programmers squeezed whatever could be squeezed to save space – and money! One of the easiest ways to save space and money was to shorten all yearly dates. Therefore, for the last four decades, computers throughout the world have been deliberately programmed to keep track of only the last two digits of the year. What began as a software problem, eventually worked its way into the hardware configuration of large mainframe computers and PCs. The shortened date habit has also been programmed into tiny microchips that are embedded in numerous appliances and machinery. Furthermore, we easily forget how expensive computer memory was just a few years ago. Just compare prices over the years. A computer with 32 megabytes of RAM (32 million bytes) can be purchased today for $400 or less. In the mid-1960s, you would have paid over $1 million for a computer with just 32,000 bytes - a mere one-tenth of one percent of the memory of your current computer

- Lack of International Date Standards

The same numbers do not necessarily mean the same date in different countries around the globe. There just are not any internationally accepted standards to express dates. For example, 6/1/98 means June 1, 1998 to Americans. In Great Britain, however, 6/1/98 means January 6, 1998. Big difference. Fortunately, at least the year is the same. Many Asian countries, however, do not accept the Gregorian calendar used by Western nations. Without any internationally accepted standards, computer programmers tended to use the method that was convenient in their own country.

- Make It Easy. Take A Shortcut

  It is just human nature to do things easier and faster. We abbreviate things. Look at your checkbook. The bank automatically prints "19" on your checks. We tend to say "the nineties" when referring to the 1990s. We even abbreviate the Year 2000 crisis term to simply "Y2K!" Allowing people to key in the last two digits saved time in the workplace. People in the 1960s and 1970s assumed you were talking about the same century.

- Applications Were Not Expected To Last To The Year 2000

  Programmers in the early days fully expected their code to be replaced long before the dawn of the Twenty-first Century. Programmers felt justified in using a date algorithm (Webster's Dictionary: a rule of procedure for solving a mathematical problem that frequently involves repetition of an operation.) which would fail when processing dates outside of the Twentieth Century because they didn't think the application would last beyond the era.

- The Market Demands Backwards Compatibility

  The explosion of new computer applications requires that a degree of compatibility be maintained with previous software. Windows 3.1 was designed to run DOS applications. The newly released Windows98 must support Windows95, Windows 3.1, and DOS. Consumers are simply unwilling to totally scrap working applications when they upgrade them with the latest software releases. Therefore, the date algorithm has remained safely embedded in new software packages. The immense problem arises when we realize that the date algorithm is rooted in layer upon layer of software designs.

- Marketplace Pressures

  Even in the 1980s, information technology professionals still assumed there was enough time to solve the Year 2000 problem. After all, in 1985, it was still 15 years away. What nobody foresaw in the 1990s was the combination of a technology explosion and a simultaneous business restructuring process. First, a serious recession hit the nation in 1990. Companies were under pressure to pull out of the economic downturn. Then, the realities of the new global marketplace forced companies to downsize quickly. Every department – including information technology – was required to do more with less. Especially less people – which meant fewer IT programmers available to work on long range problems such as Y2K. Additionally, the explosion of new technologies accelerated rapidly in the mid-1990s as the Internet, wireless communications, and DBS television took off. Consequently, companies focused on short-term profits instead of long-term problems. Hence, we are only months away from a global computer crisis.

- No Networks

    We live in the age of the Internet, local area networks, frame-relay networks, modems, and electronic data exchanges. How quickly we forget that just a few years ago most computers were not connected to others throughout the nation and around the globe. In fact, most computers were not even networked to other computers in the same building. Although designed to operate on a "stand alone" basis, computers are now globally linked. Therefore, computer "B" now shares the programming flaw in computer "A".

- Old Fashion Procrastination

    We humans put things off. "Tomorrow," we say. This isn't a problem that has sneaked up on the IT industry. No, it has been widely recognized for decades. Mostly, a favorite topic of conversations at geek parties. There was always something more important, more exciting to do. Going into a large corporation's entire computer system and looking for two-digit dates sounded really BORING. Kind of like deciding whether to play golf on a Saturday afternoon or cleaning out your grandfather's garage and making an inventory of everything he owned during his 85 years of life. Well, golf always wins. Likewise, IT professionals – and their corporate superiors - have simply postponed the inevitable. Unfortunately, we're out of time. The inevitable is here.

The Computer Collides With the Calendar

The Calendar keeps track of time – days, weeks, months, and years. It is one of mankind's earliest and most simple devices. Computers perform calculations using dates – days, weeks, months, and years. Computers are one of mankind's most recent and technologically advanced inventions. Mankind invented both devices. Both inventions are about to collide at a pivotal juncture in the history of the human race – the imminent arrival of the Third Millennium.

What will happen?

Very simply, when the clock strikes midnight on New Year's Eve in 1999, most computers will roll over to "00." That's not "00" as in 2000. Instead, it will be interpreted erroneously as "00" as in 1900. When this happens, computers – including embedded microprocessors – will detect that something seriously is wrong with their calculations.

One of three things will happen. The three possibilities are plainly described in a February 7, 1997, report by the Federal government's Office of Management and Budget. "Unless they are fixed or replaced, they will fail in one of three ways: they will reject legitimate entries, or they will compute erroneous results, or they will simply not run." The report goes on to state in stark terms the potential for trouble for the government. "Every federal agency is at risk of widespread systems failures."

Software is the language code computers use to "think." Computers that can not recognize dates beyond 1999 will malfunction in one of the three methods mentioned above.

How could something so simple as MM/DD/YY be so menacing?

The very simplicity of the problem is one of the greatest obstacles in mobilizing people to take the threat seriously. The danger is in the fact that many computers hold dates in a six-digit format - MMDDYY. Thus, the date April 10, 1998, is stored as 041098 is a classical MMDDYY format that is missing the two digits that are the century indicator. In a eight-digit format - MMDDYYYY - April 10, 2000, would be stored as 04102000.

Computers use dates for various functions and calculations. The list of date-related functions is endless: To sort data by sequence; to calculate interest on a loan; to determine the age of a person; to determine the last time equipment has been serviced; to determine payroll functions such as earnings, taxes, retirement contributions; and so on.

If calculations are performed using faulty dates, then the results will be faulty also. Consider the impact on your personal life just from the miscalculation of your birthday. Stop and think about how many times and places your birth date has been entered into a computer system since you were born: At the hospital, enrollment in school, Social Security, college, military service, your employment history, your first auto loan, credit cards, bank accounts, mortgages, retirement accounts, investments, etc. Now imagine what happens when computers at these government agencies and business enterprises that have created a file on you containing your birth date start miscalculating your age.

Here's an example. Let's take a person born in 1964. It is easy to figure the person's age. In 1998, just subtract 64 from 98. The answer is 32. Your computer would arrive at the same conclusion. In 1999, the calculation is 1999 - 1964 = 33. Again, your computer prints out the same number. In the Year 2000, however, something goes wrong. When you subtract 64 from 00, you know that the person's age is 34. Your computer says the person is -64. In many systems, the minus sign would be lost. Therefore, the computer would say the person is 64 years old. Unable to process this simple date, some computers will stop functioning. Others will continue to operate, but the data will be corrupted.

To further complicate matters, not all malfunctioning computers will assume that "00" is 1900. Some computers with Intel chips will say it is 1980 or 1984. Consequently, it may not be possible to develop a single correction that works on all computers. Because different computers have different chips inside, a company's networked computers could reset to different dates. Computers assuming the data is too old to be stored could erase crucial files.

The truth is that dates are a crucial component of every day life. Accurate calculation of dates is crucial in every business and government agency. Schools, hospitals, tax collectors, insurance companies, warehouses, food processing plants, banks, the Social Security Administration, accountants, investors, personnel departments – every group relies on the correct calculation of dates to function properly.

Can Two Missing Digits Really Upset the World System?

If anybody should know the gravity of the situation, it would be Andrew S. Grove, who recently stepped down as the Chief Executive Officer of Intel Corporation. In an interview with editors and reporters at the Washington Post on April 23, 1998, Mr. Grove said the federal government faces an "ugly" situation if it does not speed up its efforts to correct the Year 2000 error in government computers.(4)

Mr. Grove gave a very pessimistic assessment of the federal government's chances of successfully dealing with the crisis. He said government agencies have "no chance" if they don't have a plan in place to deal with the problem by the end of 1998, and have their systems thoroughly tested in 1999.

"The problem's going to be pretty bad," Mr. Grove lamented.

Other corporate executives in the United States share his growing concern. CIO Magazine released the results of a poll taken in the Spring of 1998 which shows that chief information officers think the Year 2000 millennium bug problems are getting worse. (5) Almost two-thirds (63 percent) of the responding executives say they will not fly in January, 2000.

A key executive for the world's largest information technology research and advisory firm isn't very optimistic either. John Bace is Research Director for the Gartner Group, Inc., which employs over 750 analysts in 49 countries around the world to advise 33,000 individual clients about the latest trends in technology. In his May 7, 1998, testimony before the House Committee on Ways and Means Subcommittee on Oversight, Mr. Bace told the Congressmen, "As a citizen of the Republic and an investor in the economy, I wish I could be more optimistic. However, as a technologist who wrote his first computer program in 1968, I am painfully aware of the impact even two simple digits can have on the operation of any IT system. As a result, this is a very real problem that needs to be addressed quickly." (6)

In Europe, Robin Guenier, head of Britain's Taskforce 2000, is sounding the warning bells. "Government is underestimating the seriousness of this extraordinary problem," proclaims Mr. Guenier. "We are surely facing an emergency the same magnitude as a war." (7)

On January 14, 1998, the BBC News in London reported that more than 60 business executives and academics wrote a stark warning to government leaders in Great Britain, Canada, and the United States. The letter expressed "acute concern" about the approaching Millennial bug. Among the executives signing the letter were the CEOs of British Aerospace, Unilever, Lloyds of London, and Cellnet. The executives wrote that they fear financial chaos if governments don't do more to solve the crisis. The letter warned that "malfunctions in critical areas, such as air traffic control and defense, may put safety at risk."(8)

The looming Millennial Meltdown is being taken seriously by a growing number of leaders. The cold reality that this train is about to jump the tracks is sinking into more politicians and business leaders.

Utah's United States Senator, Robert Bennett heads a new Senate committee helping government agencies deal with the problem. Senator Bennett clearly sees the potential for serious economic problems ahead. "There's going to be significant economic disruption," he predicted during a news conference on May 22, 1998.

"We have to act like Paul Revere," says Sen. Bennett. Citizens must be prepare, he advised, for the Year 2000.

"Get ready. Take precaution," Senator Bennett warns.

4 Doomsday Dates: "Houston, We Have a Problem."

"It's worse than we thought."

J.P. Morgan Securities Inc. Equity Research Report
by Mr. William D. Rabin and Mr. Terrence P. Tierney
May 15, 1997

On the fateful evening of April 14, 1912, experienced maritime Captain Edward Smith steered the British luxury liner *Titanic* through iceberg-laden waters 95 miles south of the Grand Banks of Newfoundland. For some reason, perhaps under pressure by the cruise line to set a record time, Captain Smith abandoned his years of experience. He ordered the *Titanic* to proceed at full-speed.

The *Titanic* boasted of 16 watertight compartments. Prior to departing New York City, the pride of the White Star Line had been declared "unsinkable."

Just before midnight, the ship struck an iceberg. Five of the compartments were punctured by the iceberg, one more than the ship's builders had considered possible in any accident. There were 2,220 people on board, yet the experts had only furnished lifeboats for half the ship's passengers and crew. "Why have a contingency plan if the ship would never sink?," they reasoned. Another ship, the *Californian*, was nearby, but did not aid the *Titanic* because its radio operator was asleep. More than 1,500 people died that night in the icy Atlantic waters.

Today, the world is steaming across the vast sea of the Information Age. Straight ahead is an iceberg of immense size – called Y2K. At the helm of many huge corporations are experienced captains of enterprise. They have been under daily pressure by stockholders to ride the waves of Wall Street's monstrous bull market of the 1990s. They knew better. Yet, they cast aside years of management experience, and gave the orders, "Full speed ahead!"

These proud CEOs believe their company's own PR hype. They actually believe their corporate ships are unsinkable. Even if they took a hit, the company's multiple airtight divisions could withstand the shock. Like the confident builders of the Titanic, the management crews of these corporate ships never anticipated the remote possibility that five or more airtight compartments could be punctured at once.

Disregarding the obvious dangers in the iceberg-laden waters, the CEOs order the vessels to proceed at full-speed to break the next P/E rating.

Somebody should warn them. The crew on the USS Government ship, however, is asleep at the wheel. Surprisingly, these corporate ships have no contingency plans. They never expected to go down. Regrettably, because their pride told them it could never happen, they only have lifeboats for half their employees.

Like the *Titanic*, warning signals are around us as we approach the end of the 1990s. More and more, we will hear about computer-related failures. These reports are the tremors before the quake. A prudent person would take precaution. Only fools would ignore the signs of the times.

The Millennial Meltdown Will Start Before January 1, 2000

If you're fretting about the consequences of the Great Computer Crash of 2000, relax. You won't have to wait until January 1, 2000 to see if dire predictions come true.

Stuff is going to start happening in 1999.

Actually, stuff has already started to happen.

Tangible date field crashes have already occurred that are directly related to Y2K. Additionally, previous hardware and software failures, unrelated to Y2K, give us a preview of things that could go wrong in the Year 2000. Together, these glitches are early warning signals that should be heeded.

For example, there was the case reported by the Associated Press in 1993 of a 104-year-old resident of Winona, Minnesota. Mary Bandar received an invitation from the local school system to enroll in kindergarten. The school's computer was triggered to send the invitation when it perceived that the elderly lady was only five years old. It seems the computer read her birthday as being in "88" as in 1988 – not 1888.

Consider other real-life computer failures. These computer foul-ups were documented in the book *Computer Related Risks* by Peter G. Newmann (ACM Press, New York, 1995). Although the following foul-ups were not connected to Y2K, they are serious examples of what can happen with computers make errors.

- Military leaders found a serious computer software glitchin the flight simulator of the F-16 fighter jet. The minus sign was missing for latitudes south of the equator. During testing, the missing minus sign caused the flight simulator to fly the plane upside down whenever it crossed the equator.

- Several automobiles were accidentally crushed in the parking lot of a cement factory. Large boulders were taken to the top of a rock crusher by a 3-stage conveyor belt. A technical flaw in an embedded microprocessor chip caused the second conveyor to shut down, but did not shut off the other two belts.
- Six known deaths have been attributed to cancer patients receiving overdoses from radiation. The malfunction in the radiation equipment was in the software, which allowed lethal doses of radiation.
- Up to 20 people died in London when ambulances did not respond in time. The delays were caused by glitches in new software, which was not thoroughly tested before implementation.
- A massive power outage in 1984 affected 10 western states in America. The power shutdown was caused by a computer error in a substation in Oregon.
- Despite the press stories during the Gulf War, the Patriot missile system had serious accuracy problems in shooting down Scud missiles. An unrecognized clock drift over a 100-hour period resulted in a tracking error of 678 meters.
- On September 17, 1991, an electrical power brown out in New York City shut down the city's airports and telephone service. Because of a hookup failure, AT&T's back-up generators didn't come online. The system was then operating on standby batteries. Warning signals were sent to the emergency center. Ironically, technicians did not respond to the emergency signals because they were attending a meeting discussing what to do in case of an emergency. Furthermore, the alarms had been disabled because nearby construction kept setting them off. When the batteries went dead, so did New York City's phone service.

Fruit Store Finds Y2K Pits in Credit Cards Terminals

Visa and MasterCard made a lot of merchants, bankers, and investors happy in August 1997, when both companies proudly proclaimed they had whipped the millennial bug. Previously, the two largest credit card companies had imposed a moratorium on cards with a 2000 or later expiration date after computers had rejected the cards. Come October, 1997, Visa and MasterCard said they would allow banks to issue Year 2000 credit cards.

Meanwhile, back in Warren, Michigan, the announcement that credit card companies had solved the Y2K problem was news to the owners of Produce Palace. Mark Yarsike and Sam Katz, owners of the Produce Palace International supermarket, had a bad taste in their mouth. The shop owners had purchased for $150,000 a new computerized electronic checkout system from All American Cash Register, a subsidiary of Tec America.

According to Mr. Yarsike, the two-year-old system repeatedly crashed, along with the store's 10 cash registers, every time a customer attempted to pay for groceries with a credit card that had a 2000 expiration date. "Whenever a card with the 2000 date is swiped, the wrong figures still appear on the screen. People were starting to be charged crazy amounts, which annoyed them, and also messed up our record," he said. (1)

Produce Palace International filed a lawsuit against Tec America and All American Cash Register – the world's first Year 2000 lawsuit.

Although MasterCard and Visa say their cards of Year 2000 compliant, they also realize problems will arise "out in the field" among their hundreds of thousands of local merchants. The credit card giants have been working overtime to help local merchants around the world to upgrade their validation terminals. The validation systems used by merchants have been rejecting cards with a 2000 or later expiration date. The validation systems' process "00" as 1900 when the merchants swiped the magnetic strip through the machines. According to the companies, any existing problems stem from noncompliant local merchants.

Visa and MasterCard are going forward with their Year 2000 conversion of credit cards. As of April 1, 1998, 10% of MasterCard credit cards had expiration dates in 2000 or beyond. By December, 1999, the company expects that 100% of its issued cards will have an expiration date of 2000 or later.

While Visa and MasterCard claim Y2K compliance, others are still testing the waters. As of May, 1998, American Express had yet to issue a card with a 2000 expiration date. The company says it is testing its infrastructure.

Of course, just because the cards are compliant at the issuer's end, it doesn't mean everybody is out of the woods. The data must pass through several channels. Once the merchant swipes a card, data about the purchase and card holder is sent through a central processing center. It is then transmitted to the merchant's bank, then into the credit card company's network, then to the bank that issued the card. Then, the data is sent back through the system to the terminal at the point of sale.

The more hands that touch the data, the more chances of problems occurring. Credit card companies also have to solve their internal Y2K issues involving billing, customer records, and other administrative functions. Which means that throughout 1998 and 1999, credit card companies will keep their fingers crossed and hoping that other major problems don't spring up.

"Even if we're ready, its important that all the folks who have to touch us and all the folks we have to touch are also ready," Charles M. Hegarty, president of Wachovia Bank Card Services Inc., stated in *The American Banker.* "This is not something we can do in isolation." (2)

IT Managers Report System Failures

Evidence that Y2K problems are popping up throughout the country was substantiated in a Spring '98 survey of U.S. companies. Conducted by the Information Technology Association of America (ITAA), the survey revealed that a substantial number of companies have already experience Year 2000 failures. Forty-four percent of the respondents said their companies have experienced Y2K failures under actual operating conditions. Sixty-seven percent of the respondents said their organizations experienced failures while testing for Y2K problems.(3)

The percentage of companies reporting Y2K failures is increasing each month. In December 1997, a survey commissioned by Cap Gemini America, a large IT consulting firm, reported that 7% of 108 IT directors and managers surveyed said their companies had already experienced a Year 2000-related failure.

"The failures have been occurring every year in increasing numbers," said Jim Woodward, senior vice president of Cap Gemini America's TransMillennial Services. (4)   In 1995, one client couldn't issue five-year credit cards; in '96, there were problems with four-year leases; in '97 systems that processed three-year insurance policies had problems; at the beginning of '98 already we've been contacted by a company whose purchase-order system has failed significantly due to a two-year projection of a purchase order," Mr. Woodward was quoted as saying in a January 10, 1998, article by *Info World Electric*.

Nine Dates That Will Rock Your World

Just when you think things couldn't get any worse, consider that the rollover to the Year 2000 is not the only date on the calendar that will trigger trouble for computers. In addition to January 1, 2000, nine "dangerous dates" await us in the coming months. Like solid icebergs, these nine dates are immovable too.

We're going to hit them soon. We just don't know much disruption they will cause. Eight of the dates will be tremors before the Big Quake on January 1, 2000. The last date will be an aftershock.

• ***Dangerous Date #1: Jan. 1, 1999 – Event Horizon Failures/ Euro Dollar***

The first day of 1999 will mark two important factors that will greatly impact our economy. January 1, 1999, will be a significant *event horizon*. The term refers to the last date that applications will process dates correctly. For example, the software used by a warehouse to track inventory projects inventory levels 12 months in advance.   In December 1998, the Event Horizon would be December 1999 – one year ahead. When the calendar turns over to January 1999, however, the Event Horizon will be January 2000. If the software and computer hardware are not Year 2000 compliant, it will malfunction. (Actually, problems could begin occurring in some companies in 1998 if their software applications have two-year Event

Horizons.) The second significant factor that will kick in on January 1, 1999, is the introduction of the Euro dollar by the European Monetary Union. The timing of the Euro currency is one of the worst public policy decisions ever made by politicians. The impact of this event is more fully explained in Chapter 8.

• ***Dangerous Date #2: Feb 1, 1999 – New York City Begins Fiscal Year 2000***
Brace yourself for this tremor. The government of the nation's largest city – the Big Apple – begins its Fiscal Year 2000. The city government has identified 687 mission-critical systems such as welfare, public housing, utilities, police protection, tax collection. All must be made Y2K compliant and thoroughly tested by January, 1999. As of April, 1998, the city said 234 mission-critical systems were in the process of being made compliant or tested. Another 453 critical systems remain. So far, the city says it spent $76 million on Y2K compliance. It expects to spend another $200 million by the end of 1998. Keep your eyes on this one.

• ***Dangerous Date #3: April 1, 1999 – New York State Begins Fiscal Year 2000***
A month later on the heels of New York City, the state government of New York begins its Fiscal Year 2000. The state has huge problems. State politicians have actually cut the governor's budget to deal with Y2K. So far, not much has been done to get the state ready. Another "hot spot" to watch.

• ***Dangerous Date #4: April 6, 1999 – UK's Corporations Begin Fiscal Year 2000***
Here's our first chance to see how major businesses will handle Y2K applications. Corporations in the United Kingdom begin operating on a Fiscal Year 2000 basis.

• ***Dangerous Date #5: July 1, 1999 - FY00 Begins In Most States and Businesses***
Forty-six state governments start their Fiscal Year 2000 budgets on this date. (Texas is Sept. 1, Alabama and Michigan are on October 1) This means the Event Horizons will be affected for numerous government and business applications such as budgeting, accounting, receivables, inventory, scheduling, etc. This is when the rubber meets the road for most state government agencies.

• ***Dangerous Date #6: August 22, 1999 - Global Positioning System Rolls Over***
Trail hikers, yachtsmen, highway travelers, and many others will lose their world-wide GPS on August 22, 1999. The Global Positioning System, operated by the   Department of Defense, is used for navigation in everything from nuclear missiles to sport utility vehicles. GPS is used by average citizens to determine precise location, to plan trips such as wilderness hikes, by hunters finding their way

home, and by highway truckers. The GPS started as a military project, but like the Internet, quickly spread to commercial and private use. Comprised of 24 Navstar satellites mounted on six orbital planes, GPS provides continuous access   to precise time and frequency to ground receivers anywhere on earth. The system transmits data to receivers on earth needed to determine precise time and position (latitude, longitude, and altitude). Two cesium and two rubidium clocks are aboard each satellite. The clocks synchronize time output as the satellites completes two earth orbits per day. The signal – a composite of a time signal transmitted by the satellites' clocks and by atomic clocks located in international time-standards bureaus on earth – is accurate to within 300 nanoseconds of Universal Coordinated Time. GPS sets the standards for the world's clocks. So precise is its measurement of time, financial institutions use GPS time is use to synchronize major international fund transfers to ensure that interest payments are calculated to the nearest second. Telecommunication companies use GPS to establish precise timing for switching. The problem involves the way the GPS accounts for time. GPS keeps track of dates by recording the number of weeks from an arbitrary starting point to the point when the system's "date buckets" overflow. At that point, the system resets to zero. The "date bucket" on GPS is 1,023 weeks. Therefore, on week 1,024 the "date buckets" will return to zero. The current GPS system begin counting at midnight on January 5, 1980. So, at midnight on August 21, 1999, the "date buckets" will overflow and reset to 0000. The U.S. Air Force is responsible for the operation of the GPS. All software dependent on the GPS must be rewritten. The Air Force is repairing the software and expects to have it ready by late 1998 or early 1999. The U.S. Air Force Space and Missile Systems Center issued a memo in 1997 warning of possible "catastrophic mission failure" if systematic checks of GPS systems are not made to ensure Y2K and GPS rollover compliance. As for private citizens and commercial users, basically the Pentagon recommends that you call the vendor   where you purchased your GPS receiver. Older ground receivers will fail to pick up the GPS signal.   Many local emergency response systems, however, use GPS to track emergency vehicles for 911 systems. This could be a very serious problem after August 21, 1999. The "date bucket" rollover is just one problem for the GPS. The Defense Department still must make GPS Year 2000 compliant. DoD must replace the date code software at the Boeing Mission Operation Support Center (MOSC) with the Integrated Mission Operation Support Center (IMOSC). The military expects to finish the project by December 1999. That's cutting it really close. The military realizes how important GPS has become to our national defense, having become the source for precise targeting information for today's smart weapons such as the Tomahawk cruise missiles. In April, 1997, Emmett Paige, Jr., assistant secretary of Defense for command, control, communications, and intelligence, told a Congressional committee, "The most significant system today that is not (Year 2000) compliant is GPS, which would have more impact than anything else."

- **Dangerous Date #7: Sept. 9, 1999 – End of File Logical Flag**
  Decades ago, many programmers assumed their software would not be in use by the year 1999. Because software applications need to indicate the ends of files, in order to shut down properly, many pro-grammers used the number "9999" as a file termination code. The digit "9" or a series of nines has always been used in the computing industry to signify various meanings: end of file, end of record, can-cellation, error return, missing date, etc. The problem is that "9999" was never meant to be an actual date. When we reach September 9, 1999, computers will read the date as "9999." Obviously, calcula-tions could be faulty if the computer misinterprets the "9999" sequence. The "99" problem is the wild card of the crisis. Nobody knows how many older programs contain strings of nines. A November, 1997, report by Data Dimensions, a large IT consulting firm, states the problem clearly: "This systemic failure due to "the nines" is potentially very damaging. It is no major exaggeration to say that every date processing program is potentially vulnerable to this error. And, it is almost too late to fix the problem before fail-ure occurs. Unless immediate action is taken to address and solve the 1999 date problem, computer failure is inevitable."(5)

- ***Dangerous Date #8: October 1, 1999 – Federal Government Begins FY00***
  The federal government officially begins operating under its Fiscal Year 2000 budget. The feds are extremely behind in efforts to make government computers Y2K compliant. Watch out for fireworks.

- ***Dangerous Date # 9: February 29, 2000 – The Forgotten Leap Year***
  To the surprise of many programmers, the Year 2000 is a leap year. Leap years were introduced first by Julius Caesar in 45 BC. Upon the advice of Sosigenes, a Greek astronomer, Julius Caesar instituted a purely solar calendar. The Julian calendar fixed the normal year at 365 days. Every fourth year was declared a leap year. The Julian year, however, was 11 minutes and 14 seconds longer than the solar year. By the time of Pope Gregory XIII's reign in the 1500's, the vernal equinox was occurring on March 11 instead of March 21. In 1582, Pope Gregory XIII issued a degree dropping 10 days from the calendar. He also instituted the Gregorian Calendar, which stated that century years divisible evenly by 400 should be leap years, and that all other century years should be common years. The effect of

this change is to make the average length of a year to be 365.2425 days. This will amount to one day's error after 4000 years. While companies and computer programmers have been focused on solving the Year 2000 problem, many have overlooked the fact that 2000 is also a leap year. If only they would have read the official leap year rules as posted by the National Institute of Standards and Technology. If the year is divisible by four, but not divisible by 100, or if the year is divisible by 400, then it is a leap year. It is the second part of the algorithm that many programmers have missed, which is that if the century year is divisible by 400, then it is a leap year. Therefore, the year 1600 was a leap year, but 1700 was not. The Year 2000 is a leap year! The problem is two fold: First, we don't know how many older software programs are still being used that mistakenly assumes that 2000 is a normal year. Second, many companies that are feverishly working to make their systems Y2K compliant may be overlooking the leap year factor - which means their systems will malfunction on February 29, 2000. Being off by one day can pose serious risks. The New Zealand Herald reported on February 22, 1997, about a malfunction at an aluminum smelter in Southland. All 660 process control computers in the factory shut down, destroying five pot cells, when the computers could not handle the extra day from the 1996 leap year. A humorous example of leap year miscalculations is the true story of a man who parked his car at the San Diego, CA, airport. His ticket was stamped February 30, 1992. Upon his return on March 10, he was presented at the parking lot gate with a bill for $3771.00! The parking lot computer had charged him $11 per day for 342 days.

5 Embedded Microchips: What You Can't See Will Hurt You

"On a Friday night less than two years from now, a tsunami will build in the Pacific and roll westward through all major hydrocarbon producing fields before reaching Prudhoe Bay, Alaska. We know the exact date, not to mention the hour, minute, and second. We do not know its size."

> *Feature Article on Year 2000 in World Oil Magazine*
> *April, 1998 by*
> *Scott Shemwell, Jerry Dake, and Bruce Friedman*
> *Executives with MCI Systemhouse*

The Big Quake is coming.

It will trigger a massive Tidal Wave. A silicone tsunami.

A tsunami, a Japanese word meaning "harbor wave," is a seismic sea wave produced by an undersea earthquake. A tsunami can have wavelengths of up to 120 miles, reach speeds of up to 500 miles per hour, and travel hundreds of miles across the deep ocean.

What makes a tsunami so dangerous is that its size and force is hidden below the surface of the sea. When it began out at sea, it was only a foot high. Upon reaching shallow coastal waters, however, it grows quickly to 50 feet or higher - unleashing a horrendous force of destruction upon a unsuspecting coastal community.

There's a subsea tidal wave heading toward us. The overwhelming majority of people on the beaches of today's high-tech societies have not an inkling of awareness that this massive wall is moving toward them. Despite the warnings of a few voices, the "experts" say there is nothing to worry about.

It will deliver the debilitating blow to man's massive monument to the gods of technology.

Few are aware of its existence, and its potential to wreck havoc on our society.

Like a deadly virus lurking in an unsuspecting person's body, this attacker waits silently, like a ticking time bomb, for the appointed time to explode with a furious force.

There are billions buried beneath the surface of gadgets, tools, appliances, machines, missiles, fire trucks, power generators, and oil rigs. So many that experts don't even know how many exist around the world.

Twenty-five billion is the most commonly accepted estimate. Some embedded chip experts say it's really 40 billion. That's 25,000,000,000 to 40,000,000,000! A percentage will malfunction - between 2% to 10%. That is potentially four billion malfunctioning chips on January 1, 2000! Maybe earlier, if the predictions of some Y2K analysts are correct. Some experts think many will crash on September 9, 1999.

What are these hidden miniature mines that are poised to sabotage our economic system?

Embedded Systems Drive Today's Technology

Over the last decade, computer chips have become dramatically smaller and cheaper. Engineering breakthroughs in the design and manufacturing of computer chips has been the catalyst behind the revolution in cellular telephones, laptop computers, bank debit cards, and a multitude of other products.

Computer chips have become so sophisticated that the term "embedded system" now refers to any "non-compute" device used to control or monitor the operation of an appliance, equipment, or machinery. "Embedded" means simply that the devices are implanted inside the appliance or machine. Often, the chip's embedded presence is obscured to the casual observer - and even to more skilled technicians.

At the low end, the simplest embedded chips perform a single function, or a simple set of functions, to produce a specified end result. The low end "embedded chips" perform very simple tasks, such as timers that count seconds or minutes until it receives an electronic signal to stop or reset. They are commonly referred to as "non-compute" devices or black boxes. Even the most simple of black boxes, however, can be deceiving. Upon closer inspection, it may contain a multitude of black boxes embedded with its circuitry also. Different vendors manufactured these smaller black boxes, most likely. Inside these smaller black boxes might exist an even smaller black box. Each black box can have up to ten layers of technology - each from a different manufacturer.

More complex "embedded chips" function as miniature computers - "computers on a chip." They don't appear to be computers in the eyes of laymen - no key board, no monitor, no hard drive, no printers. To IT engineers, however, these chips are very much real computers. The more complex chips have a greater degree of "intelligence" which means they are capable of conducting different functions in a variety of purposes. The chip's input comes from a sensor. Its output goes to an activator which activates the device or machine to perform a specific function such a controlling the flow of fuel to an engine or closing a valve in a million-dollar cooling system. In industrial control systems, embedded systems take feeds, such as temperature and pressure readings, from the plant's instruments and then pass the readings up to a supervisory data acquisition and control system.

Typically, the chip's functions are written in a low-level code. The code is then "burned" into the chip's ROM memory. Once it is burned in, it can not be altered. It will do what it was programmed to do.

"Embedded systems" are miniature circuits that contain microcontrollers running computer code, usually Assembler, stored on a chip.

What troubles many Y2K analysts is that nearly all programmable logic controllers (embedded systems) contain real-time clocks. These timing devices are used in factories and plants to start production of the next batch runs, or to schedule equipment maintenance checks. Many of these internal timing mechanisms are so small they may only register two digits. Therefore, the timing devices will clock on from 97 to 98 to 99. When they reach 2000, many of these embedded chips will read the new year as "00." Like their big-brother PCs and mainframes, many chips will misbehave - either by shutting down or error messages.

Embedded Systems Can Be Found Everywhere

There were four billion microprocessors manufactured in 1996. Ninety percent - 3.6 billion! - went into embedded systems. The problem is nobody knows where they were embedded - or which ones are Y2K compliant. Guess we'll have to wait until January 1, 2000 to discover the answer!

Embedded chips have worked their way inside thousands of products. Microwave ovens, VCRs, cellular telephones, laptop computers, electronic calculators, and cameras are just a few of the consumer applications where embedded chips have brought about technological advancements. Malfunctions by embedded chips in these consumer products will be an annoying inconvenience, but hardly life-threatening.

It is the presence of embedded chips in jet aircraft, guided missiles, nuclear power stations, petrochemical plants, and electric utilities that should alarm us. Malfunctions in these applications will be more than minor inconveniences. It will be disaster.

The "computer age" has so penetrated our society that most people are oblivious to their overwhelming presence throughout our technology-dependent world. Here's a partial list of products, equipment, and machines that contain hidden embedded microchips:

- Automobiles
- Heart monitors
- Thermostats
- Elevators
- Diesel locomotives
- Offshore oil platform
- Sprinkler systems

- Smoke detectors
- Answering machines
- Prisons
- Security systems
- Building electrical systems
- Pagers
- Traffic lights
- Mail sorting equipment
- Photocopiers
- Fire trucks
- Guided missiles
- Electrical utilities
- HVAC machines (heating, ventilating, air conditioning)
- Water purification systems
- Sewage systems
- Airport security systems
- Air traffic control
- Factory robots

Embedded Chip Detection Will Be Monumental Global Task

Even among people knowledgeable about Y2K issues, few people fully comprehend the enormous complexity of the embedded chip issue. The truth is that nobody knows how many of the 25 to 40 billion embedded chips will fail on January 1, 2000 – or earlier on September 9, 1999. The most common conservative estimate is 5%. At first glance, that doesn't sound like it's a big deal. Five percent of 25 billion, however, is over 1.2 BILLION!

If we only knew which 5% would fail!

That's the heart of the problem. Nobody has any idea which chips are not Year 2000 compliant. "For every 1000 embedded chips you look at, you'll find two or three that need correction. But those two or three are the ones that can close a blast furnace at the cost of one million (dollars) a day, or stop power production," says Anthony Parish, director-general of the Institution of Electrical Engineers in Great Britain. "The problem is finding those two or three that are not compliant."(1)

There's only one way to find out. Test every chip. Room by room. Building by building. Unit by unit. Machine by machine.

The problem is that embedded chips are, well, embedded! They are not easy to find or remove. In fact, most manufacturers soldered them into the circuit boards with no intentions of ever needing to remove the chips.

Because an embedded system's "black box" may contain layers of additional black boxes each made by a different manufacturer, the process of locating, analyzing, testing, correcting, or replacing the chips requires an enormous amount of time, money, and expertise. A company doesn't just send its building maintenance man around the complex with a flashlight and screwdriver. The task of reviewing one embedded system in a factory or electric utility may require a swarm of high-paid consultants: firmware engineers, microprocessor architecture specialists, chip vendors, operating system engineers, and the engineers who supervised the installation of the "black box" into the next "black box."

There are problems, though, in getting everybody together to examine the little chip. First, the biggest problem is just finding the little rascals. Will companies dismantle, piece by piece, a $10 million high-tech factory machine looking for embedded chips? Just how will they locate the chips? The recommended procedure is to call the vendor who sold the equipment. Managers, however, are finding it difficult to get answers.

Many of the older chips are no longer being manufactured. Even more troubling is that many of the manufacturers themselves are no longer in business. This is a highly competitive industry. Five years is a long time in the computer industry. The bulk of the non-compliant chips are older ones. "Many of the Ministry of Defense embedded systems are 15 to 20 years old," warns Robin Guenier, executive director of Great Britain's Taskforce 2000.(2)

Further complicating the assessment process is the lack of international standards in producing microchips. There are no standards for manufacturing motherboards. Actually, chip manufacturers like to know their design is different than their competitors' designs, so they work hard to make sure their products will be different. Even similar chips in the same equipment can not be assumed to be the same. You can not test just one "typical" chip and then extrapolate the results to apply to other chips with similar functions.

Another contributing factor is the inability to obtain solid information from the chip manufacturers. They are not about to open their mouths for fear of litigation. Chip manufacturers are increasingly unwilling to go on record about what they know about their chips' Y2K compliance. Lawyers are telling companies to put nothing in writing about Year 2000 compliance. "You know NOTHING! Keep your mouth SHUT!," is the advice of corporate attorneys. Everybody sees the big lawsuits coming. Forget about things like responsibility and duty. Just watch out for your own self-interest is the motto. "Let civilization collapse!," is the advice of the legal profession. "We just need to stay out of court."

Even if you can locate the chip, you must first test it to see if it is, indeed, faulty. In a large factory or utility company, it means shutting down production. You run the risk that the test itself may shut down your entire operation. Once you and your herd of consultants determine that a chip is not Y2K compliant, you have two choices: Rewrite the chip's program or replace the chip.

Chips are not socketed into circuit boards. They must be carefully removed, and a new one soldered back in without damaging the board.

All of this testing and replacement of chips takes time. Lots of time. In the race against the clock, time is quickly running out.

Time is not the only scarce commodity facing corporations and government agencies. Finding experienced, trained experts to access the risk and who are capable of fixing the problem is not easy. There are only about 20 firms in the entire United States that specialize in solving Y2K embedded chip problems. That's a very small pool of professionals to deal with 25 billion embedded chips. The dearth of competent IT engineering professionals with knowledge of embedded systems has companies and government agencies around the world feeling the pinch. "We're also running out of professional support. There aren't many of us in the field," said Mark Greig, director of Lincolne Scott, a large engineering consulting company in Melbourne, Australia.(3)

The sad truth is that businesses and government agencies will not get their embedded chips replaced before January 1, 2000. It's just not going to happen. Especially for those companies that are just getting started in dealing with the Year 2000 bug in their mainframe and PC computers. Worse still, many companies and government agencies simply are not aware of the embedded chip menace.

"There isn't enough time to make an inventory," warns David Spinks of England's Atomic Energy Authority. "We did an inventory when we were privatized; we only have 4,000 embedded systems. It took us 12 months to inventorize them, and the inventory was out of date before we finished it." (4)

Time has run out. That is reality.

Expert Says Embedded Chips Pose Global Threat to Population

How many appliances, products, machines, gadgets, and widgets need to checked for noncompliant embedded chips?

Everything that's plugged into electricity. Whether or not it comes from the utility company, batteries, or a generator. Everything must be considered "guilty until proven innocent," says Ann K. Coffou, managing director of the Year 2000 Relevance Service for the Giga Group, a large international information technology consulting firm to a Congressional committee on Capitol Hill.(5) Especially equipment or machinery that is crucial to life and death - either to people's lives or the financial life of your organization. She warns that embedded chips represent a huge risk to the life and well-being of the global population.

Early assessment of the embedded chip issue indicates that problems occur in about two or three in every 1,000 chips. The implications are staggering. If the failure rate is one or two per million chips, companies and agencies could take the risk that nothing serious will go wrong. Because many experts expect the failure rate will be much higher, organizations can not ignore the risk of major failures.

That means everything - every crucial equipment, machine, and system in each nation's core infrastructure - must be inventoried, examined, assessed for risk, and replaced if warranted. The process isn't simple. The embedded logic on a silicon chip is entombed deep in the system. Because PLCs (Programmable Logic Controllers) have numerous chips, and are highly interdependent upon each other, analyzing and repairing them is an extremely tedious and expensive endeavor.

Testing isn't fail safe either. According to a November 28, 1997, article in _The Independent_, a weekly business journal in New Zealand, an Auckland company tested its building's lighting management system by changing the clocks and running it up to the Year 2000. The lighting system performed without error in the rollover. On the surface, everything looked fine. The system, however, became locked into its nighttime cycle. An alarm sounded every hour, then turned off all the lights in the building until it was reset. Because of the test, the entire system had to be permanently turned off.(6)

Just because a piece of equipment has a system without a date clock doesn't mean you're out of the woods. Like a spreading disease, date-related data can worm its way into other systems. Jim Stewart, senior systems engineer at ExtenSys in Toronto, Canada, says he is "finding problems in strange areas." (7)   In a March 23, 1998, article in _Computing Canada_, Mr. Stewart said he was aware of one system without a date clock. A date, however, made its way into the process due to maintenance equipment connected to the machinery.

Our Nation's Core Infrastructure Is At Risk of Collapse

The potential for serious trouble by January 1, 2000, can not be overstated. The issue of embedded chips literally threatens the core infrastructure of our nation – and the rest of the world. Electricity, oil production, national defense, communications, natural gas, health care, manufacturing, public water and sanitation, food processing, transportation – each core segment of our society is at serious risk of failing as we enter the Third Millennium.

How long will our society function without an adequate supply of oil?

Embedded systems are crucial in the exploration, shipping, refinement, and production of oil and petrochemical products. The petrochemical industry faces a mammoth undertaking before January 1, 2000, to locate and replace embedded chips that are not Y2K compliant. Just one offshore oil platform may have over 10,000 embedded chips that govern the rig's automatic processes. Worse yet, many of these chips are embedded in the platform's below-surface structure. Having to locate and replace chips under water will become a logistical nightmare for oil companies.

Consider the economic ramifications of a January shutdown of the Alaskan Pipeline. On Alaska's frozen North Slope, a malfunctioning embedded chip could possibly shut down a pumping station or close a main valve. Minute by minute, hour by hour, crude oil in the Alaskan Pipeline stops flowing as the oil turns to frozen sludge. In Alaska's Arctic climate, nothing will thaw until Summer.

Top oil company executives are already planning for major problems. They know that all the noncompliant chips will not fixed in time. Quietly, they are preparing contingency plans to lessen the damage. "It is estimated that the average oil and gas firm, starting today, can expect to remediate less than 30% of the overall failure points in the production environment. This reality shifts the focus of the solution away from trying to fix the problem, to planning strategies that would minimize potential damage and mitigate potential safety hazards," says MCI Systemhouse, a Houston-based oil company in an April, 1998, article in *World Oil* magazine. (8)

What about electric utilities?

Embedded systems are widespread throughout the electrical power industry. From fossil-fuel plants to nuclear power plants, the nation's entire electrical power grid is exposed to extreme risk from malfunctioning microchips. Electric utilities are like a factory – they produce electricity as a product. They have three essential elements in the operations: administration, power production, and power distribution. Computerized automation based on microchips is prevalent throughout the three elements.

So pervasive are embedded chips in the electric industry, that the Electric Power Research Institute says, "Embedded operating systems are the building blocks used throughout the power enterprise for energy production, control, and distribution." (9)

Rick Cowles is the Year 2000 program manager for Digital Equipment Corporation. He is considered the leading authority on the impact of Year 2000 on electric utilities. He says that within a typical electric utility, "embedded logic control is prevalent in every facet of operation; from load dispatch and remote switchyard breaker control to nuclear power plant safety systems and fossil boiler control systems." (10) Mr. Cowles says gas turbine generating units are "controlled from miles away by personnel adjusting system loads in response to peak demands."

Embedded logic control, warns Mr. Cowles, is the "dirty little Y2K secret of all production facilities...that has the most significant potential to bring whole companies to their knees."

As to be expected, government regulatory agencies are just starting to comprehend the gravity of the embedded chip threat to our nation's electrical power supply. The Federal Energy Regulatory Commission is now gathering data, Kathleen Hirning, the Chief Information Officer for the Federal Energy Regulatory Commission explained to a Congressional committee on May 14, 1998, of the role of embedded chips in the electrical utility industry:

• "Embedded systems are used to control and monitor power production and delivery equipment in electric utilities. Computer controlled equipment includes many date-sensitive components, from very small programmable logic controllers to extensive network control systems. Many of the systems that have a date function may pass through the critical date without causing a fault. But they could later refuse to accept a modified instruction or even a new date entry. Other systems may have faults that could result in power outages."(11)

Mrs. Hirning admitted that the federal government doesn't have accurate data on the potential impact of Y2K-related embedded chip failures on America's electric utilities. Don't be too alarmed over the prospect of the nation experiencing a massive power blackout after January 1, 2000. The federal is moving into action! Mrs. Hirning announced on May 14, 1998, that the Commission is "exploring how to mount an effective Year 2000 outreach program" to the nation's thousands of electric utilities to find out what they know about embedded chips.

Mrs. Hirning and the Federal Energy Regulatory Commission may want to start the Commission's outreach program with a trip to England. South Western Electricity, is owned by the Southern Company, which is based in Atlanta, GA. The British utility company has posted on their Web site a list of physical assets, which may be impacted by embedded microprocessors: (12)

• operational equipment
• equipment in sub-stations
• relays and other protection devices
• auxiliary equipment, i.e. battery chargers
• mobile plant
• test equipment
• pole mounted reclosers
• generators
• disturbance analyzers
• fault recorders
• building management controls
• environment control systems, i.e. heating, air conditioning, lighting
• access and security systems
• fire alarms
• building facilities, i.e. lifts, elevators
• office equipment
• photocopiers, fax machines, dictation, and associated devices
• franking machines
• televisions and video recorders
• cameras and projection equipment
• kitchen equipment
• metering equipment

- credit meters
- budget meters, including keys and vending machines
- NGC metering
- Hand-held metering devices
- Meter test station equipment
- Transport systems
- Helicopter systems
- Vehicle engine management systems
- Garage equipment
- Inventory of sundry assets impacted by date
- Pre-printed stationary
- Date stamps.

The Commission's next stop should be the Florida Power and Light company. The utility posted the following admission on its Web site: "Assessment 14% complete, renovation 1% complete." (13) Translation: As of April 1998, the Florida Power and Light company had assessed only 14% of the utilities embedded chips. Only 1% of the chips have been fixed. The company only has until December 31, 1999, to assess the remaining 86% of the chips and repair another 99% of any noncompliant chips.

City water purification systems are at risk too. Water treatment plants use hundreds of embedded systems. Programmable Logic Controllers (PLCs) operate a variety of devices such as water level, temperature, pH level, and the release of chlorine and ozone. Chlorine and ozone are poisonous in lethal doses.

Telecommunications is also highly vulnerable to embedded chip failure. Large organizations that rely on telephone call centers may be in for a nasty surprise on January 1, 2000. Call centers are vital links between corporations and nonprofit organizations and their customers and supporters. Banks and financial institutions use call centers for customer account services. Car rental firms, hotels, and airlines use call centers to handle huge volumes of calls for reservations. Charitable and religious organizations operate call centers to receive calls from donors. Mail order and home shopping services use call centers to process telephone orders for goods and services.

According to Dataquest Inc., a market research firm in San Jose, CA, as much as 25% of installed call-center equipment may need to be replaced before January 1, 2000. "Practically every function on a private branch exchange (PBX) phone system is ultimately controlled by the date," says Bart Stanco, an analyst with Gartner Group, the world's largest IT consulting group. (14)

Embedded chips will also adversely impact transportation. Automobiles, trucks, jet aircraft, diesel locomotives, air traffic control systems all rely on embedded systems.

The advanced electrical systems of new automobiles and trucks are highly dependent on embedded chips. The Big Three automakers are not giving out much detail about embedded chips in their products. It is estimated that newer models have between 14 to 100 embedded chips inside their engines, emission controls, and electrical systems. So far, only General Motors has indicated that their vehicles will be Y2K compliant. As of late Spring, 1998, neither Ford nor Chrysler have made statements about embedded chips.

Public Safety Is Threatened By Embedded Chips

The danger to our society is more than financial. There is a serious public safety risk too.

Embedded chips are used in many manufacturing plants to control the functions of massive machinery. Imagine the catastrophic danger to employees at a petrochemical plant when the microprocessors that control the plant's cooling processes fail to work. There is a real possibility of explosions around the world in workplaces.

Hospitals have serious Y2K problems too. Embedded chips are in numerous medical devices – such as the equipment that electronically tracks signals from heart monitors that are implanted in patients.

Many sensors that detect fires and gas leaks are extremely vulnerable to embedded chip failure. Fire trucks, too, may not run. A major Canadian city government recently discovered that up to half of the city's fire trucks contain embedded chips in the engines that are not Y2K compliant. In Texas, the Department of Public Safety estimates that as many as 25% of fire trucks manufactured since 1985 may be inoperable after January 1, 2000.

Owners of high-rise apartment and office buildings are worried about elevators with embedded chips. After January 1, 2000 rolls around, many high-tech elevator systems will shut down, assuming that the elevators haven't been serviced since the Year 1900. An April 29, 1998, article in the Australian Financial Review said that in most modern buildings there are more than 25 independent services that may be affected by noncompliant computer chips. The article stated, "According to consultant engineer Norman Disney & Young, the potential computer problems when the century date changes to 2000 have the potential to shut down crucial building services such as lifts (elevators), fire protection, air conditioning, and may empty whole office buildings." (15)

Concern for safety (and liability) prompted the National Science Foundation to issue an "important notice" to the presidents of universities and colleges, and heads of other scientific organizations. The June 27, 1997, letter from the Office of the Director, warns recipients of National Science Foundation (NFS) grants about "potential problems associated with Year 2000." The letter told NFS grant recipients that they should "also be aware that the Year 2000 may affect electronic devices utilizing embedded microchips that perform date-based calculations. Biomedical devices and other laboratory equipment may depend upon embedded date functions. If the chip receives what it perceives to be an invalid date, it may fail, impacting important experiments. False date comparisons may invalidate test results, leading to false conclusions." (16)

The United States Food and Drug Administration (FDA) issued a letter on June 25, 1997, reminding medical device manufacturers that some computer systems and software applications currently used in medical devices, including embedded microprocessors, may experience problems as a result of the turn to the new century. In addition, the letter indicated that computer-controlled design, production, or quality control processes could be adversely affected. (17)

State governments are also belatedly starting to assess the impact of embedded chips on state-owned facilities and equipment. At a November 6, 1997, meeting of New York State's Year 2000 Project Managers and the Office for Technology, the group decided that each state agency should designate a project manager for the task of bringing their agency's embedded systems into compliance. Going into action, the group said it would send memos to other state agencies.

One state government that is tackling their embedded chip problem is Washington. The state's Department of Transportation (WSDOT) advertised that the agency was looking for a consultant or two to help work on the DOT's Embedded Chip Project. The posted notice in early 1998 was seeking Request for Proposals (RFP) "for the purpose of obtaining department-wide Year 2000 Embedded Chip Services." The official notice stated that "embedded chip issues permeate all WSDOT operational areas. These operational areas include ferries, facilities, vehicles and equipment, traffic signals and systems, and bridges." The state wanted the contracted project managers to start "as early as April 8, 1998, and be available through July 31, 1999." Apparently, Washington State's Department of Transportation isn't real confident the state will solve all their embedded chip problems in time. The notice said the project managers might have to be available "potentially through July 31, 2000." (18) Obviously, they expect to have some last minute clean up.

Embedded Chips Will Wreck Havoc On Global Economy

Our economic system is highly interdependent. Disruptions in the supply of electricity, oil, gasoline, and natural gas will have powerful repercussions throughout the economy. Likewise, disruptions in the supply chain will adversely impact manufacturing companies if a supply of parts and materials are not readily available.

It is not only that we, as a nation, are interdependent with each other. We are now part of a global economy. What happens in Japan affects us. South America, Australia, Africa, and Europe too.

Every facet of modern life will be impacted by date-related failures in microprocessors. In the United States – and around the world. Everywhere. At one time. This is an unprecedented occurrence in world history.

Most of the world is just now starting to pay attention to the Year 2000 problem with mainframe computers and PCs. Few have even heard about the disaster waiting us from billions of embedded microprocessors.

Even if the entire world woke up tomorrow and declared embedded chips as Public Enemy Number One, there just isn't time to solve the problem. There are billions of chips embedded in products throughout the world. Nobody knows which chips are going to fail on January 1, 2000. The only way to find out is to locate each chip, machine by machine, and test for compliance. Even after you find the noncompliant chips, there's no guarantee you can replace it without damaging the main unit of machinery or equipment. Besides, the chip's manufacturer may have gone belly up ten years ago. Then there is the critical shortage of trained professionals who can be hired to find, assess, and repair the embedded systems. Finally, there are only months until we slam head on into the Year 2000.

At some point in the near future – probably after September 9,1999 - when the first wave of embedded systems crash – reality will sink in when large corporations and government agencies admit they're not going to find and replace hundreds of millions, may billions, of embedded chips before January 1, 2000.

Complacency will turn to panic.

The stark truth will be evident.

Our time is out. Game over.

Mankind's silicone-plated Tower of Babel will fall.

6

A Last Minute Solution: What Do You Mean Bill Gates Joined A Monastery?

They call it the *silver bullet* delusion.

A simplistic presumption that "they" will fix it.

For most people, "they" means Bill Gates and his legion of brilliant programmers at Microsoft.

Forget it.

Bill's got his own Y2K problems.

Following a speech in Seattle in 1997, Mr. Gates was asked about Y2K. He said that personal computers don't use two digit dates, therefore PCs would not be vulnerable to Year 2000 failures.

That was then.

This is now.

On January 28, 1998, Microsoft admitted some of its software products do, in fact, have Y2K problems.

ComputerWorld magazine reported (January 26, 1998) that Microsoft Y2K strategy manager Jason Matusow admitted that the company's lack of responsiveness "has been a mistake." Mr. Matusow said Microsoft had "failed to grasp the importance of how its products are date-sensitive and critical to customers' operations."

"In the past, Microsoft has told customers that all of its products were Year 2000 compliant. Those statements were ...inaccurate."

Are you waiting for Bill Gates to unveil *Windows 2000*?

Hmmm...Believe in the Tooth Fairy too?

Unfortunately, Mr. Gates and Microsoft will be wearing a huge bull's-eye in 2000. Every greedy trial lawyer in the world will be gunning for him. Mountains of lawsuits will be filed against Microsoft claiming outrageous damages from Mr. Gates' negligence in selling software with Y2K errors.

So, forget about Bill Gates saving us. He'll be too busy saving himself.

Denial: We're Not Talking About the River in Egypt

Folks, there just isn't a Y2K silver bullet. Nothing will miraculously solve the Year 2000 computer problems before the meltdown. Accept it. It's not going to happen.

What you need to do is prepare for the crash landing.

In the face of indisputable facts, however, hundreds of millions of people will foolishly go about their daily lives as though nothing is wrong. Such thinking is the product of our culture of convenience. We naively believe "they" will come up with an instant fix. Just pop in a CD – and – *presto!* – the computer is ready for the Third Millennium!

The very simplicity of the problem – two missing digits – is what makes it so difficult for the general public to grasp the threat to modern society. When people are told the problem - that is, most computers can read 12/31/99, but not 01/01/00 – the typical response is, "Well, just add two digits and be done with it!"

It isn't that simple.

Perhaps, too, the enormity of Y2K – that computers around the world will fail at the same time - is too bizarre to comprehend. Our conscious mind can't cope with such a scary thought. Therefore, we childishly hold onto false hopes. If we wish hard enough, the problem will go away.

Its called denial.

The refusal to admit the truth or reality.

The coming computer crash, however, is real. Very real.

A poll by *CIO magazine* revealed how much the American public is in denial about the ramifications of Y2K. The consumer awareness survey – released on June 12, 1998 – showed that 38% of the people polled admitted they were not aware of the Year 2000 problem. Among the 62% who had some knowledge of Y2K, half (50%) said they were "not at all concerned" about Y2K affecting them personally.

An astounding 80% of the poll's respondents said Y2K would be solved before the Year 2000!

The attitude of the general public, however, is in sharp contrast to the responses by technology and business executives.

An earlier survey by *CIO magazine* revealed that a mere 11% of technology and business executives are confident Y2K will be solved by December 31, 1999. Whereas 53% of the general public stated they would be willing to take a flight on January 1, 2000, only 28% of technology and business executives express such willingness to fly.

The more you know about Y2K, the more alarmed you become.

Dealing with Y2K is too hard for many people.

The consequences of failure are too frightening to consider. Therefore, we just don't think about it. Ignorance is bliss.

Americans ignore anything that's inconvenient.

Individually, we refuse to confront difficult family problems such as a misbehaving teenager in the house. Corporately, we refuse to confront unpleasant national problems such as a misbehaving President in the White House.

Globally, we've never been confronted with a worldwide deadline to fix our technology.

Never before has the entire world unilaterally faced a deadline.

So, we pretend it isn't happening. The days and months pass by. We suppress our fears. Inwardly, we know the inevitable date is fast approaching. Yet, we go on with everyday life as though nothing is going to happen.

"They" will fix it. Right?

A global meltdown of computers. Simultaneous collapse of vital public services. Blackout of the electrical power grid. Panic-stricken consumers withdrawing their savings from banks. Civil unrest. Accidental launch of nuclear missiles.

Oh my.

It's just too ugly to think about such things.

Denial is safe.

We're like a leper, his flesh rotting and dropping to the ground, who looks in the mirror and says, "Hey good look'n!"

Its not reality, but it makes us feel good.

We Fix Computers the Old Fashion Way

Still confused about the fuss over two digits in a computer?

Can't understand why people are in a tizzy over a calendar date?

Mr. Peter de Jager, one of the world's earliest computer prophets to warn about the coming crisis, explains the problem in great simplicity.

"The code is broken. The deadline is fixed. We're not good at meeting deadlines." (1)

There's no argument about the two-digit date problem. That's a given. Most computer software will not be able to handle the year 2000. Therefore, the code is broken. It must be fixed. December 31, 1999 is a "drop dead" date. The deadline is immovable. Like an airplane flying toward a mountain, the rock will not move. The plane will crash, but the rock will not move. It can't be wished away. Congress can't pass a law and change the date. The deadline is fixed. Therefore, corrections worldwide must be completed before the deadline.

Information technology professionals are notoriously late. Seldom do they complete any major project on time. Typically, only 9% to 16% of all technology projects come in on time. Has Microsoft ever introduced new software on its original target date? Enough said. The computer geeks will be late. Really late. You can bet your floppy disks on it.

Unfortunately, there is no easy way to solve this global mess.

There's only one way to fix it.

The old fashion way!

Search every single line of computer code. Find each date-related glitch. Then manually fix each tainted line of code.

Solving the problem is not overwhelmingly complex.

It is overwhelmingly time consuming. And very expensive.

Consider the enormous scope of the task. Around the world, there are millions of corporations, factories, businesses, stores, banks, electric utilities, military bases, government agencies, colleges, schools, homes, churches, and other organizations that use computers. There are **hundreds of billions** of lines of computer code written inside those tens of millions of computers. The code is written in over 2,500 different computer languages, some of it dating back to the early 1950s. Much of the early source code has been lost forever. Few programmers from those days are still around today. Complicating matters, many of the world's computers are linked to other computers through networks. They electronically exchange data. Therefore, any programming flaws will be passed on to other computers, just like a flu virus. That means every computer must be fixed – or the virus will spread. A company could spend millions of dollars to correct its systems, only to crash after exchanging data with another company that failed to find all the Y2K glitches.

Your job is to search each computer – line by line – and find each line of code that has six digits instead of eight digits for dates! Furthermore, your computers must be fixed by December 1998 so your IT staff can have a year to conduct extensive tests. Throughout 1999, you must test every computer – and every computer network system – to make sure they operate properly. By fall 1999, you must interface with your third party partners to make sure your computers work with their computers. If there are any problems, you'll have just months – or weeks – to solve the problems and test again! Finally, you must verify that every computer in your organization is fixed and ready before December 31, 1999.

The process is the same. There are no shortcuts. Whether the computers are in California or China, the process remains the same. Each organization, regardless of size, must complete the same five-stage process: INVENTORY, ACCESS, CONVERSION, TEST, AND COMPLIANCE.

And the later it gets, the less chance it will get done.

Stage One: Inventory

How many computers, systems, networks, appliances, and pieces of equipment could be affected by Year 2000 problems? That's your first assignment. Nothing can be done until you conduct an exhaustive inventory. The inventory must dutifully log all computer hardware, software, embedded microchips, databases, networks, languages, utilities, hardware and software vendors, and every mechanism or system for receiving, storing, translating, and transmitting data. This inventory must take place room to room, department to department, building to building, until every square foot of the organization has been dutifully examined and noted.

Stage Two: Assessment

A critical assessment is the next step. The organization must frankly assess what it faces in becoming Y2K compliant. Which computers, networks, systems, software, and embedded systems are not Y2K compliant? Who are the manufacturers and distributors of the noncompliant hardware and software? Since the vendors know where the problems are, their feet must be held to the fire to provide the needed information. (Assuming the vendor is still in business!) Most importantly, in this phase the organization must realistically determine which equipment, systems, and functions are mission-critical. In other words, which things are absolutely necessary to the functioning of the organization? Those are the organization's core mission-critical systems. They must work on January 1, 2000, or the organization will cease to function.

Stage Three: Conversion

The conversion process is time-consuming, labor intensive, and expensive. There's no quick and easy method. The task is to identify the problem data fields and correct it. It's difficult because many uses of the two-digit date are hidden deep inside the software code. The IT team must find every location where software programs might miscalculate data or completely fail because of century date rollover problems. Hardware and software must be corrected or replaced. Line by line, file by file, program by program, computer by computer, every single noncompliant date-related item must be carefully examined. If it can't be fixed, or is too old to be worth fixing, it must be replaced. For most large organizations, however, replacement is no longer an option. It is too late. If the organization is going to rewrite the code, then time is running out for that option too. Most Y2K experts say the conversion process must be finished by late 1998. Why? Because the next stage needs at least 12 months or more.

Stage Four: Testing

Testing is the biggest and most time consuming phase – possibly accounting for as much as 70% of a Y2K program's time. Testing will bring organizations face-to-face with stark reality. If it doesn't work, what will they do in the few remaining months or weeks? Parallel testing is considered the most exact exercise. It requires, however, two separate sets of computer systems. The only way to test with confidence is to run the same data into two separate computers, the old computer and the repaired computer. The purpose of parallel testing is to verify that the new system and the old system produce the same results. But there's a Catch 22 trap in parallel testing for 2000. First, there's no excess computer capacity for the entire world to conduct parallel testing at the same time. The only accurate tests will be whether the computers run in the year 2000. Simulation in 1999 is not enough. Nothing can replace real operations under real conditions. Companies can test computers until they turn blue, but nobody will know for sure if they are fixed until the clock strikes midnight on December 31, 1999.

Stage Five: Compliance and Monitoring

This is where the "rubber meets the road." Organizations will learn if their systems work in the real world. The final stage introduces the repaired or replaced systems into the business world on January 1, 2000. Even if an organization's systems work on January 1, 2000, they are not "out of the woods" yet. Vigilant monitoring will take place throughout 2000 to make sure no contaminated data enters the system from outside sources such as vendors, suppliers, and other parties that are connected to the organization's computers.

Contingency Plans and Triage

There is another stage – a stage that corporate and government executives don't want to talk about. It is called CONTINGENCY PLAN-NING. It is the big "What IF?" *What if* we don't fix the computers in time? *What if* our systems are recontaminated by data exchanges with noncompliant computers? *What if* our suppliers and vendors don't fix their computers in time and we can't get parts and supplies? *What if* the electricity goes off and telephone lines are down? *What if* the banks are closed? *What if* satellites go dark?

There's another term you'll be hearing in the days ahead. It is called *triage*.

Triage is a medical term that refers to the decision to allocate a finite amount of resources and attention during an emergency to critically injured victims. In other words, if you can't keep everybody alive, then decide which patients should be chosen for medical care. The medical concept of triage places patients in one of three categories:

a. Those who will survive if they get no medical treatment.

b. Those who will survive if they get medical treatment.

c. Those who will die even if they get medical treatment.

Most importantly, in times of crisis, triage forces medical authorities – especially in battlefield environments - to decide which victims *must be kept alive*. Major corporations, government agencies, and large organizations will be forced to make that decision by January 1999. Privately, they already know time is running out.

Facing the inevitable reality of system failures will compel many organizations to deal with plans for triage. "What will we do if the systems go down on January 1, 2000? How will the corporation or agency function? What are our most critical functions? What temporary plans can be implemented to circumvent the loss of computers?"

These are tough – and for many, very troubling – questions that must be asked now.

The Magnitude of the Situation

For most people, grasping the enormity of the repair process on a global scale is beyond comprehension. Imagine an incredibly complex medical operation on a patient – an operation that is absolutely necessary for the patient to live but could kill the patient in the process.

Consider the amazing complexity of the human body – in particular, the circulatory system. The circulatory system is the human body's main transportation highway system. The circulatory system's main functions are to deliver oxygen and nutrients to all parts of the body, and to transport toxins and waste materials for elimination. This biological highway system consists of many one-way streets. Veins carry blood to the heart. Arteries carry blood away from the heart.

Amazingly, this great transportation process travels through 60,000 miles of blood vessels to the heart, which pumps more than 2,000 gallons of blood through its chambers each day. Our circulatory highway system includes a multitude of smaller roads and tiny streets. Known as the venous system, it includes venules, and capillaries – all which carry the blood back to the heart.

Now, imagine an operation that requires the surgical team to remove all of the patient's veins, arteries, venules, and capillaries. All 60,000 miles of blood vessels must be examined for contamination – vessel by vessel. Complicating the process, each vessel must be examined to see whether it has touched a contaminated vessel. Every contaminated vessel must be repaired. Furthermore. the entire medical procedure must be done within an irrevocable time constraint. The deadline for completion cannot be altered. If the operation is not successfully completed before the clock strikes midnight, the patient will die. Most of all, the patient must be kept alive during the entire operation. Finally, all the vessels – every vein, artery, venule, and capillary – must be placed back into the patient's body in exactly the same order!

That is what the world is facing in the remaining months before January 1, 2000.

The world's computers contain hundreds of billions of lines of computer code. Every line of code must be examined – line by line – for non-compliant Y2K data. Additionally, every line of code must be checked to see if it has been contaminated through electronic contact with a non-compliant program. There is an irrevocable deadline: December 31, 1999. It cannot be altered. If the entire process is not successfully completed by the deadline in every nation – in every corporation, bank, electric utility, hospital, and government agency – the patient will go into cardiac arrest.

And through all the conversion and testing, every organization must be kept alive and well during the process!

It's not going to happen.

The present "world system" will die on the operating table.

Mankind's technological Tower of Babel will collapse.

For a number of years, chaos and confusion will rule the world.

People will be desperate. Somebody will have to solve the world's mess.

In time, a new global economic system will be built. A global, cashless financial system will rise from the rubble.

Are you ready?

The Trillion Dollar Repair Bill: Yikes! Will You Accept A Post-Dated Check?

"Inevitable difficulties are going to emerge. You could end up with...a very large problem... Before we reach the year 2000, there is economic loss."

Federal Reserve Chairman Alan Greenspan
Comments before the Senate Banking Committee
On the Year 2000 computer problem.
February 25, 1998

The inventor of the Equatorium didn't plan on the century date change at the dawn of the Third Millennium.

Built around 1600, the 400-year-old brass instrument is believed to be the oldest piece of equipment to be affected by the Year 2000 computer bug.

Housed in England's Time and Space Gallery of Liverpool Museum, the Equatorium calculates time by charting the position of the sun and moon based on a dateline inscribed in stone.

The inventor, unknown to British historians, never considered the century date change in the year 2000. Apparently he never envisioned that the device would still be working four centuries later. Therefore, the dateline stops at the year 2000.

Consequently, when the clock strikes midnight on December 31, 1999, the Equatorium will stop working. The museum's staff says there is no way to alter the device to extend its lifespan.

"It's a little sad to think the working life of this 400-year-old totally unique instrument comes to a close in 18 months," said Martin Suggett, curator of Earth and Physical Sciences at Liverpool Museum, said in a June 5, 1998, interview on the British Broadcasting Corporation. (1)

"I find it extraordinary to think of the vision of the maker who made sure the instrument could be used 400 years into the future," commented Mr. Suggett. "But now those 400 years are coming to an end. He must have been the first person to put the millennial bug into a piece of equipment."

Whoever designed and built the Equatorium had great scientific and mathematical intelligence. Despite his or her intelligence, the inventor didn't have the foresight to look beyond 1999. For some unknown reason, the inventor chose to not deal with the Twenty-first century.

The inventor's omission of the Year 2000 comes with a price tag. Four hundred years of flawless calculations of dates and time will cease because of a simple programming flaw made in 1600.

Programming Flaws Are Expensive

At least the Equatorium functioned for 400 years. Our mainframe computers will only make it about 40 years.

Just like the Equatorium, our Millennial Meltdown will come with a price tag too.

A BIG price tag! A trillion dollars worldwide. Some Y2K experts speculate the final bill may climb as high as six trillion dollars by the time all the damages are tallied, lawsuits, and lost income and productivity are tabulated.

"In pure financial terms, the worldwide estimate for Y2K impact is greater than $1.3 trillion," says Howard Rubin, editor for IT Metrics and consultant for the Cutter Consortium, a Massachusetts information technology consulting firm. "This is equivalent to about 16% of the U.S. gross domestic product for 1997." (2)

The trillion-dollar estimate includes the cost of repairing or replacing old computer systems, the replacement of noncompliant embedded microchips, and litigation expenses that will surely gusher from Year 2000-related lawsuits.

Massive repairs will introduce new expenses too. The rush to fix so many computers in so little time will expose systems to other dangers. Mistakes will be made.

Mr. Capers Jones, Chairman of Software Productivity Research, says the 50-year record of the computer industry proves that a significant percentage of Y2K errors will not be removed. In his report, *Probabilities of Year 2000 Damages*, Mr. Jones says no large organization has achieved a 100% success rate in removing software defects in the last 50 years. The average success rate for removing defects is 85%. He says it is "naïve to think that thousands of companies who were never very good in software quality control before the year 2000 problem will suddenly achieve higher than average defect removal rates for one of the toughest software problems in history." (3)

Cap Gemini, another respected information technology consulting firm, estimates that for each 10 million lines of computer code, Y2K repairs will introduce 1,200 new errors into the system. Capers Jones says the introduction of new bugs can be as high as 10% of the lines of code repaired. Regardless of the number, employees under extreme stress and pressure to reach the December 1999 deadline will introduce millions of new programming errors into computers around the world.

Wall Street Told To Face the Music

The warnings about impending economic trouble are not the prophecies of "doom and gloom" ranters. Instead, the most alarming warnings are coming from respected world leaders in finance, government, and business.

"The Year 2000 problem will touch much more than just our financial system and could temporarily have adverse effects on the performance of the overall U.S. economy as well as the economies of many, or all, other nations if it is not corrected," Edward W. Kelley, Jr., testified before a U.S. Senate committee on April 28, 1998. (4)

Mr. Kelly, who is a governor of the Federal Reserve Board, told the Senate committee that the Federal Reserve Board doesn't really know what to expect because nothing like Y2K has ever happened. "The spectrum of possible outcomes is broad, for the truth of the matter is that this episode is unique. We have no previous experiences to give us adequate guideposts."

This isn't a false alarm, says Governor Kelley. "The problems presented to the world by the potential for computer failures as the millennium arrives are real and serious," said Mr. Kelley. Because the Y2K crisis is unique to the world system, Mr. Kelley warned, "the event is unlikely to be trouble free."

Despite growing awareness about the looming crisis, most American businesses have yet to accept the naked truth: Y2K will be extremely expensive. Credible voices of concern have been sounding the warnings about the magnitude of expense corporations and government agencies will face before January 1, 2000. One such warning was a Y2K white paper issued by Wall Street's J.P. Morgan Securities, Inc. The report's authors, William Rabin and Terrence Tierney, wrote in May, 1997, that U.S. corporations were growing in awareness of Y2K, but were slow to act. "Refusing to believe that cost estimates for complying with Year 2000 requirements can really be so huge, many corporate executives seem to be in a state of denial. But guess what? The true costs will almost certainly be even higher than current estimates, and that's not even the worse news!" (5)

And what is the "worse news" that J.P. Morgan's analysts foresaw?

"It is becoming clear that the cost of satisfying Year 2000 requirements will be significantly larger than anyone thought, with some companies spending hundreds of millions of dollars," the Wall Street report warned in early 1997.

Even more ominous was the report's comments about governments and corporations around the world. "Governments worldwide and international corporations appear to be even further behind than U.S. companies." According to J.P. Morgan, the "U.S. Federal Government has made little progress in actually addressing the problem."

J.P. Morgan, Inc., issued that warning in May, 1997.

Nothing has changed, except the number of days remaining before the clock strikes midnight on December 31, 1999.

U.S. Corporations Confronted With Monumental Task

How much will it cost worldwide to fix the computers?

More than the United States spent on the Vietnam War over 10 years.

At least $600 billion says the Gartner Group, the world's largest information technology consulting firm. Matthew Hotle, Y2K analyst for the Gartner Group, estimates that the total costs related to the Year 2000 computer bug could climb as high as $4 trillion. Mr. Hotle's estimate includes the cost of making mainframes, PCs, networks, and embedded chips Y2K compliant - and the cost of litigation and lost income. (6)

For America's largest corporations, the size of the task is staggering. Capers Jones, chairman of Software Productivity Research, a respected Y2K expert, estimates the repair and remediation costs alone will top $70 billion for U.S. companies. The Federal Reserve Bank estimates a lower price tag - $50 billion - for American corporations. (7) The United States federal government will spend another $50 billion on Y2K.

While the experts debate the estimates, the actual repair bills are coming in.

Merrill Lynch raised its estimate of how much the Year 2000 computer virus will hit their bottom line. The latest figure is $375 million. That's $100 million more than the nation's largest securities firm planned to spend.

Citicorp raised its estimate too. The global bank had previously expected to spend $600 million. That number has been increased by another $50 million.

America's major telephone companies will spend over $1.2 billion combined. Ameritech will spend $280 million. Bell South's Y2K repair costs could reach $200 million. Sprint estimates it will spend $200 million too.

As the remaining calendar days flee, one thing is clear.

"Everybody is behind," says Mr. Howard Rubin, a consultant at Cap Gemini. (8)

Mr. Rubin says no corporation in America has done enough to prepare for the Year 2000.

Y2K Labor Shortage Driving Up Costs

It's a great time to be a computer technician.

A severe global shortage of trained computer technicians and software programmers is causing Y2K repair costs to soar. In fact, there's a Y2K brain drain. High salaries and generous bonuses are luring many of the world's most skilled computer professionals to the United States.

From Russia, Europe, and India, many of the world's very best high-tech professionals are coming to America. Fighting the Y2K bug is good money.

The foreign exodus is good news for American corporations. It is bad news for companies and governments around the world. A shortage of trained staff is hampering Y2K projects in Europe, Australia, Asia, Africa, and South America.

Despite America's attraction of skilled labor seeking to exterminate the Y2K in return for big bucks, the United States critically needs another 700,000 programmers now. With so little time remaining, there's no chance of recruiting and training so many programmers.

That's one reason the U.S. Congress raised the immigration cap in 1998 so more programmers could enter the States immediately.

Wages are good too. Entry level programmers are earning $30,000. A person with five years experience can easily get $60,000. It is rumored that a major high-tech corporation in Dallas is paying top programmers $20,000 per month to keep them on the job until January 2000. Chief Information Officers are commanding as much as $450,000 in salary and bonuses.

They call such packages "golden handcuffs."

Offer them an extremely generous package on the condition they commit to staying with the organization until the Year 2000. Loyalty bonuses are running from 50% to 100% of salaries.

In Great Britain, Prime Minister Tony Blair is recruiting an "army" of 20,000 bug-busters. Deep-pocketed American corporations, however, are competing with him. The _Sunday Times_ newspaper reported that U.S. corporations are offering the UK's best brains lucrative salary packages that include free flights each weekend to England on the Concorde super sonic jet.

Clearly, the laws of supply and demand clearly still work.

Because so many companies and government agencies have waited so long to start working on their Year 2000 problems, the demand continues to rise for experienced computer professionals. With a shortage of trained workers, labor costs are soaring.

Consequently, many companies and government agencies are discovering that they've seriously underestimated the costs of fighting the Y2K bug. Sticker shock is hitting local governments particularly hard. When COBOL programmers can earn $100,000 or more in private enterprise, the chances aren't good for a city or county to attract professionals to repair their bulky, outdated mainframe computers.

At this late date, the only choice American employers have is to recruit more foreign talent. That strategy has a flip side. While the brain drain brings desperately needed talent to American corporations, it leaves foreign corporations and governments without their best people.

If the best IT professionals are flocking to America, who will fix the computers in their home countries?

Will it really matter if every American company becomes Y2K

compliant, and the rest of the world crashes?

Thousands of Small Companies Could Go Out of Business

Presently, the United States is experiencing one of the most robust economic expansions in our history. Inflation has almost disappeared. Unemployment is at a 30-year low.

Y2K will change everything overnight.

Many businesses will collapse.

Some very respectable experts are sounding the alarm.

Capers Jones, a prominent Y2K expert from Massachusetts, says the Year 2000 will have a substantial negative impact on the global economy. According to Mr. Jones' estimates, one percent of very large corporations will go belly up. That means at least five Fortune 500 companies will fail in the Year 2000.

Mr. Jones also predicts five to seven percent of mid-size companies will fail. Approximately 30,000 American companies fall into this category, each employing between 1,000 to 10,000 people.

Three percent of small companies will fail also. Employing less than 100 people, there are six million small companies within the U.S.

Other respected authorities echo similar dire predictions about the impact of Y2K on U.S. companies. Mr. George Colony, CEO of Forrester Research, expects 15% of the Fortune 1000 to fail in the Year 2000.

The United States Small Business Administration is concerned about the nation's small businesses. It is feared that 75% of the nation's small businesses are ignoring the Year 2000 threat. Small and medium-size businesses are the most likely to brush aside Y2K warnings. Lacking manpower and funds, small and medium business owners may mistakenly think they can escape Y2K's fury.

If the estimates of top researchers are correct, America's economy will take a direct hit.

It doesn't take many Fortune 1000 companies filing bankruptcy to make a dent in the Gross National Product. Like falling dominoes, companies will fail throughout the world.

Millions of people will be out of work. Possibly 40% or more of the American workforce could be unemployed between 2000 and 2002.

8 The Global Economy: We're Not In Kansas Anymore

"I feel the global economy has reached a dangerous zone."

Mr. Taichi Sakaiya
Chairman of Japan's Economic Planning Agency
Comments at a news conference following the
devaluation of the Russian ruble.
August 25, 1998

It was the day the world rumbled as the ruble crumbled.

Half the stores in Moscow's GUM, Russia's largest shopping complex near Red Square, locked their doors. Outside, desperate elderly Russians wandered the Russian capitol's streets searching for anybody willing to trade their meager stash of rubles for American dollars.

In front of the SBS-Agro bank, frightened Muscovites shoved and jostled to enter inside to withdraw their deposits. Alarm and panic spread among ordinary Russians following President Boris Yeltsin's decision 10 days earlier to devalue the nation's currency. With the Russian ruble's value plunging steeply, financial chaos overtook the Motherland.

Just the day before, the Imperial Bank went belly up. With so many banks lacking hard currency reserves, more bank failures were feared.

The story was the same throughout Russia.

At Siberia's Omskpromstroibank, worried Siberians rushed to get their money out of the bank. Spurred by the Central Bank's decision the previous day to halt dollar sales, the panic spread when the media circulated reports that Russia's hard currency and gold reserves had dipped to a mere $15 billion.

Once again, store shelves in Russia were empty. Because Russia imports over half her food, importers were having trouble paying for goods with quickly eroding rubles. Suppliers wanted American cash, not Russian money. Their inability to withdraw rubles from the banks, thus depriving businesses of needed working capital, only aggravated the food shortage.

As expected, backlash from the day's events channeled the

populace's growing anxiety toward the Kremlin. Throughout the day, the situation only became uglier. Financial instability turned into political instability. Embattled President Yeltsin fought off demands from the powerful Communist Party for his resignation.

With American economists predicting the Russian ruble would lose as much as 75% of its value, investors around the world fled financial markets.

The truth was evident. The giant Russian bear was flat broke.

Many of the bear's soldiers and military officers had not been paid wages for months. Retired workers hadn't received meager pension checks either.

The Russian government had borrowed billions of dollars from the world's banking systems. German banks, alone, lent over $30 billion to Russia. Despite the huge loans from the International Monetary Fund to prop up the Russian economy, the money was all gone.

Now the bills were due.

The day's painful developments bloodied financial systems around the world. An infectious fear over Russia's inability to repay her loans set off a surge of panic selling in stock markets in the United States, South America, Asia, and Europe.

Rumors that American investor George Soros lost $2 billion in his investment funds following President Yeltsin's devaluation sent shivers down the spines of nervous traders. London's *Financial Times* reported that holders of Russian bonds would lose $33 billion.

Asia, already battling its own financial crisis, watched as Russia's mounting woes pushed the Tokyo stock exchange to its lowest level in six years. Stock markets in Singapore, Malaysia, and Indonesia fell too. Shares on Australia's stock market slumped as Russia's bad news dragged down investor confidence.

In Frankfurt, Germany's stock index dropped more than 4% as the news media reported about Russia' s troubles. German bankers and politicians warned the Russian government not to expect a cash bailout from Germany.

On Wall Street, investors stampeded the market to sell off investments. By the close of the trading day, the Dow Jones Industrial Average had dropped 357 points.

By the close of August 27, 1998, the world's financial leaders had a new appreciation for the term *global economy*. Yes, the world has become one. The day's fast developing events clearly illustrated the new dynamics of globalization.

What happens in one nation does, in fact, impact economies around the world. And very quickly! With the Internet and global television, bad economic news is reported instantly.

Globalization: The World Becomes One

During World War II, the Chrysler Corporation built jeeps to transport American GIs to meet Hitler's Nazi troops on the battlefield.

At the same time, Germany's Daimler-Benz Corporation built tanks for the Nazi blitzkriegs across Europe to defeat American troops.

In May 1998, Daimler-Benz bought Chrysler.

There have been plenty of other global marriages too.

British Petroleum purchased Amoco Oil. AT&T and British Telephone have formed a globalized telephone network. Royal Ahold NV, a huge Dutch retailer seeking to build a worldwide food distribution company, bought Giant Foods, the largest grocery chain in suburban Washington, DC. At the same time, American food processors such as Sara Lee and Kraft are expanding worldwide by aggressively buying European food companies. Kellogg now controls 50% of Europe's cereal market.

With the rapid movement towards globalization, world political leaders are pushing for a new set of global regulations. When world business leaders met in London in April 1998, British Prime Minister Tony Blair told the summit the time has come for worldwide rules for the new global economy. "As markets go increasingly global, so the need is rapidly growing for more global rule-setting," stated Mr. Blair. "And that means more global decision-making and leadership." (1)

The belief that world governments must regulate the global economy was evident when two American companies – MCI and Worldcom – were forced to get approval from the European Union for their merger.

Federal Reserve Chairman Alan Greenspan says world financial and political leaders must design a new "architecture" for the emerging global financial system. Mr. Susumu Saito, director of the Trilateral Institute in Tokyo, says we need a world bank. "The world will have to start serious discussions toward the creation of a world central bank in the true sense of the word for the first time in history." (2)

Today, global financial integration is a reality.

Treasury Secretary Robert Rubin described this integration in a speech before the Brookings Institution. "Over the past 10 to 15 years, we have seen the rapid evolution of a new era of the global economy and global financial markets, an era that presents enormous opportunities for workers, farmers, and businesses around the globe," Secretary Rubin stated. "And the changes have been truly dramatic. Greatly increased flows of trade, capital, information, and technology have helped promote global output. Most large businesses, both here in the United States and elsewhere, have become global." (3)

Since the travels of Marco Polo and Christopher Columbus, mankind has been moving towards a global system of trade and commerce. The "global village" envisioned by poet Marshall McLuhan in the 1960s has now arrived.

Globalization is a fundamental redesign of our world's political, financial, and social systems.

We are now one.

"In today's global village, what happens in one country affects another," said United Nations Secretary-General Kofi Annan. (4)

When Japan catches the flu, America sneezes.

How will this new global economy be managed for the benefit of all the world's people?

The United Nations is the answer, according to Mr. Annan.

The Secretary-General says the "business of the United Nations involves the business of the world." (5)   "Globalization has knit us together and helped generate a sustained period of economic expansion."

Kofi Annan says this new global economy can only flourish if it works "from shared norms and objectives."

And where will we find these shared norms and objectives?

The Declaration of Independence?   The Constitution of the United States of America?

Hardly.

The answers to the global economy are found the United Nations' charter.

"Fortunately, the basis of that common understanding already exists; it is found in the United Nations Charter," declares Mr. Annan. (6)

Canada's Finance Minister Paul Martin was correct when he warned that globalization has created a world market "that outstrips the power and values of national government." (7)

The Year 2000 and the Global Economy: Falling Dominos

World trade is booming.   At the present rate of growth, world trade will reach $11 trillion by 2005.   That's nearly 30% of the world's Gross Domestic Product.   Compare that to global trade's share of the world's GDP twenty years ago – just 9.3%.

Driving this unprecedented explosion in global trade are two powerful currents of change.   The two forces are feeding each other to reach higher levels of achievement.

First, an explosion in creativity and information has unleashed a revolutionary surge in technological innovations.   In research and development laboratories around the world, scientists and inventors are pushing the limits on the frontiers of science.   From biotechnology to advanced digital communications, science is advancing at a speed that is unrivaled in the human history.

The boom in high-tech innovation shows no signs of slowing down. "There's going to be a fundamental change in the global economy unlike anything we've had since cavemen started bartering." (8)

On the cutting edge of scientific innovation are microelectromechanical systems (MEMS).   Combining tiny motors, sensors, and digital transistors on a minuscule piece of silicone, MEMS will someday become the internal "intelligence" in computers, automobiles, biomedical devices, and countless applications.

Today's scientists are evangelists for the Molecular Revolution. Known as nanotechnology, this rapidly developing science discipline seeks to replicate nature's molecular designs in minerals, plants, animals, and human beings. The ultimate aim of nanotechnology's proponents is to become "gods" by using their knowledge in chemistry, biology, physics, and electrical engineering to create artificial life. Animals that grow twice as fast as normal. Cows that produce disease fighting drugs in their milk. Human cell implants. By mastering the secrets of DNA and atoms, anything will be possible in tomorrow's laboratories.

The second powerful force driving globalization is the amazing growth in information technology and communications.

Through the Internet, consumers now have access at the stroke of a keyboard to a digital avalanche of information never imagined by Albert Einstein. Venture capital firms, flush with cash from soaring investments, poured $3.7 billion into white-hot Silicone Valley start-up ventures in 1997 seeking to satisfy the public's insatiable thirst for more and faster information.

The Internet is turbocharging globalization through electronic commerce. Forrester Research, one of the world's leading Internet research firms, estimates that e-commerce will top $327 billion in the United States by 2002. Start-up companies such as Amazon.com have "come out of nowhere" to upset traditional industries. New e-commerce Web sites are springing up as fast as entrepreneurs can dream of new applications. Internet auctions, stock trading, travel agencies, financial services, and music stores are cutting out middlemen and invading the turf of companies doing business "the old way."

At the heart of this astounding revolution in global commerce and communications are computers. Information is the life-blood that flows through the electronic veins of the global network. It's a wired world.

Global interdependence is the key word. Over one trillion dollars electronically flow around the world every day. The world's financial systems – including bank, corporations, universities, and governments -are united in a tangled web of an electronic network by computers. Because the Internet gives investors and financial traders real-time information, massive amounts of money can be electronically shifted across continents on the whim of a rumor.

Consequently, the global economy's volatility in Asia and Russia means the whole world is sitting on a powder keg. Troubles in Japan and Russia are so dangerous that a global depression could erupt any day.

With the global economy on such shaky ground, the slightest disruption could trigger worldwide panic. As with dominoes, anything can set off a chain reaction.

If our system is so fragile, what will happen when the Y2K computer bug strikes?

Take away the computers and the global economy will crash.

Thousands of years have passed by since King Nimrod's followers built their ill-fated Tower of Babel.

Their trust was in human intelligence and ability: "In technology we trust."

"Anything is possible", they proclaimed.

They had it all wrong.

The Bible says "*with God* all things all possible."

God will not be excluded from the affairs of mankind. He has a way of making his presence known.

9

Euroland:
You Picked A Fine Time To
Leave Me, Lucille!

*"I believe we're aboard the Titanic. The sea is calm, the dining
saloon sumptuous, everything very comfortable and luxurious,
the orchestra playing...Then the Titanic smashes at full speed
into the ice. When we see the iceberg, it will perhaps be too
late... 'Nearer my God to Thee' was the hymn tune the band
played aboard the Titanic as it sank. Very brave, that band...
We can only sing and pray for Europe."*

> *Jean-Pierre Chevenement — Interior Minister of France*
> *Remarks to a German magazine regarding the new*
> *European Monetary System*
> *April, 1998*

Its birth was unexpected.

As late as 1997, world leaders were saying it seemed inconceivable
that 11 nations could unite to launch a new currency.

On May 1, 1998, the unthinkable happened.

The unprecedented historical meeting took place with little notice
by the news media in the United States. Some American leaders, however, clearly noticed the global impact of the decision. Michael Castle,
chairman of the Banking Committee in the U.S. House of Representatives
understood the significance of the meeting.

"The implications of this action are nothing short of revolutionary,
but by our standards, there has been remarkably little public debate,"
commented Congressman Castle. (1)

On one of the most momentous days in Europe's history, powerful
political leaders of European nations gathered in Brussels for the summit.
Inside the meeting, France and Germany - bitter rivals in two of the
20th Century's most destructive wars - heatedly argued over control of
a new central bank. The debate was intense. Alistair Campbell,
spokesman for British Prime Minister Tony Blair, graciously described the
arguments inside the meeting as "heavy pounding." (2)

Finally, at 12:30 A.M, more than seven hours later than scheduled,
the European leaders emerged for the photo opportunity. News

reporters from around the world gathered to hear the late-night announcement. The deal was complete. Agreement had been reached, the political leaders proudly proclaimed, to economically unite Europe into a single new currency.

Romano Prodi, Prime Minister of Italy, astutely summed up the summit's significance when he said, "A page has turned, and a new chapter opens in our history." (3)

A new power is rising in the world.

The Roman Empire is awakening from centuries of slumber.

"Euroland" is here

Euroland: A 50-Year-Old Vision Becomes Real

On January 1, 1999, eleven nations will begin a three-year process to surrender a central pillar of any government's sovereignty: control of their money. In place of the 11 separate currencies will be a new money system: The Euro.

The first members of Europe's economic and monetary union (EMU) were officially chosen at the summit in Brussels on May 1, 1998. Austria, Belgium, Finland, France, Germany, Ireland, Luxembourg, the Netherlands, Italy, Portugal, and Spain were admitted into the EMU. Greece couldn't meet the standards set by the European Commission. Great Britain, Sweden, and Denmark decided to opt out of the Economic Monetary Union – at least for now. Despite strong opposition in England, Britain's Prime Minister Tony Blair, who maintains close ties with Bill Clinton, is slowly moving his nation closer each day toward eventual surrender to Euroland.

When the European Commission voted to unite 300 million Europeans under a single money system, a 50-year-old dream of European leaders finally came true. First voiced by a few visionaries in the 1920's, the dream of an united Europe has been touted by various European political and financial leaders since the end of World War II.

The war left Europe devastated. Some European leaders hoped the reconstruction of Western Europe would compel the nations to create an unified European state. West Germany's suspicions about its neighbors, and the start of the Cold War, seriously dampened enthusiasm for unification. Setbacks, disputes, nationalist rivalries, suspicions, and grass roots resistance from voters has marked the long march toward unification of the continent since the end of World War II. The first step came with the Treaty of Paris signed by six nations in 1951 to create a common authority to regulate coal and steel industries. In 1957, the six nations – France, Belgium, Italy, Luxembourg, the Netherlands, and West Germany – signed the two Treaties of Rome which created the European Economic Community (EEC). Over a 12-year period, the treaties eliminated trade barriers, developed a common tariff for imports, and created a common policy for managing agriculture. Great Britain, which politically clashed with French president Charles De Gaulle, voted to stay out of the EEC.

In 1967, the EEC was merged into a new organization: the European Community (EC). Following the 1969 resignation of De Gaulle as president of France, Great Britain finally joined the EC. Greece joined in 1981, and Spain and Portugal entered the EC in 1986.

The first real step toward achieving an economic and monetary union came with the development of the European Monetary System (EMS) in 1979. Europe's leaders mistakenly believed they could achieve an economic and monetary union by 1980, a goal they soon realized was too optimistic. The principal purpose of the EMS was to curb inflation and stabilize exchange rates among member nations.

Led by Jacques Delors, president of the European Commission from 1985 to 1995, the campaign for unification gathered support. The Single European Act, approved by the EC in 1987, significantly sped up the process toward creating an unified market. Following the fall of communism in Eastern Europe, supporters of European unity pursued the goal in the wake of the political upheaval caused by the collapse of the Soviet Union.

Although fraught with controversy, the dream of European unity dramatically moved forward with the 1992 adoption of the Maastricht Treaty. The treaty set down a detailed calendar for creation of a single currency before the year 2000, the creation of a European Central Bank, a common foreign policy, and cooperation on security, justice, and immigration policies. On October 2, 1997, 15 members of the European Union adopted the Treaty of Amsterdam, which replaced the Maastricht Treaty. In addition to new policies on borders and immigration, the treaty calls for increased cooperation between national police forces.

While the Maastricht Treaty established a fixed timetable to create a European Monetary Union, many political leaders – in Europe and the United States – didn't believe it would be possible to persuade the nations to give up their currencies. "The EMU, that's like that flightless (Australian) bird that runs along the ground making lots of noise and never taking off," scoffed David Heathcoat-Amory, Britain's shadow secretary of the Treasury and a Conservative member of Parliament. (4)

To the surprise of many observers, the bird did take off.

"An entire continent is attempting something that's never been done before," said Richard Woodruff, a Euro specialist with the Arthur Andersen consulting firm. (5)

Opponents Say EMU Will Lead To Takeover of All European Nations

Never before has a group of nations united to introduce a common currency without forming a political union. That's something that has not escaped notice by many of the Euro's most vocal opponents – especially in Great Britain. "Euroskeptics" warn that the EMU will eventually lead to a federal state, thereby destroying the sovereignty of nations, wiping our national borders, blurring national distinctions, and homogenizing distinct European cultures.

While most leaders of the pro-Euro campaign carefully avoid speaking words that would raise suspicions, there are already numerous statements and steps being made that point toward a new "United States of Europe" – or Euroland. Dr. Helmut Kohl, chancellor of Germany, openly boasts that the euro will become an alternative to the dollar as a global currency. Valery Giscard d'Estaing, the former president of France, threw fuel on the fire when he said, following the Brussels' summit, that the launch of the euro is a step towards the creation of a federated Europe. The former French president said that the euro's launch "is a federal act." (6) President Giscard d'Estaing chided those who said that the European Union would be a "Europe of Nations," saying it was a contradiction.

Giscard d'Estaing wasn't bashful about the intentions of supporters of the European Union. "One day or another things will have to be said clearly. The contradiction will be dispelled." The former French president then stated the obvious: The establishment of a central bank and a monetary system is the act of a federal government. Make no mistake about it. An "United States of Europe" was being formed. Giscard d'Estaing's words left no room for doubt. "Having a sole common central bank managing a single currency is a system of federal management," said Giscard d'Estaing. The launch of the euro is "a very important step towards a federally-based Europe."

This movement toward a "one Europe government" is precisely what frightens many conservative political leaders in England, who have steadfastly resisted pressures to join the European Union. "If you have a currency, you have a government controlling it," Britain's David Heathcoat-Amory emphatically declares. (7)

Backers of the single currency denounce as "scare-mongering" the claims of opponents that the Amsterdam Treaty will lead to gay marriages and the conscription of young men into a "European Army." The treaty allows the European Union to take action against member states that discriminate against their citizens on the grounds of sexual orientation, thus leading opponents to predict that legislation governing homosexual rights will be mandated throughout Europe.

Already, the "euroskeptics" have plenty to point to as evidence that supporters of the European Union have a hidden agenda.

The new European Union has a lot of the trappings of a federal government. It now has a powerful central bank that answers to no one, and carries out its deliberations in secret meetings. The European Union has a flag too. Since flags are an important symbol used for centuries by kings and rulers to establish loyalty among conquered foes, many patriotic Europeans are wondering if they've already been conquered. European officials are even proposing adoption of an European constitution and universal language.

It seems the European Union flags and symbol is showing up everywhere too. The EU flag now flies alongside the national flags of member nations. The EU symbol is also mandatory on car license plates in some countries such as Portugal and Luxembourg. At major sporting events, the EU symbol is prominently displayed on the field so millions of television viewers will see the new look of Europe.

The European Union will also soon have its own coins and bills. Since money has always been a central function of a sovereign state, many citizens who still patriotically remain loyal to their own country are beginning to wonder what sinister plans the European federalists have in store.

Further alarming the euroskeptics is the upcoming election of the president of the European Union. The position will be the highest office in all of Europe. Already, candidates are jockeying for the political plum. Some euro supporters are touting Germany's Helmut Kohl for the job, while others are backing Felipe Gonzalez, the former prime minister of Spain. Italy's prime minister, Romano Prodi, and Peter Sutherland, a former European commissioner from Ireland, are also mentioned as possible candidates. Whoever wins the coveted election in 1999, could become one of the most powerful politicians in the world as the new king of "Euroland."

Of course, a powerful king needs a powerful army. An army that can dispatch troops around the world to enforce European Union and United Nations' sanctions.

Despite assurances from euro backers that they harbor no secret plans for a unified European Army, the framework for such an army is already in place. With headquarters in Strasbourg, the Eurocorps has a military staff of more than 1,000. Created in 1993 by French President Mitterand and German Chancellor Helmut Kohl, the Eurocorps now has 60,000 troops under its command. Belgium, Spain, and Luxembourg have joined France and Germany in supplying soldiers. The fledgling European army is amassing military hardware too. As of July 1998, the Eurocorp has 650 battle tanks, 600 anti-tank missiles, 400 artillery guns, 1,000 armored fighting vehicles, and 700 troop carriers. (8)

Eurocorps military commanders deny that their ultimate goal is to replace NATO as the supreme Allied military force in Europe. They say their role is to only augment NATO. While Eurocorps officials are coy about the unit's purpose, other European Union supporters are being far less guarded in their comments about plans for a fully equipped independent European Army.

Demos, a think tank with close ties to Britain's Prime Minister Tony Blair, issued a document in June, 1998, that has infuriated the "euroskeptics." The proposal calls for establishment of a European army as "a permanent EU peacekeeping corps" (9) which would respond quickly to military situations around the world. The report also recommend the establishment of a pan-European police force, similar to the United

States' FBI. Ultra liberal Neil Kinnock, former leader of Britain's Labor Party, and now a European commissioner, has endorsed the report's recommendations.   Britain's conservative political leaders are enraged by the report's proposals. David Davis, a Tory leader, said the report was a "federalist wish list full of dangerous ideas." (10) Fearing that Britain's ruling Labor Party leaders are quietly giving up England's sovereignty, Mr. Davis branded the concept of a permanent European Union peace-keeping force as "simply a formula for a European army by another name." (11)

More fuel to the fire came with a proposal in June, 1998, to gradually scrap national borders in the election of members of the European Parliament. The Parliament is the only democratically elected supranational institution in the European Union. Seats in the legislative body are distributed among the EU member nations based on their populations. Since the Parliament poses a direct threat to the sovereignty of the governments of the member nations, the proposal to abolish national boundaries in the elections sends a chill up the spine of many euroskeptics who fear the rise of a federal state.

This flurry of federal activity is making some Europeans feel a bit uneasy, especially with the sudden rise of EU symbols everywhere. "There is a conscious attempt to manipulate the way in which we think of ourselves, " wrote Norman Lamont in an editorial in London's Daily Telegraph newspaper on June 11, 1998.

"That tells us more about where the EU is intending to go than any politicians' speeches," Mr. Lamont warns. (12)

The loss of national sovereignty and governmental rule by unelected bureaucrats wielding power at the EU headquarters in Brussels , however, does not worry most Europeans.

"So long as the system delivers, it's not a problem," is how Matthhias Dembinski, a senior researcher at the Peace Research Institute, shrugs off concerns about a new federal state rising to power in Europe. (13)

The Euro: New Coin of the Realm

The unprecedented currency transformation begins on January 1, 1999.

A new form of money will appear on the Earth. The euro.

On that date, the newly formed European Central Bank takes control of the monetary policies of the 11 participating nations. Like the U.S. Federal Reserve Bank, the European Central Bank will be the cornerstone of the new currency since it holds the power to set interest rates.

The European Central Bank will be the pinnacle of financial power in the emerging super economic trading zone. The new bank is the first financial institution in world history that 11 nations have voluntarily surrendered control of their money to an independent body that answers to nobody.

With headquarters in Germany, the aggressor nation in the two bloodiest wars of the 20th Century, the European Central Bank will wield enormous financial power in the new millennium. After a contentious, messy battle with France over control of the new bank, the European Union finally chose Wim Duisenberg, former head of the Dutch central bank and Germany's candidate, as the bank's first president. At the official ceremony where Mr. Duisenberg assumed control of the bank, the new euro czar boldly proclaimed that, for the euro to succeed, it would be necessary for the European Central Bank to speak with "one voice." (14)

Under terms of the Maaschicht Treaty, the European Central Bank will be responsible for managing the seismic shift from multiple national currencies to a single European monetary system. The treaty set down strict economic standards that nations had to achieve before joining the European Monetary Union. The selection process for EMU membership elaborately prescribed the criteria for "convergence" into the new currency system. For example, each country had to reduce its budget deficit to 3% of Gross Domestic Product (GPD), meaning the nations had to cut government debt/spending to within 3% of what the country earned. Among the nations that applied for charter membership, only Greece's economy was judged as too weak to meet the strict standards for entry into the EMU. Other stipulations mandated strict entry requirements regarding inflation rates, interest rates, and the ratio of government debt to the GDP.

The Madrid European Council, meeting in December, 1995, established a detailed three-year timetable for the member nations to integrate their economies into the new euro monetary system. The complicated convergence process is called "triangulation." First, the 11 founding nations – Austria, Belgium, Finland, France, Germany, Spain, Ireland, Italy, Luxembourg, the Netherlands, and Portugal – will phase in the euro currency for the financial and banking markets.

While existing national coins and bills will remain in circulation for three years, the exchange rate between the participating countries will immediately become irrevocably locked against each other and the euro. EMU supporters say consumers will benefit from stability in exchange rates. They say a tourist with $1,000, under the present system, who changes the money to local currencies in 15 EU nations, and doesn't buy anything, will end up with just $500 because of exchange rate fees.

The European Commission adopted a "neither obligation or prohibition" policy so as not to provoke hostility from common people to a too rapid changeover. The commission has stipulated that those who want to start paying in euros – through credit cards or specially requested checkbooks only – can do so as of January 1, 1999. Consumers and merchants are not required to use euros until January 1, 2002.

The national currencies of the 11 nations will, however, cease to be legal tender on July 1, 2002. On that date, 300 hundred million Europeans – from reindeer herders in Finland to pasta makers in Italy – will be using the same coins and bills. Prior to the official elimination of existing national coins, merchants and shop owners will be required to post prices in both denominations – the country's national currency and the euro.

European corporations, however, will immediately feel the effects of the euro. Beginning on January 1, 1999, companies will electronically deposit in employees' checking accounts paychecks based on euros. The first "euro keyboards" have appeared too. The euro symbol – an epsilon, which is a Greek letter "E" which looks like a "C" with two horizontal lines drawn across its middle – now joins the standard U.S. dollar sign and the British pound sign.

Government mints throughout Europe are working overtime to produce billions of the new euro coins and bills in anticipation of their introduction on January 1, 2002. To avoid nationalistic arguments, the European Union voted to allow each nation to mint its own version of the euro. The participating nations will produce the new money with the European Union symbol on one side, while the other side will feature a design that represents that particular nation's heritage.

The images on the bank notes – in denominations of five, 10, 20, 50, 100, 200, and 500 euros - will depict seven European historical architectural styles. The chosen designs are classical, Gothic, Romanesque, Baroque, Renaissance, Rococo, and a modern glass and steel image. The bills will be inscribed with the word "EURO" and printed in different colors based on the denomination. Along with its face value, the front side of the euro bills will prominently depict the blue European Union.

A historical change of epic proportion is coming quickly. Currencies that have been in circulation for centuries are about to disappear. The German mark, French franc, Italian lira, and the Spanish peseta – plus guilders, schillings, and all other currencies – will fade into history in what one Brussels-based diplomat says is "the greatest experiment in political economy since the Russian Revolution." (15)

"This is the biggie," states British economist Peter Coldrick, who works in Brussels at the European Trade Union Confederation. "It's going to affect all avenues of life." (16)

The Euro: Powerful Challenger to the Mighty American Dollar

Europe doesn't want to be Uncle Sam's dancing partner anymore.

In fact, Europe wants to have her own party.

With the Year 2000 crisis just ahead, this is a lousy time to pack up and leave. Unfortunately, Europe is head-strong right now to have her own way.

Since the end of World War II, Uncle Sam has been running things around the world. Now, if Europe's powerful leaders have their way,

America will have to move over to make room for a new major player: Euroland.

"Our European colleagues are marching – possibly galloping – toward federal destiny," warns Michael Portillo, former British defense minister and an influential member of the Conservative Party. (17) Mr. Portillo believes that the adoption of the euro is the first step toward the dissolution of national boundaries of European nations.

He sees the movement to political union as anti-American. "Europe is intent on creating a political union in a very short period time...In the long term, it is reasonable to expect that a common EU foreign policy will be un-American and will not be as supportive as British policy is now. Many in Europe resent dependency on American support for security. Also, there is an appetite in certain parts of Europe to be free of U.S. influence and free of U.S. troops," says Mr. Portillo. (18)

Other analysts see something bigger looming ahead.

A cashless world.

Peter Huber, a senior fellow of the Manhattan Institute, says "the world isn't moving into euros, it's moving out of cash...Cash is an obsolescent technology, the last financial refuge of criminals and the very poor." (19) According to Mr. Huber, legal tender is shrinking in importance. While people still feel comfortable seeing their paychecks "quoted in good old dollars," says Mr. Huber, "that reflects yesterday's habits and technology, not tomorrow's."

For the immediate future, however, many global investors and multinational corporations will seek to ride the Euro wave.

Perhaps, the euro will topple the Almighty Dollar, European investors speculate.

If the most ardent supporters of the EMU have their way, the euro will be where the buck actually stops.

For the first time, the U.S. dollar will have real competition. The United States, with a population of 268 million people, has a Gross Domestic Product of $7.2 billion. America's share of world trade is 19.6%. Over 47% of world trade is executed in American dollars. Even more importantly, 61.5% of all world currency is held in U.S. dollars.

A unified Europe will present the first serious challenger to the supremacy of the American dollar during the 20th Century. The single currency and elimination of trading barriers will make Europe a forceful global competitor by making the European economy more efficient. In comparison to the U.S., the emerging Euroland has more people – nearly 300 million. The Gross Domestic Product of the 11 nations rivals the U.S., nearly $7 billion. When all 15 EU members are counted, their combined share of world trade exceeds America, totally 20.9%. Euroland will be the world's largest exporter and importer. If the EMU is extended to all 15 EU nations, the euro area will become the world's largest economy.

A huge economy means a huge capital market. Financial analysts are preparing for dramatic effects on liquidity. "Transaction costs will collapse overnight," predicts Avinash Persaud, head of currency research at J.P. Morgan. (20)

An international think-tank for academic economists, the Centre for Economic Policy Research based in London, issued a report in April, 1998, that predicts the euro will rival or overtake the dollar. The report says the currency will be attractive to international investors by turning Europe's many nations into one giant trading zone.

What troubles many U.S. financial experts the most is the euro's serious threat to the dollar's dominant position as a reserve currency. Acceptance of the U.S. dollar is universal. The dollar accounts for more than 80% of all foreign exchange transactions. The dollar is the one currency that all parties engaged in world commerce find acceptable – importers and exporters, governments, multinational corporations, banks, stock brokers, and even criminals.

The euro will dramatically challenge the dollar as an acceptable global currency. Ease of use and lower transaction costs will be big attractions to corporations and governments around the world when dealing with Europe. Presently, almost all currency transactions between Japan and Europe are transacted through U.S. dollars. For example, when an Asian exporter sells products to France, Germany, and Italy, the trade would, most likely, be transacted in U.S. dollars to reduce expenses in dealing in multiple currencies. After January 1, 1999, the same company will be able to transact the trading in euros.

Many financial experts expect the euro to make its presence felt very quickly. Richard Portes and Hele'ne Rey, who authored the report for the Centre for Economic Policy Research, say the introduction of the euro will shock the international financial system. The two academics believe the financial shock "is likely to be substantial and relatively sudden." (21) Others concur that the euro will rise to global influence with meteoric speed. "The euro will become an international currency within a matter of months, not years," states Mr. Persaud of J.P. Morgan. (22)

The immediate result will be a new bi-polar global world order where the euro and dollar compete against each other for world supremacy. Long term, the rise of Euroland could mark the beginning of a long slide of the American economy to a second-rate power. If America is dethroned as King of Reserve Currencies, the effects will roll across the United States like dominoes. Stock prices and interest rates will be hit first. Consumer prices, jobs, savings, and real estate values will be jolted too.

What happens to the financial well-being of average American citizens when international investors pull their money out of U.S. stocks, real estate, and banks? With a vast, unified trading zone, Euroland will give investors another place to go to place their investments. Foreign banks, too, which hold more than 60% of their reserves in dollars, could pull out large sums of money from America. Foreigners also own about 37% of marketable U.S. Treasury notes. Foreign capital has, for many years, subsidized our government's debt spending ways. A sudden loss of foreign capital would dramatically lower the standard of living for all Americans.

As much as $1 trillion of international investment may shift from dollars to euros after January 1, 1999. A financial shift of such magnitude will have an enormous impact on the United States economy, with particularly strong effects on interest rates, government spending, and taxes.

Euro Conversion Costs: Y2K Has A Big Brother

When New Year's Day arrives in 1999, J.P. Morgan's 1,000 employees in London won't be celebrating the holiday with feasts and football games. Instead, they will usher in the New Year working to convert billions of dollars of financial data from EU nations into euros. The giant securities trading firm expects to spend up to $65 million on euro conversion.

Euro conversion will be expensive.

Very expensive.

The Gartner Group estimates the cost of software conversion and restructuring will reach $400 billion for businesses worldwide.

The advent of the euro will radically impact all European companies – and any company in the world that does business in Europe. For any business not fully prepared, the first business day of 1999 could be a nightmare.

Particularly troublesome will be the three-year period of "dual currencies." From 1999 to 2002, existing national currencies will circulate alongside of new euro bills and coins. "Dual pricing" will also be the common practice – stores listing each item in their national currency, and its equivalent price in euros.

For consumers, it means learning to recalculate everything into euros – milk, bread, medicines, gasoline, cigarettes, beer, and the prices of all the other basic staples they know by heart. Learning the new currency will not be easy. Take Italy, for example, where consumers are not use to decimal point transactions. A U.S. dollar equals 1,500 Italian lira. So, when an Italian housewife walks into her neighborhood grocery store, in January, 1999, to purchase a bar of soap, the purchase will be 1.2 euros.

Even more confusing – to both consumers and merchants – will be the process of "triangulation." The European Commission decided to phase-in the euro to give people time to get accustomed to the new currency. During this three-year period, every organization during business in Europe will have to deal with two different currencies. Transactions must be processed according to a complicated three-step conversion formula. For example, an Italian company doing business in Germany will first convert Italian lira into euros using a six-digit conversion rate. The euro amount will then be rounded to at least three decimals. Then, the euros are converted into German deutsche marcs using another six-digit conversion rate.

Because every decimal place counts, such complicated transactions are bound to create serious data processing headaches for information technology managers. The EMU requires the first step of the conversion to be carried out to six decimal points. The second step, however, can be rounded to three decimal places. This rounding process could result in as much as a half-cent difference. While a half cent discrepancy on a purchase of chewing gum will not be a big deal, an order of five million manufactured parts will add up to a lot of missing money. For young start-up firms, such losses can be devastating.

"Triangulation" means every business in Europe – and every company in the world doing business in Europe – needs to be upgraded for the duel currency pricing, multi-currency trading, and complex rounding and balancing transactions required by the European Monetary Union by January 1, 1999. Only large banks and financial service firms will have the massive computer power to run the off-the-shelf software needed for this "triangulation" conversion process. Small and medium-size companies will face major problems in computing the "triangulation" conversion process.

The massive costs to convert operating systems to handle the dual currency transactions will spur a furious round of corporate mergers throughout Europe. As the day approaches, corporate consolidation is expected to sweep across Europe's business landscape, especially among banks and financial service firms. The new euro currency will also force companies to establish uniform pricing in all nations. Gone will be the days when a company gets away with selling its widgets for more in the Netherlands than it does in Luxembourg. With price transparency, once your widget prices are quoted in euros, your customers will immediately be able to determine price differences in other parts of Europe.

Another serious problem facing European businesses is the need to redenominate debts and financial securities. The EMU politicians forgot to spell out the methods to redenominate, so banks and investment houses will do so on a country-by-country basis. Bonds and other security instruments must be recalculated into euros. The process in each country is complicated enough by itself, but, many investors have bonds and securities from different countries. Such multi-country debt and equity portfolios mean that once the institution changes the currency unit of the securities instrument, you may have to repackage the portfolio. Consequently, repackaging could disrupt the investment strategy of the investor.

Conversion to the euro will also cost European businesses billions of dollars to changeover cash registers, vending machines, and toll booths to handle the new coins. In Germany alone, vending machine industry experts say it will cost $550 million to convert the nation's approximately three million cigarette machines, parking lot payment machines, and other coin-fed vending machines.

While many business executives see major pitfalls ahead with euro conversion, some see golden opportunities. Leaders of the "smart card" industry are betting that technical headaches caused by the EMU will dramatically increase acceptance of smart cards by consumers. Citing the estimated $12 billion cost to European banks to switch to the euro, smart card executives say the cards will allow holders to conduct transactions in a number of currencies, thus saving banks money in the transition. "One Europe, one money, one card" may become the motto of Europe's banks.

U.S. Companies Lag Behind in Europe Conversion

With the European Monetary Union deadline rapidly approaching, few U.S. firms are fully prepared to handle the new currency. Many firms are hardly aware of the need to be euro-compliant by January 1, 1999.

Ernst & Young, the large U.S. accounting firm, surveyed 200 multinational U.S. corporations in mid-1998. To their surprise, only 45% had set up teams to evaluate how the euro would affect their bottom lines. Even more depressing was the realization that only 18 of the 200 multinational corporations had begun to serious analyze the consequences of not being ready for the EMU – a market that will account for 35% of all global transactions by 2002. (23)

Clearly, U.S. companies are far behind their European counterparts in preparing for the pitfalls and opportunities that the EMU will present to the global business community. The Securities Industry Association warned in April, 1998, that the launch of the euro poses a "substantial risk" that U.S. firms involved in European markets will be unable to manage the dual currency system.

U.S. banks and financial service companies are far from ready for the euro. According to the Financial Times, "U.S. securities firms have not yet prepared their computer systems for the introduction of the single European currency." (24)

For companies doing business in Europe, conversion and restructuring is mandatory if the company plans to stay in business. "If you're an organization with multinational business interests doing trade with Europe, if you have a system today that is single currency, you're in trouble," warns Lauren Hills, senior vice-president of marketing at Prestige Software International, an Australian software firm. (25)

Everything is affected. The euro currency will render virtually every major computerized accounting system in the world obsolete by the end of 1998. Companies will be forced to operate two accounting systems from 1999 to 2002. Accounts receivable systems must be capable of maintaining customer data in multiple currencies. Whole systems managing accounts payable, project estimates, payroll, taxes, logistics, inventory, and human resources will have to be rewritten. Foreign exchange and tax software will need to be modified. Vital historical data must be converted. Financial statements must be remodeled to fit the dual currencies.

Some U.S. companies, however, are wasting no time making the switch. Microsoft has moved quickly to prepare for the new European monetary system. The giant software developer will start doing business in euros in 1999. The company will adopt dual accounting procedures, publish price lists in euros, and accept the currency on January 2, 1999. Furthermore, Microsoft promises that its software applications will feature the new euro symbol.

U.S. companies that ignore the fast-approaching European Monetary Union will quickly find themselves as outcasts in a fast-changing global marketplace in the New World Order.

The Euro and Y2K: Technology's Twin Terrors Threaten Global Economy

"Europe is on track for a computer-generated disaster," is the stark warning issued by Robin Guenier, executive director of Taskforce 2000, the British group spearheading the campaign to prepare England for the Year 2000 computer crisis. (26)

Taskforce 2000 was established in 1996 by Ian Taylor, a member of Parliament, and former Minister for Science and Technology under the government of former Prime Minister John Major. The organization was the first government-backed Y2K taskforce anywhere in the world.

Mr. Guenier, who was formerly chief executive of Britain's Central Computer and Telecommunications Agency, claims Europe is making the Y2K crisis worse by diverting so much money and manpower into euro conversion when the Year 2000 millennial computer bug threatens their survival. "This is a global problem," says Mr. Guenier, "but made worse in Europe by the diversion of scarce computing resources to handle the now inevitable introduction of a single currency."

"The issues Y2K and EMU really, are quite different. And yet they are similar, observes Paul Eastwood, a business development manager at JBA International, a London-based application specialist firm. "The Year 2000 crisis is a technical problem that will have business ramifications, and the euro problem is a business issue that will have technical ramifications." (27)

For companies doing business in Europe, the logistical task to restructure computer systems is staggering. Graham Lloyd, a managing consultant with PA Consulting Group in Australia, warns that multinational companies are "scarcely awakening" to the euro challenge. (28)

Euro conversion will not be a simple process. Mr. Lloyd clearly sees the two-fold danger posed by the euro conversion. "First, we are not just adding another currency," explains Mr. Lloyd. "We are adding one huge one, removing 11 and, for up to three years, interchanging between them."

Mr. Lloyd also points out that the euro conversion process is far larger than just an information technology problem. "The guts of the work ahead at the IT level will involve some hard questions dealing with the basis on which systems are structured," he says. "The complexity arises because many of the systems were established on concepts we thought would never change."

The introduction of the euro is unprecedented in world history. It is the first currency with no base country, and, until 2002, 11 EMU countries will have two currencies. The IT capabilities companies will need during the three-year transition period are extremely complex. Moreover, the solutions will never be needed again after the third year. Mr. Lloyd says the massive work necessary to prepare computers for the dual currencies will be an expensive investment that has only a three-year lifespan. "Some estimates compare it at up to 150 per cent of the millennium workload with less than half the time frame for completion."

Estimates for euro conversion of U.S. banks are mind boggling. Solving the Year 2000 problem will seem "like a walk in the park" when compared to what it will cost to make corporations euro-compliant, according to Michael Donahue, an executive with KPMG Peat Marwick LLP. (29) "Euro conversion," says Mr. Donahue, will cost "Wall Street banks six times the investment of the Year 2000 issue."

European Businesses Lag in Y2K Preparedness

The single-minded determination of the European Union to launch the euro is blindly diverting information technology professionals and corporate resources to focus on preparing European businesses for the new currency. Hundreds of billions of dollars in computer industry resources are being drained away, and a serious shortage of qualified IT personnel is being aggravated by the European obsession with launching the new single currency. With so much attention focused on euro conversion, the Year 2000 computer bug is being virtually ignored in Europe.

"The experts contend there are not enough people with the technical know-how to handle the Y2K problem at the same time as creating a parallel accounting system using the euro and the local currency," warns a report issued by Lafferty, Harwood & Partners Ltd., a financial analyst firm in Montreal, Canada. (30)

The complexity and magnitude of successfully managing euro conversion and Y2K compliance at the same time is almost beyond comprehension. Working on both massive projects is like a doctor simultaneously performing a heart transplant and brain surgery on a patient, and having to complete both operations within an extremely short deadline.

"The euro and year 2000 are competing for scarce software resources," says Capers Jones, president of Software Productivity Research, Inc., a high-tech consulting firm in Massachusetts. Mr. Jones, who has been one of the foremost leaders in alerting the world to the Y2K threat, strongly criticizes the timing of the euro introduction. "The timing of the euro conversion with the year 2000 is disastrous. It is one of the worst public policy decisions in human history." (31)

Because big IT computer projects are rarely completed on time, Robin Guenier, England's Y2K Paul Revere, says the chances of Europe successfully completing at the same time the two largest computer projects in world history is "ludicrous." (32) "Everybody knows it's true, but nobody dares say so," Mr. Guenier laments.

In comparison, Europe and the United States are opposite each other in their readiness for the euro conversion and Y2K. In the United States, many of America's largest corporations are feverishly working to overcome the Y2K computer virus. Conversion to the euro, however, is getting little attention in the U.S. On the other hand, European corporations are intensely focused on preparing for the arrival of the euro. The Year 2000 threat is not receiving much in resources or personnel by European companies.

Most troubling to Y2K experts watching Europe is the dismal lack of preparation by Germany. Among industrial nations, Japan and Germany are considered the least prepared for the Year 2000 computer meltdown. "Our major areas of concern are Germany and Japan," says the Gartner Group's Andy Kyte. (33) "In these two highly sophisticated countries, with very heavy dependency on information technology and very short supply chains...there is a danger the year 2000 problem is not treated sufficiently."

What makes Germany's nonchalant attitude about Y2K so menacing is that Germany is the center of financial power in the new European Monetary Union. The most contentious battles fought by European politicians during the launch of the euro was deciding where to base the new European Central Bank, and who would be elected as its first president. Germany won both fights. If Manhattan is the banking capital of the United States, then Frankfurt is the capital of Euroland's banking system.

While other European cities are famous for food, wine, architecture, and culture, Frankfurt, Germany, is famous for the concentration of powerful financial institutions within the city. The old city along the Main River has been a financial power center for centuries, including being the home of the famed Rothschild dynasty.

Now, Frankfurt has re-emerged as the most powerful financial center in Europe. Nearly 400 domestic and foreign banks – including the colossal Bundesbank, Duetsche Bank, Dresdner Bank, and Commerzbank – employ over 60,000 people, 13% of the city's workforce, in Frankfurt.

Frankfurt is the banking center of the new European Monetary System, yet Germany is ignoring Y2K. What economic calamity will befall Europe when Y2K and euro conversion collides head-on?

Y2K Meets the Euro: Double Trouble Just Ahead

A horrific global financial collision is just ahead.

Two high-speed locomotives are racing toward each other, with the entire world population on board.

Soon, these two colossal computer trains – Y2K and the euro - will collide. The sudden impact threatens to wreck the world financial system, producing a global catastrophe of epic proportions. The aftermath of the collision will be a historic worldwide financial meltdown. Upon the rubble of the old financial system, a "superpolitician" will emerge to pave a silicone highway to a new digital, cashless global economy where no national borders exist. One world. One money system.

"Merging Year 2000 and EMU is an absolute road to disaster," warns Darlene Brown, an IT analyst for the Gartner Group in Stamford, CT. (34)

Some European leaders, seeing the impending train crash ahead, are calling on the European Union to hit the brakes now.

William Hague, the leader of Britain's Conservative Party, is warning that a global economic crash caused by the euro will trigger civil unrest across the European continent.   As the youngest Tory leader in 200 years, Mr. Hague reminds European audiences that the European Union treaties irrevocably bind nations to the single currency with no way to leave the EMU if things go wrong. "One could find oneself trapped in the economic equivalent of a burning building with no exits." (35)

So alarmed are computer industry officials, that many are begging European governments to not enact any more laws that require large-scale changes to computers. While some leaders are openly calling on the European Union to delay the entry of the single monetary currency, few believe Europe's politicians will heed the warnings.

The likelihood of European politicians delaying the arrival of the EMU is almost nonexistent. Their cherished dream of an united European continent blinds their eyes to reality. Without regard to the impending disaster looming ahead for Europe and the entire world, they are hastily rushing toward unification as though some unseen hand is compelling them toward a predestined appointment in time.

"There is no point calling for postponement of the single currency," concludes John Clayton, chairman of Eurim, the British IT trade association. "You can't step in front of a moving train." (36)

Other responsible leaders are urging government leaders to concentrate resources on essential services. "What has to be fixed are the key utilities like the electricity supply and telecommunications," states Stephen Ing, Project 2000 manager for British Petroleum. "If they go wrong, then civil unrest is not far away." (37)

Robin Guenier continues to press the British government to call on the European Union to postpone the euro's arrival. "It is increasingly obvious that inadequate time and resource are making it impossible to deal with the EMU and Year 2000 computer projects at the same time. The euro is the only one that can be deferred," Mr. Guenier says. (38)

Mr. Guenier, however, is not optimistic about the chances of slowing down the euro's introduction. With so little time ahead to solve two massive computer projects, he fears the devastating impact their failure will wreak upon the planet.

"The outcome will be a ghastly and damaging mess," sadly concludes Mr. Guenier.

10 The Dow Jones 10,000: Just When the Stock Market Goes Through the Roof, the Computers Go Through the Floor.

"Ensuring that securities industry systems are ready for the Year 2000 is too important to the continued functioning of the industry to risk failure."

Mr. Thomas McCool — Director of Financial Institutions
United States General Accounting Office
In Testimony Before A Congressional Commerce
Subcommittee on Finance
May 8, 1998

The Y2K computer bug has an ugly little stepsister.

It is known on Wall Street as DJ10K

The Gartner Group, a respected worldwide information technology consulting group, warns that DJ10K could trip a few unsuspecting Wall Street brokerages and banks on their trek to see the Dow Jones reach the cherished 10,000 peak.

The Dow Jones industrial average, which tracks the fortunes of 30 major corporations, has been steadily climbing in recent years. First published in 1896, the Dow Jones industrial average didn't hit the 2,000 mark until 1987. With America's steroid-pumping economy surging forward in recent years, the Dow Jones has shot skyward like a meteor to the delight of investors. In 1996, the index reached the 6,000 mark. By April, 1998, the Dow Jones was over an historic 9,200 points.

By early summer 1998, the Big 10 was just ahead. Investors were salivating like stray dogs in heat. Economic troubles in Asia and Russia, however, put a damper on investors' hopes to see the Dow Jones hit the magical 10,000 mark. Following Russia's devaluation of the ruble, the Dow Jones Industrial Average fell below 7,700 points by late August 1998.

Investors have grown accustomed to handsome returns during the last 10 years. Few are willing to settle for single-digit performance on stocks.

Will the stock market rally for one more gallant charge to reach the magical 10,000 mark? One big death gurgle before the collapse? Nobody knows.

If the market does foolishly ignore the warning signs from Asia and Russia, it may discover another computer software problem waiting ahead. David Cappucio and Andy Kyte – two research executives from the Gartner Group, reported that they might have uncovered another potentially threatening software virus waiting to explode.

It is nicknamed DJ10K – meaning the Dow Jones 10,000 problem.

Some Wall Street computer trading systems, the company warns, only recognize a four-digit Dow Jones index. It seems many Wall Street computer-trading programs never contemplated the possibility that the Dow Jones industrial average would ever reach 10,000. Like the programmers who used two digits instead of four digits for the century date, these programmers shortsightedly assumed the Dow Jones would never climb to the 10,000 mark.

The Gartner Group is worried that when the Dow Jones does hit 10,000 or higher, the computers will mistakenly think there's been a horrendous stock market crash. Designed to compute only four digit Dow Jones averages, many systems will read the extra digit incorrectly, dropping the first or last digit. It seems to affect companies basing operations on old equipment originally programmed in such computer languages as COBOL, JCL, and PL/1.

Let's say the Dow Jones soars to 11,528. Some Wall Street computers with old software may read it as 1,528. Assuming that a catastrophic stock market crash has occurred, the computers would trigger automatic trading systems to immediately respond to the "crisis" in the stock market. When computers perceive the Dow Jones has fallen to a preset amount, many automated trading systems will suspend trading to prevent "panic" trading.

There we go again! Computers control everything.

This computer-controlled automated trading system on Wall Street was designed by information technology gurus to be a fail-safe way to prevent a stock market meltdown. Ironically, it may actually help trigger a wave of panic selling.

A Computer Generated Sell-Off Could Mean Chaos On Wall Street

This software glitch looms over Wall Street as an ominous sign that our complex financial system is precariously vulnerable to simple foulups by electronic gadgets.

A "false alarm" by computers would spread confusion, and eventually panic, across the nation, exposing investors to huge financial risks. "This is a real and present threat," (1) the Gartner Group warned in a May, 1998, report that was aimed at companies that make extensive use of the Dow Jones Industrial Average. The report strongly warned such companies to immediately investigate their systems to determine the level of exposure. Gartner says companies that incorporate the Dow

Jones average in their rules-based decisions should "immediately constitute a crisis management team" to determine if they could be affected by DJ10K. The crisis management team should make a thorough inventory of all information technology systems to locate data fields that cannot handle the extra digit, and locate all technical systems that support those processes.

These crisis management teams "should behave as though the barrier could be breached tomorrow," (2) Mr. Kyte apocalyptically warns. The truth is, it could happen tomorrow. Unlike the Year 2000 problem, the DJ10K doesn't have a fixed deadline. The Dow Jones Industrial Average could reach 10,000 well before January 1, 2000. In fact, some Wall Street analysts believe the stock market will make one final surge, topping the magical 10,000 mark, before falling up to 30% in a serious correction that ends the current raging bull market.

"Trading organizations face massive exposure if the Dow passes 10,000 and their systems interpret it as 1,000 or 0,000," says Andy Kyte, an analyst for Gartner. (3) "Computer-based trading systems could interpret the '10,000 event' as a catastrophic crash."

While the Gartner Group admits nobody knows for sure what will happen, the potential exist that the glitch could precipitate a stock market crash. "You could well see some triggered trading and people making entirely wrong decisions in the stock market on the basis of their computerized trades," explains Mr. Kyte. "We could be talking about very, very significant losses, certainly in the tens of millions- hundreds of millions – of dollars." (4)

Many Wall Street investors and information technology managers smugly dismiss the warnings.

"We can handle it," is the confident collective response echoing Wall Street's blustering bravado.

Nothing is going to get in the way of making more money. That's their idol.

The folks at the Gartner Group, however, say such replies are strikingly similar to initial responses to early warnings about the Year 2000 problem. Now, reality has sunk in as companies face the facts. The Year 2000 crisis will happen whether they believe it or not.

While Wall Street's biggest banks and brokerage firms publicly say they're not worried about DJ10K, Gartner Group executives say there are large firms that privately express their concern. "A few who say they might have the problem are not going to go public with it," explains David Cappucio, Gartner's vice president of research. (5) Mr. Cappucio said that two of the nation's 10 largest trading companies "believe they might have a problem."

In a May 4, 1998, interview with CNNfn, Mr. Kyte said one of Gartner's major clients had reassigned some employees from the Year 2000 problem to work on the DJ10K problem. Mr. Kyte said the client was "one of the top ten banks in the world." (6)

Who would have ever thought financial experts would have so much trouble with numbers?

11

Meteors:
What Will Hit Us Next?

*"And there shall be signs in the sun, and in moon, and in the
stars; and upon the earth distress of nations, with perplexity...
Men's hearts failing them for fear, and for looking after those
things which are coming on the earth: for the powers of heaven
shall be shaken. And then shall they see the Son of man coming
in a cloud with power and great glory."*

> *Jesus Christ*
> *Luke: 21: 25-27*

A spectacular explosion on December 9, 1997 suddenly interrupted
the tranquillity of the predawn Arctic skies above southwest Greenland.
(1)

Fisherman Jens Nielson was aboard the fishing trawler Nicoline in
the waters of the Davis Strait when, just after 5 a.m., an enormous fireball illuminated the darkened sky. The orange-red glow was so bright,
he could see the distant mountains along the coast.

Three hundred miles away at the southeast tip of Greenland, another sailor on the trawler Regina C saw the fireball too. He described the
cosmic event as being like "the center of an electrode welding on iron."
The sailor added that a brilliant flash occurred after the fireball dropped
below the horizon.

The red-hot fireball was captured on video by a parking lot surveillance camera in the town of Nuuk along Greenland's southwest coast.
As it streaked across the early morning sky, the fireball's brilliance flooded the parking lot with light. A silhouette of distant mountains briefly
appeared during the burst of light.

Numerous eyewitnesses claimed they heard a "sputtering" when the
meteor broke into smaller pieces as it streaked across the Arctic sky.
Even rumblings and tremors along coastal Greenland were reported to
authorities.

The brilliant flaming meteor that made Greenland's nighttime sky
glow was just one of an unusually large number of fireball reports sent
in late 1997 to Sky & Telescope, a magazine for amateur astronomers.

The magazine said it wasn't clear whether the high number of reports was the result of increased meteor activity, or because more amateur astronomers are watching the sky.

Regardless, reports of fireballs are pouring in from around the world.

On June 11, 1998, hundreds of frightened people called British police departments after a spectacular fireball changed colors as it blazed across the night sky. Initially, the fireball was a single white-yellow glow, then turned to green-blue before breaking up in a shower of sparks. The Ministry of Defense told frantic callers that the object was from "an unusually large meteor shower."

British astronomers, however, ruled out a meteor shower since meteors are produced by the debris of comets. One prominent British astronomer raised the frightening possibility that the fireball was an advance warning of something much bigger heading our way. "This object was probably a chunk of an asteroid," said Robin Scagell, vice president of England's Society for Popular Astronomy. (2) Mr. Scagell said he could not completely discount the remote possibility that the fireball had arrived in advance of a much bigger asteroid in outer space on a collision course with Earth.

"There's no way we could know if there isn't some monstrous lump of material heading for us out of the direction of the Sun," Mr. Scagell conceded. "It might be small enough for us not to have noticed it, but big enough to do some serious damage. However, it's very unlikely."

While a monster-size asteroid capable of wiping out civilization is unlikely, smaller fragments of asteroids have recently made their way through the earth's atmosphere. On October 9, 1992, a driver was startled when a chunk from an asteroid smashed the car fender. Another asteroid spread fragments over Gila Bend, Arizona, in June, 1998. During the same month, a homeowner in west Texas found a piece of an asteroid in his yard. In late May, 1998, astronomers discovered a 100-foot-wide asteroid that passed within 476,000 miles of Earth – slightly less than twice the distance between the moon and Earth.

On June 13, 1998, a meteor entered the Earth's atmosphere over the United States, scattering fragments over a distance of 1,000 miles. Fragments of the same meteor crashed through a couple's roof in Tennessee, and two different properties in Portales, New Mexico. Houston Woods, a resident of Nashville, was in his kitchen drinking coffee when a meteorite crashed through his roof and lodged in the springs of his bed. Moments later, Nelda Wallace heard explosive sounds over her house in Portales, NM. She then saw a large rock whistle in and crash in a cloud of dust in her back yard. Mrs. Wallace said the 37 pound rock was "too hot to handle." Four miles away, Robert Newberry, a Portales farmer, discovered a meteorite that crashed through the roof of his barn.

All this fireball stuff is giving NASA a bad case of the heebie gee-bies.

In fact, it making NASA downright edgy. NASA slapped a 72-hour gag order on astronomers and scientists regarding public announcements about any asteroids or comets hurtling toward Earth. In April, 1998, NASA drafted "Interim Roles and Responsibilities for Reporting Potentially Hazardous Objects." Concerned about public hysteria, the space agency wants scientists to wait 72 hours before publicly announcing findings about a comet or asteroid on a potential collision coarse with Earth.

Perhaps the increased sightings around the world of fireballs explain NASA's growing interest in asteroids. The American space agency, which prefers to refer to approaching asteroids and comets as Near Earth Objects (NEOs), is planning to spend $1 billion over the next 10 years to locate and track more than 25,000 asteroids and comets. The objects getting NASA's attention are those that are more than a half mile in diameter and or in Earth-crossing orbits. So far, about 2,000 large aster-oids and 700 comets have been officially identified as Near Earth Objects.

What are the odds of a gigantic asteroid striking Earth? About one in 1,000 within the next century says Cark Pilcher, NASA's director for solar system exploration.

According to Mr. Pilcher's estimates, asteroids capable of global destruc-tion strike the Earth every 100,000 to one million years. Smaller aster-oids, however, large enough to wipe out miles of land, hit the Earth about every 3,000 years. Such an asteroid hit Tunguska, Siberia, in 1908, and the shock wave flattened trees across an area bigger than New York City.

Whether or not a mile-wide chunk of rock plows into the Earth within the next 100 years is debatable. Only time will tell.

One thing, however, is certain.

A intergalactic artillery barrage will pelt Earth's atmosphere in 1998 and 1999.

It is the Leonid meteor shower – an annual extraterrestrial event. This time, however, rocket scientists and satellite manufacturers will be holding their breath.

November 1999 is bad timing for a really big meteor shower. Just 43 days before the clock strikes midnight on December 31, 1999!

Return of the Leonid Meteor Showers

It is one of the most spectacular displays of "shooting stars." Every autumn dedicated sky watchers vigilantly gaze into the chilly November nighttime heavens toward the constellation Leo. "Maybe this year," is the heartfelt wish of amateur astronomers worldwide as they focus on the the curved hook of Leo's celestial sickle.

Usually around November 17 or 18, meteors appear to streak forth from Leo's sickle. Typically, perhaps as many as eight or 10 per hour will dash across the sky. The annual shower was given the Latin name of Leonid because the meteors seem to radiate from Leo the lion.

The actual source of the Leonids is the comet 55P/Tempel-Tuttle. The comet was discovered in 1866 by Ernest Tempel and Horace Tuttle. Today, we know that "shooting stars" are actually, in most cases, the trail of space dust from crumbling comets. It was the Italian astronomer Giovanni Schiaparelli who first identified the source of the Leonids. Following the discovering of Tempel-Tuttle in 1866, Schiaparelli established that the orbit of the August Perseids, another famous meteor shower, closely followed the orbit of Comet Swift-Tuttle. About the same time, two other astronomers, Urbain Le Verrier and Theodor von Oppolzer, noticed a resemblance of the Leonid orbit to that of the newly discovered Temple-Tuttle comet. The combined observations of these astronomers led them to calculate the orbit of the Leonid meteor stream, and eventually led to the formulation of a theory on the origin of meteors.

The Leonids are responsible for producing some of recorded history's most awesome meteor storms. Meteor storms are not common. While the typical annual Leonid shower produces up to 10 meteors an hour, a Leonid storm unleashes a torrent of brilliant flashes of light across the November sky. It is not unusual for tens of thousands of meteors to streak across the sky during an intense meteor storm.

Such storms periodically materialize when the Earth crashes head-on into the thickest part of the river of rubble that precedes and follows the orbit of Comet Tempel-Tuttle. The sparse scattering of meteors during most years are the strays that are widely scattered along the comet's orbit which stretches as far as the planet Uranus. A narrow, dense ribbon of debris, however, remains close the comet itself. The spectacular showers occur when the Earth's orbit intersects with this thick cloud of comet dust.

For almost a hundred years, the comet Tempel-Tuttle was lost. It was rediscovered in 1965. Calculations revealed that the comet would pass closer to the Earth's orbit than on any occasion since 1833.

On November 17, 1966, the Leonids produced an incredible pageantry of celestial fireworks. Within a few hours, skywatchers in the central and western United States witnessed an historic display of Leonid's firepower. Eyewitnesses reported that the "rain of fire" sent as many as 150,000 meteors across the sky within one hour.

The Leonids: King of Meteor Storms

Meteor storms are rare heavenly events that have never been observed and recorded with today's sophisticated astronomical observatory equipment.

Historical accounts of such events date back as far as 902 AD when Chinese astronomers first recorded a Leonid storm. Through the centuries, many accounts that "stars fell like rain" have been recorded.

South American natives told of a "rain of stars" in 1766. Prussian explorer Alexander von Humboldt observed from his camp in Cumana, Venezuela, such an event on November 17, 1799. Humboldt wrote that there was "no part of the sky so large as twice the Moon's diameter not filled each instant by meteors." On the same night, another observer in Florida noted that the meteors were "at any one instant as numerous as the stars." In Germany, a witness said that "bright streaks and flashes" made it appear as though daylight had already broken.

The Leonids erupted again on November 12, 1833 in a memorable demonstration of its firepower. The incredible firestorm was recorded by Victorian astronomy writer Agnes Clerke:

"On the night of November 12-13, 1833, a tempest of falling stars broke over the earth...the sky was scored in every direction with shining tracks and illuminated with majestic fireballs. At Boston, the frequency of meteors was estimated to be about half that of flakes of snow in an average snowstorm. Their numbers...were quite beyond counting; but as it waned, a reckoning was attempted, from which it was computed, on the basis of that much-diminished rate, that 240,000 must have been visible during the nine hours they continued to fall."

The night was clear and starry. The meteor hailstorm was seen by trappers in Halifax to Plains Indians in the western frontier. According to published newspapers reports, the light of the flaming fireballs was so bright that families were awakened from their late night sleep. "Imagine a constant succession of fireballs, resembling rockets, radiating in all directions from a point in the heavens," wrote Denison Olmstead, a Yale professor who witnessed the great storm.

The fascination of astronomers about that memorable night prompted them to research the history of this historical outburst from the heavens. They discovered accounts of the Leonids in ancient Chinese, Arab, and European documents. German astronomer Heinrich Olbers suggested in 1837 that the storms occurred in cycles of 33 or 34 years. In 1863, Hubert Newton, a Yale professor, traced accounts of the Leonids for almost a thousand years, with fiery displays in the years 902, 934, 967, 1037, 1202, 1366, and 1533. Later, astronomers calculated in 1866 that the dense cloud of debris does, indeed, revolve around the sun in an orbit that is 33.25 years.

The last spectacular hailstorm from the Leonids came on November 17, 1966. Like the event of 1833, the Leonids shot off a fiery pageantry of celestial fireworks. Within a few hours, skywatchers in the central and western United States witnessed an historic display of Leonid's firepower. Eyewitnesses reported that the "rain of fire" sent over 150,000 meteors across the sky within one hour. At New Mexico State University Observatory, Thomas Kirby and Thomas Pope estimated the barrage to be from 200,000 to one million per hour.

They're Back! Meteor Storm Will Be The Most Severe in 33 Years

A full-blown meteor storm is a rare occurrence. During the 19th century, seven meteor storms were recorded. Within the 20th Century, only four meteor storms have been observed. Seven storms since 1799 have been produced by the Leonid meteor showers.

The Earth is on course for another head-on encounter with the Leonid dust stream very soon.

The most intense meteor showers will be November 17, 1998, and November 18, 1999, as Earth passes through the dense tail of comet P/Tempel-Tuttle. Both dates will set off a considerable display of cosmic pyrotechnics. Many astronomers believe, however, that the 1999 encounter will be the most severe of the two upcoming encounters with the Leonids.

Regardless, it will be the most spectacular bombardment of Earth's atmosphere in 33 years.

This time, the "rain of fire" will be visible in 1998 across the Western Pacific and Eastern Asia. In 1999, the meteor storm will be seen by skygazers in the Middle East, Eastern Europe, and Central Asia.

It promises to be quite a show. Tens of thousands of meteors will pelt the Earth's atmosphere. The heat from friction entering the atmosphere will cause them to glow before burning up in the denser air.

So, what on earth does a meteor storm have to do with the Year 2000 computer virus?

One word.

Satellites.

It is causing sleepless nights for a lot of folks.

During the last major meteor storm 33 years ago, there were few satellites orbiting the globe. Most were military satellites. In 1966, before the dawn of the information age, there was little likelihood that a meteor would strike any of the few satellites hovering in the sparsely populated outer space.

Now, as we approach the Year 2000, there are about 550 satellites orbiting our planet at varying altitudes. Besides military surveillance, these hundreds of satellites link nations together with high tech communications, navigation, and weather-watching capabilities. Satellite technology is a vital link in today's technology-driven economy and culture.

Scientists, military leaders, and corporate executives are worried. Nobody wants to be an expensive high-tech causality in a meteoric hailstorm of fireballs.

"This will be the most severe storm we've had in the past 33 years, and there are many more spacecraft up there," warns Bill Ailor, director of the Aerospace Corporation.

So worried are these chieftains of space that they assembled together at Manhattan Beach, CA, on April 27, 1998, to collectively wring their hands about the fiery darts of the Leonid showers. About 200 commercial, government, and military satellite operators, insurance executives, astronomers, and scientists convened the Leonid Meteoroid Storm and Satellite Threat Conference to pool their ideas on how to deal with the upcoming cosmic attack.

There's one undesirable thing shared alike by scientists, insurance agents, and corporate CEOs: Uncertainty.

"The consequences are still virtually unknown," said Peter Brown, an advisor to satellite operators, and a physics and astronomy graduate student at the University of Western Ontario. "There has not been a meteor storm since the onset of the modern space age. Nobody planned for it," stated Mr. Brown. (3)

Nobody planned for it?

Mankind didn't.

God did.

Meteor Storm Poses Serious Threat To Valuable Satellites

Surprisingly, most of the meteor particles are tiny. Most of them are not much bigger than grains of sand. Small rocks travelling racing at a velocity of 40 miles per second, however, can inflict serious damage on a $300 million satellite. In fact, these small meteoroids can have the destructive power of a .22 caliber rifle.

While military satellites are better shielded, space experts say no satellite has a prayer of a chance to avoid being hit All satellites can expect to be bombarded during the upcoming Leonid meteor storms. The question is, "How much damage will be done?"

"This is probably the most potentially significant threat we've seen to spacecraft in many years," stated Donald Lynch at the satellite threat conference. Mr. Lynch, an astrophysicist and a key organizer of the conference, warned that the comet's debris can damage satellites in different ways. "It's a quirky thing, the damage isn't usually explosive, but debris works in ways that we can't simulate or anticipate on Earth." (4)

Obviously, the greatest threat would be a direct hit by a large meteoroid that seriously punctures the satellite. The millions of small meteoroids, however, can inflict damage in numerous ways. They could punch holes in solar panels, blast reflective coating off mirrors, pit sensitive lenses, and short out delicate electronics.

"The damage can be out of proportion to the number of hits, depending on the timing," explained Mr. Lynch, a researcher with Aerospace Corporation's Center for Orbital and Re-entry Debris Studies in El Segundo, CA. "For instance, a particle hitting a satellite once a day for 10 days probably wouldn't matter, but 10 hits in a millisecond could have a very different result."

Scientists know firsthand the damage that can be done. During a fairly light Perseid meteor shower in 1993, the Olympus communications satellite, launched by the European Space Agency, lost its directional control and was disabled by meteoroids. In 1991, meteoroids ended the mission of a Japanese solar research satellite when particles punctured the sun filter. The Mir Space Station and the Hubble Space Telescope have sustained dings too. In early 1998, a Global Positioning System satellite sustained numerous hits.

Scientist Warns "Pencil Eraser-Size" Meteoroid Could Be Catastrophic

Aren't killer meteors suppose to be the size of a flaming high school gymnasium?

Not so, say scientists.

A meteorite just the size of a pencil eraser traveling at 156,000 miles per hour can pierce the thin lining of a $500 million satellite and knock it silly.

Mr. Lynch says space experts assume that satellites won't be hit by anything larger than specks of comet dust. If one the size of a pencil eraser strikes a satellite, he warns, the result would be catastrophic.

He says the potential for damage "varies from none at all to totally destroying or disabling a satellite...There's a low possibility of something major happening. But if it was major, it could be catastrophic."

Catastrophic, like losing a GPS navigational satellite, shutting down a weather forecasting satellite, destroying a satellite that delivers television programming to broadcast stations, cable systems, and DBS customers, knocking off a vital communications satellite, or even disabling an important military satellite.

Considering that many satellites these days cost hundreds of millions of dollars, it's no wonder so many folks are biting their nails when they think about November 18, 1999. With over a hundred billion dollars worth of inventory floating in geosynchronous orbit 22,000 miles above the Earth, a lot is at stake.

"What if you get unlucky?," asked Delbert Smith, a Washington lawyer who represented internal satellite operators at the conference. "Who's going to explain to the major corporations your satellites aren't there anymore?" (5)

Well, stuff happens.

Life goes on. Maybe not life as we know it now, but life goes on.

All that satellite operators can do is try to minimize the damage.

That means evasive actions such as turning the satellite's solar panels on edge so there's less surface area as a target. Controllers of the giant Hubble Space Telescope plan to protect the expensive mirror by turning the spacecraft around so the back end is facing the storm. Some spacecraft might be temporarily moved into safer orbits, but the competition for these safe parking spots is extremely intense.

Worried that the Leonid shower will damage the *Haruka* satellite, Japan's Institute of Space and Astronautical Science will shut down the telescope satellite for two days in November 1998 and 1999. Launched in 1997 to study black holes in the center of the galaxy, the Japanese satellite's parabolic antenna and eight solar battery panels are in danger of being sandblasted by hundreds of thousands of meteorites. During the peak of the Leonid storm, Japan will turn off the satellite and align the equipment to the same angle as the falling meteors.

Despite the precautions, there really is no place 550 satellites can hide. While scientists hope they come through this meteor storm with few losses, they are prepared for the worst-case scenario. John Pike, a member of the American Federation of Scientists, warns that the precautions don't add up to much. "Half the satellites are boxes with wings," says Mr. Pike, explaining that the satellite's solar panels can be turned on edge to minimize damage. "But the spin-stabilized satellites are basically big drums, and there's not a heckuva lot they can do to reorient them in space." (6)

Other operators may choose to shut down for the three hours when the storm is expected to be at its peak.

Shutting down, though, has its risks too.

They may not start up again.

Its not like you can jump-start them with a set of battery cables.

Sensitive things, those expensive satellites!

"Once they're in orbit, you're pretty limited in what you can do to protect them," says Mr. Lynch. "These are mostly 24-hour-a-day, operational satellites, and if you turn them off to protect them, there's always a small chance you won't be able to turn them back on." (7)

That's why military officials have zipped their lips about their plans. It's a serious dilemma facing the Pentagon. "There are meetings going on all over the United States to decide what action people will take and under what circumstances," says Lt. Col. Don Jewell of the United States Air Force Space Command in Colorado Springs, CO. (8)

U.S. military leaders are very concerned about protecting the Pentagon's fleet of top secret spacecraft. The Air Force Space Command operates 50 satellites, including GPS satellites, communications satellites, and weather satellites.

Spy satellites are operated by the National Reconnaissance Office, a spy agency based in Chantilly, VA. NRO officials say they've been studying the upcoming Leonid meteor storm for years. Today, satellites are vital to America's national defense. The Pentagon relies on satellites, both military and commercial, for communications, reconnaissance, navigation, weapon targeting, and weather forecasting.

The best way to protect the military's expensive and vitally important defense satellites is to shut them down and face their sensitive sensors away from the pelting meteor storm. That's not easy for the Pentagon. During those three or four hours, the Pentagon would lose critical intelligence, navigational, and communication functions. A major part of our national defense system would be down. That would provide America's enemies with a window of opportunity for mischief.

Like start a war.

Edward Tagliaferri, a consultant to the Aerospace Corporation, told the conference that military satellites "can't afford to be off the air." (9)

Aside from direct punctures and shock wave damage, a fierce meteor storm can inflict serious damage to satellites in other ways. The most serious threat is "space sandblasting," the stressful abrasion satellites suffer when they pass through the ultrafine dust cloud of a comet's tail.

Sandblasting can cause satellite computers and gyroscopes to be scrambled by electromagnetic pulses caused when the particles turn into plasma upon impact. These high-energy plasma jets can fry delicate electronic equipment, leading to massive computer failures. Experts also warn that electromagnetic energy may produce chaotic and erroneous readings from satellite computers. Additionally, endless abrasions by a cloud of sandy particles can significantly reduce the satellite's life span through excessive wear and tear.

The serious threat of losing one or more expensive satellites has caught the attention of large corporations. "Certainly people are taking it seriously," says Susan Gordon, a spokeswoman for Intelsat, a huge satellite operator based in Washington, DC,
Intelesat operates 20 communications satellites providing crucial voice, data, and video links for television networks and international telecommunications companies. The company's 20 satellites cost about $200 million each, and generated more than $960 million in revenue in 1997.

Year 2000 Computer Crash Meets A Monster Meteor Storm

The dawn of the space age began with the Russian launch of Sputnik in 1957 and the American launch of Echo I in 1958. Slowly, mankind began to link his civilization with high-tech satellites in space. The missions of spacecraft such as Vanguard and Explorer became a part of our dinner table talk. Those early flights were followed by the manned missions Apollo and Gemini. America was leading the space race!

Today, the missions of hundreds of satellites connect daily with our lives, providing television signals, transmitting telephone conversations, and relaying vital data around the world. Weather satellites such as the Synchronous Meteorological Satellite transmits temperatures and cloud patterns on the Earth. Two SMS satellites cover the entire United States and adjacent oceans, sending detailed pictures back to Earth every 30 minutes. Other satellites such as the Landsats observe the Earth with multispectral optical scanners, sending color images back to Earth with vital information about soil characteristics, water and ice quantities, coastal-water pollution, and insect blights upon crops and forests.

We're so comfortable with satellite technology that it is taken for granted.

All kinds of people use satellite technology daily. Military spy agencies, telephone companies, cable television systems, farmers, weather forecasters, credit card companies, and so on.

Do we ever stop to think about how dependent we have become on technology? How would we function – our businesses, military, banks, communication systems – if we loss a major portion of all these high-tech gadgets?

We have over a hundred billion dollars worth of fancy hardware orbiting above the Earth. Our society has become highly dependent upon the technology provided by these satellites. The loss of Galaxy IV in April, 1998, which disrupted service to 90% of America's pagers, highlighted mankind's increasing reliance on satellites.

Astronomers know there's no such thing as a typical meteor storm. How severe will the next attack of the Leonids be when they arrive in November, 1998, and again in 1999? If the vastly increased number of meteor sightings in late 1997 and early 1998 are any indication, then we're about to experience a galactic shooting gallery.

Without the Year 2000 crisis looming ahead, the coming Leonid meteor storm would be, in itself, a very serious threat to our society's 550 satellites. It has been 33 years since the last major meteor storm. With so many satellites above, our exposure to risk has risen greatly.

What happens if several critically important satellites go haywire during the Leonid storms? Multiple satellite failures would be unthinkable. Such technological failure would have severe economic impact on our nation and the rest of the world, possibly even threatening our national defense.

The upcoming Leonid meteor storm is a very real threat.

Military leaders, corporations, and NASA scientists are worried. And rightfully so. Our high-tech satellite system has never been stress-tested during a major attack of meteorites.

"They are approaching very, very quickly, which means they pose a very large threat to satellites," warns Nicholas Johnson, a NASA satellite expert, in Houston, TX. (10)

November 18, 1999, is only 43 days before the century date change at midnight on December 31, 1999. If anything goes wrong in space, it will only add to the general state of confusion and panic on Earth. Especially if the financial system has collapsed in late 1999 when folks suddenly realize the Millennial computer virus won't be fixed in time. Who will have time to deal with a crisis in the heavens when life on Earth becomes a living hell?

A lot of unexpected surprises await us in the final days before the Year 2000.

Computers crashing on Earth. Computers crashing in space!

My! My! What's this old world coming to?

What a lousy time for a meteor storm! Who planned this, anyway?

As the old margarine commercial use to say, "It isn't nice to fool Mother Nature!"

Well, it isn't smart to sin against Father God.

Our society has rejected His laws, renounced His commandments, forsaken His ways, and forgotten His blessings.

More than anything, we've lost our fear of a holy God.

Like a spoiled brat, we've asked for this. Now we're going to get it.

We deserve it.

Get ready.

12 Solar Tornadoes: Isn't This Crisis Hot Enough?

"And the fourth angel poured out his vial upon the sun; and power was given unto him to scorch men with fire."

The Revelation 16: 8

Big things are happening in space.

Big things that can't be explained.

On May 6, 1998, astronomers announced they had detected the brightest cosmic explosion documented in human history. The biggest explosion since the "big bang" 15 billion years ago briefly illuminated for several seconds the entire universe in December, 1997.

The magnitude of the explosion astounded scientists.

The explosion detonated in the center of a galaxy 12-billion light years from Earth. The gamma ray burst equaled the combined energy emitted by all of the 10 billion trillion stars in the entire universe exploding at the same time!

"I was astounded when I heard these results," said Stan Woosley, an astronomy professor at the University of California at Santa Cruz. (1) "This was the brightest explosion in history," Mr. Woosley stated.

"The energy released by this burst in its first few seconds staggers the imagination," said Shrinivas Kulkarni, of the California Institute of Technology in Pasadena. (2)

What produced this mega galactic explosion?

Basically, all scientists could do was shake their heads in wonderment and say, "I dunno."

What could it be? A massive explosion as powerful as the beginning of the universe?

Perhaps a new heaven and new earth?

Who knows?

One thing is certain. Whoever detonated the first "big bang" surely set off the second "big bang" too.

There are other big things happening in space too. Like massive tornadoes on the Sun. Powerful sunquakes too.

It seems things are really cooking on the Sun these days.

Things will get hotter too. Especially in the Year 2000.

Why?

Because Cycle 23 has begun. Just think of it as the sun having PMS.

Solar Cycles: The Sun's Turbulent Life

Consider it the El Nino of space weather.

Every 11 years, the Sun has a hysterical conniption fit.

The Sun goes through a 22-year cycle from a period of relative calm for 11 years, to a period of numerous sunspots and violent storms for 11 years. Then the Sun returns to calmness again.

During these furious eruptions of solar energy, sunspots form on the face of the sun. Giant bubbles of hot gas try to escape, but the sun's magnetic field ties them to the sun's surface. The pressure from the gas continues to build, winding tighter and tighter. Finally, the gas explodes, violently ripping away from the magnetic field, and spewing into space huge amounts of material from the sun's corona.

A solar flare is born.

These coronal mass ejections (CME) contain supercharged atomic particles. Deadly Xray particles are carried along with the atomic particles.

Obviously, scientists are fascinated by the sun's violent cycles. A fleet of spacecraft is focused on the sun, giving scientists a fresh, new look at the turbulent atmosphere of Earth's nearest star. They hope to greatly improve their understanding of events on the sun, especially powerful solar storms and flares.

Recently, scientists have made exciting discoveries about the sun's surface - a place where the temperatures range between a "cool" 6,000 degrees Fahrenheit, to a slightly hotter region where the thermometer hits 16million degrees Fahrenheit on a hot day.

Fortunately, there's no humidity. Otherwise, it would be really miserable.

New research has yielded images so striking and unexpected that scientists are now revising their solar theories.

What have they discovered?

The sun has powerful tornadoes and sunquakes.

So far, over a dozen tornadoes have been recently detected. These huge gyrating solar storms are 1,000 times faster than tornadoes on Earth. The tornadoes were unexpectedly discovered by scientists using the Solar Heliospheric Observatory satellite (SOHO). They occur most frequently near the north and south poles of the sun. These rotating funnels travel upside down across the surface of the sun, spewing forth super—heated gases. The solar tornadoes are nearly as wide as the Earth, and roar across the sun's surface at speeds up to 300,000 miles per hour.

Because of these breakthrough observations of solar flares through the SOHO satellite, scientists now believe these eruptions are the major source of solar wind. Gusts and shocks in the solar wind buffet the Earth's environment, producing the "northern lights."

Scientists have also confirmed that the sun has powerful quakes too. These sunquakes are much more powerful than any terrestrial quake on Earth. Researchers with the SOHO project recently observed a sunquake that produced seismic waves in the sun's interior. The flare-generated sunquake contained 40,000 times the energy released in the great San Francisco earthquake in 1906.

The quake produced waves two miles high. Unlike a stone dropped in water that produces ripples that eventually dissipate, waves from sunquakes act in an opposite manner. Within an hour, the waves travel a distance equal to 10 times the diameter of the Earth. The waves accelerate from an initial speed of 22,000 miles per hour to reach a maximum speed of 250,000 miles per hour within one minute.

Cycle 23: The Most Severe Solar Storms Have Started

Our sun is having another conniption fit.

According to scientists, this will be one for the history books.

Scientific observations clearly show that the sun is awakening from its long, dormant phase. So far, it is off to an auspicious start. Already, the increase in solar activity is the most abrupt and rapid rise recorded during the last half of the 20th century.

The sun is now on the upswing of its 23rd activity cycle. This numbering system dates back to 1848 and the astronomical work of Rudolf Wolf of the Zurich Observatory in Europe. Solar magnetic fields reverse at the peak of each 11-year cycle. Therefore, Cycle 23 is officially the last half of the current cycle – composed of Cycles 22 and 23 – which began in 1986.

Peak sunspot activity spans a period of two to four years.

Cycle 23's peak interval starts in 1999.

Experts say Cycle 23 will peak in March 2000. Some say it may be the worse ever recorded.

"You can expect fireworks anywhere from Christmas of 1999 and 2000 for the next three years," according to Donald Trombino, curator of solar astronomy at the Museum of Arts and Sciences in Daytona Beach, Florida. (3)

"We're welcoming in the millennium with a bang," says Mr. Trombino.

Already, the U.S. satellite TRACE (Transition Region and Coronal Explorer), surveying the upper layers of the sun's atmosphere, has sent back fascinating photos of massive releases of red-hot fiery magnetic energy. Researchers report observing a single solar flare release as much energy in seismic waves as the entire United States consumes in 20 years. The incredible energy stored in magnetic fields in the sun's outer layer is violently spewed out during these powerful solar flares. These outburst create strong electric fields which greatly accelerate electrons and protons. The blast produces a sunquake, violently shaking the sun and sending the high-speed waves across the solar surface.

Scientists are closely monitoring the amount of sunspot activity. There isn't, however, any reliable way to predict solar weather. All scientists can do is rely on statistical data gathered over 150 years and try to make predictions.

Might as well use the Farmer's Almanac.

"It's like saying we're going to have a mild or cold winter, says Dr. David Hathaway, a solar scientist at NASA's Marshall Space Flight Center. "We're in a similar state in predicting what the sun's climate is going to do." (4)

The reason scientist can't predict the severity of the Sun's cycle is because sunspots are driven by the dynamo that lies hidden beneath the photosphere. They simply don't know what controls the dynamo. What they do is study measurements of several related solar activities, then look for patterns that proceed the sunspot cycle.

After that, all they can do is guess.

"There's no real physics involved," explains Dr. Hathaway. "It's all statistical inferences."

Which means nobody knows for sure how big this next cycle of solar storms will be when it peaks in March 2000.

Early indications, however, have scientists expecting a whopper of a sun storm.

It is coming in late 1999.

Just in time for the big New Year's celebration.

Oh boy!

Solar Storms Threaten To Cause Major Disruptions on Earth

You guessed it.

Scientists are now worried about the consequences of the sun having a hyperactive thyroid gland.

When something on fire as big as the sun gets a stomachache, there's bound to be negative side effects.

If the sun belches, the whole solar system feels it.

The sun has already started to belch. Really nasty stuff, too.

In recent months, the cameras on the SOHO satellite have been zapped by blasts of high-energy protons. These solar blasts have struck the spacecraft's instruments like snow on a windshield, generating plenty of static noise. Also, SOHO's LASCO telescope has recorded powerful coronal mass ejection too.

Solar flares are classified according to measurements of released energy – B, C, M, and X. Each class is 10 times stronger than the last. Normally, solar flares are in the B and C class. As the sun's cycle proceeds toward maximum, solar flares will become M and X giants.

During the sun's last cycle, the biggest flare was an X13. The scale runs from X1 to X10. Flares greater than an X10 saturate the detectors, leaving scientists only estimating the intensity of the flare.

Already, several Class X flares have erupted.

Solar flares look like nuclear explosions. The flares throw off a huge cloud of magnetically charged particles big enough to envelop the Earth. Upon arrival on the Earth, these highly charged clouds produce atmospheric light shows. The aurora borealis – the Northern Lights – is a breathtaking by-product of solar storms.

Other by-products, however, aren't so pretty.

Solar flares produce your garden variety of radiation bursts – X-rays, gamma rays, visible light, and even chunks of the sun itself. These solar-proton events are short-lived, lasting about a day or two. The Earth's protective magnetic field is disrupted too. The level of impact upon the Earth depends on where the flare was pointed when it erupted from the sun's surface. If it was pointed toward the Earth, then it will be a direct hit.

Severe solar storms are extremely dangerous to satellites. Electrically charged protons become trapped in the region of space near the Earth. Nearby satellites get sprayed by hyperactive electrons. When the electrons strike the satellite, they penetrate partially through the satellite. Upon stopping, the electrons make a spark similar to static electricity. If the satellite is drenched in enough electrons, the electrical energy builds up inside the satellite. Finally, the satellite will discharge the energy in what looks like a lightning bolt, with electrical energy arcing between parts of the satellite.

According to their service manuals, surface charging really isn't good for satellites.

Too many electrons zap satellites silly.

The electrical discharge causes the satellite to short-circuit. Consequently, the satellite will experience a major memory meltdown.

The satellite gets amnesia.

The next you know, they're lost in space.

Satellites that don't know where they are just aren't worth much.

Solar Storms Threaten Communications and Electrical Power Systems

Over the next three to four years, the sun could cause billions of dollars worth of damage to satellites and communications systems on Earth.

"It's space weather El Niño," (5) says George Siscoe, a Boston University professor.

The upcoming geomagnetic storms will disrupt television and radio transmissions, mess up cellular telephone reception, scramble aviation navigation systems, and pose a life-threatening radiation hazard to astronauts and high-altitude military pilots. Spacecraft are also exposed to more atmospheric drag and to greater erosion by atomic oxygen when the Earth's outer atmosphere is heated up. Even flights of the supersonic Concorde may have to be diverted during an intense solar flare-up.

"Even though we can't see it directly, space weather has an effect on many technological systems," (6) according to Gary Heckman, a senior forecaster at the National Oceanic and Atmospheric Administration's Space Environment Center in Boulder, Colorado. "High-energy protons can penetrate satellites and damage electrical (components)."

In 1995, a $220 million Canadian communications satellite, Anik E-1, suddenly went dead. Plenty of Canadian businesses and government agencies relied on Anik E-1 for all sorts of critical data. Scientists later determined that an arcing spark shorted out the connections between the satellite's solar panels and its radio relays. The surface charging was caused when a cloud of highly charged electrons from an electromagnetic solar storm broadside the satellite. Additionally, six other satellites were temporarily disabled by the solar blast.

Interestingly, the 1995 Canadian satellite failure happened during a solar minimum - the period when the sun is calm. We are now into the beginning of the next solar maximum - one that scientists suspect may set the record for violent activity.

This may explain what knocked out Galaxy IV in May, 1998, and disrupted 45 million pagers and disrupted signals to public radio stations and several cable television networks. Galaxy IV, a nine-foot cube with a wingspan of 100 feet - unexpectedly lost its main computer. Then the backup computer didn't start either. Although the space weather was fairly quiet when the satellite's computers went down, readings of electron particles were very high in the days preceding the failure.

The unexplained demise of Galaxy IV has satellite operators worried. The new solar maximum - which peaks in March 2000 - could unleash a torrent of electromagnetic energy and radiation that produces nightmares for our technology-dependent society. So powerful are these blasts from the Sun that even buried pipelines can be corroded.

With telephone companies using new regions of the electromagnetic spectrum for wireless communications, users can expect to increasingly experience static, interruptions, and fade-outs over the next few years.

Intense solar activity also affects FM and AM radio signals. "All radio wave communication will be affected," warns Alan Title, principal investigator for the Stanford Lockheed Institute for Scientific Research in Palo Alto, CA. (7) "Every time there's a solar flare, there's a disruption of some kind...We're dealing with things we can't control." Disruptions to radio waves occur when solar energy is trapped in the Earth's ionosphere, thus making the ionosphere much more electrically charged. Rather than passing through the ionosphere, radio waves will be bent back towards the Earth. This "skip" causes interference with transmissions. For ham radio operators, however, the "skip" will increase their transmission distance to thousands of miles.

As the sun's storms become more ferocious and frequent, we may experience widespread blackouts when electricity grids are overloaded by the sun's energy. The electromagnetic pulses from solar eruptions can overload entire electrical power systems, disrupting electricity for millions of people. During the last solar maximum in 1989 to 1991, electric utilities in Canada and Sweden were knocked out.

A massive solar cloud hit North America in the very early morning hours in March, 1989. Power loads in the United States were low at the time. Unfortunately, the Hydro-Quebec electrical plant in Canada was caught off-guard. The power surge triggered the plant's protective devices to shut down, one after another, until the entire system crashed. Over 6.5 million people were without power for nine hours. The crash cost Hydro-Quebec over $10 million.

According to a report by the U.S. Department of Energy, the 1989 flare could have knocked out power throughout the East Coast. U.S. power grids are highly interconnected. Hydro-Quebec exports excess electricity to American utilities across the boarder. Had the solar surge arrived a few hours later in the day, when electricity use would be at its peak, Hydro-Quebec would have been exporting power south to American utilities. Most likely, power systems would have fell like dominoes. The Department of Energy's report said a similar solar flare hitting at peak time could topple electrical power grids from Maine to Maryland. The overload could cost utilities up to $8.3 billion.

Solar Storms and Y2K: The One, Two knockout Punch

"We're becoming increasingly tied to space programs," warns Gil Klinger, Deputy Undersecretary for Defense. (8)

Clearly, more leaders are becoming increasingly alarmed about our society's vulnerability to a massive technology failure. The growing dependence of the world's population – from military generals to high school students – on satellite communications exposes our technology-addicted society to potentially catastrophic consequences should a worldwide computer meltdown occur in the Year 2000.

"Since electrically enabled technology is getting more and more pervasive, the impact of it is going to be more noticeable," says Boston University professor George Siscoe.(9)

Like the Leonid meteor storm, the Cycle 23 solar maximum poses a very serious threat to the 550 satellites hovering above the Earth. Two factors must be considered. Since the last solar cycle in the late 1980s, we now have many more high-priced satellites circling the globe. Also, advances in microprocessors mean the electrical components of satellites are much smaller. The smaller components are more easily damaged thus making today's satellites even more vulnerable to the sun's nasty bad weather.

Increasingly, many scientists are warning there's a danger in relying too much on tiny microprocessor chips. Its not just the use of micro-processors in space satellites that worries scientists, but our society's reliance on the chips in everything from telephones to medical equip-ment.

Dr. Richard Harris, a member of the British scientific team that dis-covered the solar tornadoes, warns that we should add the "sunspot bug" to our list of worries because of the possible adverse effects solar storms may have on the tiny microprocessors in all types of devices.

Dr. Harris' concerns are shared by Louis Lanzerotti, a technology expert for Bell Labs, the research arm for Lucent Technologies. "Our technologies have become more sophisticated, and we've become more vulnerable over time. The danger to the chips is unpredictable." (10)

The vulnerability of technology to violent solar activity prompted scientists to look to SOHO, the solar observatory satellite, as an early warning system for dangerous blasts of radiation. Following a solar erup-tion, scientists know they have about one hour before the radiation cloud strikes the Earth. At the beginning of Cycle 23, scientists were counting on SOHO to provide critical observations of solar storms in the Year 2000, the peak of sunspot activity. Such information from SOHO would be critical to provide early warnings to satellite operators, telecommunication companies, and especially electrical utilities. Without such warnings, electrical power systems could be overwhelmed by the electrically charged particles striking the Earth, thus producing blackouts.

SOHO's voyage, however, hasn't been entirely sunny.

On June 24, 1998, SOHO died. During maintenance operations, the $1.2 billion satellite began spinning out of control. Scientists speculated that a computer error in instructions sent to SOHO caused the satellite to turn too far. The change in direction would have its solar panels pointing away from the sun, thus having no energy supply. Further complicating rescue operations were the failure of the satellite's emer-gency recovery system. Apparently, a critical gyroscope had been turned off earlier. As SOHO went spinning out of control in cold, black space, scientists feared its hydrazine fuel and batteries might be frozen, not to mention structural damage from the spinning.

Controllers at the Goddard Space Flight Center received a signal from the crippled satellite on August 3, 1998. Engineers fear the satel-lite's small batteries are too weak to power the spacecraft. They hope to salvage the mission if the frozen hydrazine fuel thaws later when the satellite's angle toward the sun changes.

Meanwhile, NASA is scurrying to launch a replacement for SOHO, nicknamed *Goresat* for Vice President Al Gore. If everything goes on schedule, the spacecraft will be launched in 2000 in time for both the peak of the sun's solar activity schedule and the Year 2000 presidential elections.

They can try, but don't be surprised if the mission fails.

It just seems things aren't going right as we approach the Year 2000. What other surprises await us ahead? In technology we trust, but our idol will fall.

The signs are around us.

Look at what is coming upon our high-tech world.

A worldwide computer crash! The most severe meteor storm in 33 years! Possibly the most violent solar storm in recorded history!

And it's all converging upon mankind at the same time. None of it can be stopped or delayed. It's almost like a timetable written by somebody outside this world!

Is this a script for a weird science fiction movie?

What is happening to this world?

13

Our National Defense: Hey General, I'm Push'n The Buttons, But Nutt'n Is Happen'n!

"We don't want to enter the nightmare scenario where everyone's screen suddenly goes blank. That would be a very uncertain and worrisome environment for all of us."

> *John Hamre — Deputy Secretary*
> *United States Department of Defense*
> *In testimony before the U.S. Senate Armed Services*
> *Committee*
> *June 4, 1998*

It was a top military secret.

President Clinton had ordered the Pentagon to prepare to launch air strikes against Iraq's Saddam Hussein.

In the early morning hours of Monday, February 2, 1998, military and civilian analysts on the Air Force's Computer Emergency Response Team in San Antonio, TX, noticed unusual warning flags popping up on their computer screens.

Instantly, they knew the meaning of the flags. Unauthorized intruders were attempting to enter a half dozen military networks around the nation. Accustomed to hundreds of attempted intrusions each day, the analysts quickly realized there was something different about these intruders. There was a pattern to the electronic attacks. It was a full-blown, organized cyber attack.

Appearing to originate from universities in Massachusetts, Texas, and Utah, the intruders entered unclassified military networks through the Solaris operating system used at many U.S. military bases.

Even more alarming to the Air Force was how quickly the electronic attack became global. Computers around the world were being programmed to illegally enter the Pentagon computer network.

The Pentagon's top brass was alerted to the computer attack. A crisis coordination team was immediately set up at the Pentagon. John Hamre, Deputy Secretary of the Department of Defense, promptly briefed President Clinton that an electronic attack was under way.

Military leaders feared that Saddam Hussein had launched a worldwide sneak cyber attack against the Pentagon. Perhaps it was the first electronic cyber war.

The persistence of the intruders and the vast number of computers worldwide they were attacking stunned Pentagon officials. "They wouldn't go away," said Air Force Colonel J.C. Massaro, commander of the Information Warfare Center. "It kept happening and kept happening." (1)

In all, over 750 military computers were illegally penetrated by the electronic attackers, including computers that would schedule and monitor the movement of troops and supplies, and the launching of aircraft during a war with Saddam Hussein.

The FBI was brought in to help trace the origins of the cyber attack. After a month long investigation, the FBI found the cyberterrorists.

The terrorists turned out to be two 16-year-old California high school students.

Assisted by another teenage cohort in Israel, the boys left the Pentagon badly shaken. The teenage hackers are members of a worldwide ring of computer hackers called *Masters of Downloading*. This global computer gang shares information over the Internet on how to penetrate computer systems by stealing passwords and probing network vulnerabilities. The worldwide search for the attackers was made more complicated by numerous privacy laws protecting the identity of Internet users. Because the attackers utilized multiple Internet servers in the United States, Germany, France, Taiwan, Israel, and the United Arab Emirates, federal investigators were forced to obtain nine court orders to pursue the trail of the cyber attackers.

The surprise cyber attack stunned military leaders and the White House. Clearly, military officials were caught off guard as they were planning military strikes against Iraq. Gaping holes in our military defense system was starkly evident. Systems to detect intruders on computer networks at military installations were severely deficient. Even more troubling was the lack of a plan to coordinate the Pentagon's response to a global cyber attack.

In today's globalized communications network, how safe are the citizens of the United States of America?

Could an "electronic Pearl Harbor" surprise us?

If our computer systems collapse, how vulnerable are we as a people?

Could America's enemies already be planning to take advantage of massive systems failure at the Pentagon in January 2000?

What horrific devastation would befall American cities if we had no warning that a nuclear attack had been launched against the United States?

Contrary to what the Pollyanna optimists say, Y2K is deadly serious.

Y2K and the Pentagon: Federal Government Admits It Won't Be Ready
The Year 2000 computer crisis seriously threatens our survival as a nation. Protecting its citizens from foreign enemies is the federal government's primary purpose for existence. Despite the dire possibilities that could befall this great land, America's politicians find little reason to be alarmed.

Nobody wants to sound the alarm for fear of disrupting the bull market that enthralls Wall Street's investors. Suggestions that we should go into a national state of emergency in preparation of Y2K are glibly shrugged off as "alarmist" thinking. "Good old American ingenuity will come to our rescue," is the typical response to any calls for "wartime" action.

Let's face it. Americans – including many preachers and church members – just don't think anything disastrous could ever strike the USA. "God bless the USA," proclaim our bumper stickers.

Well, what if God stops blessing the USA? America has never suffered wartime destruction within her borders from an outside force. We've never witnessed foreign troops on our beloved soil.

What if God lifts his hand of protection?

Has America crossed the line where God is forced to punish us for our gross sins? What makes us so confident that America can escape judgment?

What if today was December 31, 1999? What would happen tomorrow? If – God have mercy on us – a foreign enemy launched a nuclear attack against the United States, are we absolutely confident our high tech defense system would adequately alert the Pentagon to the incoming nuclear warheads, and successfully launch a counter strike?

If our banks fail, the stock market crashes, the electrical power grid goes down, telephone systems fail, then civil unrest and panic will spread like wildfire through every major U.S. city. Cities will burn.

For a brief period of time, America will be vulnerable. A window of opportunity will exist for America's enemies to bring us to our knees.

Add to this boiling pot of social chaos the uncontrolled mayhem that would race through America if terrorists and foreign espionage agents, working secretly within our borders, launch a coordinated campaign of sabotage. Major dams destroyed, whole towns flooded. Nuclear power plants blown up. Irreparable damage to vital communications centers. Water supplies in major cities poisoned.

America has never suffered, within her borders, at the bloody hands of enemies. America, however, has never been so rebellious toward God either. Are we really so confident that God would never lift his hand of protection from this great land?

What if tomorrow is January 1, 2000? What would be the capability of the Department of Defense to defend the United States of America?

Presently, at the time of this book's writing, the situation would be frightfully grim.

Alarmingly, a major portion of our national defense would simply fail.

When Congressman Stephen Horn, a California Republican who has been sounding the alarm in Congress for several years, issued in early June 1998, his quarterly "report card" for federal government agencies, he gave the Pentagon a "D."

"D" as in doomsday.

The problem at the Department of Defense is simple to understand. Our military has a lot of computers. A lot of very old computers. Old computers with two-digit dates. In fact, the Department of Defense has a staggering 358 million lines of computer code to examine, fix, and test before December 31, 1999.

"The Department of Defense is peculiarly vulnerable to this problem (Y2K) because it has such a grotesque set of legacy (older) systems," explains John Stephenson, who headed a major study by the U.S. General Accounting Office of our military readiness for the Year 2000. (2) "It has an awful lot of systems that have been around for an awfully long time," Mr. Stephenson says.

The U.S. Department of Defense has more than 1.5 million computers, 10,000 computer networks, and 28,000 computer systems. Over 2,800 systems are designated as "mission critical." These critical systems include computers that control our nuclear missiles, military satellites, communications, and the movement of troops and supplies during a war.

The Pentagon alone accounts for a third of all the critical computer systems in the entire federal government. With just months before the arrival of the new millennium, how many of the Pentagon's mission-critical systems have been corrected to be Y2K compliant?

So far, the military has spent over $2 billion on Y2K compliance. Congress authorized, in June, 1998, an emergency appropriation of an additional $1.6 billion for Year 2000 repairs at the Pentagon. Money, however, is not the problem. Time is the problem. It is running out quickly. As of May 15, 1998, by the Pentagon's own admission, a whopping 29% of its mission critical systems were Y2K compliant! Additionally, the GAO reports that, as of February 1998, "more than half of the over 730,000 personal computers they had checked had a Year 2000 problem."

The implications of this admission are astounding. If January 1, 2000, were tomorrow, an unbelievable 71% of America's most critical defense systems would not function. At the Pentagon's present rate of repairs, the U.S. military will not be ready for the Year 2000 until 2002!

That means for two years, America will be defenseless!

Even more frightening is the magnitude of the military's task to locate and repair an estimated 600,000 to 900,000 embedded microchips in critical components of our defense system, including weapons such as

Tomahawk cruise missiles and nuclear submarines. Embedded micro-processors are also used by the military in a variety of equipment such as telecommunication equipment, traffic control on military bases, security systems, base street lights, medical equipment, and elevator control systems. (3)

How serious is the situation?

"It is unsolvable," retired Brigadier General Ed Wheeler emphatically declares. (4)

General Wheeler, an Oklahoma patriot who led National Guard troops in Desert Storm, believes it's too late to stop the Y2K crisis. He says the federal government should be focusing, at this late stage, on contingency plans to deal with an inevitable crash.

Just what are contingency plans for a world super power? How do we defend our population during a two-year period when our defense systems are down? How do we maintain peace and order around the world if Uncle Sam can't launch missiles and transport troops across the seas?

What about our troops stationed overseas? How will they defend themselves? Will we just abandon them, defenseless and alone, into the bloody hands of terrorists with nuclear and chemical weapons?

The potential ramifications of the Y2K crisis threaten our very survival as a people. A two-year gap in military preparedness is absolutely unthinkable. With weapons of mass destruction threatening us from every direction, even a two hour period of being defenseless could mean death for tens of millions of American citizens.

Sadly, America is asleep. "All is well in the USA," is the soothing mantra of the news media. With the economy this good, what is there to worry about?

Stop worrying about President Clinton's low moral standards and lack of character, shouts the media. "It's the economy, stupid!" that really counts, we are reminded each day.

Don't listen to the President's critics, advise the liberal media and Mr. Clinton's spin-doctors.

"Just chill," is their advice to the American public.

GAO Issues Chilling Warning

"Chill out" may be the advice of Bill Clinton and Al Gore, but the message contained in a recent report from the General Accounting Office was entirely different.

The GAO's report is more like "bone chilling."

The GAO is the federal government's auditor. The independent agency audits the spending of federal government agencies and issues unbiased reports. The agency prides itself on issuing reports that are untainted by political pressure. The GAO tells it like it is.

And how is the GAO telling it about the Department of Defense?

Entitled "*Year 2000 Computer Problems Threaten DOD Operations*," the GAO states in unambiguous terms the dismal condition of our national defense in facing the Y2K millennial meltdown. "Time is running out to correct Department of Defense systems that could malfunction or produce incorrect information when the year 2000 is encountered during automated data processing. (5)

Saying that "most of Defense's automated information systems and weapon systems are vulnerable to the Year 2000 problem," the GAO report clearly identifies the dependence our modern military has upon computers. "The Department of Defense relies on computer systems for some aspect of all of its operations, including strategic and tactical operations, sophisticated weaponry, intelligence, surveillance and security efforts, and routine business functions, such as financial management, personnel, logistics, and contract management."

What are the consequences if the government fails to prepare the Department of Defense before December 31, 1999?

In accountants' language, the GAO states the hard, cold reality: "Failure to successfully address the Year 2000 problem in time could severely degrade or disrupt any of Defense's mission-critical operations."

Hmmmm?

How much fighting can a defense force do that is severely degraded and disrupted?   Hand-to-hand combat, perhaps?

The GAO auditors found the DOD in disarray in dealing with Y2K. Even by the time of the report's release in April, 1998, the military was still in the very first stage of compliance, which is assessment.   In fact, the Department of Defense is a year behind its own schedule. The report states, "the department is still assessing systems even though it originally anticipated this would be done in June, 1997."

Furthermore, the GAO charges that the DOD's "progress in fixing systems has been slow." Amazingly, there is "no program office or full-time executive in charge of the department's effort" to prepare the Department of Defense for the Year 2000!   According to the GAO report, the DOD "has not determined...which systems have the highest impact on its mission," nor does Defense "issued adequate guidelines to its components on key issues concerning status reporting, interfaces, and testing.   The report also reveals that "information being reported to Defense by components does not provide a reliable indication of program status because it is not being validated for accuracy or completeness."

Whoa!

Read that again!

According to an official report by the General Accounting Office of the United States Government, the Department of Defense is a year behind in even figuring out which computer systems are critical to its mission of defending our nation, nobody is in charge, progress in repairing computers is painstakingly slow, there are no guidelines telling each military division just what constitutes Y2K compliance, and the information being reported by military commanders to the Pentagon is not reliable because it is not being validated for accuracy and completeness!

There you have it! Nobody is in charge! Our Department of Defense will be defenseless on January 1, 2000.

Clearly, the GAO report warns that our entire defense system is in jeopardy of failing around the world when the calendar rolls over to the Year 2000. "The impact of these failures could be widespread, costly, and potentially disruptive to military operations worldwide." Any parent with a son or daughter stationed overseas should be unequivocally demanding that our federal government get serious about this threat to our military forces. With bases in South Korea, Europe, Saudi Arabia, Kuwait, Japan, and the Philippines, anti-American forces may be incited into a violent frenzy should global chaos ensue at the turn of the new millennium. It is a shuddering thought to imagine America's young soldiers stranded on foreign bases, without back-up support or even communications, defending themselves against hordes of zealous Yankee-hating fanatics equipped with weapons of mass destruction.

Saying that the DOD's dismal Y2K preparations "seriously endangers Defense chances of successfully meeting the Year 2000 deadline for mission-critical systems," the GAO outlines some of the pitfalls that Y2K will confront the military. The report points to the Global Command Control System as a prime example of how dependent the military is upon computer technology. The GCCS is deployed at 700 sites worldwide. The system is used by military strategists to "generate a common operating picture of the battlefield for planning, executing, and managing military operations." During a operational exercise in August 1997, the Global Command Control System failed testing when the date was rolled over to the year 2000. The GAO warns that the U.S. and its allies "would be unable to orchestrate a Desert Storm-type engagement in the year 2000 if the problem is not corrected."

Another serious problem is the August 21, 1999, date rollover of Global Positioning System. "Smart bombs" – those marvelous missiles that could strike Saddam Hussein sitting on the toilet – aren't too smart without the Global Positioning System. Besides being used for aircraft and naval navigation, military leaders use the GPS for precision targeting the designated impact of the "smart bombs." Dates are very important to "smart bombs." The GAO report says "ground control stations use dates to synchronize the signals from the satellites and maintain uplinks to the satellites."

And what would happen if the GPS date problem is not fixed?

"Failure to correct Year 2000 problems could cause these stations to lose track of satellites and send erroneous information" to users of the GPS system.

"Smart bombs" soaring through the sky with erroneous information?

Hmmm.... that's bound to liven up anybody's day.

What else does the GAO warn could happen?

The Automated Digital Network (AUTODIN) is an aging electronic messaging system that provides secure messaging for military commanders. The system is being replaced by the Defense Message System (DMS). Both systems provide messaging for important operations such as intelligence gathering, diplomatic communications, and military command and control. Pretty important stuff, eh? Especially during a war. So, what if Y2K shuts down AUTODIN and DMS? The GAO, our nation's watchman, cautions us with this ominous warning, "Should Year 2000 problems render DMS or AUTODIN inoperable or unreliable, it would be difficult to monitor enemy operations or conduct military operations."

Now that's bound to put a severe crimp in your best planned military strategy. It just seems logical to assume that "to monitor enemy operations or conduct military operations" are two big priorities in fighting a good war.

The GAO report is equally blunt about how Y2K could drastically impair the readiness of our defenses by cutting off the supply lines to our troops. "Aircraft and other military equipment could be grounded because the computer systems used to schedule maintenance and track supplies may not work. Defense could incur shortages of vital items needed to sustain military operations and readiness – such as food, fuel, medical supplies, clothing, and spare and repair parts to support its over 1,400 weapons systems."

Y2K will also impact the Defense Department's accounting operations, the GAO says, affecting payments on defense contracts, the pay checks to active duty soldiers, and pensions to retired military personnel. "Billions of dollars in payments could be inaccurate because the computer systems used to manage thousands of defense contracts may not correctly process date-related information...Active duty soldiers and military retirees may not get paid if the systems used to make calculations and prepare checks are not repaired in time."

What was the Defense Department's response to the GAO's stinging analysis of our military's preparation for the Year 2000?

They agreed with everything.

"In reviewing a draft of this report, the Acting Principal Deputy of the Office of Assistant Secretary of Defense for Command, Control, Communications and Intelligence concurred with all of our recommendations to improve Defense's Year 2000 program," the GAO report concludes.

The report, however, ends with a somber postscript to the Defense Department's agreement to the GAO's recommendations. "However, in concurring with several of our recommendations, Defense did not indicate how it would implement them. Instead, it reiterated current practices which to date have not resulted in reliable and complete inventory, progress, and cost data."

So, the Pentagon agrees with the GAO's analysis, pledges to implement the agency's recommendations for Y2K compliance, then says it will keep doing the same things that got the Defense Department so far behind!

Might be a good time to dust off your dad's old 1962 blueprints for a bomb shelter.

Pentagon Finds Novel Way to Become Y2K Compliant: Fudge the Numbers!

One way to make your department look good on paper is to play "fast and loose" with the numbers. A hardware store manager in a small country town might get away with bit of fudging when doing an inventory. Whether there's 128 boxes of bolts in stock or 160, its no big deal. When its nuclear warheads you're counting, well, that's a completely different matter.

Fudging is just what the Defense Department was caught doing. The Defense Department's Inspector General discovered the bogus numbers in an investigation of the DOD's list of "compliant" mission-critical systems.

DOD's Year 2000 policies state that the military cannot automatically assume a system will successfully operate in the next century until it has been certified by a system manager. Only after the system manager signs a Year 2000 compliance checklist can a computer system be officially declared "Y2K compliant."

The investigation revealed that computer system managers turned in reports listing mission-critical systems as Y2K compliant, even though they knew the systems had not received such certification. In November 1997, the Pentagon reported that 430 mission critical systems were Y2K compliant. Upon inspection of the 430 systems by the Inspector General, however, it was discovered that between 265 and 338 of those systems were not compliant after all. The investigation also revealed that "the existence of a completed and signed Y2K compliance checklist did not always mean that the system was Y2K compliant." (6)

Hey, "compliance" means different things to different people! "I say 'too-may-toe,' and you say 'too-mat-o.'" We're only talking about our national defense! Let's not quibble over semantics!

While the official report did not identify the affected systems, the Washington Post reported that the computers were believed to be systems used by large Defense agencies, such as the Army, Air Force, the Finance and Accounting Service, the Special Weapons Agency, and the Defense Logistics Agency. (7)

"Senior DOD management cannot afford to make Y2K program decisions based on highly inaccurate information," the Inspector General reported to the Pentagon. "If DOD does not take the action that it needs to obtain accurate information as to the status of its Y2K efforts, we believe that serious Y2K failures may occur in DOD mission-critical information technology systems." (8)

Now that's a comforting thought when you go to sleep tonight. Make sure you say your prayers!

U.S. Armed Forces Facing Potential Disaster

The scope and size of the United States Department of Defense is awesome. Within its ranks, both uniformed and civilian, are more people than the entire population of metropolitan Washington, D.C. Much of the early development of computer technology in the 1950's and 1960's came from research and development by DOD. As a nation, we owe so much to the men and women of the American Armed Forces who have built the most powerful military machine on Earth to protect this nation.

Our modern-day military defense system has been built layer by layer, since World War II. It has taken 50 years to construct an immensely complex system that now heavily depends on technology. Much of today's defense structure relies on old legacy computers systems dating back to the early 1960's.

It is no wonder that John Hamre, the Deputy Defense Secretary, calls Y2K "an especially large, complex and insidious threat for the Department of Defense." (9) In testimony before the U.S. Senate Committee on Armed Services, Mr. Hamre outlined for the Senators the width and breadth of DOD's Y2K problem. It addition to weapon systems, Mr. Hamre pointed out that Y2K will affect "command and control systems; satellite systems; the Global Positioning System; highly specialized inventory management and transportation management systems; medical equipment; and important universal systems for payment and personnel records." (10) Mr. Hamre also reminded the Senators that the Department of Defense "operates a multitude of military bases, which are much like small towns, where the infrastructure is also vulnerable to Year 2000 problems. Power grid, heating systems, air filtration, embedded chips that may not be compliant. The problem will also extend to all forms of commercial communications and mass-transportation systems (traffic lights, trains, subways, and elevators) which affect our men and women in uniform."

Today's high-tech world makes information technology critical to winning a war. Desert Storm was the world's first "smart weapons" war. Without superior technology and information, the U.S. would have been forced to fight an entirely different war against Saddam Hussein. In his Senate testimony, Deputy Secretary Hamre said that the "superior ability of the United States warfighters to obtain, process, analyze, and convey information is our most powerful weapon on the battlefield." (11) He bluntly admits that the Year 2000 problem is "a threat to the core of our military superiority."

Anything that disrupts the flow to battlefield commanders of vital information needed for decision-making poses a deadly threat to our uniformed men and women. Likewise, any systems failure in crucial military hardware – tanks, jet fighters, battleships, satellites, missile launchers – would leave our soldiers defenseless in the heat of battle.

Our dependence on technology is what makes Y2K so terrifying. As a nation, we have yet to fully comprehend the deadly seriousness of a massive technology collapse in our national defense system. Defending the citizenry of America is the highest priority of our federal government. Y2K has the potential of exposing the USA to attacks by foreign enemies and terrorists. Failure to fix Y2K could result in disastrous consequences.

Pentagon officials are aware of the gravity of the situation. "We must make sure the American people know that they are safe and that our potential adversaries know that the Year 2000 does not pose a vulnerability that they can exploit," says William A. Curtis, the Pentagon's Y2K oversight director in the Office of the Assistant Secretary of Defense for Command, Control, Communications and Intelligence. (12)

The Day NORAD Stood Still

In 1993, military commanders at the North American Air Defense Command (NORAD) wanted to see what would happen if the USA was attacked with nuclear weapons on January 1, 2000.

NORAD is the United States' top-secret military installation that watches the skies 24-hours each day for incoming nuclear missiles. The computer-dependent installation is designed to provide America with an early warning of a nuclear attack. NORAD is the linchpin of our strategic forces. Without NORAD, we'd be in big trouble.

A simulated test was conducted at NORAD's highly classified base at Cheyenne Mountain, just outside Colorado Springs, CO. The dates on computers were rolled up to December 31, 1999. As the simulated computer clocks struck midnight, the computers rolled over to the Year 2000.

Guess what happened?

"It all locked up at the stroke of midnight," recalled Robert Martin, a top computer specialist with the Mitre Corporation, a leading defense contractor. (13)

Everything froze.

The computer screens that monitor missile-detecting satellites. Radar screens. The early warning communications systems. It all froze.

Fortunately, it was a test. If it happens again on January 1, 2000, we could all be crispy critters before breakfast. Happy New Year!

Government Official Voices Concern About Nuclear Missiles

President Clinton's advisor on the Year 2000, John Koskinen, warned in March 1998, that he could not rule out "doomsday scenarios" where America's nuclear defenses cease to function. (14)

Mr. Koskinen worries about nuclear missiles, especially "if the data doesn't function and they actually go off." (15)

If it makes you feel better, the presidential Y2K advisor doesn't think our nuclear missiles will accidentally explode. He thinks they just won't do anything. Just sit there in the silos like nuclear-tipped duds. "It's more likely that they won't function because the systems don't recognize what happened." (16)

What good are nuclear warheads if you can't launch them during a full-blown nuclear attack by Russia or China?

Our nuclear defenses will be fixed in time, says John Hamre, Deputy Secretary of Defense. "We have a dedicated task force working to ensure all systems required for nuclear command and control are secure," Mr. Hamre states. "Everything from the early warning satellites down to the custodial codes required for fusing and arming. That will be OK." (17)

Others aren't so sure.

No one really knows what will happen after midnight on December 31, 1999.

John Pike, an analyst with the Federation of American Scientists, has serious concerns about the world's stockpile of nuclear weapon systems. When Y2K compliance involves nuclear warheads, Mr. Pike says that is "where the margin for error, the fault tolerance should be pretty close to zero." (18)

Mr. Pike says there is a big difference in the Federal Aviation Administration having a Y2K-related disaster, and the Pentagon having a Y2K-related disaster. "If FAA fouls up, some 747s crash. If STRATCOM fouls up, they incinerate the northern hemisphere." (19)

Well, there go the property values. Talk about a "fire sale" on American and Canadian real estate!

It is the overwhelming task of carefully reviewing 358 million lines of computer code that troubles experts such as Mr. Pike. "It is a great steaming heap of spaghetti code, which means that it works but nobody knows why anymore," (20) Mr. Pike explains. "And nobody wants to look too closely for fear that they might break it. When they go in there to start looking at this code, it turns out that half the code doesn't even execute anymore," Mr. Pike states. "Which would basically be your car having a dozen cylinders instead of six and only six work, and you have no idea which six. And no one can explain to you why this seems to be the case."

Despite the daunting task confronting U.S. military forces with so little time remaining, David Knox – a NORAD spokesman – says NORAD will be Y2K compliant by the end of 1998.

"We're going to be as confident as we can be," Mr. Knox says. (21)

Confident as we can be? We're talking about the nuclear defenses of the United States of America!

Perhaps NORAD isn't real confident either. Mr. Knox says NORAD has made extensive contingency plans in case some errant computer code remains in the system.

Somebody needs to tell the good folks at NORAD that being "confident as we can be" could lead to the destruction of the United States of America. With it comes to our national defense, "almost compliant" is not enough.

NORAD's contingency plans may mean heading for the fallout shelters. That is, assuming we still have any fallout shelters!

Y2K Spurs Armageddon Fears

The scenario sounds like the plot for a new James Bond movie, but U.S. military officials are becoming increasingly worried that it could happen. At midnight on December 31, 1999, Russia's aging defense computers go haywire. Fear-stricken Russian military leaders, believing the United States has launched a first-strike nuclear attack, retaliate by launching Russia's massive nuclear arsenal to destroy America.

Such a Y2K nightmare is being taken seriously at the Department of Defense in Washington, D.C. The Pentagon's concern has prompted the Clinton Administration to offer to share early warning information with the Russians to prevent the outbreak of nuclear war triggered by a Year 2000 computer meltdown.

Awareness of Y2K has been almost nonexistent in Russia and China. "Our concern is that Russia and China have only a very rudimentary understanding of the Year 2000 problem, which is why we need to reach out to them to make sure they have custodial confidence in their own systems." said Deputy Defense Secretary John Hamre. (22)

"We have been in discussions with them on this," said Pentagon spokesman Kenneth Bacon told reporters on July 13, 1998. (23) "We have offered to share or engage in joint early warning projects with Russia and maybe with other countries as well." U.S. Defense Secretary William Cohen raised the Y2K issue with Russian Defense Minister Igor Sergeyev at a meeting in Brussels on June 12, 1998.

Both Russia and the United States rely heavily on computerized early warning systems. These early warning systems collect data from ground-level sensors, radar, and satellites. If Russia's system collapses after December 31, 1999, error messages could be sent to Russian nuclear missile command sites.

Whether the systems display false or confusing data – or completely shut down – the situation could suddenly plunge the world on the brink of a nuclear holocaust. The situation in Russia is particularly troublesome because of the age of the country's defense computers. Furthermore, Russia's growing economic instability reduces the cash-strapped government's ability to provide funds to fix the Y2K problems, and poses the risk that a financial collapse would trigger social anarchy within the nation. Widespread social unrest following an Y2K-induced economic collapse would seriously threaten the control of Russia's nuclear arsenal.

John Hamre, Deputy Secretary of the U.S. Department of Defense, told the United States Senate Armed Services Committee he wants to calm Russian nuclear forces during the change to the Third Millennium. Mr. Hamre told the Senators that sharing early warning information was important so "we don't enter into the nightmare condition where everybody is all of a sudden uncertain and their screens go blank." (24) Such a nightmare "would be a very worrisome environment for all of us."

Mr. Hamre also testified that the Pentagon is worried about the Russian government's ability to deal with the Year 2000 computer problem. He said U.S. military officials are "very concerned that the military leadership in Russia right now is coping with very serious funding constraints. They are increasingly falling back to rely on nuclear weapons as a safeguard for their national security, and their early-warning system is fragile, and they don't have any program to deal with the year 2000." (25)

U.S. Navy Vice Admiral Richard Mies, nominated by President Clinton to be Commander-In-Chief of the U.S. Strategic Command, is also worried about Russia's lack of concern about Y2K. During his confirmation hearing, he told the Senate Armed Services Committee that he is "concerned about the effect the Y2K problem may have on our other nuclear powers such as the Russians." (26) Vice Admiral Mies assured the Senators that the subject of Y2K and nuclear weapons has been brought up to the Russians for consideration. Although the Russians have sent U.S. military officials assurances they are taking measures to address the problem, Vice Admiral Mies said he doesn't "have as reassuring a feeling about their measures as I certainly do about our own."

Vice Admiral Mies certainly has good reason to be concerned about how serious the Russians are taking Y2K. The Russian government didn't even start considering the problem until mid-1998.

On May 13, 1998, Russian Prime Minister Sergei Kiriyenko issued an order to government agencies to access their computers for possible Y2K problems. Coordination of the program was assigned to the State Telecommunications Committee. When asked in late June 1998, whether the Y2K problem would be solved in time, the committee quoted a software research company that said the problem wouldn't be solved until the year 2050. In a written statement, the agency said, "The Russian State Telecommunications committee considers that the '2000 problem' cannot be resolved entirely in the remaining time." (27)

Americans shouldn't worry about an accidental nuclear launch, says Marshal Igor Sergeyev, Russia's Minister of Defense. Mr. Sergeyev, former commander of the Strategic Missile Forces, says Russia's military computers are safe from Y2K because "special computer technology is used." (28) He didn't explain what he meant.

The real threat of nuclear war in the Year 2000 is being raised by growing chorus of respected experts. Edward Yardeni, chief economist for Deutsche Morgan Grenfell, Inc., is calling on world political leaders to deal with the situation. "Military leaders of the United States, other NATO members and Russia must jointly assess the risk of an accidental nuclear missile launch or a provocative false alarm." (29)

Such nations "must rapidly develop a fail-safe joint communication and intelligence network to eliminate any such risk," Mr. Yardeni wrote in a report issued in April 1998. Mr. Yardeni, who was recognized by the Wall Street Journal in January 1998 as the Economist of the Year, warned "Measures must be taken to thwart terrorists, hackers, and other malevolent opportunists from taking advantage of any Year 2000 chaos."

The American Chamber of Commerce in Russia is also sounding the alarm. Warning of "catastrophic" consequences in Russia if computers are not fixed in time, the American Chamber of Commerce particularly cited the Russian military's lack of Y2K preparation. In a June 17, 1998, news release, the Chamber said, "Efforts to address the year 2000 problem for the defense industry appear to be in their natal stage." (30)

Sobering words about the threat of nuclear war have also been spoken by Mr. John Pike of the Federation of American Scientists. For both the United States and Russia, Mr. Pike says there is a "real risk though that we could see the sort of computer malfunctions that we've seen in previous years, where the command and control systems erroneously report that an attack is in progress; erroneously direct missiles to shoot at the wrong target; and at a minimum, cause all of the countries to put their missiles on much higher levels of alert, because they're concerned about their unreliable warning systems." (31)

This uncertainty produced by the Year 2000 computer virus has prompted the Physicians for Social Responsibility to issue a nuclear war alert. The group, which is the American affiliate of the International Physicians for the Prevention of Nuclear War, issued a report saying, "some analysts are concerned that computer defects in the year 2000 could cause further problems in Russian nuclear controls." (32)

The group of medical doctors urged people to be "skeptical" of any claims by both the U.S. and Russian governments that Russia's nuclear controls are still good. The report says the risk of an accidental nuclear war is high. "U.S. and Russian arsenals remain on high alert," says the report. "This fact, combined with the aging of Russian technical systems, has recently increased the risk of an accidental nuclear attack."

Ira Helfand, a co-author of the report warns that such an accidental nuclear attack would lead to "an all out nuclear war." (33) Such a war "would be the greatest disaster that we have ever known."

CIA Warns Y2K Poses Security Risks

Government agencies and corporations, under intense pressure to meet deadlines, are cutting corners on security procedures. The Gartner

Group has warned that major organizations are failing to conduct extensive background checks on computer programmers hired to solve Y2K problems.

The FBI uncovered a scam by the Mafia to steal millions of dollars from companies through computers. In the scam, the Mafia set up a Y2K consulting company to help legitimate businesses solve Year 2000 problems.

The mob-controlled "consultants" told companies they would fix their computers.

The "fix" meant the Mafia computer programmers, with access to the clients' computers and files, busily rewrote the software to redirect money from the clients' bank accounts into the Mafia's bank accounts.

Mr. George Tenet, Director of the CIA, however, has warned of a more sinister plot. America's top spy is worried that foreign nations – such as Russia, China, and Iraq – could send agents to the United States as programmers for the purpose of sabotaging critical computer systems. Mr. Tenet said the vast number of foreign computer programmers and foreign produced software programs makes it easy for a hostile nation to implant viruses in American computers.

The CIA director said the agency is concerned that so many foreign persons are gaining unrestrained access to vital and sensitive computer systems in government, banking, financial services, and other important sectors of the nation's infrastructure.

"We are building an information infrastructure, the most complex the world has ever known, on an insecure foundation," stated Mr. Tenet before the Senate's Governmental Affairs Committee. (34)

Pentagon Covers Its Flank Against Cyber Terrorists

Nothing illustrated America's perilous risk to cyberterrorism more than a top-secret government exercise that stunned unsuspecting senior Pentagon leaders.

Code-named "Eligible Receiver," a team of computer specialists from the National Security Agency began the exercise in June 1997. During a two-week period, the team used software obtained from computer hacker sites on the Internet to conduct information warfare attacks on secret military computer systems.

The NSA "Red Team" of 50 to 75 make-believe computer hackers posed as agents for North Korea. Their goal was to penetrate secret U.S. military computer systems, and thereby, terrorize the U.S. government into changing its policies toward the communist regime in Pyongyang, North Korea.

The National Security Agency test was launched without the Pentagon's knowledge. The NSA wanted to see how far cyber terrorists could actually go into military computer systems without being spotted and stopped.

What happened?

Groups of NSA "cyberterrorists" glided in and out of military systems around the world without detection. The test results were frightening. With ease, the make-believe hackers penetrated military computer networks in Washington, D.C., Chicago, St. Louis, Colorado, and Hawaii.

Just how dangerous was the U.S. military's exposure to risk from these "cyberterrorists?"

They were so successful at penetrating military computer systems during the two-week period that they could have shut down the command-and-control elements of the entire U.S. Pacific Command. The Pacific Command is in charge of 100,000 American troops stationed in the Pacific that would fight China or North Korea if war would break out.

Even more frightening is the fact that these would-be terrorists could have shut down the entire electric-power grid in the United States!

Needless to say, "Eligible Receiver" gave the Pentagon a fresh dose of anxieties about the perils facing us in the Year 2000. Infowar attacks against military computer networks exposes America to the ugly threat of an "electronic Pearl Harbor."

One group that is giving the Pentagon a bad case of heartburn is the Masters of Downloading. They claim to have penetrated numerous sensitive Pentagon computer systems. In October 1997, the MOD stole software from the Defense Information Systems Network Equipment Manager, which controls the Global Positioning System satellites that provide American bombers with pinpoint accurate coordinates. In addition to stealing software that controls the GPS, the MOD accessed classified software used to monitor and manage an assortment of military computer hardware. The Masters of Downloading also brag they've broken into U.S. submarines.

Pipe bombs are no longer the weapon of terrorists. Instead, the chosen weapon of today's terrorists are "logic bombs" which can be dropped into computer networks. Many national defense experts warn that a terrorist group or enemy nation could launch an "infowar" attack against the United States capable of devastating the network of computers that our nation depends on for daily life. In addition to shutting down the electric-power grid, cyberterrorists could bring down Wall Street by blocking banking and financial transactions, send missiles off-course, shut down 911 emergency call centers, bombard military computers with error messages, and even turn off traffic light signals in hundreds of cities.

For small nations, waging a conventional war against the United States of America is totally unrealistic. Infowar will be the war of the Third Millennium. "Many of the countries whose information warfare efforts we follow realize that in a conventional military confrontation against the U.S., they cannot prevail," CIA Director George Tenet told the

Senate Committee on Governmental Affairs. (35) "These countries recognize that cyber attacks...represent the kind of asymmetric option they will need to 'level the playing field' during an armed crisis against the United States."

So tantalizing is the potential of infowar attacks to wreck havoc on nations that scientists and computer programmers in several countries are feverishly developing cyber weapons. According to the CIA, nations working to acquire information warfare technology include Iran, Iraq, and Libya. One such weapon is a HERF gun. Both the U.S. and Russia are developing their version of electronic weapon. The High-Energy Radio Frequency gun sends electromagnetic pulses to garble data stored on computer disks or tapes. HERF guns can also disable computer networks by disrupting the flow of electrons.

Tales abound around the world about HERF gun attacks on government and financial computer systems such as banks. In fact, the United States used HERF guns against Saddam Hussein during the Gulf War to disrupt Iraq's communications. Major banks are "hardening" their computer systems with shielding to repel HERF attacks. "SEV Bank in Stockholm has hardened its computer centers against HERF guns," said Manuel Wik, strategic specialist in the Swedish Electronic Systems Directorate. (36)

Year 2000 Could Unleash Mayhem Around the World

We do not live in normal times.

Unlike other calamities in past times such as the Great Depression, we exist in a world that has lost its moral code that held together the fabric of society. Close-knit communities helped and protected each other. Together, they pulled through the troubles.

They didn't have nuclear, chemical, and biological weapons either.

Today, we are racing toward an unprecedented global meltdown of computer technology. Nobody knows what will happen after December 31, 1999. Will the world's computers glide into the Third Millennium with only a few glitches, or will they send an electronic time bomb cascading through the world's interconnected computer networks?

Whether we like to think about it or not, there are people in the world who hate the United States with a burning passion. They think Americans are a bunch of fat, spoiled Yankees consuming the Earth's resources while the rest of the planet's population just barely survives.

The destruction of America is their goal.

The Year 2000 could give these madmen the opportunity they need to cripple America. Knowing that the United States and other industrialized nations will suffer tremendous trouble from the Y2K bug, these rogue nations and an assortment of terrorists could be planning right now to take advantage of the coming computer crash.

Communist China, with 13 nuclear missiles pointed at U.S. cities (thanks to President Clinton allowing the Chinese to obtain sensitive

American missile guidance technology!), may perceive the Year 2000 computer crash as the way to tip the world's balance of power. Russia's remaining die-hard Communists, likewise, could see the Year 2000 as their last chance to destroy Capitalism and reinstate totalitarian communism throughout the world.

Even more menacing is the threat of Russia's aging defense system's computers melting down at midnight on December 31, 1999.

The Year 2000 threat to our national security is real.

This is not a test.

High-ranking Pentagon officials openly admit the United States Department of Defense will not solve its Y2K problems in time. "DOD components are applying extraordinary efforts to meet the technical challenges associated with Y2K compliance. Despite these efforts, however, there is no guarantee all DOD systems will be free of risk by the immovable deadline of January 1, 2000," Deputy Defense Secretary John Hamre told U.S. Senators on June 4, 1998. "Systems whose risks have been mitigated through renovation and testing could fail, and the failure of one system could disrupt many others." (37)

Amid the concerns by the General Accounting Office that the Pentagon was in trouble, the Department of Defense admitted in August 1998 that it is falling further behind schedule in fixing its computer systems. That news followed the DOD Inspector General's report in July 1998 that critical systems were not Y2K compliant. The report mentioned the U.S. Central Command, which directed the missile attacks against Osama bin Laden's terrorist base in Afghanistan and the chemical factory in Sudan, "faces a high risk that Year 2000-related disruptions will impair its mission capabilities." (38)

Further evidence that our military defense system might not be ready for the Year 2000 came in a letter from Secretary of Defense William S. Cohen. His official memorandum addressed to the Joint Chiefs of Staff and the Pentagon's top brass admitted that DOD is behind schedule. "The Department of Defense is making insufficient progress in its efforts to solve its Y2K computer problem," the Secretary wrote. (39) Secretary Cohen warned U.S. military officials he was prepared to order a stop to every other computer project inside the Pentagon. "We will take a hard look at progress in November and December (1998). If we are still lagging behind, all further modification to software, except those needed for Y2K remediation, will be prohibited after January 1, 1999."

In today's volatile world, the failure of U.S. military systems would surely open Pandora's box for mischief and mayhem by political misfits around the globe.

"What kind of unrest will occur around the world is of great concern," (40) says U.S. Senator Robert Bennett (R-Utah).

Deputy Defense Secretary John Hamre says that Y2K is "going to have implications in the world and in American society we can't even comprehend." (41)

"I will be the first to say we're not going to be without some nasty surprises," Mr. Hamre warned the Senate Armed Services Committee.

Nasty surprises indeed.

Will America be humbled and brought to her knees?

Better that we fall to our knees now in submission to God, then fall to our knees in surrender to foreign enemies.

14 *Electric Utilities:* It's Sure Dark In Here!

"Energy provided by our electric utilities is a critical catalyst to the operation of virtually every sector of our nation's economy. If power shuts down, the rest of our society will shut down in its wake."

> *Congresswoman Constance A. Morella (R-MD)*
> *Remarks before the House of Representatives*
> *Committee on Science — Subcommittee on Technology*
> *May 14, 1998*

It lasted 10 weeks.

The downtown business district of the city, teeming with commerce and trade, abruptly came to a halt.

Auckland, a city of one million people in New Zealand, went without a full and constant source of electrical power almost 10 weeks.

The trouble began on January 22, 1998, summertime in the land down under, when a gas-filled cable failed during a spike in electric consumption. An excessive heat wave was blamed for overly stressing the aging cable owned by the Mercury Energy utility company. February 1998 was the hottest month since New Zealand began keeping records in the late 1880s. The lack of rain contributed too. Company officials said the dry soil kept heat from dissipating away from the underground cable.

Power was shut off throughout the city's downtown center. Residents in high rise apartment complexes had no air conditioning. Employees in office buildings were stranded in elevators. Restaurants and cafes were forced to quickly pack meat and perishable foods in rapidly melting ice.

For the next 18 days, employees and residents suffered in the unbearable, sweltering heat. People wondered how it could get worse.

It did.

Like falling dominoes, Mercury Energy's decrepit 110- kilovolt oil and gas filled cables failed. On February 9, 1998, the second cable failed. Then, the third and fourth cables failed on February 19 and 20.

The unthinkable had happened. Without warning, Mercury Energy suddenly had no backup power supply for Auckland's downtown.

Downtown Auckland was without electricity.

Chaos filled the city's business district.

One in twenty of Auckland's residents are employed in the business district. Over 6,000 residents live in the downtown area. Eighty thousand commuters stream into the business district every weekday.

Mercury Energy struggled to restore power. Working with only half its normal workforce due to cost-cutting employee reductions, Mercury Energy officials were embarrassed by the revelation the utility didn't even know which side of the streets the cables were buried.

At times, partial power was intermittently restored – only to fail again without warning.

The broken promises of Mercury Energy frazzled the nerves of everybody working and living in the downtown district. At Auckland Hospital, a child under anesthesia was being scanned for an acute spinal condition. Lights went off in the hospital again. The doctors, with scalpels in hand, fearing the girl needed immediate surgery, kept the child under anesthesia and quickly transported her to another hospital.

In the city's center that once hummed with international commerce, the only hum was the sound of huge portable diesel generators, which lined streets. In streets that had bustled with traffic, the only bustle were the fuel trucks hustling to keep the generators' diesel engines roaring. Makeshift signs in parking garages warned people to avoid the choking clouds of diesel fuel fumes.

The loss of power left downtown Auckland devastated. It soon became a ghost town. Even criminals fled for better working conditions.

Air conditioners stopped pumping cool air. Elevators were stuck. Computers crashed. Food spoiled in powerless refrigeration units. Without running water, toilets didn't flush. Lights went dark. Gasoline pumps froze. Cash registers locked. Traffic signals ceased blinking. Security gates remained open. ATM machines became useless tin tellers. Telephones, computers, printers, fax machines, photocopiers – every high tech business machine fell silent.

The resourceful New Zealanders improvised.

A cargo ship docked in the harbor. Cables were strung to the ship's generators and connected to the city's power lines. Hundreds of portable generators were rushed in for temporary duty, providing minimal electricity for security systems and emergency lighting. Temporary cables were hung overhead through the city's downtown in a desperate attempt by Mercury Energy to restore full power.

Major employers had two choices. Attempt to keep operations running in powerless offices, or move employees to temporary facilities in other parts of the city. Employees packed up computers, printers, copiers, fax machines, and supplies in the sweltering heat. Everything that could be carried was moved to other locations. Some executives turned their homes into makeshift offices, with employees taking over living rooms, dens, and spare bedrooms to the dismay of many wives.

Retailers sold their wares on sidewalk tables. Merchants made change from shoeboxes.

Apartment dwellers, fearing they'd be trapped in stranded elevators, let rotting garbage pile up in apartment hallways. Residents cooked with portable gas stoves and barbecue grills. Without refrigeration and sanitation, restaurants and cafes had no choice except to lock their doors.

Companies that chose to remain in their downtown offices told employees to bring bottles of drinking water and plastic bags for their human waste. One news article reported a businessman with a broken hip forced to descend 12 flights of steps on crutches in a hot staircase without ventilation. Barefoot employees scurried about in modern offices with windows that could not be opened. To obey government occupational safety regulations, managers roamed offices with thermometers. New Zealand's health and safety rules prohibit keeping employees on the job when indoor temperatures climb to 90 degrees or higher.

The ordeal put enormous stress on everybody.

"We have had people trapped in elevators, overcome by fumes, there have been fires..." reported Auckland's Mayor Les Mills. "People have been hurt." (1)

Under intense duress, Mercury Energy's chief executive officer, Wayne Gilbert, collapsed and died at his desk from a massive heart attack. His unexpected death came on the evening prior to the release of a report from a government investigation into the electric power debacle, which was highly critical of Mercury Energy's negligence.

Meanwhile, Mercury Energy's Chairman, Jim Macaulay was stricken with terminal cancer and given only months to live.

After weeks of turmoil and suffering, Aucklanders gathered for prayer. Pastors beseeched God to lift the darkness that plagued the "Wall Street" district of New Zealand's economy.

Not all churches, however, joined in the ecumenical prayer services.

A group of conservative, Bible-quoting Christian leaders said the blackout was God's judgment on the city of Auckland. They cited the gay rights "Hero Parade" and celebration that marched through the city's center the weekend before the power failure. Led by New Zealand Prime Minister Jenny Shipley and numerous politicians, over 100,000 people turned out for the homosexual celebration.

A written statement from the Wellington For Jesus Campaign said the Bible made it clear that nations will fall under God's judgment for sodomy.

"The power failure in Auckland should serve as a reminder

that Man's systems are fallible," the statement said. (2)

"This spectacular and unexpected failure should serve as a call to repentance."

Auckland's Power Disaster is a Harbinger of Year 2000 Woes

Civilized societies require ample electricity.

Without a full, uninterrupted flow of electricity, modern civilization ceases to be civil.

Auckland's recent 10-week encounter with no power is an omen of the trouble ahead for our high-tech world and its precarious dependency on electricity.

All essentials of modern life – cooking, sanitation, water, heating and cooling, communications, manufacturing, transportation, commerce, food production, medical care – entirely depends on a continuous and abundant supply of electrical power.

Americans, spoiled and demanding, quickly become irritable when air conditioning and cable television go off for an hour. How would millions of people in New York City or Los Angeles react if power goes out for 10 weeks in 2000?

It is not a pretty thought.

If American society was still held together by Christianity's moral code, citizens would ban together and help each other make it through the crisis.

Neighbor helping neighbor.

Forget it. We're not Christian any more.

We're pagans.

Americans shoot Americans over the smallest items.

Every man for himself. That's the moral code of many Americans on the eve of the Third Millennium.

Electric utilities are extremely endangered by Y2K problems.

The electric utility industry is just waking up to the coming crisis. It's too late. There's not enough time to fix all the power plants, generators, switching stations, transformers, and power lines.

Like Auckland's negligent Mercury Energy company, American utilities should have seen Y2K coming. It is pretty late in the game to start thinking about it now.

There will be power outages. You might as well get prepared now.

Government officials are beginning to know it too.

"We're no longer at the point of asking whether or not there will be any power disruptions, but we are now forced to ask how severe the disruptions are going to be," United States Senator Christopher Dodd (D-Connecticut) said on June 12, 1998, at a Senate hearing investigating the Year 2000 problem.

The Senate's Special Committee on the Year 2000 Technology Problem, chaired by Utah's Robert Bennett, kicked off the hearings by releasing a survey of 10 of the largest electric, gas, and oil utility companies in the United States. The survey's purpose was to ascertain the level of preparedness of the nation's utilities for the Year 2000 date change.

The results were not reassuring.

"Based on the results of this survey, I am genuinely concerned about the very real prospects of power shortages as a consequence of the millennial date change," concluded Senator Bennett. (3)

The survey revealed that a mere 20 percent of the utilities contacted had completed an assessment of their computerized systems ,- the very first step in making an organization ready for the Year 2000. One utility did not even know how many lines of computer code it had within its systems!

The survey also discovered that none of the utilities had been assured that its third party providers of parts and supplies would be Y2K compliant by December 31, 1999. Even more disturbing was the fact that none of the utilities had back-up plans for Year 2000-related power failures, despite federal and state requirements that they maintain up-to-date emergency response plans.

Keep in mind that the Committee surveyed the nation's largest utilities! If these guys are behind, how far behind are the rural co-ops and small town municipal-owned power plants?

To the Senators' dismay and astonishment, the head of the Federal Energy Regulatory Commission admitted that nobody even knows whether the nation's 6,000 electric utilities are close to being prepared for the Year 2000. It seems nobody in the government has bothered to ask. "The state of year 2000 readiness of the utility industry is largely unknown," reported James Hoecker at the Senate hearing on June 12, 1998. (4)

"Evidence is completely anecdotal," FERC Chairman Hoecker confessed to the Senators. "We can't get a handle on where companies are at regarding the year 2000."

Another federal bureaucrat told the House of Representatives' Science Committee the same thing. "The magnitude of the potential year 2000 problem in the regulated energy industries is not yet known," said Kathleen Hiring, chief information officer at the Federal Regulatory Commission. (5)

Just when do federal regulators plan to get around to asking? December 1999, perhaps? Let's not get alarmed! After all, it is only an industry that can leave multitudes of people – including children and senior citizens – shivering in below zero temperatures in January 2000.

The dismal lack of regulatory oversight troubles computer engineers who are keeping a close eye on the electric utility industry. "It is very disconcerting that at this point in time, we are just now starting to take a look at the whole industry," lamented Rick Cowles, an outspoken critic of the electric industry's readiness for the Year 2000, and author of *Electric Utilities and Y2K*. (6)

The scary truth is that the electric utility companies, themselves, don't know how vulnerable they will be to Y2K malfunctions. The Year 2000 computer bug has caught a lot of utility executives and engineers by surprise. Unfortunately, preparing for a massive technology meltdown wasn't taught in business school.

"For many of them, it is analogous to the deer caught in the headlights," said Roleigh Martin, a Minnesota computer engineer and Y2K expert. "This is a new problem to them, and there's not a lot of good information available about where they stand." (7)

With the clock ticking toward the new millennial, too many utility executives have brushed aside warnings by "Y2K alarmists" who have predicted economic and social chaos after January 1, 2000.

"Not a big deal," is the way Jim Davis, Nuclear Energy Institute Director of Operations, described the century date rollover exercise at nuclear power plants. (8)

Fortunately, not all power company executives and managers feel the same way. An increasing number of utilities are becoming aware how daunting a task it is to guarantee that power will continue flowing after New Year's Day 2000. They're working hard to exterminate the Y2K computer bug before the deadline. "Let's just say it is a big deal," said Steven Savati, Atlantic Electric's Y2K program manager in a local New Jersey newspaper interview. (9)

"Did they start in time?" is the nagging question.

For many utilities, especially rural co-ops and municipal-owned systems, it may be too late.

"The window of opportunity is beginning to close," warned Peter De Jager, a Canadian computer programmer and one the world's earliest Y2K experts. "If you're not working on this by now, you are being grossly negligent," Mr. De Jager warned utilities in an interview in the March 1998 issue of *Electrical World*. (10)

As the Grid Goes, So Goes the Nation

It has been described as the largest and most complex machine in the world.

The national power grid. An interconnected maze composed of 6,000 electric power plants, a half million miles of high-voltage transmission lines, about 112,000 substations, and countless computers, sensors, microprocessors, and a host of other sophisticated monitoring gadgets along the way. There are also a lot of human beings throughout the system closely monitoring the flow of electricity every second of the day.

Most of the time, it works beautifully.

Despite its reliability, the grid is extremely fragile.

It doesn't take much to mess it up.

As long as the computers keep humming, the juice keeps flowing. From Texas' Rio Grande Valley to Montana's big sky country. From

Baltimore's Inner Harbor to San Francisco's Golden Gate Bridge. Every day, zillions of electrons sizzle through high-voltage transmission lines to power everything from simple kitchen appliances to expensive factory machines, dairy equipment, hospital life-support systems, airport runway lights, ATM machines, and just about everything we rely on in today's high-tech society.

We simply take it for granted. Flip on the switch and – presto! – the automatic coffee maker starts brewing the morning's fresh pot of gourmet java. We don't think about it. We just assume the power will always be there – an invisible energy force ready to make our life more comfortable and convenient in every imaginable way.

But where does all this juice come from? And how does it get into your curling iron or electric shaver in the morning?

Like any commodity, electricity is bought and sold every day. Actually, every minute. Unlike other products, electricity can't be stored for sale later in the month. There are no warehouses to store unused electricity. It must be used now. If you are in the business of making electricity for profit, it means you've got to find somebody to buy your excess electricity this very moment – not tomorrow.

That's where the national power grid comes in.

You may think the friendly utility company on the other side of town produced the electricity that toasted your morning muffins. The truth is they purchased the electricity from another utility 500 miles away in another state.

America's national power grid is a highly integrated, complex web of electric generating plants and transmission systems. There are 109 regional power grids in the United States tied together into four major Interconnections. Ever since a massive blackout on November 9, 1965, darkened New York City, most of the East Coast, and parts of Canada for 13 hours, the electric power industry has relied on regional systems that can transfer excess electricity to other utilities during their peak usage periods.

The 109 grids belong to one of nine major regional councils. Those councils form the national North American Electric Reliability Council (NERC). Membership in NERC includes private investor-owned, city-owned, rural cooperatives, and federal power facilities such as the Tennessee Valley Authority.

Following the catastrophic 1965 East Coast blackout, the complex grid emerged to make sure that if any power plant or major transmission line goes down, surplus energy from other generating plants could quickly be transferred to the affected area.

The system stands out as a marvelous testimony to the reliability of America's electric utility industry. While consumers go about their daily business with faith the electricity will always be there, what they don't see is the hour-by-hour hustling by energy company managers to keep the juice flowing. In peak usage times, it means utilities scrambling to find additional power outside their areas.

In a major grid zone, such as the East and West coasts, there are literally thousands of transactions happening each hour to acquire surplus electricity from other regions and to move it to where its needed at the moment.

Keeping the juice flowing, however, demands second by second monitoring of the entire grid. Utility managers must keep a tight handle on how much electricity their system needs each hour. To match the power coming in with the power in demand, managers dispatch by computer instructions to generating plants to crank up the juice, or to shut down.

The grid system is a very efficient way to produce and transfer electricity to all parts of the nation. It is also an efficient use of our natural resources. Without out it, communities would be forced to build many new power plants to meet demand during peak periods. That would be both costly and environmentally unsound. Because the new plants would be idle during low usage times, utility rates would skyrocket. Also, large metropolitan regions would suffer from more pollution if more fossil-fuel generating plants were constructed instead of purchasing unused power from other utilities.

So, when there's below zero temperatures in Chicago, surplus electricity can be pulled out of Arizona. The reverse is true also. When Washington, DC, is baking during the summer's hot, steamy "dog days," power can be transferred from the cool regions of upper New England.

The complex interconnectedness of the national power grid, however, means that when something goes wrong in Pittsburgh, it could unexpectedly impact the folks in Toledo in a very negative way. Likewise, a tree falling on a high voltage line in Oregon can turn off the air conditioners in Phoenix on a 115-degree afternoon.

That's what happened in 1996 when two major blackouts hit the Western states.

The first blackout struck on July 2, 1996. Residents in normally cool northern California, Utah and Idaho were baking in unusually hot weather. With air conditioners continuously running, massive amounts of power was being sucked out of the western power grid which covers 14 states and 112,000 miles of transmission lines.

The extremely hot weather caused an expanded 345,000-volt power line in Idaho to droop. When the sagging power line touched a cottonwood tree in the forest, an electrical arc short-circuited the line. Over the short period of 35 seconds, power lines across the western United States failed like dominoes.

Two million customers in 14 states were suddenly without power.

Six weeks later, the West was hit by an even bigger power failure. This time, the blackout cut off power to four million customers in a region stretching from the Canadian border to Mexico. The blackout was caused by a serious of snafus. It began with heavy demand in southern California caused by hot temperatures. Meanwhile, Oregon's forests were abundantly rich with green foliage caused by heavy Spring rains. When the heat wave hit Oregon, the high demand load and hot temperatures caused power lines to sag. That's when a group of high-voltage lines drooped in a forest 60 miles east of Portland, sparking a "flashover."

Coincidentally, 41 minutes later another sagging line caused another flashover in a filbert orchard west of Portland. Five minutes later, an important generating plant at the McNary hydroelectric plant in eastern Oregon malfunctioned. The unexpected loss of 600 megawatts of electricity added more instability to the grid. Within minutes, the combined malfunctions cascaded through the power grid, triggering the entire Pacific Intertie to shut down. That's happens to be the main artery that feeds power throughout the region from southern California to the upper Northwest U.S.

Everything from country grocery stores in rural Oregon to Space Mountain at Disneyland was disconnected. Power was not restored to all customers until the next day.

Like water, electricity follows the path of least resistance. When something goes wrong, it cascades through the entire system.

Something like Y2K would be a good example.

Those who think Y2K is a lot of hype may be left in the dark.

If a heat wave, sagging power lines, and a lush tree can conspire to trigger a massive blackout covering 14 states, then what impact will numerous Y2K-related power plant failures have on the national grid in 2000?

"The grid was never programmed to handle an abundant number of simultaneous failures," says Roleigh Martin. (11)

Mr. Martin, a computer engineer and consultant, says Y2K power failures are inevitable. "The odds are overwhelming that there will be failures in some places. The question for every individual is, 'Will it be my area?'"

Michael Gent, president of NERC, cautiously admitted to the Senate special committee investigating Y2K, that "Year 2000 poses the threat that common mode failures...or the coincident loss of multiple facilities could result in stressing the electric system to the point of a cascading outage in a large area." (12)

Mr. Gent says the possibility of such a widespread meltdown is extremely low, but "conceivable."

That's "bureaucrat mumbo jumbo" for covering your hind end. "Yes, it could happen. No, I don't think it will."

How do they know if they are just starting to ask power plants if they are ready for Y2K? What evidence does Mr. Gent present to guarantee that simultaneous blackouts will not shut down the grid throughout the nation?

One federal bureaucrat testifies before U.S. Senators and says nobody knows the present state of readiness of the American power industry for the Year 2000.

The next bureaucrat says, "Don't worry. Trust us."

How can you jump from "not knowing" to "trust that we've got it under control"? Where's the logic?

Congresswoman Connie Morella knows the seriousness of the threat. "When you consider how important our electric utilities are to everything we do in life, then you'll recognize that if we do not have our compliance for the Y2K and as things fall apart, it's going to be devastating in our entire society." (13)

Embedded Microchips May Unleash Power Plant Panic

The smooth operation of America's electricity infrastructure requires precise production and flow of power. Every generating plant – from rural co-ops to nuclear plants and wind-powered turbines – are plugged into the grid. Each power generating facility is set with millisecond precision to the same clock using the Global Positioning System. Many utility systems are dependent on time signal emissions from GPS. (Remember, the GPS dates roll over on August 21, 1999!). Like hearts beating in perfect unison, the power plants pump out the juice at 60 cycles per second.

In control rooms around the nation, utility employees sit behind computer consoles closely monitoring the spikes and ebbs of all this alternating current. Huge air conditioners and fans hum to keep the computers from overheating. Sudden surges in demand or unexpected malfunctions cause warning arrows to flash on the computer screens.

The whole flipp'n thing runs on computers.

And it not just big computers with monitors and keyboards.

It is thousands of tiny embedded microprocessors hidden throughout the system.

Yes, America's national power grid is joined at the chip.

Power companies heavily depend on computers in all aspects of the production and transmission of electricity. From sending out electric bills to monitoring radioactive leaks at nuclear power plants, computers are a vital component of the system.

No computers. No electricity.

What is so troublesome to many Y2K-aware individuals is that the power industry is just starting to wake up to the threat. One such utility, the Orlando Utilities Commission, didn't launch a Y2K project until September 1997. So far, the OUC has discovered up to 400 computer systems at the utility that could be vulnerable to Y2K. "As you get into checking each system and subsystem and component, the overall number could run into the thousands," says

Sheridan Becht, a spokesman for OUC. (14)

Look at a utility company as a "electricity factory." The products of General Motors are Chevrolets, Pontiacs, and Buicks. The product of Consolidated Edison, Texas Utilities, and Allegheny Power is electricity.

They make it and sell it for money.

For any profitable business, the core administrative infrastructure is computerized. Customer billing, vendor invoicing, payroll, customer service, inventory, purchasing, financial control, government regulatory reporting - its all done on computers. Without computers, utilities would go back to the 1950s. If the utility's internal operating computers crash, can they pay their bills? Can they collect money owed to them? Can they buy fuel and supplies? Can they pay their employees? Will they be able to schedule repairs, maintenance, and trouble shooting?

The generating plant - whether coal burning or nuclear - is the factory. To achieve maximum production cost efficiencies, the "factory" is highly automated with computers, embedded microchips, and microcontrollers. The fewer employees, the smaller the payroll expenses. The higher the profits, the higher the stock sells on Wall Street.

Just as GM has a network of local auto dealers to distribute their products, utilities have a distribution network too. If you can't get the product distributed, nobody in the marketplace can buy it. For utilities, the distribution network is the web of substations, relays, transformers, and transmission lines. Again, "critical missions" throughout the entire process are highly dependent on computers and microchips.

There's the problem. Many of these embedded microchips and microcontrollers have been programmed with dates. And date-sensitive microchips mean trouble in the Year 2000.

Real Time Control and embedded logic perform vital functions in every facet of the production and distribution of electrical power. Embedded chips are programmed to perform specific functions, often on a predetermined timetable. The system response to those preprogrammed instructions can also be "time-stamped" on embedded chips, creating a process called a "logic ladder." The time-stamp then feeds data into other control systems throughout the generating plant.

Modern utilities simply could not efficiently operate without embedded microchips. For example, managers hundreds of miles away can tweak turbines to produce more or less energy by adjusting system loads. Embedded chips are also in flow control and feedwater systems, load dispatch computers, fossil plant boiler control systems, and in nuclear plant safety systems.

Because energy production requires precise time-based functions, embedded chips hidden in sensors, relays, valves, and switches often use clocks for exact millisecond synchronization with other equipment.

Hidden embedded chips will be a major headache for utilities. In a very short time span, every utility must completely assess their plant infrastructure, identify every embedded chip, conduct tests, and replace noncompliant chips before December 31, 1999.

Quite frankly, the prospects for successfully completing such a massive undertaking are not very good.

"When you consider the number of chips that need changing, outages are almost a certainty," concludes Andrew Pegalis, president of Next Millennium Consulting. "Embedded systems require a monumental effort. They first must be located, they must then be tested, and some of the manufacturers of these chips have gone out of business, which means you often don't know how they were programmed." (15)

The electric industry is just now compiling a database of chips suspected of being vulnerable to Y2K troubles. The magnitude of the task is overwhelming. A typical coal or gas-fired power plant may have thousands of embedded microchips hidden throughout the system.

Amazingly, many utilities still are in the dark themselves about the serious threat posed by embedded microchips.

"When a company sends us two sentences telling us they've addressed the year 2000 by replacing their customer billing system, and they show no concern about embedded systems, then I have a concern," says Brenda Buchan, Y2K coordinator for Florida's Public Service Commission. (16)

Y2K experts, however, loudly warn companies and government agencies that the only sure-fire way to be sure embedded chips don't fail after January 2000 is to test now for problems.

With remaining time fleeing quickly, will the power industry test everything for trouble?

"There is no way that we can test the entire system and make sure that every problem is fixed," Dennis Eyre honestly admits. (17) Mr. Eyre is executive director of the Western Systems Coordinating Council, a regional division of NERC, and the largest regional grid covering about 50 million people.

Y2K Tests Crash Electric Power Plants

There are 6,000 mission-critical components in the production and distribution of electricity that are vulnerable to Y2K failures.

That's the conclusion of Susan Thomas, worldwide director of Unisys' Y2K project. She says it doesn't mean all 6,000 systems and components will fail, but that the potential for loss is present.

"On a rule of thumb, the failure rate may vary, at the high end, between 8 per cent to 11 per cent of the 6000 or, at the low end of expectations, between 1 to 2 per cent." (18)

And what is the challenge?

"The challenge is finding and testing which of those 6,000 is going to fail."

There's no other way to prepare electric utilities for the Year 2000 except to test them for mission-critical Y2K vulnerabilities.

So far, only a few electric utilities have conducted tests.

Each one crashed.

"Every test I have seen done on an electrical power plant has caused it to shut down. Period. I know of no plant or facility investigated to this date that has passed without Y2K problems." (19)

That stunning statement was made spoken by Mr. David Hall, an embedded-chip expert at Cara Corporation, to a group of Congressional leaders in Washington, D.C.

Ponder the significance of his words.

First, you have to realize that the United States Department of Energy didn't even have a formal Y2K plan until May 1998. This is the government agency that is supposed to be the people's watchdog over the energy industry.

These Y2K-enlightened regulatory bureaucrats tell us there'll be nothing to worry your little heart over about 2000 problems. These same bureaucrats, however, admit they are just learning about embedded microchips.

Oh well, with President Clinton motivating all his appointees to shake down big companies for political contributions, who in Washington has time to brush up on technical things like Y2K and embedded chips? There are just too many fund-raising cocktail receptions to attend!

Compare the blissful ignorance of Washington's bureaucrats with those of a highly trained expert in embedded chip technology who categorically states that every test of a utility for Y2K problems shut it down.

Who do you believe?

(This is a good time to place a bookmark here and go order a portable generator!)

Y2K experts say testing is 60 % to 80% of the job of becoming Year 2000 compliant. They also say at least one year of testing is mandatory to have enough time to correct any problems that arise.

If that is the case, then it is really scary that so few utilities are even close to testing their systems. As of Fall 1998, too many utilities – especially small rural coops and municipal plants – had not even started a Y2K compliance program! They're entering 1999 – the last year before the millennium change – totally unprepared for the troubles ahead.

According to a state Public Utility Commission survey of Texas utilities, some said they would not "be able to complete the required testing and repair until the last quarter of 1999." (20)

One utility that decided to test its systems was Hawaiian Electric Company (HECO). The company's engineers temporarily reset its master clock to December 31, 1999. When the clock turned over to midnight, HECO's entire energy management system froze.

What troubles many business executives in other industries is the reluctance of power companies to share their information with customers who depend on utilities to run their businesses.

"Utilities are so far unwilling to share the results of the (year 2000) tests, said Cathy Hotka, vice president of information technology at the National Retail Federation. (21) "One company is unwilling to rat on the other, and they seem to think they'll have legal trouble if they do..." she told Congressional members of a House subcommittee.

Unwilling to rat on each other?

What are they afraid to tell us?

Nuclear Power Plants and Y2K: That's A Nice Shade of Green You're Wearing!

The nuclear power industry is tight-lip about their Y2K readiness. Nobody wants to talk publicly about his or her worse case scenarios.

The Nuclear Regulatory Commission, the federal agency that watches over nuclear plants in the U.S., says that it is "working to ensure that all of our systems critical to our mission will by Year 2000 compliant so that our communications and data interfaces will function well." (22) The NRC makes specific reference to "the one mission critical system that is directly linked to operating nuclear power plants is our Emergency Response Data System (ERDS)." It probably is important. The NRC says the "application performs the communication and data transmission functions that provide near real-time data to NRC incident response personnel during declared emergencies."

Wow. Wonder what it's like to experience a "declared emergency" at a nuclear power plant? Oh well, there are more important things in life to worry about.

Fortunately, you can sleep sound tonight because the NRC says it is "currently upgrading ERDS to be Year 2000 compliant..."

Hey, take your time. No need to get bent out of shape over a silly deadline!

So far, the NRC doesn't seem to be getting too worked up anyway. The agency waited until May 8, 1998, to send out to nuclear plants what the agency calls a "Generic Letter." In other words, it was a "Dear Nuclear Power Plant Operator" type of letter. The response was due from the power plants by mid-August 1998. (23)

Wow, the NRC really came down hard on the nuclear power plants! The "generic letter" stated that nuclear power plant licensees "should indicate whether they are pursuing a Year 2000 program." "

"Should indicate?"

What about telling them something like this? "You MUST tell us NOW what you're doing to ensure the public's safety at your nuclear power plant?"

But to show their toughness, the NRC says all nuclear power plants "are required to submit a written response no later than July 1, 1999, confirming that the facility is or will by Year 2000 ready by the Year 2000."

So, the NRC is going to wait until six months before the millennial date change to require nuclear power plants to tell the government and the general public if they are going to be ready before the end of the year!

(This is another excellent place to stop reading this book and order a portable back-up generator for your house! Maybe a hazardous material radiation suit with matching gloves too!)

The NRC says that Y2K could impact nuclear plants depending on the types of computer systems in use. The agency outlines five computer systems that could be affected: (1) Software to schedule maintenance and technical specification surveillance; (2) programmable logic controllers and other commercial off-the-shelf software and hardware; (3) digital process control systems, such as a feedwater control or valve control; (4) digital systems for collecting operating data; and (5) digital systems to monitor post-accident plant conditions. (24)

Some of the systems and equipment that are "most likely to be affected by Year 2000 problems" are plant security computers, plant process systems (data scan, log, and alarm and safety parameter display system computers), and, oh yes!, radiation monitoring systems.

Then the NRC laid down the law to nuclear plants by telling them that "the majority of the program remediation, validation, and implementation activities should be completed at a facility by mid-1999, leaving only a few such activities scheduled for the third and fourth quarters of 1999." (25)

Want to know what's going to happen with nuclear power plants in the United States? Here's a pretty good guess.

The NRC will keep tiptoe'n through the tulips until the written responses come back in July 1999. Suddenly, reality will sink in. "We're not going to make it!" will be their shared cry.

By Fall 1999, the NRC and the nuclear power industry will realize that their exposure to risk is just too high. Federal law strictly prohibits nuclear power plants from operating if there are any questions about safety. The threat of colossal lawsuits will be too much to risk.

The NRC will order America's nuclear power plants to shut down.

A federally ordered shutdown of nuclear power plants in the U.S. is a real possibility. The subject is being openly discussed in some European countries. Sweden has already declared that it is taking no chances with its nuclear power plants. "We don't exclude problems during the change of the century," said Staffan Forsberg, deputy director of reactor safety at the Swedish Nuclear Power Inspectorate. (26)

"If we are not satisfied or convinced safety problems are solved, then we will shut them down," he promised.

In Great Britain, inspectors have discovered Y2K problems in alarm and monitoring systems in several British nuclear power plants.

And a lot of nervous eyes are on Russia's aging nuclear power plants. Western experts say computer failures could trip Russia's nuclear plants to shut down. Some fear another Chernobyl-style disaster is in the making.

Some U.S. nuclear plants will voluntary close. Nervous investors sensing trouble over the horizon will dump plants from their portfolios. The GPU Corporation announced in August 1998 that it plans to shut down its Oyster Creek nuclear power plant in New Jersey by the year 2000. The 620-megawatt plant is the second oldest nuclear power plant in the United States. The plant, which serves two million customers in 13 counties, has been for sale, but no buyers could be found. (27)

When the NRC shuts down the American reactors, our country will lose a significant portion of our electricity supply.

There goes 40% of the East Coast's power supply – and 20% of the entire power supply for the United States.

By October 1999, a genuine, old fashion panic will spread through America like wildfire when people finally wake up to the realization that January 2000 is only days away.

Maybe that explains why the Nuclear Regulatory Commission will distribute to states with nuclear power plants supplies of potassium iodide, a drug that blocks radiation that causes thyroid cancer. (28) State governments are stockpiling the medicine at evacuation centers. The NRC does not require states to stockpile the drug, but is now strongly encouraging civil defense officials to store supplies. Maine, Tennessee, Ohio, and Alabama were among the first states to accept supplies of potassium iodide.

When the Trains Stop, the Electricity Stops Too

Fossil-fuel burning power plants need fossil fuels. Lots of fossil fuels like coal and oil. That's simple enough to understand.

The overwhelming portion of coal and oil are delivered to utilities by railroads such as Burlington Northern/Santa Fe.

Guess what? Railroads need electricity!

There's a serious Catch-22 problem brewing here. In order for fossil-burning power plants to keep cranking out the juice, they've got to have a daily supply of coal or oil. Has anybody checked to see if the railroads are Year 2000 compliant? Don't you think it might be a smart thing to do before New Year's Day rolls around?

You'll discover in another chapter of this book that railroads have very serious Y2K problems of their own to deal with.

One major problem is that all the signal and switching systems are now computerized. In fact, it is impossible to manually switch the tracks today!

With all the mega-mergers taking place on Wall Street, railroads are already having major problems uniting their computerized systems.

Logjams of boxcars have piled up in numerous terminals. Manufacturers and retailers are complaining about late deliveries of products.

If embedded microchips in railroad systems shut down major train arteries, then stockpiles of coal at utilities will dwindle fast. We're talking January 2000 here! It's cold in January in most parts of the country.

Furthermore, if utilities shut down because of Y2K problems – and later because of a lack of fuel supplies – then the railroads will be immobilized too. If railroads need electricity to operate signals and switches, then power blackouts through the nation will prevent railroads from making timely deliveries of much-needed fuel supplies.

Geomagnetic Storms Could Imperil Utilities

Nature impacts utilities. Heat waves, like the 1995 heat wave that resulted in over 730 deaths in Chicago, greatly strain power plants to produce record-breaking amounts of electricity to keep millions of air conditioners pumping cool air. On August 3, 1998, energy consumption broke its all-time record during a heat wave, prompting the California Independent System Operator to initiate a state Electrical Emergency Plan.

When bitter cold fronts sweep over a region, folks turn up the electric heat. Even worse, Arctic weather sometimes brings ice storms. Heavy ice will quickly bring down power lines. Such was the situation in Canada in January 1998 when a four-day ice storm dumped up to seven inches of ice on some regions of eastern Canada and parts of New England. Several million Canadians and Americans endured frigid weather for weeks without power after heavy ice snapped electric poles in half, leaving their top sections swinging in the air. In Quebec alone, over 4,000 electric poles were knocked down.

There's another kind of weather that threatens electric utilities too.

It is called Space Weather.

Scientists are learning more about solar wind and other showers of high-velocity electrons. They believe that someday they'll be able to accurately predict Space Weather just like meteorologists on Earth predict hurricanes and thunderstorms.

For years, scientists have known that the sun spews out billowous clouds of electromagnetic particles that can affect Earth's communications and electricity.

Recently, scientists identified Jupiter as the mystery source of another periodic shower of electrons that sometime "rain" on the Earth.

These electron storms from Jupiter's magnetic field can disrupt electricity on Earth. If power plants have no advance warning, a severe electron storm can actually spark a blackout.

It is the new Solar Maximum – Cycle 23 – that has scientists, satellite operators, and electric utility executives watching the skies for signs.

As described in an earlier chapter, our sun has now entered its new

11-year cycle of violent activity. Early indications point to an extremely volatile solar maximum this time.

It peaks in March 2000. Just in time for the big Millennial Meltdown!

John Kappenman, head of Transmission Power Engineering at Minnesota Power, says the North American power grid resembles "a large efficient antenna that is electromagnetically coupled to the disturbance signals produced by fluctuations of the earth's magnetosphere." (29)

Mr. Kappenman explains that "the network depends on remote generation sources linked by long transmission lines to delivery points. The effects of GICs (Geomagnetically Induced Currents) build cumulatively over a large geographic scale, overwhelming the capability of the system to regulate voltage and the protection margins of equipment." (30)

That means solar storms can knock power plants off-line.

It has happened before. During the last solar maximum, a geomagnetic storm in 1989 resulted in a blown voltage regulator on the Hydro-Quebec power grid in eastern Canada. The blackout left millions of residents without power for several days.

Cycle 23 – the current solar maximum – is shaping up to be the worse on record. According to Sunanda Basu, an atmospheric scientist with the National Science Foundation, the Year 2000 could see large solar flares trip circuit breakers in power grids throughout northern latitudes. (31)

According to Mr. Kappenman, "many portions of the North American power grid are vulnerable to geomagnetic storms." He says much of the grid is located "in northern latitudes, near the north magnetic pole and the auroral electrojet current and in regions of igneous rock, a geological formation with high electrical resistivity." Mr. Kappenman warns that utility systems in the upper latitudes of North America are "at increased risk because auroral activity and its effects center on the magnetic poles, and the Earth's magnetic north pole is tilted toward North America." (32)

Combined with everything else happening around the Year 2000, geomagnetic disturbances could trigger cascading power blackouts throughout the nation, and other parts of the world.

"You can't believe how much it's going to affect our lives within the next few years," warns Michael Kelly, a geophysicist at Cornell University. (33)

Loss of Power Grid Will Paralyze Nation

Will we have power after January 1, 2000?

That's the big question on the minds of utility executives, politicians, investors, and business owners around the world.

John Catterall, the West Australian manager for Infrastructure Control Systems, says Australia's power grid is "extremely vulnerable to the year 2000 and...the potential could be catastrophic." (34)

In Great Britain, utility companies are urging the government to institute World War II-style emergency broadcasts to deal with nervous customers clamoring for information about blackouts and service disruptions. Utility executives fear that phone banks will be overwhelmed with calls from citizens demanding information about Y2K-related failures.

The _Sunday Times_ of London reported on February 15, 1998, that England's National Health Service advised Parliament to prepare the public for possible loss of infrastructure services in 2000. The Times article said that the NHS report told Parliament that the NHS "must draw up contingency plans for a utilities breakdown and food shortages which could be caused if computer failure cripples distribution systems." (35)

The disturbing truth about the matter is that nobody truly knows whether the lights will stay on after New Year's Day 2000.

An uncanny confluence of events and pressures are rushing toward a critical juncture. Decisions by the federal and numerous state governments to deregulate the electric power industry are exposing utilities to market pressures to reduce employee payrolls and maintenance costs. Abnormal weather patterns over recent years, coupled with increasing consumer hunger for more power, are straining the capacity of utilities to meet peak load requirements. Mergers by huge railroad companies are creating logjams of railway cars loaded with coal. Year 2000 problems – especially embedded microchip technology – has caught many utilities by surprise. Finally, the eruption of the sun's violent storms, sending massive waves of electrons over the Earth, will peak in early 2000. Scientists were counting on SOHO, an expensive scientific satellite heading toward the Sun, to help them predict the eruption of Cycle 23 violent storms in time to warn utilities. Something went wrong and scientist lost control of the satellite in July 1998.

The potential for widespread power failures is a real possibility.

The facts are what prompted Senator Bob Bennett to declare there was "a 100 percent chance" the U.S. power grid would collapse if January 1, 2000, was the day of the Senate hearing which was on June 12, 1998.

Senator Bennett fully understands the grave danger Y2K poses for our society's future.

"If the power grid goes down because of connections in the computers or because of embedded chips in certain power plants that shut those power plants down because of bad software somewhere, then it is all over," Senator Bennett surmised.

"It doesn't matter if every computer in the country is Y2K compliant if you can't plug it into something." (36)

15 *Water and Sewage:* Water! Water! I Need Water!

"A drought is upon her waters; and they shall be dried up: for it is the land of graven images, and they are mad upon their idols."

Jeremiah 50:38

"It could have killed the entire town!," so exclaimed David Fletcher, Utah's Year 2000 project manager. (1)

He was referring to reports of a Y2K test at a water treatment plant in an Australian city.

The city's engineers wanted to test the water purification system by turning up the computer clocks to January 1, 2000. As the computer's clock rolled into the year 2000, a large dose of chemicals dumped into the city's drinking water.

Water and sewage treatment facilities are the forgotten stepchildren of Y2K preparations. Hardly anybody is asking whether these public facilities in small towns and big cities are Year 2000 compliant.

That's why this chapter is really short. There's just not very much information available on preparations by local governments to check their public water and sanitation facilities for Year 2000 vulnerabilities. If serious action isn't taken soon, urban populations around the world are in for major trouble.

Like their electric utility counterparts, the silent enemy of water and sewage treatment plants is embedded microchips.

Embedded chips regulate such things as the level of chemicals that are added to drinking water supplies. At sewage treatment plants, out-flow systems, which allow sewage or raw waste to flow into a river or sea, are regulated by embedded microchips.

In the Middle East, entire urban populations in Arab nations totally depend on desalinization plants for fresh drinking water. In Saudi Arabia, there are about 30 desalinization plants drawing salt water from the sea and purifying it for human consumption. Twenty-one of these plants are located along the Red Sea coast, with the remaining plants along the Arabian Gulf coast. In 1997, Saudi Arabia's desalinization plants purified 776 million cubic meters of water. The country has 16 more plants planned for future construction.

Water is an extremely scarce commodity in all Arab nations such as Bahrain, United Arab Emirates, Kuwait, Qatar. These arid nations, without rivers or large lakes, pump millions of gallons of desalted water through hundreds of miles of huge pipelines on the desert. Automated pumping stations control the flow of this life-sustaining precious liquid all along the way. Embedded microchips regulate the automated functions of the process.

What is alarming about the dependency of Arab nations on desalinization plants is that the Middle East is one of the least aware regions in the world about Year 2000 problems. Millions of Arabs without water will be catastrophic.

Whether the silence by governments about municipal water and sewage treatment plants is intentional or evidence of their ignorance, it is not known.

A few voices, however, are waving warning flags.

Don Cruickshank, England's Action 2000 chairman, has voiced his concern about the lack of attention to public water facilities. "The water industry is relatively late approaching the problem of embedded systems," he was quoted in Computer Weekly. (2)

Another Computer Weekly article (March 5, 1998) reported that British water companies "are drawing up contingency plans to prevent supplies being hit by the date bug." (3) The article stated that "water and sewage treatment plants contain hundreds of embedded systems, controlling everything from hardware to the programmable logic controllers that supervise the plant's operations."

Andrew Scudamore, Business Development Director at England's South Staffordshire Water Group of Companies, said that any water company "runs the risk of not recognizing the full extent of the problem, and therefore may miss many other Y2K angles of its business that could be catastrophic to the overall operation of that company." (4)

The United Kingdom's water utilities and its government water regulator are refusing to guarantee that water supplies will be available in January 2000, even to hospitals. Ros Vickers, Y2K coordinator for nine of Great Britain's 10 largest water utilities, said that service guarantees are impossible. (5)

In the United States, the Los Angeles Department of Water and Power, the largest municipal system in the world, hired TAVA Technologies to study LA's Year 2000 embedded system issues. The contract, announced on July 27, 1998, was for a period of 24 months. That means Los Angeles expects to have TAVA still working on their embedded chip problems until at least July 2000. Wonder what millions of thirsty Californian will drink between January and July 2000?

A Canadian federal Y2K task force, led by the CEO of Canada's biggest telephone company, recently issued a warning that the health and safety of the Canadian public may be threatened because of slow attention to Year 2000 problems.

"We are now urging all firms to develop effective contingency plans to prepare for possible failures and to protect themselves from unprepared partners," warned Jean Monty, CEO of Bell Canada Enterprises, and chairman of the national task force studying Y2K's effects on Canada.

Mr. Monty said that while Canadian banks, telephone companies, and airlines have been closely cooperating to address Y2K problems, "that is not yet the case for providers of other essential services such as electrical power, oil and gas, food, and water supplies, and other essential services." (6)

Water, food, and air are the three essential necessities for life. Without any of the three, life ceases to exist.

Besides drinking and sanitation, water is necessary for the production of electricity, fire protection, food processing, and most manufacturing operations.

This isn't funny.

Somebody should get serious about this.

Will city water treatment plants stop working after January 1, 2000? Nobody knows. Worse yet, hardly anybody is even trying to find out!

When God brings judgment upon nations, He sends war, famine, pestilence, and drought.

God instructed the prophet Ezekiel to admonish the people of Israel to ration out their water. Judgment was soon coming to Israel! The Lord told the prophet to tell the Israelites that their cities would be destroyed, their farmlands deserted, and that people would sip their tiny portions of water in utter despair.

> "Son of man, eat thy bread with quaking, and drink thy water with trembling and with carefulness; And say unto the people of the land, Thus saith the Lord God of the inhabitants of Jerusalem, and of the land of Israel; They shall eat their bread with carefulness, and drink their water with astonishment, that her land may be desolate from all that is therein, because of the violence of all them that dwell therein."

Ezekiel 12:18-19

"Never in America!," you declare. "Rationing drinking water? Impossible!"

Be careful what you think.

In the next Scripture verse, God warned Israel to stop saying the proverb, "The days are prolonged, and every vision faileth?"

We would say it today like this, "Every day that passes by makes the prophets into liars!"

God told Ezekiel to inform the people that soon he would put an end to that saying. In fact, God gave them a new proverb that basically said, "The time is here for these prophecies of judgment to be fulfilled."

The Lord said He was sending judgment because their land was filled with violence.

So is America.

God knew when food and water supplies dried up, He would get their attention. "And the cities that are inhabited shall be laid waste, and the land shall be desolate; and ye shall know that I am the Lord." (Ezekiel 12:20)

Does America, with her streets filled with murder and violence, need to be reminded that God is Lord?

16 Telecommunications: Hello! Hello! Anybody There?

"In the past two months many witnesses have come before this committee professing their industry or their company will be year 2000 compliant. My conversations with chief information officers and key executives of long distance and regional telephone companies have convinced me those claims of compliance may be based more on hope than on actual fact."

> Gary Beach — Publisher
> CIO Magazine
> Remarks before the Senate Special Committee on the
> Year 2000
> July 31, 1998

If electricity is the "lifeblood" of our modern economic system, then our telecommunications network surely is the central nervous system.

Communication has been the cornerstone of all of civilization's advancement. For centuries, communication was slow, transmitted only by word of mouth or the written page. Following the invention of the telephone by Alexander Graham Bell, the technological advancements in methods of communication have been responsible for improvements in most of our modern day life.

During the Twentieth Century, we constructed a highly complex, interdependent communications network that now allows anybody to send messages around the world. The same "baby boomers" who sat in front of television sets as children watching Neil Armstrong speak to Earthlings from the moon, hardly give a second glance to "live" Photographs of the Martian landscape by the Pathfinder probe.

We've come a long way, baby!

We live in an age when everyday folks carry pocket-size cellular telephones, get pages from employers a thousand miles away, are bored with 100 cable TV channels, surf the World Wide Web with high-speed modems, and have two telephone lines and a fax machine in their homes.

Every day, 270 million Americans take for granted this

marvelous array of communication gadgets.

What would we ever do without it?

This highly complex, interdependent global web of voice, data, and video transmission networks, however, does a lot more than connect your once-a-year holiday telephone call to Aunt Lucy in Gun Barrel City, Texas.

Around the clock every day of the week, vital components of our nation's government and economy totally rely on the global telecommunications system. There can be no down time. It must work every second of the day.

From New York City, the financial heart of the world, a trillion dollars of the world's wealth are electronically transmitted around the world each day. Each electronic transfer of cash is done over date-sensitive communication networks by computers using date-sensitive software.

Wall Street investors, the Federal Reserve Bank, global banking institutions, large insurance conglomerates, and the world's multinational corporations depend on the global telecommunications network to transact the world's business deals.

The Pentagon counts on it too.

American Airlines, the Internal Revenue Service, America Online, the Red Cross, Harvard, the National Institute of Health, the Billy Graham Evangelistic Association, NASA, the QVC shopping channel, the National Weather Service, and every other major organization depend on the system too.

So much of our daily lives depend on the telecommunications network, that any large-scale failure would severely impact our standard of living.

The telecommunications network also transports electronic command and control signals for the regional electric power grids, gas and oil pipelines, hydroelectric dams, and water treatment plants.

It's all done with computers, satellites, and telephone lines.

And it all requires electricity! And electric utilities require the telecommunications network! And the telecommunications network requires electricity!

Get the picture?

This could be a big mess.

Nobody Knows If the Infrastructure Will Survive Y2K

The telecommunications infrastructure is made up of a myriad of systems. It includes local and long distance telephone companies, the Internet "backbone" and Internet service providers, cellular networks, cable television systems, satellite operators, TV and radio broadcasters, the Pentagon, universities, and millions of computers around the world.

No single entity owns the global telecommunications network.

In America alone, there are five long distance carriers and a growing horde of resellers, six Regional Bell Operating Companies (RBOCs), six national broadcast television networks, a thousand or more local telephone companies, 4500 Internet Service Providers, 16 communication satellite operators, thousands of local TV and radio stations, hundreds of wireless and cellular companies, eleven thousand cable television systems, and hundreds of communications equipment manufacturers.

If no single entity owns the entire network, that means nobody is in charge of making it ready for the Year 2000.

Apparently, that includes the Federal Communications Commission.

The FCC didn't get around to holding a Y2K meeting until April 29, 1998.

The FCC sprang into decisive action by launching a Y2K Web site. Then they sent letters to 200 major telecommunications companies advising them that Y2K would be a big deal.

Oh, the joy of seeing our tax dollars at work!

Here's a huge iceberg straight ahead, and the FCC is playing shuffleboard on the deck of the Titanic!

In late April 1998, the federal government's General Accounting Office gave the boys at the FCC a friendly call. "Hey, can you tell us what is the current Y2K preparations of the telecommunications industry?"

Seems like a sensible request from the government's auditors. After all, you would assume that the guys over at the FCC were right on top of the problem, right?

Well, the FCC said, "Duh, we don't know!"

In testimony before the House Ways and Means Committee, the GAO's "bug man," Joel Willemssen, told Congressmen that the "FCC was unable to provide us with information on the current status and anticipated readiness dates in areas such as satellite, cable, broadcast, and wireless services." (1)

Mr. Willemssen, Director of Civil Agencies Information Systems in the GAO's Accounting and Information Management Division, continued with his astonishing revelation by telling the Congressmen that the "FCC could not provide us with data on when major interexchange (long distance) and local exchange carriers were expecting to be Year 2000 compliant."

The Federal Communications Commission did not even know when the nation's local and long distance telephone companies would be ready for the Year 2000?

What were they spending their time doing?

Is there a bigger threat to society that we don't know about?

Guess how the GAO obtained the needed information? They picked up the telephone and called the companies themselves! According to the information gathered by the GAO, most of the major carriers say they'll be Y2K compliant by mid-1999.

At least they're not going to wait until the last minute!

They'll have a good six months to kick back and relax.

No sweat!

Will the global telecommunications network be 100% ready for the Year 2000? Everybody does not share the FCC's cool confidence in Washington.

People like that skeptical old Senator from Utah, Bob Bennett.

"It is too great a leap of faith to believe that all the elements of an endeavor this complex will be ready at the stroke of midnight...especially in light of the limited readiness the industry has shown to this committee," said Senator Bennett following his committee's hearing on the telecommunication industry's Y2K preparations. (2)

Y2K Expert Predicts Y2K Telcom Failures

If Lou Maroccio's projections are on target, there's a good chance a lot of your calls won't go through after January 1, 2000.

Mr. Maroccio is a Y2K research director for the Gartner Group, the world's largest computer consulting firm. He says there's a 50% to 60% chance each major telecommunications carrier will suffer at least one failure of a mission critical system.

Such failures could be everything from billing snafus to a total loss of dial tones.

His prediction comes in spite of the billions of dollars being spent collectively by telephone carriers to become Y2K compliant. According to Security and Exchange Commission documents, the combined expenditure of seven of the nation's largest telecommunication firms had exceeded $2 billion by March 1998. AT&T plans to spend almost a half billion dollars. GTE is spending $350 million and has over 1,200 employees assigned to the problem. SBC Communications is spending $250 million on its systems.

Despite billions spent to prevent disaster, there's no guarantee that one noncompliant source of electronic data won't bring everybody else down. "Year 2000 is truly a 'weakest link' problem," Gerald Roth, Vice President of technology programs at GTE, explained before the House Ways and Means Oversight Subcommittee. "The single system or date conversion we miss may be the undoing of the 99% we did find." (3)

The "weak links" could be the 1,400 small telephone companies serving America's small towns and farming communities. While the big companies such as AT&T and MCI plan to be ready for testing by December 1998, many of the small telcos are falling behind schedule, or worse, just getting started on the Y2K remediation projects.

And there's the problem.

The telecommunications network is an immensely interconnected global gridiron that electronically interweaves thousands of telcoms with each other. In the U.S., public telephone companies process millions of calls each minute. A simple long distance call requires a multitude of complex electronic and computerized transactions to take place.

Consider what must happen when you make a long distance call to an old college friend. You don't think about the process that must take place with millisecond precision. You just hope that Tim or Karen will be home when you call. Within milliseconds, your call races to the nearest Private Branch Exchange, then to your local phone company's central office switch. From there, it travels with lightning speed through your local carrier's components and systems that route your call to an inter-exchange carrier. The long distance carrier passes your call through trunk lines across the country – or maybe sends it by satellite or fiber optic lines – to your friend's local exchange carrier's central switch. Next, the local company routes your call through their components and systems. Finally, the telephone rings in your friend's home. All within seconds!

This complicated interconnected system must be checked, repaired, and tested before the end of 1999.

Testing is essential.

"Because a single noncompliant component could potentially shut down the entire network, rigorous testing will be necessary," (4) the House Ways and Means Committee Oversight Subcommittee said in a report.

Testing might be essential, but it's easier said than done. The knotted, tangled construction of the network makes testing a complicated and difficult endeavor.

"The permutations and combinations of calling events, service requests and routing possibilities exceed the industry's ability to 100% testing of Y2K," Gerard Roth, Vice President of GTE's Technology Programs, told the House Oversight Subcommittee. (5)

Besides, you can't turn off the world's telephone systems for a week or two of testing. "Testing cannot be done on the live network...testing would disrupt current operations, create unacceptable outages," Mr. Roth explained to the Congressmen.

The work being done to remediate and test the public telephone network, Mr. Roth assured the Congressmen, is the "best known solution to Y2K we are able to accomplish."

In other words, it's the best they can do at this late date.

Big Customers Demand Answers

It is beyond question that our entire society greatly depends on the reliability of our telecommunications system.

If you don't think so, imagine dialing 911 and there's no dial tone. Even worse, imagine your local police, fire, and rescue departments having no dial tones too.

Businesses have everything at stake too. They're counting on the telephone companies to have their systems 100% compliant soon.

One vital component of the global economy is getting impatient with the telephone companies. The banking industry absolutely depends on a robust electronic data transfer system for daily commerce. Hundreds of billions of dollars flow through the telephone lines every day.

Several high-level banking officials have openly complained that the telecommunication companies are stonewalling in giving them information about their Y2K projects. Federal Reserve Board member Edward Kelly, Jr., warned a Senate committee that the nation's telecommunication companies are at risk. He complained that they've been less than generous with internal information concerning their Y2K results. "They have been very tight with providing information, especially on the testing of interconnectivity between systems," Mr. Kelly stated. (6)

One major bank that is getting antsy is Citicorp.

At a Y2K conference sponsored by the General Accounting Office in October 1997, Citicorp executives ripped into third-party vendors and suppliers who are dragging their feet in getting ready for the Year 2000.

Citicorp, and all other financial institutions, have good reason to be impatient. They can't test their systems until the telecommunication companies are 100% Y2K compliant! Because banks, investment brokerages, and insurance companies rely on telephone lines to conduct business, their Y2K test plans, obviously, depend on testing their systems over the telephone lines. The banks and Wall Street could spend billions to fix their systems, only to get contaminated by computer bugs on the telephone lines!

Among Citicorp's demands, the company said telephone companies must agree to certify that each service is Y2K compliant by December 1, 1998. Citicorp also wants the telephone companies to give the banks access to their Y2K plans and test results.

The threat of telephone companies passing the Y2K bug to other businesses like a deadly flu virus concerns many top corporate chief information officers. "The Great Paradox" is what Gary Beach calls the threat. Mr. Beach, who is publisher of CIO magazine, told Senator Bennett's special Y2K committee, "Let's say the telecom industry's Y2K remedial efforts are 100% compliant...and the system works as advertised. The telecommunications infrastructure then becomes a powerful conduit for spreading Y2K problems. Technical problems will be passed down the information technology food chain as quickly as telephone connections occur. On the other hand, if the telecommunications system experiences significant Y2K problems, not only businesses but lives could be lost." (7)

Mr. Beach's magazine readers are the top information technology experts for major corporations. His readers' livelihoods depend on the telephone companies. He's heard their promises to be compliant by December 1998.

He is skeptical.

"In the past two months, many witnesses have come before this committee professing their industry or their company will be year 2000 compliant. My conversations with chief information officers and key executives of long distance and regional telephone companies have convinced me those claims of compliance may be based more on hope than on actual fact." (8)

Forget About Reaching Out To Touch Somebody in Asia (or Europe, South America, and Africa too)

By everybody's estimates, telephone companies in the United States are far ahead of the rest of the world in getting ready for the Year 2000. American companies are closely followed by Canadian, British, and Australian companies.

After that, it doesn't look good.

A survey by British Telecom showed that only 23% of its partners in Asia and the Pacific Rim were working on Y2K solutions. In Africa and the Middle East, a mere 11% of its interconnected partners had Year 2000 programs.

Other surveys are turning up similar discouraging news.

Another British Telecom survey in October 1997 discovered that a third of 160 telecommunications managers in Great Britain didn't think the Year 2000 would be a problem for their systems. More than half of the managers admitted that all they knew about the problem was what they heard and read in the news media.

The U.S. State Department released a report in March 1998 that confirms the dismal number of telecommunications companies in other countries that are working on Y2K. The State Department survey 113 nations and found that 22% expected to be Y2K compliant by December 1998; 23% expect to be compliant by December 1999; 29% said they are working on it, but having problems; and the remaining 26% had either never heard of Y2K or hadn't started to do anything. (9)

Assuming the 22% meet their December 1998 deadline without any glitches, that means 78% of the telecommunications firms around the world just aren't going to make it.

International carriers are also discovering the threat of embedded microchips in their systems. Some underwater seabed based repeaters may need to be replaced.

In Asia, where Y2K has not been taken seriously, Telkom Indonesia announced in late July 1998 that the Year 2000 virus would threaten a substantial portion of its infrastructure. Indonesia's telephone company said it would spend $200 million to repair its backbone and nonbackbone transmission systems, local exchange and switching systems, billing systems, and network management systems.

The impact on the U.S. economy could be devastating if foreign telephone companies are not running after January 2000. Most major U.S. manufacturing companies have plants around the world or rely on foreign suppliers for parts. If you can't call them, you can't order anything. For example, Illinois-based John Deere & Company has 60 manufacturing plants around the world.

No foreign parts being shipped to America means nothing will be built in America.

The FCC's chairman, Bill Kennard, said, "This could have a huge impact on international trade, foreign investment, the global economy, and even national security." (10)

Huge impact indeed!

Perhaps another Great Depression!

Don't Forget About Those Fiery Meteors and Nasty Solar Flares

More than Y2K is threatening the global telecommunications network.

Meteor showers and violent solar storms may wreck havoc on Earth's communications systems too.

The Leonid meteor showers are returning in November 1998 and November 1999 when the Earth passes through the dense debris of the tail from the comet P/T Temple-Tuttle. In 1966, the last major Leonid meteor storm, over 150,000 meteors per hour streaked across the sky.

Thirty years ago, we had few satellites above the Earth. Today, we are extremely dependent on satellites for all types of communications, both military and civilian. If the upcoming Leonid showers are as heavy or heavier than the 1966 event, there's a high likelihood one or more important satellites will be destroyed or seriously damaged.

Scientists believe the worse bombardment of meteors will be in November 1999.

The sudden loss of several vital communications satellites a month before the rollover of 2000 could severely impact the world's efforts to keep the global network running. A sudden shock is the last thing telecommunications companies need with less than a month to go to the Year 2000.

The sun has some hot things cooking too.

Cycle 23, the current solar maximum, looks like its going to be a real scorcher. Violent storms on the sun and giant flares will send vast clouds of magnetically charged electrons toward the Earth.

These geomagnetic storms will seriously hinder communications systems on Earth, especially wireless telephone calls and broadcasting by radio stations. Solar storms can also damage satellites, rendering them useless.

The Year 2000 computer virus, the heaviest meteor shower in 30 years, and the most violent solar maximum in recorded history will be too much for the world's fragile telecommunication's network.

The global telecommunications network is essential for the world's money system based in New York City. Without it, the world's money system will collapse.

God destroyed the Tower of Babel.

He made it impossible for men to communicate with each other.

God is ready to judge New York City's financial kingdom.

The global telecommunications system will collapse.

Once again, God will make it impossible for men to communicate on the Earth.

17 The Global Financial System: Bank Holidays? What Are We Celebrating?

"We need a world-class leader to emerge, and give the people of the global information society, true and positive leadership."

*Alan J. Simpson — President, Communication Links, Inc.
Remarks before the House Government Reform and
Oversight Committee Subcommittee on Government
Management, Information and Technology
June 22, 1998*

It was the best of times.

The "Roaring Twenties" produced unprecedented wealth in the American economy.

During the presidency of Calvin Coolidge, both production and consumption soared. At the top of the economic ladder, America's wealthiest families saw their investments soar to new heights. The emerging middle class witnessed many of their peers becoming rich "overnight." Factories churned out shiny new automobiles, ice boxes, radios, and a never-ending flow of new technological inventions.

The Twenties was a time of selfish spending on the attainment of material goods, and satisfying personal pleasures. People adopted new fads, chased wealth, bought new inventions, and opened their minds to new ideas. While rural America was troubled by the abandonment of traditional values, upwardly mobile young men danced the jitterbug with women who smoked cigarettes and wore short skirts. It was a decade of having a good time, illegally sipping liquor privately in "speak easies," and idolizing the glamorous motion picture stars shining from Hollywood.

Despite the wealth and good times, all was not well in America.

Beneath the surface of the prosperous economy, trouble was brewing. People were so busy making money and enjoying the good times, nobody saw the warning signs.

Confidence reigned supreme. Unbridled confidence in Yankee ingenuity was the engine that sustained the economic growth. Consumption of goods - automobiles, new housing, appliances, furniture, and new gadgets called radios – fueled the stock market. Ownership of automobiles tripled during the decade. Having convinced Americans to discard conservative principles such as thrift, frugality, and postponing pleasures, America's rising corporations, teeming with profits, urged people to buy on credit. Experts assured the lower and middle classes that "buy now, pay later" was the way to go. As President Coolidge proclaimed, "The business of America is business."

Investors marveled as the value of stocks soared. One new corporation – Radio Corporation of America – was launched to seize the new medium of radio communications. Few Americans owned a radio at the start of the Twenties, but sales soared during the decade. By 1930, more than 30% of American families owned a radio. In 1928, the price of RCA's stock multiplied by nearly five times, even though the "high tech" company had not even paid a single dividend. Stocks were trading at prices far beyond the worth of the companies. Average folks watched the net worth of relatives and neighbors skyrocket as stock prices continued to climb to dizzying new heights.

The artificial high of the stock market deceived many. The growing beliefs that the Twenties were an "once in a lifetime" chance to get rich spurred many levelheaded wage earners to abandon their financial common sense. As the stock market euphoria overtook the heartiest soul, especially between 1927 and 1929, people stampeded to get into the stock market "gold rush" while the "gett'n was good." People emptied their savings, mortgaged their homes, cashed in their World War I Liberty bonds, and borrowed money from banks so they could dump money into risky ventures with the hopes of "striking it rich."

During the last two years of the Bull Market, the Dow Jones Industrial Average doubled in value. Nobody had ever witnessed anything like this! Industrial production per hour increased by 63% during the Roaring Twenties. Investors poured millions of dollars into the stock market. Unwilling to be left out of the buying frenzy, many bought stocks "on margin." The speculative scheme allowed people to buy stocks on credit. Eager investors put down a small amount of the purchase price and borrowed the rest, gambling the stock prices would continue to climb.

Besides growing consumer debt and "margin" buying, there were other warning signs too.

Wall Street lenders made unwise loans to European governments, especially Germany, left devastated by the World War I. These huge international debts extended by American banks further destabilized the world's economy.

While the good times were making the rich even richer, the poor were getting poorer. The gap between the "haves and the have-nots" was getting wider. The top 0.1% of Americans had a combined income equal to the bottom 42%. Even though increased productivity caused corporate profits to shoot up by 62% between 1923 and 1929, average wages for manufacturing jobs rose only a scant 8%.

America's corporate chieftains were accumulating unprecedented amounts of wealth. Henry Ford's compensation in 1929 was $14 million – which would be about $350 million in today's economy. Compared to the average personal income of $750, the overwhelming majority of Americans could only imagine what it was like to earn fourteen million dollars.

Farmers were suffering too. As many families migrated to urban areas to find jobs in America's bustling factories, people failed to notice that the Roaring Twenties' prosperity had passed by the farmers. During World War I, farmers greatly expanded their crop production to fill the void left by agricultural cutbacks in Europe. After the war, agricultural prices fell as the international market filled with fresh supplies of crops. Average annual farm income was only $273 at the peak of the Roaring Twenties' boom.

The glitter of gold obscured other inequalities too. Membership in organized labor fell dramatically between 1920 and 1929. Over a thousand corporate mergers swallowed up 6,000 independent companies, leaving 200 corporations controlling half of all U.S. industry by 1929. By 1929, the richest 1% of Americans controlled 40% of the nation's wealth. Several hundred thousand employees saw their jobs permanently disappear as cost-efficient machines replaced humans in America's new "automated" factories.

Investor frenzy continued in the stock market through the first half of 1929, in spite of the unsold factory inventories growing to three times larger than in 1928. This was the boom that would never end!

Between August and October 1929, factory production plummeted. Wholesale prices declined. Personal income fell too. Again, the euphoria blinded the eyes of most people. They couldn't see what was about to strike them down. Speculators continued to invest money in the remaining days of the bull market.

Stock market prices fell dramatically on Monday, October 21, 1929.

As the market plummeted, large investors began selling stocks. Prices stabilized on Tuesday and Wednesday. Fear, however, overtook investors on Thursday, October 24, 1929. In their hearts, Wall Street investors knew the bull market was over. A group of leading bankers attempted to calm the market on Friday, but prices dropped again when the market opened for trading on Monday.

The next day was Black Tuesday. On October 29, 1929, any remaining hope of recovery evaporated. Investors stampeded to sell off quickly depreciating securities. It is estimated that stocks lost between $10 billion to $15 billion on that day. So furious was the selling that at times there were no buyers on the floor.

Suddenly, the boom was over.

Millions of families were deep in debt.

Prices fell. Real estate values plummeted. Available credit dried up.

Confidence succumbed to despair. Over the next three years, the nation plunged into darkness.

Unemployment climbed from 3.2% to 25% as 15 million Americans lost their jobs. In Toledo, the unemployment rate hit 80%. In Akron, 60% of the city was out of work. Men who had earlier brokered big business deals found themselves selling apples or shining shoes just to feed their children. Housewives and young teenagers left the security of their homes to find any kind of work to help their husbands and fathers keep the family together.

Proud men, who had never taken anything from anybody, were reduced to the humiliation of standing in line for handouts. Bread lines stretched for miles around Salvation Army kitchens. Many formerly employed men sifted through garbage cans for food. Nearly two million men became hobos, riding trains and hitchhiking across the country in search of work.

The already meager income of farmers fell 60% between 1929 and 1932. Mortgage foreclosures evicted one-third of America's farmers from the land. Like a Biblical plague, a scorching drought hit the Great Plains. Stretching across Kansas, Oklahoma, Texas, New Mexico, and Colorado, the severe drought and massive soil erosion created the Dust Bowl. The gusting winds of Black Blizzards piled up drifts of blowing topsoil and sand against farmhouses, barns, and fences.

The first bank panic hit in late 1930. Frightened, desperate men and women frantically pulled their savings from the banks. A second bank panic hit in the spring of '31. By 1932, an astounding 10,000 banks had closed, 40% of the all banks in the United States. Another panic hit banks in early 1933. President Franklin Roosevelt ordered banks to be closed. In total, depositors lost over $2 billion in savings during the Depression. Their stocks, purchased at all-time highs, were worth only 20% of their value prior to the great crash.

Despair and hopelessness gripped the nation.

The supply of money dried up. Bankers refused to lend to home-owners and business owners. Instead, they foreclosed on multitudes.

Shopkeepers boarded up their stores on mainstreet. Factories and mills closed. Their smokestacks ceased billowing black smoke. There simply were no jobs.

Families were evicted from their homes. Shantytowns sprung up in towns and cities. People called them "Hoovervilles" in mocking refer-ence to President Herbert Hoover.

America remained in the Great Depression until the Great War.

The bankers opened their treasuries once again to loan millions to the U.S. government and factories to prepare for war. The same moneychangers who had no loans for farmers and factory workers suddenly had hundreds of millions for war.

1999: The Next Great Depression

America in 1998 looks a lot like America in 1928.

The question is, "In 1999, will we look like America in 1929?"

We are now experiencing unprecedented prosperity. Federal Reserve Chairman Alan Greenspan says this is the best economy in his 50-year career as an economist. Inflation has almost disappeared. Unemployment is at a 30-year low. The Dow Jones Industrial Average, to everybody's amazement, breaks new records. High-tech startup firms attract hundreds of millions of dollars in the first day of an Initial Public Offering, despite having never earned a nickel. Financial magazines abound with stories touting the success secrets of 25-year-old whiz kids striking it rich with new Internet-related companies.

Millions of Americans now have their retirement savings invested in 401K plans. By 1995, 41% of all families owned stock. The value of stocks owned by households in 1998, either directly or through retirement plans, topped $13 trillion. Everybody wants to be in this hot market! Factory workers, cab drivers, college students, housewives, ranchers, and people from every walk of life pour millions each day into mutual funds.

Nobody wants to miss out on this "once-in-a-lifetime" opportunity to get rich!

Like 1928, the warning signs are everywhere.

Consumer debt is now at an alarming all-time high, doubling since 1990. American families are awash in a sea of debt. They owe a whopping $1.2 trillion – not counting their home mortgages. New car loans pushed total new installment credit card debt in June 1998 to an unbelievable $6.7 billion!

The lust for more consumer goods, high-tech gadgets, luxury items, shiny $40,000 sport utility vehicles, and exotic vacations have tempted level-headed husbands and wives to hock their houses for equity loans. Advertisements entice the weak with unheard of deals of equity loans up to 125% of the home's value.

The mortgaging of American homes is growing to alarming heights. Responding to TV sales pitches from Dan Marino and Jim Palmer, homeowners have hocked their homes to feed their high spending habits. They use the loan money to buy new cars, fast boats, new furnishings, and maybe a European vacation. From 1996 to mid-1998, over four million American homeowners converted a whopping $26 billion of credit-card debt into home equity debt. Although the 4.2 million homeowners borrowed to consolidate credit card debts, only 1.5 million were still free of credit card debts two years later.

Bank regulators warned in July 1998 that lenders are becoming too lax in lending standards. They pointed to increased lending to risky real estate investment trusts (REITS), increased consumer installment debts, and the rising number of home equity loans. Regulators say they see too many banks approving too many weak loan applications. While banks and credit card companies aggressively lend more money to consumers, personal bankruptcies are at a record level.

Meanwhile, other parallels to 1928 are clearly evident. Membership in trade unions has declined over the last 10 years. Millions of jobs permanently disappeared over the last decade through corporate downsizing and automation. Smaller companies are being gobbled up in a frenzy of mergers. Merger mania is sweeping Wall Street as globalization compels large corporations to join forces to become global giants, such as AT&T and TCI.

Executive compensation is reaching astronomical proportions. Sanford Weill, CEO of the Travelers Group, is the most highly paid executive in America. Mr. Weill's salary in 1997 was $227 million, not counting bonuses and stock options, according to Forbes magazine. With shareholders concerned only about achieving higher stock prices, corporations are dangling hefty pay increases and bonuses in front of their top executives. For example, Charles Wang, CEO of Computer Associates International, and two other executives were given $1 billion worth of stock to split in 1998 as a bonus. Mr. Wang's portion was worth $675 million. .

While CEOs are awarded salary increases averaging 34%, American workers have been inching forward with meager 3% wage increases, just enough to stay even with the cost of living. Despite the record earnings posted by corporations, most of the wealth is going into the hands of a few. For America's poor, the average income of the poorest fifth of American families actually dropped in 1996, although the American economy soared.

Like the farmers of the 1920s, America's farmers are in the throes of troubling economic currents. The American economy is flourishing, but farmers are struggling. And nobody notices! Farms are getting bigger, but profits are smaller. Net farm income is about the same as 20 years ago, yet operating expenses have soared. Huge food processing companies, under pressure by shareholders to increase stock prices, are squeezing farmers by paying less for crops and livestock. Farm prices have dropped 30% from 1996 to mid-1998 for corn, wheat, and soybeans. Increasing pressure on farmers is the Freedom to Farm Act, which eliminates farm subsidies by 2002. Faced with a worldwide grain glut, exports have plummeted. American farmers face competition, too, inside the U.S. as the NAFTA agreement has opened the U.S. market to crops and beef from Mexican, Latin American, and Canadian farmers. Adverse weather and disease have taken their toll too. Reminiscent of the Dust Bowl of the Great Depression, the entire state of Texas was declared a disaster area in Summer 1998 as triple-digit heat and drought left Texas ranches parched, contributing to an estimated $2.1 billion worth of damages to Texas agriculture.

Exposure to high-risk credit deals has caught the eyes of federal regulators. As American banks extended risky international loans to European governments and businesses during the 1920s, today's banks are now scrambling to sell risky credit derivatives.

Credit derivatives are contracts that transfer risk, which is any loss that comes from a change in a borrower's ability to repay a debt. Simply, it allows banks to trade and insure against the risk that borrowers will not repay them. Also known as default swaps, these financial devices provide insurance to lenders that they'll get their money back if the borrower goes bankrupt. Major financial institutions, such as NationsBank, are furiously buying and selling the contracts. The global market for credit derivatives exploded to $170 billion in 1997, triple over '96 totals. The market is expected to double in 1998.

Alarmed by the risk to the American banking system, the chairwoman of the Commodity Futures Trading Commission, Brooksley Born, has threatened to put stringent federal regulations on default swaps. Treasury officials from the Clinton Administration, however, have urged her to delay any regulations on credit derivatives until October 1999.

By October 1999, it may be too late.

Wall Street Expert Forecasts Global Failure

Edward Yardeni is no wild-eyed, "loose cannon" radical.

Nor is he a charter member of the Montana militia.

Chief economist for Deutshe Morgan Grenfell, the global investment subsidiary of Germany's Deutsche Bank, Mr. Yardeni is one of the most respected economists in the world.

The Yale educated thinker is admired by Wall Street for his ability to foresee powerful trends and changes in the global economy. He has been a vocal cheerleader for the belief that technology, a conservative Federal Reserve monetary policy, and higher productivity by American workers would create an unprecedented period of strong economic growth and low inflation.

Edward Yardeni's economic forecasts have been on the mark. So precise have his forecasts been over recent years, the Wall Street Journal, the voice of America's investors, bestowed on him in January 1998 the title of "Economist of the Year."

Accolades from other respected Wall Street institutions have been bestowed on Mr. Yardeni too. ABC News described him as "the best economic forecaster in the country." *Investor's Business Daily* calls him "one of the top market forecasters of the decade." *Barron's* magazine wrote, "Few, if any, market seers have had a better stock-market forecasting record over the past decade than Yardeni." (1)

Wall Street has a problem.

Their favorite bull market cheerleader now describes himself as an "alarmist." (2)

"The entire Y2K problem will not be solved," says Mr. Yardeni. "We must prepare for the possibility of business failures and the collapse of essential U.S. government services including tax collection, welfare payments, national defense, and air traffic control."

Heavy stuff!

Did he say "business failures" and "collapse" of federal government services?

Yep.

Here's the guy who everybody was patting on the back in January 1998, telling him how smart he is about the economy. By summer 1998, Mr. Yardeni was warning there was a 70% chance of a severe global recession.

What happened?

And why aren't more people listening to him?

He realized there's "simply too many computers that have to be fixed and not enough time." (3)

Mr. Yardeni says our "global and domestic markets for financial securities commodities products and services depend completely on the smooth functioning of the vast information technology infrastructure." He says to understand the financial impact of Y2K, we need to "Imagine a world in which these systems are either impaired or completely broken." (4) "Suddenly, people will be forced to do without many goods and services that cannot be produced without information technology."

He says a Y2K-induced stock market drop will be deflationary. He predicts a $1 trillion loss in stock market capitalization.

Mr. Yardeni has pleaded with world banking and government leaders to deal with the Year 2000 crisis. He warns about the possibility of an accidental launch of nuclear missiles too. The respected economist says military leaders of the G-8 nations (the world's most industrialized countries) "especially the U.S. and Russia, must jointly assess the risk of an accidental nuclear missile launch or a provocative false alarm." He implores the world's nuclear superpowers to "rapidly develop a fail-safe joint communication and intelligence network to eliminate any such risks." (5)

Mr. Yardeni shakes his head in bewilderment at the optimists who glibly dismiss his dire warnings. He believes "that so much is at risk that there is no way there won't be significant disruptions, malfunctions, and crashes in vital computer systems." Those who say the Year 2000 will not be a problem are "naively optimistic to conclude that everything will be fixed in time just because the consequences of failure are obviously so grim."(6) Such people "just don't get it."

"It is time to prepare for failure," Mr. Yardeni wrote in the Harvard Business Review (July-August 1998). He says government and corporate leaders must "alert the public" to head-off panics. Leaders must deal forthrightly with the crisis by telling the public, "This is what might happen. This is how we're preparing for it. Don't panic." (7)

Without leadership from the top, "panic is likely, and panic will only lead to further disruption."

Y2K Threatens Interconnected Global Financial System

Financial institutions – banks, investment firms, mutual funds, mortgage lenders, credit card companies, and insurance companies - depend on numbers.

They also depend on computers to crunch the numbers every second of the day.

Major banks in the United States are hopelessly behind schedule in Y2K remediation. Chase Manhattan Bank, the nation's largest bank, has 200 million lines of computer codes to correct, at an estimated cost up to $300 million. The giant institution's annual report filed with the Securities and Exchange Commission in early 1998 said the bank had completed its first three phases – inventory, assessment, and strategy. That means Chase Manhattan had not even started to actually repair its 200 million lines of code. According to Y2K computer experts, over 90% of the work is repair and testing. That doesn't leave Chase Manhattan much time.

Citicorp is spending $600 million to fight the Y2K virus. NationsBank has 1,000 employees devoted to Y2K and plans to spend $380 million. Merrill Lynch, the nation's leading stock broker, is confronted with correcting 170 million lines of computer code, and forced in August 1998 to spend in $100 million more than the $275 million budgeted for Y2K. The Federal Reserve Bank, itself, is not Y2K compliant! The Fed has 90 million lines of computer code to repair. The Federal Deposit Insurance Corporation, which insures the bank deposits of millions of consumers, isn't compliant either!

Another huge bank, BankBoston, warned the Senate Banking Committee that his institution has been working on Y2K computer problems since 1995 and still had major problems to solve. Mr. David Iacino, BankBoston's senior Y2K project manager, told the Senators that time is running out for banks. "Knowing that all financial institutions must address the very same issues that we have faced with much less time remaining, I am concerned with the general preparedness of the rest of the financial services industry domestically and, more so, internationally," Mr. Iacino said. (8)

Even if every bank and financial firm in America fixed their computers before January 2000, the global financial system would collapse.

"American financial institutions deal with their international counterparts virtually every minute of the day as they settle transactions, execute currency trades, and operate offices throughout the world," Senator Bob Bennett explained at a July 1998 hearing of his special Y2K Senate committee. "Americans have invested significantly in foreign stocks, primarily through investment funds, and the stocks of American companies are traded at all hours of the day and night in markets throughout the world." (9)

For typical citizens, the scope of America's electronic payment systems is beyond comprehension. Over a trillion dollars in global foreign transactions occur daily, with 80% involving the American dollar. Global trade exceeds $5 trillion. Over 275,000 foreign-owned financial affiliates are located in local economies around the world, with 18,000 of those inside the United States. The Board of Governors of the Federal Reserve System says that "90% of all bank assets are electronic entries in data bases, and virtually all bank transactions involve electronic processing." (10) About 10,000 depository institutions use the Fedwire, an electronic transfer system operated by Federal Reserve Bank, to transfer 86 million payments valued at over $280 trillion each year. Another Fed electronic system, the Fedwire securities transfer service, transfers 13 million securities each year valued at over $160 trillion. A third service, the Automated Clearing House, is the Fed system used by banks to clear checks by 50 million consumers.

Financial institutions around the world are neglecting the Year 2000 problem. Europe's banks and corporations are obsessed with preparing for the Euro money system scheduled to start on January 1, 1999. Little attention has been given to repairing their computer codes to handle the millennial date change.

In the United States, one in five securities companies had not even started a Y2K plan for their computer systems as late as summer 1998. According to the National Association of Security Dealers, 21% of security firms - companies that sell and trade stocks, bonds, and other investments - had no plans to repair their computers. The NASD survey also showed that 43% of security firms estimated they were at least 61% finished with their Y2K repairs. The remaining 25% of financial services firms stated they've complete 30% or less of needed repairs. (11)

Asian banks are fighting for their very survival as a devastating recession has overcome the region. Riots have filled the streets of cities in South Korea and Indonesia. Japan's Prime Minister resigned in mid-1998 because of the nation's dire economic slide. Treasury Department officials fear the negative spiral that will be unleashed in Asia if Japan and China are forced to devalue their money.

The story in Russia, Latin America, the South Pacific, and Africa is even worse. Many nations are blissfully unaware of the impending danger. Even if they immediately declare a national emergency, the shortage of experienced computer programmers and dwindling days left to repair all their computers makes it physically impossible to accomplish such an enormous task.

What good will it be if America's banking system is Y2K compliant in a world economic system that has crashed all around us?

"No other event in history will so thoroughly expose the

vulnerability of our living and working in a world so interconnected by computers and telecommunications," Mr. Peter Miller, CIO of J.P. Morgan & Company, told the Senate's special committee on Y2K. (12)

Mr. Miller accurately described the problem when he told the Senators that making the solution more daunting "are the intricate, complex, and pervasive interdependencies among computers and computer networks that populate the world today." He said that it is "not enough that every computer, software application, and embedded chip affected by the Year 2000 be fixed. They must be fixed in ways so that they remain compatible with all the other devices with which they interoperate."

What if America's banks are Y2K compliant and there's no electricity and telephone service?

Will such disruptions have an impact on our economy?

You bet!

What if airports are closed for a month because the FAA's air traffic control system has crashed?

What if public water purification and sewage treatment plants are immobilized because of noncompliant embedded microchips? Think it will slow down the bull market?

And imagine the impact of thousands of manufacturing plants, warehouses, and office complexes shut down simultaneously for weeks or months.

Now consider the entire global supply chain in disarray. Commerce and government services in Europe, Asia, Africa, and South America coming to an abrupt halt. No parts and supplies shipped to American manufacturing plants. Oil drilling rigs silenced by Y2K. Cargo ships unable to navigate the seas. Shipping canals inoperable. Telecommunications and electricity shut down around the world.

Monetary Officials Fear Bank Failures Will Trigger Panics

Financial institutions around the world are at risk because of their interconnected relationships, warned the United States Deputy Treasury Secretary.

"All financial firms are potentially at risk," said Mr. Lawrence Summers at a Senate hearing. (13) "Even those entities which act responsibly to renovate their own systems can still be harmed, because of the intertwined nature of the financial system."

"If the failures are widespread, they can pose a threat to central markets such as an exchange or clearinghouse," the deputy secretary advised.

The Institute of International Finance, which represents 285 major financial institutions in the U.S., Europe, and Japan, says many of the world's banks are not ready for the Year 2000. The institute issued a report in April 1998 warning that there are "quite a number of banks that are just not adequately prepared for the Y2K problem." (14) Unless the computer problem is solved, the report warned, "essential business functions such as interest rate calculations and settlement systems may fail, data could be corrupted or inadvertently deleted."

"We are not assuming that everything is going to work well," confessed Mr. William Donough, President of the Federal Reserve Bank of New York to a banking industry panel. (15)

At the same panel, Ronald Reagan's former assistant secretary for Defense, Mr. Frank Gaffney, warned bankers "We have the makings of a national emergency on our hands." (16)

Another powerful global banking institution, the Bank of International Settlements, issued a statement at its April 8, 1998, meeting saying that banks that are not taking Y2K seriously would prevent worldwide testing, thus endangering all financial institutions. "Failure of these organizations to prepare adequately and share information on their plans in order to promote effective testing could lead to serious disruptions in the world's financial markets." (17)

Furthermore, the powerful Bank of International Settlements, considered the central bank for all government's central banks, told global financial leaders that "contingency plans should be considered for the potential failure of key parts of the financial market infrastructure..." (18)

The Governor of the Bank of England, Eddie George, told the BIS gathering that January 1, 2000 would be a "Day of Judgment." (19)

Another high level international banking supervisory authority, the Basle Committee on Banking Supervision, has warned that failure to address the Year 2000 issue could cause banks to declare bankruptcy. (20)

Increasingly, high-ranking banking officials are talking about contingency plans. Mr. Ernest Patrikis, First Vice President of the Federal Reserve Bank of New York, told the House Committee on Banking and Financial Services, that "contingency planning is something that most financial market authorities, particularly central banks, undertake regularly with regard to a wide variety of potential market disruptions." (21)

References to "contingency plans" are code words for, among other emergency steps, mandatory bank holidays. Some banks, such as New England's BankBoston, are scheduling back-up generators in case electrical power is interrupted.

It's the talk about bank holidays that is most chilling. Already, responsible leaders in the financial services industry are openly discussing Year 2000-mandated bank holidays.

Edward Yardeni has recommended to global leaders that governments "should consider requiring all non-essential employees to stay home during the first week of January 2000." Mr. Yardeni says, "Financial markets might have to be closed during this period." (22)

A news report by Reuters (January 16, 1998) said banking officials are debating whether to declare a bank holiday on December 31, 1999. According to Reuters, the president of the Federal Reserve Bank of New York, William McDonough, said the proposal "may offer meaningful benefits." (23)

In Singapore, computer experts are so worried about the country's banks that they are recommending to the Monetary Authority, Singapore's central bank, that all banks remain closed for the first several days of 2000. (24)

Great Britain isn't taking any chances. The British government has already established plans for a bank holiday. Officially billed as a "millennial holiday," the plan calls for Friday, December 31, 1999, to be declared a bank holiday. Because New Year's Day in 2000 will be a Saturday, banks will be closed on Monday, January 3. Therefore, England's banks will not open until Tuesday, January 4, 2000.

Bank holidays are under serious discussion because officials fear panic-stricken customers clamoring to withdraw their money if things go wrong in January 2000. Alan Greenspan, the Federal Reserve Bank chairman, has vowed that the Fed will pump billions of dollars, if necessary, into banks to keep them solvent.

The Federal Reserve Bank is worried about widespread runs on banks because of Y2K fear. According to Mr. Fred Breimyer, chief economist for the State Street Bank and Trust Company, in an article by the *Boston Journal*, the "Federal Reserve Bank and Treasury Department are very much aware this could happen, and they are making provisions for a substantial oversupply of currency to meet the currency drain." (25) The *Boston Journal* article said, " the Treasury Department is now printing extra currency, especially in large denominations such as $100 bills, in preparation for expected depositor demand for cash."

The Federal Reserve better get busy printing lots of cash.

People won't wait until January 3, 2000, to pull out their savings.

The panic will strike in late 1999 – perhaps September or October – as frightened citizens wake up to realize the computers will not be fixed in time.

The sum of U.S. notes in circulation is approximately $460 billion. The Federal Reserve Bank stores $150 billion in government vaults. Additionally, U.S. banks have another $30 billion in their vaults. What happens when tens of millions of Americans empty their checking and savings accounts, and their IRAs and 401Ks too? If 100,000,000 households each withdraw $5,000 from savings in December 1999, the sudden drain of $500 billion dollars from the monetary supply will spur the greatest depression in America's history.

Millions more, with substantial nest eggs in investment funds, will withdraw huge sums out of mutual funds. The fear of "wealth shock" – losing all the paper wealth their stocks have accrued during the boom years of the '90s – will spook everyday investors to get their wealth out immediately.

There's just not that much money in circulation.

As "purely a precautionary measure," stated a Federal Reserve official, the Federal Reserve Bank announced on August 20, 1998 it would print and store another $50 billion dollars for 1999. That would give the Federal Reserve a stash of $200 billion in its vaults.

It still isn't enough.

Even when you add the Federal Reserve's stockpile, the reserves held by banks, and printed money in circulation, there still isn't enough cash to supply a Y2K bank run in 1999. Basically, it means America's 100,000,000 families would have access to approximately $2,600 each.

New Zealand's central bank fears a bank run too. The South Pacific nation's Federal Reserve Bank announced on August 24, 1998, it would hold onto old banknotes that were scheduled to be destroyed next year.

And if American banks don't have enough to worry about, thousands of businesses – large and small – will default on loans in 2000. Like railway cars jumping the tracks, a massive train wreck will pile up on Wall Street and Main Street as companies file bankruptcy following Y2K crashes.

Finally, billions of dollars in high-risk credit derivatives will come home to roost.

Big banks will go under.

Godly judgment will come to the ungodly system of usury.

The World Financial System Will Collapse in 2000

Thomas Jefferson, America's third president and author of the Declaration of Independence, didn't trust powerful bankers.

He knew their hearts.

Their love of money would drive them to evil, leading them to someday destroy the republic Jefferson helped to found.

President Jefferson warned Americans about banks when he wrote these words:

> "If the American people ever allow private banks to control the issue of their money, first by inflation and then by deflation, the banks and corporations that will grow up around them will deprive the people of their property until their children will wake up homeless on the continent their fathers conquered."

Underneath the calm exterior of the Earth's powerful bankers and financiers, an unsettling sense of nervousness has evaded their private inner world in recent months.

They dare not show their worries to the common public.

For decades, they have dreamed about a globalized economic system. An economic order where parochial national boundaries do not exist. Where the wealthy, educated, privileged elite from the industrialized nations would finally be free to orchestrate world affairs without questioning from those beneath their class.

They are the chieftains of world commerce. Bankers, financiers, modern aristocracy, the noble scions of privileged and wealth. Regardless of their national heritage, they have no allegiance to any flag. They bow their knee to no god, except mammon. Their only commitment is to their shared vision of world rule.

One world. One people. One government. One economic system.

Patiently, they have implemented their carefully crafted plan of globalization. Compliant media and docile politicians have obliged them every step of the way. Their wealth and influence work an amazing change in the views of many, bringing everybody around to seeing the wisdom of their objectives. Behind closed doors in boardrooms, and in posh cocktail parties at exotic resorts, they smugly boast of their ability to shape and mold public opinion.

The struggle has not been easy, despite their power and influence. Success has required overcoming the simplistic, national pride of the common citizenry, whether in European nations or America. At times, political uprisings have needed to be squelched, lest the peasants become too bold.

Looking to the new millennium, these modern day royalty have fancied in their hearts and mind that the "new age" of a one-world system would soon dawn. Wars would end, political strife would cease, and national boundaries would disappear as reasoned men of privilege assume full control of worldly affairs.

Something, however, is seriously wrong.

Events are racing out of control, and they know it.

It is a doomsday scenario too scary for even a Hollywood thriller.

While their wealth is exploding exponentially during the bull market of the 1990s, in the summer of 1997 a two-bit Asian country's devaluation of its currency, the baht, triggered an economic meltdown that now threatens financial markets around the globe.

Thailand's economic malaise spread quickly to nearby Indonesia like a deadly virus. Rioting students took to the streets in Indonesia, demanding the ouster of long time ruler President Suharto. With its economy in a free fall and inflation at 100%, angry, hungry workers demanded food for their families. Food is available, but Indonesia's spiraling inflation rate and worthless money, the rupiah, has priced food out of reach for many citizens.

The financial typhoon left Indonesia and its 200 million citizens in social chaos. Next came the Philippines, Malaysia, Taiwan, and South Korea.

During the last months of 1997, most American economic gurus dismissed the "Asian flu" as a minor bump on the road to a truly global economy, a problem that, if "managed" correctly, would miraculously go away. By summer 1998, the Asian financial slump had infected other regions of the world, giving chills to investors. Hong Kong, which pegs its money to the U.S. dollar, is precariously holding onto its currency. Japan, the world's second largest economy, is mired in bad bank loans, bankruptcies, and currency depreciation. Prime Minister Hashimoto resigned in disgrace because of the worsening crisis. China, too, faces intense pressure to devalue its currency.

By Fall 1998, the tentacles of Asia's woes spread to South Africa, Australia, Europe, South America, and the United States. Russia's beleaguered stock market, having collapsed in August 1998, forcing Kremlin officials to suspend trading, continues to slide toward default. The value of Russian stocks and bonds dropped sharply following President Yeltsin's executive order raising interest rates to 150%. Following Mr. Yeltsin's decision to devalue the Russian ruble, widespread financial panic spread across Russia in   August 1998 as frightened citizens sought to withdraw their savings from shaky banks. Unpleasant repercussions are splashing upon the shores of industrialized nations with robust economies. The U.S. stock market fell 357 points in one day after Russia's economy crumbled. With Japan and other Asia countries sliding helplessly toward the cliff of deflation, American economists dusted off old college textbooks to brush up on the effects of deflation – something that the U.S. has not experienced since the Great Depression.

European and American businesses are bracing themselves for a flood of cheap Asian products to hit their markets as prices dropped even further.

With economists scratching their heads and wondering how to deal with falling prices in a globalized economy, many Wall Street tycoons are worrying that deflation could be so contagious, Asia may drag down the whole world into its quagmire.

All eyes are on Japan and China. Deepening gloom about Asian economies continue to weaken the Japanese yen and Chinese renminbi. Compounding the Asian troubles, North and South Korea and China were ravaged by the worst floods in early 50 years. In China, the overflowing treacherous banks of the Yangtze River swept away 17 million houses and killed thousands of people. Further north, China's Nen River overflowed in what was described as the worst flooding in China's history. The massive flooding in China and torrential rains in Korea devastated both nations' agricultural economy. Fears for the future of Asia continued to rattle fretful investors around the world. Further deterioration of Asian economies would spread more bouts of Asian contagion, triggering a global recession, or worse.

By early September 1998, the Dow Jones Industrial Average had fallen over 1,700 points from its all-time peak of 9,337 just a month earlier.

Other troubling signs are visible too. Saddled with consumer debt, more Americans filed for bankruptcy in the fiscal year that ended June 30, 1998, than any previous year in the history of the United States.

Federal Reserve chairman Alan Greenspan told the Senate Banking

Committee that "Conditions in Asia are of a particular concern..." (26) Mr. Greenspan worries about the American economy's interconnection with the global economy. "The risk of further adverse developments in these economies remain substantial," Mr. Greenspan said, "and given the pervasive interconnections of virtually all economies and financial systems in the world today, the associated uncertainties for the United States and other developed economies remain substantial as well."

It wasn't supposed to happen this way.

In the eyes of the world's financiers and investors, everything was nearing perfection. A New York broker was quoted by the Washington Times (August 12, 1998) saying, "Things are as close to perfect for the capital markets as one could have ever hoped for: a government budget surplus, virtually no inflation, sustained corporate profit growth...a multi-year big shift into equities by individual investors." (27)

"Anything," he said, "that seems to potentially threaten perfection can greatly unsettle the markets."

The new millennium was supposed to be the dawn of the New World Order.

Right before the eyes of the world's bankers and financial tycoons, the globalized economy is in a deflationary free fall.

The Asian meltdown threatens to suck the entire world into a giant financial black hole. Investors fear that the dual collapse of the Japanese and Chinese economies will, most likely, be the sucker punch to America's kidneys that drops us to our knees.

Compounding the dilemma, every business and government agency in the world must completely repair their computers to eliminate the Y2K virus before January 2000. Asian bankers and corporate executives have their hands full trying to put out the raging fires, let alone have time to fix their computers.

Likewise, European banks and corporations are enthralled in the glorious thought of the new European Monetary Union. They have little interest or time in Year 2000 computer problems. The Euro comes first.

Meanwhile, scientists are espousing serious warnings about the upcoming Leonid meteor showers and the new solar maximum geomagnetic storms.

It's all coming to a head in 1999.

Just when the world's privileged class thought they had everything under control, everything falls apart!

Life is not fair.

The world's powerful moneylenders are not prepared for the awful calamity that is about to befall them.

Earth's six billion people are not aware of the momentous catastrophe that is waiting in late 1999.

There will be substantial gut-wrenching anguish by the wealthy.

Sadly,   there   will   be   much   heartbreaking   suffering   by hundreds of millions of average folks.

The total collapse of the world's economic system will be more than some people can bear. Many will commit suicide rather than face a bleak, unknown future without life's luxuries.

Others will wonder streets like zombies, unable to emotionally and mentally deal with reality.

For the world's high-powered elite, a cruel hoax will be discovered.

While the rich and powerful manipulated the masses to help them establish the foundation for the New World Order, the privileged elite will realize that they were used and manipulated too. To their astonishment, these titans of finance will realize they've been deceived by one of their own. Having manipulated the lowly masses for years for their self-serving purposes, they will shutter at the realization they were pawns too.

A craftier, more skillful deceiver will use them to lay the groundwork for his empire. "A snake in the grass!" his former allies will call him. A snake indeed!

Yes, a New World Order will rise in the aftermath of the Year 2000 debacle, but not the world order they envisioned. It will be the New World Disorder.

Their plans will be reduced to ashes and rubble. All their wealth will evaporate. The manipulated masses will violently rise up; seeking revenge for the horrific suffering that has come upon the world. No mansion will be safe from marauding gangs searching for food and valuables.

Immediately following the worldwide computer crash, this soon-to-be global ruler will quickly ascend to a prominent position of leadership. Taking advantage of the anarchy and confusion, he will consolidate his political, economic, and military strength with blinding speed. With even the rich and powerful in shock, his calm execution of a carefully crafted plan will go unnoticed.

During the first two years, chaos will engulf the nations. Perilous times will rock the foundations of every institution. No nation will be spared from troubles.

So great will be the woes that both the modest multitudes and enlightened elite will cry out for deliverance. Anything will be better than the wretched conditions overwhelming both rich and poor.

Finally, when the suffering and despair reach unbearable levels, the world's "savior" will step forward. He'll have a plan. A new system. A way to bring order and prosperity to the nations. People will be ready.

With blinding speed, this inspiring world leader will amass enormous power. He will command unyielding allegiance.

The world's formerly powerful and wealthy elite, scions of the privileged classes, will be shocked and dismayed. They will marvel in disbelief when they see how cunning and cruel he becomes once gaining the power he covets.

They will fear him.

They will obey him.

He will wage war against many nations.

Y2K is about more than two-digit date codes. Y2K threatens more than America's economy. It threatens the entire global economic and political system.

It will crash.

A new cashless system will arise from the ashes.

People around the world will desperately cry out for a solution to the calamity. This powerful global politician will emerge to lead the world out of financial and social chaos.

To survive and prosper in the new system, you'll be required to openly show your submission and allegiance to his ultimate authority. That's the price he'll demand to alleviate the world's woes.

Billions will eagerly receive his mark.

Sounds like something from the Book of the Revelation.

Imagine that.

And you thought Y2K was a lot of hype!

18 Insurance: Sorry, Your Policy Doesn't Cover a Global Catastrophe!

"This is a very real potential insurance coverage problem...these claims are going to be severe..."

> *Joshua Gold — Law Partner*
> *Anderson, Kill & Olick*
> *Remarks at 1998 annual meeting of the*
> *Insurance Management Society*

Insurance executives fear the Y2K computer bug.

And for good reasons.

It gives them nightmares. No, they don't dream about six-foot bugs destroying their computers.

Actually, the major insurance companies got a head start over banks, brokerages, and other big financial conglomerates in getting their computers ready for the Year 2000.

So, what do executives see in their Y2K nightmares?

Trial lawyers.

Hordes of hungry, Y2K-crazed trial lawyers.

Like the wicked witch's army of long-tailed, flying monkeys in the Wizard of Oz, insurance executives toss and turn at night dreaming about swarms of shrieking lawyers descending on the front lawns of courthouses in every city and town.

Whipped into an uncontrollable litigious frenzy, trial lawyers are eagerly preparing to attack the fat cash reserves of insurance companies like a flock of starving demonic buzzards.

Yuk! It won't be a pretty site.

Embedded Chips Give Property and Casualty Companies Y2K Panic Attacks

More than two-fifths of small manufacturers in the United States have yet to implement a Y2K program, according to a survey released by the National Association of Manufacturers. As of mid-1998, a substantial number of manufacturers are seriously underestimating the threat of Y2K to their viability. The NAM study shows that one-fourth of all small manufacturers have not taken any steps toward fixing their computer systems.

At the heart of insurance companies' fears are embedded microchips in manufacturing plants. Potential microchip-related problems include damage caused by computer-controlled production systems failures, fire and explosions, malfunctioning machine safety guards, fire alarm and sprinkler failures, computer-controlled destruction of inventory, elevator malfunctions, and failures in heating/air conditioning equipment.

A real-life example of embedded microchip problems surfaced in 1996 at a New Zealand foundry. When computer systems could not deal with an unexpected Leap Year date, it shut down all the smelters at the Tawai Point Aluminum plant in Southland, New Zealand. Because temperature controls in the smelters failed, substantial damage was inflicted on the foundry's expensive equipment.

To their shock, insurance companies are discovering the unlimited possibilities for trouble caused by malfunctioning embedded microchips. There are large numbers of manufacturing machinery that operate by time-sensitive or date-sensitive embedded microprocessors. Assembly line manufacturing processes, therefore, are particularly susceptible to expensive Y2K losses. Because embedded chips are integrated into a machine's internal components, the business owner may not be aware of its existence.

Newspaper publishers using integrated computer systems to edit copy, arrange layout, and download each page directly to their printing presses could experience Y2K complications. If their software uses 9/9/99 as a code for "end of file" or "material not to be published," editors may come to work on September 9, 1999, to find that the presses ran all night printing thousands of blank newspaper pages. In such a real-life scenario, the publisher's damages would be limited to financial losses from wasted paper, ink, and lost sales at newsstands.

A similar type of potential problem would be a food processor's computer-controlled inventory system automatically ordering freshly packaged food to be destroyed since the computer thinks the January 2000 expiration date is January 1900. Again, the damages are monetary losses to the business owner.

A second type of potential business loss would be malfunction machinery, such as a metal lathe cutting into its spindle, which causes significant physical damage to the machine itself, to other machines on the assembly line, or other physical property. In this scenario, the business owner would suffer monetary damages in repairing or replacing the damaged equipment.

More worrisome to insurance companies is the potential for death or dismemberment by accidents in the workplace caused by malfunctioning embedded chips. For example, a computer-managed cooling system in a chemical processing plant could fail to regulate temperatures. A fiery explosion could result in the death or serious physical injuries to employees and nearby residents.

Property and casualty insurance companies are also concerned about potential problems caused by embedded chips in large buildings, including factories, offices, and apartment dwellings. Those expected to be at considerable risk include centralized facilities management systems, fire control systems, elevators and escalators, energy management systems, building security systems, and environmental management systems. Vaults, time clocks, mailroom equipment, and water/sewage treatment facilities are also at risk.

Manufacturers purchase equipment breakdown insurance to cover unplanned and uncontrolled equipment shutdowns. A royal battle is now brewing between business customers who believe their insurance already covers any Y2K problems, and property and casualty insurance companies who say Y2K is neither unplanned or uncontrolled.

The fight is over what constitutes "covered equipment" and an unplanned or uncontrolled "accident."

Property and casualty insurance companies offer manufacturers what are called "boiler and machinery policies." Such policies provide coverage for physical damage to "covered property, business interruption, extra expense, and spoilage." Damages must be the result of an "accident" defined as a "sudden and accidental breakdown of the covered equipment or a part of the covered equipment." (1)

Insurance companies are saying that Y2K problems are not their problem.

According to recent announcements by major insurers, the monkey is being put on the backs of small business owners. Insurance companies reason that Y2K is a "known" problem that business owners have a responsibility to fix before January 1, 2000.

Attorneys and business analysts say big insurance companies are plainly planning to shift the burden to their customers.

Insurance Companies to Customers: "We're Outta Here!"

Insurers see the storm clouds on the horizon.

They don't like what they see.

An avalanche of litigation will hit them in 2000 that will make the asbestos lawsuits of the 1980s look like a family picnic with lawyers and insurers.

Coning & Company, a Hartford-based firm providing asset management services to insurers, issued a 63-page report in July 1998 entitled "Insurers and the Year 2000 Computer Bug – The Tower of Babel Revisited." The Coning report said the insurance industry faces significant exposure from claims arising from Y2K damages. Mr. Mark Trencher, assistant vice president for the company, said the claims "conceivably could be much bigger than any hurricane or catastrophic event we've ever seen." (2)

Mr. Trencher said insurers doing business with governments, especially health insurers, are particularly vulnerable to Y2K-related lawsuits because government agencies are seriously behind schedule in dealing with the Year 2000.

Other insurance executives are echoing Mr. Trencher's warnings. "Every insurer...is terrified of the magnitude of what consequential damages will mean as the result of the Year 2000," the *National Underwriter* quoted Mr. John Love as saying, who is a principal with Armfield, Harrison and Thomas, an insurance and surety bond broker in Virginia. (3)

Insurance companies say they want to wash their hands of Year 2000 damages.

It is no wonder.

Lloyds of London says Y2K lawsuits could total $1trillion.

Nervous over horrendous damages, insurers have succeeded in persuading state insurance regulators to allow them to exclude Y2K-related damages from most insurance policies – even if they don't tell customers. By August 1998, the powerful insurance industry had won such concessions in all states except Alaska, Maine, and Massachusetts. Texas adopted modified regulations denying insurance companies permission to arbitrarily cut off insurance on small businesses with revenues under $10 million.

The Insurance Services Office, a New York City organization representing 2,900 insurance companies, carried out the dirty work for the insurance industry. Among the proposals touted by the ISO to state regulators, one calls for allowing "total exclusion for losses attributable to problems associated with the change to the year 2000." (4)

Their reasoning is simple: Y2K is not an insurance problem.

"We don't believe it's an insurance problem," said Mr. Steven Goldstein, a spokesman for the Insurance Information Institute in an interview by *Dow Jones News Service*.(5) Across the Atlantic Ocean, the response is the same. "The millennium bug is a man-made problem," says Mr. Phil Bell, technical manager for Royal & SunAlliance, a major travel insurance company in Great Britain. "The costs of putting it right should fall upon the business." (6)

Insurers also defend the policy exclusions by saying there is no precedent for a worldwide computer crash, therefore there is no way to project their exposure to risk. Since policyholders have not paid any premiums for Y2K protection, the insurance companies have no funds set aside for Y2K liabilities.

As with all disputes, the issue of liability depends on whose interpretation of the policy's contract language you decide to believe. Insurance executives believe they have no choice but to take the hard line in the Year 2000. They see legions of Y2K ambulance chasers massing at the borders, ready to lay siege to insurance companies' gold-lined coffers.

That's why major insurers are putting customers on notice that they are responsible for fixing their Y2K problems now. American International Group (AIG) sent letters in June 1998 to policyholders urging them to deal with Y2K problems. CAN Insurance Company, Travelers Property Casualty Corporation, Chubb Corporation, and Reliance National Insurance Company have mailed similar letters too.

Signed by Mr. Thomas Tizzio, senior vice chairman, AIG's letter warned policyholders that Year 2000 glitches might produce erroneous calculations or cause equipment to malfunction. "Inventory and accounting systems will be affected; so will credit-card validation, electronic data interchange, automated banking reports, pension benefit payments, drug distribution systems for pharmacies and hospitals, and mechanical systems operating everything from office building environmental controls and elevator banks to telephone switches and oil refineries." (7)

Mr. Tizzio concluded his letter by warning, "The potential for dislocation from Year 2000 problems is unprecedented."

Attorneys believe the AIG letter, and similar insurance mailings, to policyholders is a preemptive move to cover their backsides. Insurance companies can argue that they warned policyholders of the impending danger. Failure to fix their computers, therefore, is not the fault of the insurers.

When claims hit the courtrooms, the heart of the defense by insurance companies will be that Y2K is not "fortuitous," meaning an accident occurring entirely by chance. You cannot insure against something that is likely to happen. Likewise, you cannot insure, the companies argue, against something within your control. On the other hand, trial lawyers will argue, "Yes, my client heard the weather forecast for rain, but the weatherman didn't say it would be a 40-day monsoon."

Other insurers will be making exclusions prior to January 2000. Already, some travel insurance companies in England have announced exclusions to policies relating to Y2K problems. CGU, the biggest insurance group and travel underwriter in the United Kingdom, plans to exclude claims made for policyholders who die or suffer personal injuries from Y2K-related accidents. Also, several British companies have warned homeowners not to expect their homes or automobiles to be covered by damages caused by Y2K failures.

Special Y2K insurance, however, is available if you have enough money to pay the premiums. American International Group is selling a Millennium Insurance policy paying up to $100 million in claims related to Y2K business interruptions and legal liability. The circuit-blowing premiums reportedly start at $65 million.

Lawyers for insurance companies maintain that the Y2K issue needs only clarification, not a written policy change. Under such legal reasoning, insurance companies would not be legally obligated to notify policyholders that Y2K damages are excluded from coverage.

A report released by the Gartner Group (August 11, 1998) sums up the surprise waiting millions of policyholders in January 2000.

The Gartner Group report says people assuming they're automatically covered for Year 2000 disasters and damages "may be in for a rude awakening." (8)

Corporate Directors Face Serious Liability Exposure

Corporate executives and members of boards of directors are in the sights of trial lawyers.

Lawyers are expected to file an avalanche of lawsuits accusing corporate officers of negligence in failing to prepare their companies for the Year 2000.

The threat is so severe that one major insurer specializing in liability coverage for executives saw its stock price tumble after Moody's Investors Services issued a warning. Moody's report on Executive Risk Inc. triggered a Wall Street sell-off of the company's shares.

Executive Risk, and other major underwriters of directors' and officers' liability insurance, may be left paying the tab for policyholders who get sued by people claiming they were damaged from Y2K problems. Two companies, AIG and Chubb, control two-thirds of the $3 billion insurance market for executive liability insurance. While AIG and Chubb are diversified into other types of insurance, Executive Risk makes most of its money from protecting company executives.

Called D&O insurance, it is essential in today's litigious society. Banks require D&O insurance before they'll issue multimillion-dollar loans.

Major insurers are circulating reports warning that standard D&O insurance may not cover directors and officers from Y2K lawsuits. Moody's report says D&O is one of the few insurance policies tied directly to business risk, such as loss of revenue, earnings, and stock prices.

The possibilities for lawsuits against corporate officers are endless. Electric utility executives could be sued if the power plant fails, shutting off electricity to the local hospital and resulting in deaths of patients. Executives of manufacturing plants could be sued by family members of employees killed by Y2K-related accidents inside plants. Shareholders may sue directors and officers if the company's stock price falls because the firm must refund millions of dollars to angry consumers who purchased electronic products that fail to operate after January 2000.

Year 2000 Could Make Insurance Companies Insolvent

Insurance companies are in big trouble.

It is not surprising they're starting to get their wagons in a circle.

Marauding bands of war-painted savages carrying briefcases are atop the hills sizing them up for the kill.

The insurance industry has its hands full getting their own houses in order for the Year 2000. State Farm Insurance started in 1989 to tackle its 70 million lines of computer code. The company has 2,000 third-party software applications and 475,000 data processing items too. Despite their early start, State Farm was not Y2K compliant by fall 1998. Medical Mutual of Ohio, a giant $2 billion medical insurance company, started early too. The company is scrambling to meet its end-of-year deadline in 1998 to start one-year of critical testing. Prudential Insurance Company, having spent over $100 million so far on its 170 million lines of code, pledges to be Y2K compliant by the end of 1998 too.

The insurance industry is extremely date-sensitive. Becoming Y2K compliant is not an option. Its "do or die" for an industry that depends on computers to calculate life insurance cash values, policy expiration dates, and the ages of policyholders. Insurance companies are also dependent on the telecommunications industry to keep telephone and data transmission lines up and running.

The need to fix their computers is urgent. Problems will start in fourth quarter '98 and first quarter '99 when insurance companies start processing data that crosses over into the Year 2000, such as 1999 policy renewals.

AMP, a giant insurer in Australia, warned in July 1998 that the company couldn't guarantee that it would make the deadline for Y2K compliance, despite having spent over $135 million so far.

Claims management also poses severe problems for insurers. Error-free data is required for actuarial analysis, policy coverage, cost allocations, and OSHA reporting. Even without Y2K, logic errors and physical data-entry errors are common. Data error rates average between 4 and 8 per cent industry-wide. Because there are no universal standards for claims data processing, many data errors go undetected. The flow of corrupted data in the Year 2000 could crash insurance computers.

Data networks are another dangerous minefield. In addition to cleaning up their own networks, insurers must also verify third-party entities such as brokers, dealers, and state government regulatory commissions are Y2K compliant too.

Insurance companies also face federal government scrutiny in their fiduciary responsibility to handle billions of dollars worth of pension funds. Legislation is pending in Congress requiring pension plan fiduciaries to determine that no pension funds are placed in any investments that are not Y2K compliant.

Insurance companies could get burned by the sun too. And falling meteors could punch big holes in their cash reserves. Should several satellites be destroyed by geomagnetic storms from the sun's Cycle 23 solar maximum, or damaged by thousands of meteors in November 1999, satellite operators will cash in their insurance policies for big claims.

All of this could not hit the insurance industry at a worse time.

Insurance companies have been hemorrhaging huge chunks of cash for several years, paying out claims resulting from numerous natural catastrophes. Earthquakes, floods, droughts, and fires are hitting populated regions of the United States. Losses from these natural disasters are quickly depleting the once fat cash reserves of insurance companies. For example, during a two-month period in 1994, Hurricanes Andrew and Iniki – plus other weather-related damages – hit insurance companies for over $21 billion in claims. Current cash reserves in the United States are only $380 billion. With Lloyds of London predicting a $1 trillion price tag for Y2K damages, cash reserves could easily disappear.

As we race toward the third millennium, the world's insurance companies have everything on the line.

They are one of the most date-dependent, computer-dependent industries in the world. Their future business viability hinges totally on their ability to become 100% Y2K compliant soon.

Their future also depends on the telephone companies becoming compliant too.

Y2K compliance, however, is the least of their problems. Angry victims of Y2K disasters, accidents, financial losses, and inconveniences will overwhelm their claims offices with billions of dollars worth of damages.

A couple of big, expensive satellites getting knocked out could knock out insurance companies too.

Unexpected natural disasters – such as hurricanes, tornadoes, and earthquakes – would sink their ships.

Homeowners and small business owners should forget about expecting coverage for Y2K damages to their families and properties.

The insurance companies have no plans to pay up. Y2K insurance is only available to the rich who are willing to pay umpteen millions to get it.

They say your policy only covers "acts of God." And Y2K is not an act of God!

Hmmmm?

Maybe there's a loophole.

Judgment on an evil world is an act of God.

19

Aviation:
Fasten Your Seatbelt.
Y2K Turbulence Ahead!

"If all the mission critical components of the aviation system have not been demonstrated to be Y2K compliant, aircraft will not leave the ground."

> *Congresswoman Constance Morella*
> *Opening remarks at the Congressional hearing of the*
> *Technology Subcommittee of the House Science*
> *Committee Regarding the Federal Aviation Administration*
> *August 6, 1998*

Everything appeared normal on that late spring morning on June 5, 1998.

Soaring at 27,000 feet above the Earth, President Bill Clinton was onboard Air Force One. The President was on his way to Bedford, MA, to give a commencement speech at the Massachusetts Institute of Technology.

Having departed from Andrews Air Force Base in Maryland, the Boeing 747 was over Robinsville, NJ, at 8:11 AM. Suddenly, the President's aircraft completely vanished from the radar screens of air traffic controllers tracking the White House entourage.

For the next 48 seconds, Air Force One was invisible. All of the President's flight data was lost momentarily.

Air Force One was being tracked with data from Federal Aviation Administration radar in Gibbsboro, NJ, located 15 miles southeast of Philadelphia. The FAA air traffic controller handling the President's flight was stationed in Ronkonkoma, NY.

"Radar contact lost. Stay your position," the air traffic controller quickly alerted the President's pilots.

Four minutes later, radar contact with Air Force One was lost again for 37 seconds, about 10 miles south of New York City's LaGuardia Airport.

"At no time was there a safety issue," FAA spokesman, Paul Takemoto, told reporters. (1)

The FAA acknowledged, however, that the Gibbsboro ground-based radar station was the same facility blamed for a near-collision of a Swissair jumbo jet and a small plane in October 1997. The FAA also admitted the Gibbsboro station had lost Air Force One in March on another flight.

The FAA radar stations around the country have been troubled since going into operation in 1997. The Gibbsboro station was taken off-line for troubleshooting. Following repairs, the FAA returned the station to service about four months before the Air Force One error. The FAA now believes the problem is a generic flaw in radar systems used nationwide.

In an eerie coincidence, hundreds of flights were delayed for an hour on the same morning at New York City's three airports. A computer glitch at TRACON, which stands for Terminal Radar Approach Control, disrupted hundreds of the Big Apple's early morning flights at LaGuardia, JFK, and Newark airports.

A FAA spokesperson said the FAA didn't "know exactly what caused it." (2)

The New York Times, however, reported that computer technicians working on TRACON's midnight shift were testing new software intended to fix a computer glitch. According to the New York Times article, a union official said computer engineers were trying to install a software patch on about 50 workstations. After failing to properly install the software, the technicians decided to switch back to the old software.

Air traffic controllers' computer screens froze. TRACON handles arriving and departing flights within 50 miles of the airports. When the old system was brought back up, the system began losing flight data such as the altitude and airspeed of aircraft approaching New York City.

Two serious computer glitches over the heavily traveled East Coast corridor on the same morning illustrate the risks passengers unknowingly take upon boarding aircraft. Passengers simply assume that the FAA air traffic control system works without problems. After all, their lives depend on controllers handling hundreds of complicated flight movements based solely on the accuracy of data on their computer screens.

Air traffic controller mistakes are sharply climbing. During the first half of 1998, air traffic controller errors increased 20 percent. An examination of FAA reports show that the New York City region has experienced the highest error rates.

Airline industry analysts say many of the errors are contributed to mental lapses by controllers. Faced with a shortage of 2,000 controllers, the FAA's air traffic controllers are overworked and stressed. Furthermore, many controllers are approaching retirement age.

The radar loss of Air Force One, computer glitches at TRACON, and numerous near-misses are warning signs that America's heavily computerized air traffic control system is ready to snap.

Y2K will wreck havoc worldwide on air traffic.

The FAA's computer technicians are scrambling to keep the agency's aging computer system held together with rubber bands and chewing gum. It won't make it through the millennium.

GAO Warns FAA Will Run Out of Time To Fix Computers

Jane Garvey, the FAA's Administrator, says she will board a jet on the East Coast at midnight on December 31, 1999, and fly to the West Coast. Ray Long, the FAA's new Y2K director, will be onboard too.

Both say the New Year's Eve flight will demonstrate their full confidence in America's air traffic control system in the year 2000.

First class seating shouldn't be a problem for the dynamic duo. Most likely, they'll have the entire plane to themselves.

Most people possessing any reasonable amount of knowledge about Y2K don't plan to be anywhere near an airport during the first few weeks of January 2000.

So far, the FAA has amassed one of the most dismal records among federal agencies for botching computer network repairs. The FAA is also one of the most tardy federal agencies in getting started on Y2K projects.

The agency didn't take Y2K seriously until several members of Congress ripped into them in February 1998 following a scathing report by the General Accounting Office. The GAO blistered the FAA's hide, saying the agency was slow, was behind schedule in Y2K basics, didn't have a Y2K manager, and didn't even know how much the FAA would be impacted by Y2K problems.

Joel Willemssen, the GAO's Director of Accounting and Information Management Division, delivered the public scolding. Mr. Willemssen told the congressional committee:

"FAA's progress in making its systems ready for the year 2000 has been too slow. At its current pace, it will not make it in time. The agency has been severely behind schedule in completing basic awareness activities, including establishing a program manager with responsibility for its Year 2000 program and issuing a final, overall Year 2000 strategy. Further, FAA does not know the extent of its Year 2000 problem because it has not completed key assessment activities. Specifically, it has yet to analyze the impact of its systems' not being Year 2000 compliant, inventory and assess all of its systems for date dependencies, make final its plans for addressing any identified date dependencies, or develop plans for continued operations in case systems are not corrected in time. Until these activities are completed, FAA cannot know the extent to which it can trust its systems to operate safely using dates beyond 1999." (3)

A cursory examination of the scope of the FAA's responsibilities easily reveals the agencies reliance on computers. The FAA has developed a vast network of aviation technologies and interconnected systems. Foremost, the agency is responsible for air traffic control facilities at the nation's airports. The FAA also operates nearly 100 flight standards offices, which supervises airline inspections. Data exchange relationships have also been established between the FAA and the National Weather Service, the Defense Department, and numerous airlines, aircraft manufacturers, commercial pilots, and other groups.

The GAO's Y2K said without properly operating computer systems, the "FAA could not effectively control air-traffic, target airlines for inspection, or provide up-to-date weather conditions to pilots and air traffic controllers." (4)

By waiting so late to start working on their computers, Mr. Willemssen warned that "time is running out for the FAA to renovate all its systems..." and that the FAA's delays "put the agency at great risk."

The FAA's failure to repair, test, and validate all of its mission-critical systems in such as short period of time, Mr. Willemssen advised, "could result in the temporary grounding of flights until safe aircraft control can be assured."

If the GAO needed to prove their point about the FAA's disoriented approach to the Year 2000, the FAA provided the evidence themselves just weeks prior to the congressional hearing. It was a classic example of bureaucratic confusion.

One team of computer technicians at the FAA promised to have all the Y2K bugs fixed within 90 days. A second team announced in late January 1998 that the FAA would replace the computers, at a cost of $100 million, because they doubted the changes could be made and tested within the remaining time.

Other FAA officials said, however, they didn't think all the computers could be replaced with new ones in the remaining time either!

Then, at an aviation conference, Dr. George Donohue, the FAA's associate administrator for research and acquisitions, said the FAA would do both – debug and replace computers – at the same time because it was a good "belt and suspenders approach." (5) "We are trying to do both because it gives us the highest assurance and insurance," explained Drucella Anderson, a spokeswoman for the FAA.

Jane Garvey, the FAA Administrator, said in February 1998 that the agency would continue to pursue its two-prong strategy – fixing old computers and replacing them at the same time.

It is no wonder that the FAA was publicly scolded by the White House Office of Management and Budget too. The OMB issued a report in December 1997 saying that the Department of Transportation had only fixed 7% of its mission-critical systems.

Guess who is dragging down the Transportation Department's Y2K scores?

"The Department of Transportation continues to be at high risk of system failure in the year 2000, in large part because of poor progress by the Federal Aviation Administration," the OMB charged in their report. (6)

Another expert told the panel that even "if the FAA stops slipping their schedule, they would miss their deadline by more than seven months." (7) Mr. Stanley Graham, a management consultant who specializes in IBM mainframes, said that if the FAA continues to slip behind schedule at its present rate, "they would finish almost nine and a half years late."

Jane Garvey, the FAA's administrator, however, promised Congressional leaders in early 1998 that the FAA would be Y2K compliant by November 1999 – thus allowing a month to test the repairs before January 1, 2000.

FAA Ignores IBM Warning to Junk Old Computers

Complicating the FAA's task is the scope of the massive network of 657 computer systems, which is comprised of 433 mission-critical systems with 23 million lines of code written in 50 different computer languages.

At the heart of the FAA's Y2K headache, however, is its dependency on outdated IBM mainframe computers. Every day the FAA uses some of the oldest hardware and software in the world. Some of the computers were built with technology from the 1950s and 1960s, including the last vacuum tubes anywhere!

Referred to as HOST computers, the FAA is the last remaining user of ancient IBM 3083 mainframe computers. The outdated 1970s units comprise a very large and extremely important part of the National Airspace System (NAS). All 20 air traffic control centers in the U.S. are tied together by the HOST computers, which analyze and collate radar data for the nation's air traffic system.

The FAA also relies on a fleet of back-up electrical generators. Over 88% of its generators are at least 20 years old, and nearly 50% are over 30 years old. The average life span for the generators is 15 years. Therefore, if major cities are hit with electric utility shutdowns on January 1, 2000, the FAA's backup generators may blow a fuse themselves.

For years, the FAA has attempted to modernize its aging fleet of mainframes. The agency announced in 1983 plans to update its computer systems. Despite years of labor and billions of misspent tax dollars, the FAA still uses its old IBM mainframes with their outdated vacuum tubes. The GAO estimates that the FAA spent $2.649 billion on a system called Advanced Automation Service (AAS). Following numerous delays, redesigns, and cost-overruns, the program was finally canceled in 1994. Allowing for parts of the new program that were salvaged, the GAO says, "$1.5 billion in capital and support contract costs were completely wasted." (8) The GAO did not include the labor cost of 100 employees working on the project for about 10 years.

With the FAA's dismal track record on replacing computer systems, few people have confidence the agency can get ready for the Year 2000 in such a short period of time.

So it came as no surprise that IBM issued a stern warning to the FAA urging the agency to scrap the old mainframes. The giant company flatly told the FAA that the old IBM 3083 mainframes were written in hundreds of thousands of lines of computer language – called microcode – that IBM does not know how to read and interpret today! In a letter to the FAA dated October 2, 1997, IBM warned the agency, "Analysis of 3083 microcode involves reviewing hundreds of thousands of lines of microcode written in several different protocols... IBM does not have the skills employed today that understand the microcode implemented in the 3083 well enough to conduct an appropriate Year-2000 assessment. In addition, the tools required to properly analyze the microcode do not exist.' (9)

IBM concluded its letter saying, "The appropriate skills and tools do not exist to conduct a complete Year 2000 test assessment" of the computers. "IBM believes it is imperative that the FAA replace the equipment" before the year 2000.

Other aviation professionals have publicly sounded the alarm. Mr. Michael Fanfalone, President of the Professional Airways System, told a Congressional subcommittee in February 1998 that the "FAA has known for at least two years that its 1970s' vintage IBM 3083 HOST computers would become suspect after midnight on December 31, 1999." (10)

Testifying before the House Appropriations Subcommittee on Transportation and Related Agencies, Mr. Fanfalone made it clear that the FAA was playing with fire by continuing to rely on the IBM 3083 mainframes. "The Y2K threat exists in the HOST microcode, which is used to control the inner processes of the computer," Mr. Fanfalone explained. "While initial testing has been done, the FAA has not confirmed how much of the threat is real, and whether or not it is correctable. If problems with the microcode are found, IBM has said it would make its best effort to correct the problem, but would not guarantee that all the errors are found and corrected. In other words, if we use this microcode beyond December 31, 1999, the FAA would not be guaranteed that the Y2K problem was resolved. The threat is made more significant because Y2K problems were also found in the self-checking maintenance software. These systems are NOT ready for the year 2000, and the FAA does not yet have an agreed-upon plan or funding to remedy the matter."

It gets worse!

IBM told the FAA that its HOST computer system contains eight key hardware units in each mainframe that have an end-of-service life by December 31, 1999! The main processor has a September 30, 1998, end-of-service life! (11)

This means IBM is telling the FAA that its mainframe computers are nothing but "boat anchors" after December 31, 1999. The units were built in the 1970s with the expectation of never being in use beyond

1999!

"This is old equipment, and it is well past its natural life cycle," said IBM spokesman Craig Lowder. (12)

According to Mr. Kenneth Mead, Inspector General of the Department of Transportation, IBM has notified the FAA that the processor in the 3083 model uses Thermal Conduction Modules, which contain processing chips. The unit has a cooling pump system that prevents the system from overheating. The computer chip that turns on the pump is date-dependent, therefore affected by Y2K. Should the cooling system not turn on at the correct day and time, the unit could overheat – thereby shutting down the HOST computer.

Additionally, IBM specified that modules needed to be refurbished after seven years to prevent helium leaking from seals. The FAA never refurbished the modules.

Because of the age of the IBM 3083s, spare parts for repairs are almost nonexistent. According to IBM's report, the modules are failing at an increasing rate. "The total number of modules that failed in 1997 was three times the number that failed in 1995." (13) The most critical shortage is the CLVM module, which the FAA uses 96 of these modules in computers around the nation. IBM has conducted a worldwide search for spare modules.

IBM has a grand total of six modules in their entire worldwide inventory.

There's also a shortage of professionals who understand the ancient microcode – the computer's language. Mr. Fanfalone said, "There's only two folks at IBM who know the microcode, and they're both retired."

Presto! FAA Says Magic Words and Becomes Y2K Compliant Overnight

With Congress and the GAO breathing down their necks, the FAA bureaucrats felt the heat. Because they fiddled around so long getting started, they had not even completed their initial assessment of computers – the very first step in a lengthy process to become Y2K compliant. The FAA schedule called for completing its assessment by mid-1998, and having its software, hardware, and firmware Y2K-certified by November 1, 1999!

Intense public scrutiny was making life very uncomfortable.

Then, an amazing thing happened!

Those bureaucrats discovered the Yellow Brick Road.

Miraculously, the situation improved!

First, the FAA abandoned their November 1999 deadline. It was obvious the date was scaring too many folks. So, they bumped it up to June 1999. The GAO's Mr. Willemmsen, however, said the projections "are based on very optimistic schedules that may not prove to be realistic." (14) With so little time left, "it is doubtful this can be done."

Next, President Clinton's Y2K Czar, Mr. John Koskinen, determined that the FAA could still function even if all Y2K work stopped in mid-1998. Earlier in the year, the Office of Management and Budget reported that the Department of Transportation, which is over the FAA, had only 38% of its core systems compliant. Mr. Koskinen said the FAA's backup system could handle 70% of regularly scheduled flights, allowing flights to be paced equal to flights in bad weather.

As the summer of 1998 arrived, the skies over the FAA became sunnier. Jane Garvey announced on July 30, 1998, that – somehow, some way – the FAA had repaired 70% of air traffic systems, including 67% of its mission-critical systems.

The FAA was on a roll!

Maybe Bill Clinton didn't inhale, but somebody at the FAA did!

That became obvious in July 1998 when Jane Garvey announced that "aggressive testing" proved those old IBM mainframes wouldn't crash until 2007!

It seems the FAA hired, as consultants, those two remaining retired IBM computer technicians who understood the microcodes. Using a spare IBM mainframe, they conducted tests on the 23-year-old computer at the FAA's technical center in Atlantic City, NJ. Because the mainframe considered 1975 – its date of introduction – as "Year 01," they determined that the mainframes stores dates between one and 32. Therefore, the mainframe's rollover date would be 2007, not 2000.

Just think, they were going to trash those worn-out dinosaurs because the manufacturer – IBM – said there was no way they would guarantee the old computers would last beyond December 1999!

Yep! The good ol' FAA – the agency that "completely wasted" $1.5 billion on computers it couldn't figure out for 10 years how to install – certainly wasn't going to throw out perfectly good vintage 1975 mainframes just because IBM says they're trash!

What does IBM know about computers?

"We're not in a position to pass judgment on their tests," IBM spokesman Mark Nelson was quoted as saying in *ComputerWorld* magazine. (15) "IBM's position is that (the 3083s) should be replace because of age and scarcity of parts," Mr. Nelson said in refusing to endorse the FAA's tests. "They're not year 2000-compliant."

There are only two places where unreality is commonly accepted as reality: Wonderland and Washington.

Think about it when you board a flight in 2000.

Bring your family and come fly the friendly skies of the FAA!

Yeah, right!

Y2K: Bad Weather Report for Travel Industry

There's a lot of money riding on the FAA.

Airlines, hotels, travel agents, theme parks, convention centers, posh resorts, restaurants, taxi cabs, auto rental agencies, trade associations, lobbyists, sales and marketing professionals, corporate executives, professional sports teams, manufacturers, and a slew of other businesses and individuals – including the companies that package all those peanuts!

A one-month shut down of the air traffic control system would financially cripple thousands of businesses.   Even a one-week shut down would reverberate throughout the economy.

Anything over a month would send the economy spiraling into a deep recession – possibly a global depression.

Year 2000 computer problems threaten more than the FAA's air traffic control system. The entire aviation/travel industry must become Y2K compliant too.

Two aircraft manufacturers have certified that flight operations of their planes will not suffer Y2K malfunctions. Seattle-based Boeing and Europe's Airbus say their aircraft will perform normally through the millennial transition.   Boeing told an international aviation conference in London it would give a written guarantee to airlines that Boeing-built aircraft would be safe.

Delegates attending the Millennium Management for the Aviation Industry conference on March 31, 1998 were surprised Boeing would make such a bold promise.   Their surprise was based on the announcement by Lloyds of London in the same month that the insurer will not pay claims related to air travel accidents or financial losses caused by Y2K.   Lloyds and other British insurers such as the British Aviation Insurance Group have drafted exclusion clauses to limit their exposure.

American and European insurers have classified Y2K as a business risk. Insurers will exclude Y2K liability coverage for airlines, then give it back on a case-by-case basis. Airlines will be required to give detailed reports from technical audits to prove all their planes and aviation equipment are Y2K compliant.

Such stringent insurance rules have prompted airlines to reconsider their flight schedules for January 2000. Airlines have already made plans to temporary ground flights on January 1, 2000, to make checks. Some airlines have also made plans to cancel international flights to countries that have not made their air traffic control systems and airports Y2K compliant.

Insurers are worried about navigational equipment, satellites, electrical power, and telecommunications systems too. The FAA dependence on Global Position System satellites is causing heartburn for insurers. The GPS is scheduled to experience a date rollover on August 21, 1999. The GPS signal – a low-level stream of electrons - is very vulnerable to interruptions.   Interruptions could be caused by geomagnetic disturbances from the sun – such as Cycle 23 – and from deliberate attacks by cyberterrorists.

The Italy-based Centre for Infrastructural Warfare Studies (CIWARS) reported in its *Intelligence Report* (January 4, 1998) that a Russian-made hand-held device is in the terrorist marketplace that can scramble GPS signals within a 125 mile radius. (16) CIWARS also reported (January 18, 1998) about an unconfirmed report by a California television station regarding a near-miss air collision over Burbank, CA, on January 9, 1998. Following the near collision between a Southwest Airlines 737 with a Cessna 402, the station reported that a man on the ground with a small hand-held device pressed it just before the two plane nearly collided.

If the report were accurate, it would be the first confirmed report of use of a Russian-made GPS jamming weapon. It means the entire FAA air traffic control system is in serious jeopardy from terrorist attacks.

Hoping to prevent a worldwide crash of the travel industry, the International Air Transport Association is spending $20 million to encourage travel-related companies around the world get ready for the Year 2000. Airlines are spending $1.6 billion to get their internal computer systems ready. United Airlines has 40,000 computer programs. The airline estimates 11,000 are noncompliant. American Airlines has budgeted $160 million and Delta plans to spend $125 million. Air Canada must review 30 million lines of computer code. Australia's Qantas Airways is spending $147 million. In addition to its computer codes, Qantas has encountered Y2K problems in embedded microchips inside food and refrigeration equipment.

The airlines don't have much time.

The Day of Reckoning will hit airlines soon.

Since airline tickets can be booked a year in advance, all Y2K problems must be eradicated from computerized reservation systems prior to January 1, 1999. Also, airline tickets are usable for one year. Tickets issued after December 31, 1998 will expire in the Year 2000.

That explains the urgency at the SABRE Group – the world's largest airline reservation system – that maintains an extensive global data interchange with 420 airlines, 40,000 travel agents, 50 auto rental firms, and 39,000 hotels. SABRE will spend about $200 million updating its 200 million lines of code and 180,000 computer terminals around the world that connect to the giant system.

SABRE is racing to get the job done before the end of 1998. The company has already experience some turbulent jolts. SABRE went dark on June 24, 1998, for three hours. Computers crashed in the early morning hours at SABRE's high-security underground center at the Tulsa, OK, airport. Airline reservation agents and travel agents worldwide could not access the system. Passengers at airports could not get boarding passes. The company said a series of circuit breakers tripped.

A week later, SABRE crashed again. This time, everything was down for almost six hours – including SABRE's TravelCity, the company's Internet booking Web site. Officials blamed the failure on a "software issue."

A Y2K test? Perhaps at SABRE's Solana Business Park complex near the Dallas-Ft. Worth International Airport?

Hong Kong Airport Fiasco Foretells Things to Come

Finding your luggage will be the least of your problems if the grand opening at Hong Kong's new airport is any indication of Year 2000 problems.

The fiasco made new believers in Murphy's Law.

Scheduled to open in early July 1998, the Chek Lap Kok airport was touted as the world's most sophisticated airport. A $20 billion tribute to technology and engineering.

The problems started when Hong Kong's Airport Authority decided to move all operations from the city's old airport to the new airport in one night. Upon opening, the Chek Lap Kok airport suffered a series of computer foul-ups. Most of the problems were centered in the airport's cargo operations, and blamed on a poorly written software program.

Customer service is not what the airport delivered.

Flight information monitors went blank throughout the shiny new terminal. One out of two pieces of luggage were lost. Hundreds of flights were delayed. Many passengers missed their flights.

Cargo operations were so messed up that millions of dollars worth of perishable goods rotted in the terminals. An estimated $2 billion worth of cargo business was lost during the first nine days. So bad was the confusion, the cargo company finally shipped everything back to the old airport to be handled properly.

Airports in America are now discovering that they, too, have Y2K problems.

Internal operations at all airports – large and small - must be checked for Y2K pitfalls. At the Los Angeles International Airport, employees are combing the six-million-square-foot facility listing every piece of electronic equipment

At Atlanta's Hartsfield Airport, aviation officials inspected the facility in June 1998 for possible Y2K problems. Operations examined included fuel systems, security check points, baggage claims, loading bridges, ticketing systems, fire trucks, and runway lighting systems.

In Denver, the city spent billions building the "airport of the future." The Year 2000 wasn't in their future. They forgot to make the airport Y2K compliant. Apparently, the politicians who spent billions of tax dollars to build an airport for the Twenty-first Century didn't consider Y2K. Airport officials have identified over 100 computer systems that may have Year 2000 problems, including the underground transit system, airport communications, gate access, flight information monitors, fire alarms, security access, and of course, the baggage system.

Embedded microchips are surfacing at airports too. The automated underground trains that ferry passengers between terminals have lots of embedded chips. So do modern fire trucks. Embedded chips have been found in elevators and escalators too.

You may want to arrive at the airport more than an hour early before your flight!

Air Travel in 2000: On a Wing and a Prayer

Don't worry. Planes won't fall from the sky on January 1, 2000.

They just won't take off.

The reasons are very simple. Airlines need two things to fly. Passengers and flight insurance.

Only fools will endanger their lives in January 2000 by boarding a flight. When the truth gets out, few people will take the chance. Airlines will not spend millions on fuel to fly empty jets around the world.

But the lack of paying passengers at the ticket counters won't be the only thing that grounds the planes. Big insurance companies will refuse to insure the airlines against liability for Y2K-related crashes. If airlines perceive danger, they won't fly. Especially since corporate officers could be held liable for Y2K tragedies.

The risk of litigation. That will keep planes parked on the tarmac.

A monumental task confronts the entire travel industry – aircraft manufacturers, airlines, aviation suppliers, travel reservation firms, travel agents, vendors, and airports

The most troublesome concern is the Federal Aviation Administration.

The agency is a colossal mess of mismanagement and wasteful spending.

Sadly, the FAA has chosen an extremely risky course. Rather than admitting they ignored the Year 2000 crisis until the very last minute, FAA bureaucrats have embarked on a dangerous plan to certify their outdated computers as Y2K compliant – whether they're compliant or not.

FAA bureaucrats know they're hopelessly behind schedule. There is no way to repair or replace their fleet of worn-out IBM 3083 mainframe computers in the remaining time. What's worse, IBM has warned the FAA in very plain language that the old computers are NOT Y2K compliant, were not built to last beyond 1999, spare parts are nonexistent, modules are failing at a rapidly increasing rate, maintenance was never performed as required, and the company doesn't have employees who understand the early computer language.

Jane Garvey has decided to gamble the lives of all passengers by rolling the dice in a risky chance the IBM mainframes will chug along for another year, thus buying more time.

If fatal crashes occur – or the insurance industry forces airlines to shut down – the blood, economic loss, and shame will be squarely on Jane Garvey and her accomplices.

20 Manufacturing: Wish I Had Paid Attention in Shop Class!

"In my own view, it is a particularly large global disaster in the making."

> Mr. Jerry Jasinowsky — President
> National Association of Manufacturers
> June 30, 1998

"All that Y2K stuff is a bunch of baloney!"

That's the typical comment by some folks who refuse to deal with the coming crisis. "It's just a way for a lot of consultants to make money" is how they explain it away.

"Nothing is going to happen!" they rationalize.

So, what would happen if one of the Big Three automobile manufacturers rolled over the dates on their computers to January 2000?

Chrysler did it.

During a Y2K test Chrysler Corporation's assembly plant in Sterling Heights, company executives were prepared to find a few computer glitches. Computer technicians turned all the clocks to December 31, 1999. They found more than glitches.

Chrysler executives and employees were barred from leaving the plant. The sprawling plant's security system shut down the building and locked the doors. Nobody could get in or out.

General Motors Corporation is keenly aware of the Y2K menace too.

When GM hired a new chief information officer to spearhead the giant manufacturer's Y2K program, Ralph Szygenda promptly rolled up his sleeves and got to work. First, he was amazed how many people in the company didn't think Y2K problems would turn up on the factory floor. After recruiting Deloitte & Touche and Raytheon Engineers & Constructors as outside consultants, Mr. Szygenda dispatched 91 computer experts to GM's vast network of factories.

Mr. Szygenda was quoted in Fortune magazine making an incredible public confession.

"At each one of our factories there are catastrophic problems. Amazingly enough, machines on the factory floor are far more sensitive to incorrect dates than we ever anticipated. When we tested robotic devices for transition into the year 2000, for example, they just froze and stopped operating." (1)

Mr. Szygenda's candid assessment made news in business publications.

The big wigs at GM apparently didn't appreciate his openness with the media and public about their "catastrophic problems." Mr. Szygenda was silenced. He isn't giving any more interviews about Y2K problems. All news inquiries are now directed to Mr. John Ahearne, a spokesman for GM's information systems in Detroit. Mr. Ahearne was quoted in *ComputerWorld* magazine saying that Mr. Szygenda' s comments were taken out of context by *Fortune* magazine. He explained to *ComputerWorld* that what Mr. Szygenda meant to say was, "This stuff has to be fixed, or it could be catastrophic."

Oh. I see. Wouldn't want shareholders to get nervous, would we?

Time will soon tell the truth. General Motors, and every other manufacturer in the world, is racing toward a rendezvous with the Year 2000.

General Motors is confronted with the biggest Y2K challenge in the world. With hundreds of factories scattered around the world, GM has a short time to deal with a staggering 2 BILLION lines of computer code! The automaker has identified more than 500,000 devices and systems that could have Y2K problems. On top of this, the company must deal with 100,000 third party vendors that supply parts and services.

According to documents filed with the Security and Exchange Commission, GM expects to spend up to $500 million debugging their factories. Reviewing 2 billion lines of code is almost incomprehensible. As of fall 1998, no company with 200 MILLION lines of computer code has become 100% Y2K compliant. How will GM review, correct, and test 2 billion?

But what happens if GM manages to fix 2 billion lines of computer code and its 100,000 third party suppliers don't?

Inventories: Just in Time or Just Out of Time?

Like a big spider web, giant manufacturers such as GM and Ford are intricately tied to a supply chain of thousands of independent companies throughout the world. If one cog in the supply chain breaks, companies up the ladder can come to a screeching halt.

In recent years, dependency on the suppliers has greatly increased. To avoid stockpiling inventories of parts and supplies, manufacturers utilize a management system called Just-In-Time inventory. Developed by Toyota, the just-in-time inventory system drastically reduces overhead and labors costs. Under normal conditions, the system delivers parts and supplies to factories just as they are needed.

But what happens when conditions aren't normal?

The 1998 UAW strike at General Motors clearly illustrates the impact. When 9,200 United AutoWorkers went on strike on June 5, 1998, at two vital parts plants in Flint, Michigan, the repercussions hit throughout the GM empire. The sudden disruption in the flow of parts to GM plants quickly inflicted economic damage on the corporation. Within weeks, all of GM's manufacturing plants in the U.S. was crippled. Hundreds of thousands of workers were laid off. Dealerships in towns and cities across the nation hopelessly watched their supply of shiny new GM vehicles disappear.

Effects of the strikes and plant shutdowns were felt throughout the nation's economy, contributing to a 0.6% drop in the June 1998 industrial production. The ripple effect hurt plenty of other companies too. Small manufacturers supplying GM with steering wheels, bolts, car seat leather and a host of other items were hit by the shutdown of GM plants.

Just-In-Time inventory management exposes all manufacturers to financial ruin if there's any long lasting disruption in the supply chain. The more the company relies on the others, the more vulnerable it is to supply chain disruptions. GM makes about 65% of its own parts. Ford Motor Company produces less than half of its parts. Chrysler makes only 30% of its own parts.

To keep the assemblies running smoothly, manufacturers count on a precise, predictable shipment of parts and supplies from its vendors. Any failure to meet tight delivery deadlines for one part can impact the entire assembly line.

The Year 2000 computer bug has the potential to cripple supply chains around the world. In today's global economy, widespread disruptions to the supply chain would be felt in every industrialized nation. Because so many U.S. corporations now out-source numerous parts to foreign companies, Y2K's impact could deal a double blow since places like Japan and Korea are only vaguely aware of the Year 2000 problem. The Gartner Group reported in August 1998 that "Eastern Europe, Russia, India, Pakistan, Southeast Asia, Japan, most of South America, most of the Middle East, and central Africa lag the United States by more than 12 months." (3)

Manufacturers Have A Big Chip on Their Shoulders

Manufacturers have two critical problems with computer technology. Like every business, manufacturers must first make the computers that run their internal operations – such as payroll, personnel, and accounting – are Y2K compliant. The problem many manufacturers will discover is that many of their software programs were custom designed for their business years ago. For too many companies, they won't even know who wrote the programs. Without knowing how the code was written, the process will be extremely tedious.

Manufacturers have a bigger problem to tackle.

Factories are loaded with embedded microchips. Today's automated machines rely on embedded technology to control and regulate the precision and efficiency of the manufacturing process. In most plant-floor devices, chips are embedded within the machinery – making it extremely difficult to find and correct. Finding them will require extensive searches in factories throughout the world for microchips hidden in automated production equipment, machine tools, computerized valves, safety equipment, and any other equipment or system that utilizes embedded logic. Like peeling an onion, the search for embedded chips requires engineers to dig through layers and layers of embedded logic deep inside highly sophisticated equipment.

The manufacturing process uses dates and calculations to effectively manage numerous functions within the factory. From instrument calibrations to scheduling preventive maintenance, embedded microprocessors can be found at every step of the assembly line. For example, Navistar's automated manufacturing system at its Melrose Park near Chicago tracks orders and automatically orders all the necessary materials. The system also schedules which production lines will be used, how long the process will take, how much manpower will be needed, and keep track of production costs.

Factory buildings, including warehouses, have embedded chips throughout operational systems such as environmental control systems, heating and air condition equipment, fire alarms, sprinkler systems, conveyor belts, elevators, security systems, time clock equipment, and outdoor lighting systems. Sophisticated safety-related control systems are highly dependent on embedded chips too. Great Britain's government department for Health and Safety reported in January 1998 that there is a 50% - 80% chance all safety control systems will fail. The agency's report listed sensors that detect fire or gas leaks in large manufacturing plants as the systems most at risk. (4)

Despite the impending danger and risk to human life, few manufacturers are taking seriously the threat of a Year 2000 factory-floor meltdown. According to the Gartner Group's August 1998 report, only 11% of companies have even begun to investigate embedded chips inside their equipment and facilities.

Fixing everything will be enormously expensive. And just because company engineers find problems, doesn't mean they can fix or replace the noncompliant chips. In many cases, it will mean junking the entire piece of machinery.

Who Will Make New Microchips In 2000?

If conservative estimates are correct, between 2% to 10% of embedded chips may fail in the Year 2000. That means there will be a huge demand in the marketplace for new microchips that are Y2K compliant.

What a great time to own stock in the computer chip industry, right?

Think again.

It seems the wonderful folks in Silicone Valley who make embedded chips have forgotten that their own manufacturing plants are controlled by - you guessed it! - embedded microchips! Consequently, there will be a worldwide shortage of microchips after January 2000.

Mr. Lou Marcoccio, research director for the Gartner Group, says semiconductor companies are particularly vulnerable to Y2K failures. (5) Gartner has warned that the semiconductor industry's fab lines across the world may experience major disruptions due to the Year 2000 software bug. A fab is a complex, integrated network of software and manufacturing equipment.

In June 1998, the Sematech research consortium issued a warning saying that tests show 90% of fab line production gear is infected with a wide variety of Y2K problems. The Gartner study classifies semiconductor companies into three categories. Level One is the least prepared group, which means they are aware of the problem but haven't appointed anybody in the company to lead the Y2K project. Level Five include companies that are at the highest level of preparation for the Year 2000. The research company says most of the world's small semiconductor companies are at Level One. Medium-size companies are at Level One or Two. Only the world's largest semiconductor companies are at Level Three, which indicates the companies have allocated resources to fight the Y2K problem inside their fab lines.

Mr. Marcoccio says the semiconductor industry has been slow in dealing with the Year 2000 because it has "a considerable attitude of denial." (6)

Dr. Frankenstein was in denial too.

Massive, simultaneous failures by embedded microchips around the world will be tumultuous. Embedded technology is present in every sector of the economy: Oil and gas production, electric utilities, telecommunications, medical equipment, food processing, mining, and numerous others. Most of the chips are difficult to locate - not to mention replace. Many older chips can not be replaced since the chip's manufacturer has gone out of business. A lot of expensive equipment will sit idle in factories around the world.

Idle factories translate into massive layoffs.

It is the domino effect that poses such a monumental threat to the global economy. When one factory shuts down because of embedded chips, the impact will be felt immediately. Vendors that purchase products from the company must scramble to find another source. Employees will be laid off, forced to apply for unemployment compensation. Local retailers will experience a slow down in sales as people spend less. Government agencies collect less in payroll taxes too.

Now imagine thousands of manufacturing plants around the world idle at the same time.

How many wrecks on the freeway at rush hour does it take to cause traffic to grind to a halt?

Y2K will be the traffic jam from Hell.

21

Agriculture:
This Little Piggy Can't
Get to Market!

"Son of man, when the land sinneth against me by trespassing grievously, then will I stretch out mine hand upon it, and will break the staff of the bread thereof, and will send famine upon it, and will cut off man and beast from it."

Ezekiel 14:13

Famine in America?

So ludicrous is the thought, most Americans would never seriously consider the possibility. Americans throw more food in trash containers each day than many nations have available to feed their starving masses.

Famine will come to America soon.

We are an ungrateful nation.

God has abundantly blessed America's farmland with the richest harvests in the world. Our granaries are teeming with wheat, corn, rice, and soybeans. Supermarket shelves are stacked high with every imaginable food item. While children starve in distant lands, American dogs and cats feast on cans of "premium" pet food.

Soon the grocery shelves will be empty.

The unthinkable will happen in America. Food supplies will disappear. Violent men will kill for a morsel.

Americans will be reminded whose hand fed them so generously for 250 years.

Once again, families in America will bow their heads and say reverently, "Give us this day our daily bread."

Spraying Millennial Bugs Down On the Farm

Ask the typical suburban soccer mom, loading bags of groceries into her $40,000 sport utility vehicle, if farmers use computers. Most likely, you'll get a blank stare, a giggle, and a shrug of her shoulders. "Never thought about it," they'll most likely say. "Well, I guess some do, but I can't imagine why."

Living comfortably in suburbia, most Americans have lost connection with the land. How food gets from Iowa to the local grocery chain store is a mystery. Unlike their forefathers, today's Americans have no means of food production. The typical suburban 25-year-old man wouldn't know how to butcher a steer if his life depended on it. And his young bride couldn't can a jar of tomatoes if you paid her a $100 per jar.

They simply assume an endless supply of food will be in the stores and restaurants 24-hours a day. Their lives are 100% dependent on the food supply chain.

What if the supply chain breaks?

Most cities have approximately a 72-hour supply of food within stores and warehouses. That's three days. What happens then? Buy food from local farmers? Very unlikely. A study at the University of Massachusetts found that most states purchase 85% to 95% of its food from farms outside their respective boarders. (1)

Forget your stereotypes about farmers. Today's successful farmers are becoming increasingly dependent on computers, with 31% owning or leasing computers. The bigger the farm, the more likely computers are used. Among the nation's two million farms, many are large-scale business operations capitalized at $1 million in land, machinery, livestock, and other assets. Modern farmers use computers to manage their farm business, such as bookkeeping, seed inventories, accounting, crop data, and records of crop and livestock sales.

New sophisticated agricultural technology – called precision farming – utilizes data from orbiting satellites to help farmers be more efficient in land use. Using infrared photographs, the satellite transmits data to sensors in the cab of the tractor, showing the farmer field deficiencies, crop and soil assessments, and sections infected by weeds or insects. High-tech farmers also rely on the Global Positioning System and National Weather Service satellites to fine-tune their cultivation practices.

Farmers have a keen interest in the market – not the farmer's market, but the commodities market. Like other investors, they have a lot riding every day on the price of corn, wheat, rice, soybeans, fruit, hogs, beef, and poultry. Farmers track daily trading prices on the Internet. They also use computers for data about bank loans, credit rating agencies, government loans, and university research. Farm computers use specialized software, such as *CattlePro*, a sophisticated herd management program used by beef ranchers.

Computers are found all along the food supply route. Hybrid seed producers, grain elevators, fertilizer manufacturers, farm implement manufacturers and dealers, banks, farm credit agencies, extension services, transportation companies, food processors, distributors, and retail operations all depend on an intertwined network of computers.

Grocery Stores in 2000: Empty Shelves and Long Lines

Time is money in farming.

Fresh food doesn't stay fresh very long. There's not much of a market for rotted, spoiled food.

There is little time between the production of food and the sale of food. Perishable products such as fresh milk, eggs, vegetables, fruit, beef, pork, and poultry must be shipped on a very tight schedule. The journey from farmer to consumer requires quick movement through the hands of processors, wholesalers, and retailers. Railroads and trucking companies link the components of the food supply chain.

Farmers critically depend on other businesses to provide crucial products and services. Farmers depend on giant fertilizer companies to ship needed nutrients during the growing season. Hybrid seed producers must readily supply ample seeds at planting time. Seeds must go into the ground at specific times, therefore timely shipments are mandatory. Since hybrid seeds cannot be stored for long periods of time, farmers must receive a fresh supply of hybrid seeds each year. If hybrid seed producers go bankrupt, there will be nothing to plant the following year. No seed. No harvest.

Electricity is a mission-critical system on farms. Dairy farmers need electricity to run automatic milking machines twice each day. Electricity is needed to heat special barns to keep calves and piglets warm. Conveyor belts from feed storage silos and haylofts also run on electricity. Irrigation systems, temperature controls in greenhouses, and automated cattle feeding systems require electricity too. A disruption in electrical power to farms would have a devastating effect on food supplies.

Fuel – gasoline, diesel, oil, and gas – are needed to keep tractors, combines, trucks, and farm implements humming. If oil and gasoline production is halted because of embedded microchips, food production will stop too. If railroads don't move freight, then food will rot in the bins.

Dr. Yardeni Warns Senate about Food Shortages

A Y2K food shortage is not a science fiction novel.

Serious leaders are becoming increasingly concerned about the world's lack of preparation for the problems that will erupt after January 1, 2000. Dr. Edward Yardeni, is the Chief Economist, Global Investment Strategist, and managing director for Deutsche Bank Securities, a global investment firm. Mr. Yardeni says he is "amazed by the lack of alarm about Y2K, especially among our global policy makers." (2)

Dr. Yardeni says we are "especially blind about the possible problems that will hit the global food supply in 2000." (3) He told the Senate Committee on Agriculture, Nutrition, and Science that the Year 2000 "technical problem could significantly disrupt the food supply chain."

He then pointedly asked the Senators 11 thought-provoking questions about possible effects of Y2K on the global food supply:

- "Will farmers have access to the information, the seeds, the fertilizer, the feed, and the credit they will need to feed our global population in 2000?"
- "Will disruptions in our energy supply chains (electric, oil, and gas)

hamper the ability of farmers to grow their crops and feed their livestock?"

- "Will the distribution channels operate without any serious risk of delays that might spoil food products before they get to market?"
- "Can our food supply chain cope with a wave of panic buying late in 1999, similar to what always happens during localized natural disasters?"
- "Is there a risk that fertilizer plants might fail as a result of problems with embedded chips?"
- "How might disruptions in natural gas distribution depress fertilizer production?"
- "Should farmers be encouraged to stockpile the basic inputs they need to produce food in 2000?"
- "Will the railroads be able to operate at full capacity to transport grains, livestock, and finished-food products to their customers?"
- "Will ships move freely in and out of ports to deliver the imported and exported foods that are so important in global trade?"
- "Should we be ready to provide food assistance to nations overseas that have major Y2K-related problems with their food supplies?"

* Source: Testimony of Dr. Edward Yardeni. U.S. Senate Committee on Agriculture, Nutrition, and Forestry, July 22, 1998.

22 *Transportation: Is This Anyway to Run a Railroad?*

Imagine the disruption if one million traffic signals were to fail, if buses or trains couldn't run because transit management systems fail, if cargo backs up at ports or rail terminals because tracking systems break down, or if highway-rail grade crossing signals stop. The delays and risks to safety are potentially enormous."

> Mortimer Downey — Deputy Secretary
> Department of Transportation
> Comments at the Intelligent Transportation System
> Year 2000 Summit
> July 27, 1998

They said it would be better for everybody.

Farmers called it the merger from hell.

When Union Pacific gobbled up the financially troubled Southern Pacific railroad in 1996 for $3.9 billion, company executives promised it would be the biggest and best railway system in America. The merger officially joined the two railroads that once met in Promontory, UT, to complete America's first transcontinental railroad in the nineteenth century. With fewer employees and more computer automation, the new combined railroad would be more efficient, they said, and better able to compete with trucks and barges.

What Union Pacific delivered to shippers - including farmers, lumberyards, importers, and thousands of companies - was chaos on the tracks. Confronted with the enormous task of merging the two companies' railway systems internal operations, personnel, and computers. Union Pacific executives attempted to pull off one of the most complex mergers in recent history.

The result was a massive logjam of railway cars in switching yards that delayed shipments throughout the western United States. The paralysis began in the summer of 1997 when Union Pacific attempted to integrate its system with Southern Pacific's system into a single a switching yard in Houston, TX. The logistical fiasco created a traffic jam that drastically reduced the railroad's ability to move trains between the Midwest and West Coast. A year later, the bottleneck was still producing congestion from Texas and Midwestern farm states to California and far north as Seattle.

Typically moving 350,000 carloads of freight each day over its 35,000 miles of tracks, Union Pacific's troubles were compounded by a severe lack of yard space, a labor shortage, aging rail yards, weather-damaged tracks, several serious accidents, and a shortage of locomotives.

Computers were a big culprit in Union Pacific's woes. The daunting task of quickly merging two incompatible computer systems didn't go well.

Union Pacific was hit with another surprise. Record grain harvests in 1997 resulted in corn, wheat, and soybean crops piling up on the ground because of a railroad traffic jam. Grain elevators in farm towns in Nebraska, Oklahoma, Illinois, and most of the Midwest, each stockpiled massive block-long mounds of corn and wheat, waiting on rail cars. Farmers waited over a month to ship their harvests. Even when grain reached the West Coast, striking union members refused to load containers for export to other nations.

Farmers were not the only people hurt by Union Pacific's mess.

Cargo shipments throughout the Western states came to a standstill. Lumber from the Pacific Northwest, Idaho potatoes, Colorado coal, Texas oil, California vegetables and fruits, minerals from Wyoming and Nevada, and Asian imports all sat on docks for 30 days or more throughout the yearlong traffic jam. Government officials estimated the delays cost manufacturers, mining companies, and farmers more than $100 million a month in expenses and lost revenue. In total, Union Pacific's foul-ups cost the economy an estimated $4 billion.

Union Pacific is spending $2 billion to hire more employees, buy new locomotives, and install high-tech computerized scanners to speed up the process. So far, employee unfamiliarity with the new computer system, and a July computer shutdown contributed to new logjams in 1998. Currently, there is a serious shortage of cement in Texas. Also, a flood of cheap Asian imports is piling up on West Coast docks, spurred by the devaluation of currencies and economic turmoil in Southeast Asia.

Y2K Could Derail America's Railroads

The 1997-1998 railroad debacle clearly illustrates the precarious reliance our urbanized society has on prompt shipments of food, raw goods, and energy fuels. The Year 2000 computer problem will greatly exasperate our dependence on the railroads for prompt shipments of essential goods. Any serious interruptions in the delivery of grain, cattle, and coal will mean food shortages and electricity blackouts.

America's railroads are, indeed, vulnerable to Y2K computer glitches.

In 1993, Union Pacific built a $6 million computerized railcar to inspect its 35,000 miles of tracks. Onboard the high-tech railcar, a computer and sensor systems was designed to electronically transmit data to the railroad's information technology center.

After spending millions on the new railcar, an engineering manager at Union Pacific thought about the Year 2000. What will happen, he thought, if this new electronic car is not Y2K compliant? After extensive research, the company found potential Y2K problems, which are now being corrected.

Union Pacific's awakening about Y2K has led the giant railway system to find other Year 2000 problems. Computerization has changed the face of the railroad industry. Routing and tracking hundreds of thousands of railcars over thousands of miles of tracks requires dependence on sophisticated computer systems with millions of lines of code. Traffic signals are sent electronically. Signal and crossing systems must be checked for potential Y2K problems.

The modernization of railroads has replaced manual controls with computerized switching systems. Electronically controlled railroad switches are faulty, but all the manual switches have been uprooted and warehoused. If the switches fail in the Year 2000, there's no physical way to manually switch the tracks.

Besides checking their computer networks for Y2K bugs, such as Norfolk Southern's 18,000 programs and 20 million lines of code, railroads must also extensively search for embedded microprocessors. For example, embedded microchips are present inside locomotives. New Zealand's Tranz Rail has located embedded systems in fire alarms, lighting, and refrigeration systems.

In Great Britain, Railtrack is hampered by a severe shortage of signal engineers. England's railroad is forced to compete for engineers with government agencies building the Jubilee Line Extension for the opening of the Millennial Dome in London. Because signal technology is extremely dependent on computers, Railtrack officials are scrambling to find enough engineers to complete Y2K inspections and repairs. The national railroad is so far behind on Y2K repairs, it canceled 44 computer projects in May 1998. _ComputerWeekly_ reported that an internal Railtrack memo expressed fears that the rail service would not be operational by January 2000. According to the article, the memo said some mission-critical systems would not be Y2K compliant until December 31, 1999. (1) The railroad's Y2K program suffered another setback in May 1998 when its Year 2000 compliance director quit after less than six months on the job.

Railroads and electric utilities share a unique relationship, too. Railroads need electricity to operate switches and signals along thousands of miles of tracks. Likewise, fossil-fuel electric utilities depend on railroads to promptly deliver a steady supply of coal. If there are Year 2000 power outages, trains will stop running in the blackout areas. As evident in the Union Pacific fiasco, it doesn't take much to create a massive traffic jam of railcars. But what happens if other Y2K problems shut down the railroads? A month-long railroad shutdown in January will result in coal stockpiles at utilities depleting quickly. For people living in Northern and Eastern states, a prolonged power blackout in January and February will be devastating, even life-threatening.

As mentioned in the previous chapter, America's food supply chain absolutely depends on the smooth functioning of railroads. Any serious bottlenecks or outright shutdowns of rail traffic would produce food shortages in large urban areas.

Year 2000 and the Maritime Industry: SOS!

The global shipping industry is staring at potential disaster in the year 2000. Over recent years, cargo ships have been extensively computerized to reduce operational costs. Big ocean tankers and cargo ships may have 100 or more embedded chips running engine rooms, communications, navigation, and cargo handling.

After reviewing 50 Very Large Crude Carriers, Royal Dutch's Shell Trading and Shipping Company found 3,000 embedded systems. (2) Shell officials say they found embedded microchip failures in seven areas, including ballast monitoring, ship's performance monitoring, cargo handling, and radar system mapping. Another British company, London's Entropy Management Ltd., estimates up to 20% of embedded microchips on ships may fail.

In May 1998, the United Kingdom's Marine Safety Agency launched a Web site dedicated to Y2K issues for the shipping industry. Mr. Vaughn Pomeroy, head of engineering services for Lloyd's Register, said the Web site was designed to raise Y2K awareness in the global maritime industry.

It is embedded systems that trouble them the most. "We are most interested in the embedded systems which can occur in all sorts of locations, right down to intelligence within sensors such as gas detectors where it is known that certain types can fail," Mr. Pomeroy said at the news conference. "Under such circumstances, detection of a potentially hazardous situation might not be possible," he warned. (3)

The industry group said ship systems most affected include propulsion control, steering, navigation, electric power, boilers, stability computers, fire detection and alarms, radio communications, maintenance planning, passenger lifts, and automated discharging and loading of cargo.

At the Ship2000 Web site, the Chamber of Shipping lists over 34 mission-critical systems on ships that are vulnerable to Y2K glitches. The list includes compass system safety, electronic combustion control and burner management, GPS, oil separation environment, auto-pilot safety, main engine governor safety, bridge control for main engine safety, and fire detection system safety.

Y2K problems are not only at sea, but in the world's cargo ports too. Cargo handling infrastructure is especially dependent on embedded microchip technology for positioning containers both on ships and ashore. Embedded chips are installed in quayside cranes, gate barriers, and security gates. PSA Corporation, Singapore's giant terminal company, is aggressively tackling its Y2K problems. The company expects to be ready by mid-1999. PSA, however, is dependent on smaller shipping companies to be Y2K compliant too. Feeder vessels transport much of the cargo that goes through its terminals to other neighboring nations. In America, the Virginia Port Authority is tackling its Y2K problems. Terminal managers around the world say if embedded systems fail, there will be chaos in the world's ports.

The shipping industry has been slow to deal with the Year 2000 issue. Inspection of the world's fleet of 80,000 seafaring cargo ships and tankers is expensive and time consuming. _Shipping Times_ magazine reported that Chevron Oil inspected the Samuel H. Armacost tanker, built in Japan in 1982 - that had 1,800 subassemblies to be examined. Chevron found 122 to be suspect of Y2K problems. (4) Y2K inspections are costing shipping companies between $10,000 to $20,000 per ship, and takes up to nine days. Therefore, the worldwide costs of inspecting ships for Y2K problems alone will cost the maritime industry between $800,000,000 to $1.6 billion! That doesn't include repairs! Chevron estimates it is spending between $60,000 to $500,000 to repair each of its 35 tankers.

Insurance companies and lawyers are bound to keep a lot of ships docked in harbors around the world when the calendar turns over to 2000. Chevron plans to keep its ships out of restricted waterways and at dock come New Year's Eve 1999.

Chevron Captain Philip Davies was quoted saying, "As our lawyer puts it, he'd like to see every ship in the world at anchor" when 2000 arrives. (5)

The maritime industry is a vital part of the global economy. America's marine transportation system moves one trillion dollars worth of cargo each year, contributing $78 billion to our gross national product. With the exception of Canadian pipeline supplies, the maritime industry delivers nearly all of America's imported oil. Ten million barrels of crude oil and petroleum products are shipped to America every day. Through America's 355 ports, 95% of all U.S. exports move by ships – 4.5 billion metric tons annually. Ships also move 13% of all trade between American cities.

Year 2000 complications onboard cargo ships and tankers, and on land at cargo terminals, will have a substantial negative impact on the U.S. and global economy. The risks are real. Ocean vessels – including passenger cruise liners – could run aground or collide because of Y2K computer failures.

"If ships are sailing in congested areas or close to the coast and equipment fails at the wrong time," said Michael Hunter, Y2K engineer for England's Marine and Coastline Agency, "there is a risk of collision or a stranding." (6) "It is possible that in some cases, failure of systems may affect standards of safety...by causing essential machinery or equipment to malfunction."

Mr. Hunter says it is possible that a ship's automatic pilot could change direction, thus putting the ship on a collision course with other ships.

Oil Drilling Platforms Threatened by Y2K

It really doesn't matter if the world's supertankers are Y2K compliant if there's no oil to ship.

Without a doubt, there will be an extreme shortage of oil and gasoline – possibly for several years – after January 2000. If oil and gasoline supplies are severely curtailed, a major Depression will hit the world.

The oil industry faces a gargantuan task to eradicate Year 2000 computer bugs from thousands of offshore oil platforms, oil wellheads, and refineries throughout the world.

In a speech before the Sixth North Sea Conference, Mr. John Mills made the alarming disclosure that the typical offshore oil platform uses between 50 to 100 embedded systems. Mr. Mills, who is Director of Corporate Affairs Shell UK Limited, said the embedded systems are "sets of electronic code used to control equipment which are effectively sealed, and cannot be altered by the users." (7)

Then, he dropped the bombshell.

"These systems contain anything up to 10,000 individual microchips. We have found that up to half of these systems are critical in terms of production and the impact of our activities on the environment."

Think about this statement! The typical offshore oil platform has up to 10,000 embedded microchips!

It gets worse.

Many are under water!

"An offshore platform may have 10,000 or more embedded silicon chips governing all automated and even some manual processes. Many of these systems are subsurface or underwater and physically difficult to access," states an article in World Oil. (8)

In the time remaining before January 2000, do you really believe the oil companies will find and replace every noncompliant microchip in each offshore oil platform? Especially the chips that are below the sea?

It is a physically impossible task.

Since half of these chips are critical to the production of oil, a worldwide oil shortage is certain. According to Shell UK's Mr. Mills, "if the St. Fergus gas fractionation plant were to fail, a large part of the North Sea would be unable to operate." (9)

The degree of reliance on computers and embedded chips by the oil industry was clearly explained by Mr. Mills in his speech. "The impact can range from refinery process control and safeguarding systems, via pipeline control and terminal operations, through to commercial and retail activities. Pipeline control and terminal operations have become a particularly computer intensive operation, relying on computer systems to control pumping and to detect any leaks," Mr. Mill told the conference.

Shell UK's shipping terminal at Tranmere on the Mersey River handles 12 million tons of crude oil annually, yet only three full-time employees are on duty at any given time.

Oil companies are dependent on third-party vendors too. Mobile drilling, subsea engineering, seismic operations, and platform maintenance are functions no longer handled by major oil firms. The interdependence on outside suppliers makes it imperative that each member of the supply chain is Y2K compliant.

Fuel is essential to our economy and standard of living. There can be no mistakes in fixing all of the world's oil and gas drilling and refinery facilities. The Year 2000 is coming quick. There will be no second chance.

"We only have one go at getting this right..." warns Mr. Mills.

Each passing day increases the odds of an extended oil shortage. Perhaps it explains why Dr. Pat Robertson, founder of CBN, is seeking to lease a closed oil refinery and 20 acres of storage tanks in Southern California. (10)

We need more people with the vision of Joseph.

23 *Hospitals:* Code Blue!

"If there isn't more action, I'm afraid this Y2K problem could have this nation's health care system on a respirator come January 2000."

> *Honorable Christopher Dodd — United States Senator*
> *State of Connecticut*
> *Remarks before the Senate Special Y2K Committee*
> *July 23, 1998*

The prognosis isn't good.

Much of our health care system may be DOA after January 2000.

When a Senate committee gave America's hospitals a Y2K check-up, the patient was told to get in shape quickly.

"Doctor" Bob Bennett was frank. "Unfortunately, I have troubling news today," Senator Bennett said at a hearing on July 23, 1998. "Clearly, the health care industry is not yet ready for the Year 2000. If tonight when the clock struck midnight the calendar flipped to December 31, 1999, large portions of the health care system would fail." (1)

The world's greatest health care system is heavily dependent on computer technology. Our nation's extensive network of health care providers - 800,000 physicians, six thousand hospitals, fifty thousand nursing homes, VA hospitals, Medicare, Medicaid, HMOs, blood suppliers, medical equipment manufacturers, pharmaceutical companies, insurance payers, and ambulance rescue squads - are not close to being ready for the Year 2000.

Avoiding computers in obtaining health care is impossible, unless your doctor still makes house calls in a horse-drawn buggy. Upon entering a health care facility, you'll encounter computer technology at each station along the way. The emergency room's admission clerk will immediately ask for medical insurance information, which is electronically sent to the appropriate insurance company or government agency. Nurses will print out a copy of your medical history. The attending physician will electronically schedule the appropriate treatment or hospitalization. You'll be examined with biomedical diagnostic equipment that contains embedded microprocessors. If surgery is needed, the operation will be scheduled on the hospital's computer system. During the operation, you'll be hooked to a vast array of gadgets, pumps, monitors, tubes, and wires that are controlled by embedded microchips. After your release, computers will promptly send to you – or your insurance company – the astronomical bills for using all those computerized gadgets.

The range of life-threatening Y2K problems in hospitals and health care facilities is considerable. Medical records could be lost. Biomedical equipment could fail. Emergency vehicles could be delayed. Diagnostic equipment could give erroneous data. Laboratory results could be wrong, leading to incorrect treatments. Pharmacies may lack adequate supplies of medicines. Insurance or Medicare payments could be delayed or contain serious errors. IV feeders could malfunction, and electric power could go off.

The Year 2000 computer bug is a life and death issue for the health care industry. It may be a life and death issue for some patients too. Failure to correct hospital computer systems and biomedical equipment could result in deaths. A British government study predicted that there might be 600 to 1,500 Y2K-related deaths in hospitals throughout Great Britain in 2000.

Physicians! Heal Thyself!

The big problem today is that most of the health care industry simply doesn't know what will happen. Awareness of Year 2000 problems is extremely low among sectors of the health care industry. Only 30% of the nation's hospitals have a formal Y2K plan in July 1998. Ninety percent of physicians are taking no actions in their professional offices.

Voices inside the health care industry are sounding the alarm. "The healthcare community is in serious trouble due to anticipated problems of the Y2K changeover," Mr. Joel Ackerman told the Senate Special Committee on the Year 2000 Technology Problem. (2) "Patient care and patient lives are at stake," warned Mr. Ackerman, who is executive director of Rx2000 Solutions Institute, a nonprofit group helping hospitals develop a Y2K program.

For hospital administrators, time is extremely short to come to grips with what could be an operational nightmare. Hospitals will be exposed to operational disruptions caused by Y2K-related failures. Hospitals are small cities. Depending on its size, hundreds to thousands of patients may be "dwelling" inside for stays between several days to several months. With human lives depending on them, hospital administrators must first make sure the hospital's physical infrastructure is Y2K compliant. Lighting systems, fire alarms, sprinklers, heating and air conditioning systems, pagers, intercoms, food service, and telecommunications are essential services for any hospital's daily operations.

Hospitals are also dependent on public utilities such as electricity, water, and sanitation. Most hospitals have disaster plans on file, and frequently test them, for events such as hurricanes, earthquakes, and tornadoes. Consequently, hospitals have on hand stockpiles of bottled water, bandages, and critical supplies. Hospitals also maintain some type of back-up generators for emergency electrical power. What nobody knows is how severe Y2K emergencies will be, and how long will they last.

Third-party vendors are vital players in the health care supply chain. Linens, blood supplies, medicine, pharmaceutical companies, and food suppliers must also be Y2K compliant. A disruption in the supply chain will only add pressure and confusion to the daily operations of any facility.

Computer systems failure will seriously hinder the delivery of quality health care. Compared to other industries, the health care industry is far behind the curve in understanding the seriousness of the Year 2000 problem. Medical officials are just now starting to deal with the potential impact computer failures could have in patient care.

Finding qualified computer programmers to assist in tackling the Y2K bug is becoming more difficult for hospitals with each passing day. By waiting so long to get started, many hospitals are discovering there's a serious shortage of information technology professionals available. The labor shortage is also forcing hospitals to compete with large corporations that are paying high wages and bonuses to IT professionals to complete Y2K projects by mid-1999.

Health care facilities are also financially strapped with high overhead from new buildings, ever increasing operational costs, and rising liability insurance costs. Since most hospitals are nonprofit organizations, finding millions of dollars in extra cash for Y2K is causing the blood pressure to rise for plenty of hospital administrators.

The mounting financial pressure is forcing the three major financial rating agencies to monitor the debt level of hospitals. Hospitals issued bonds for nearly $27 billion in debt in 1997. Fitch IBCA Inc. says it is finding Y2K is costing hospitals between 5% to 10% of total net revenues. (3) The debt reporting agencies such as Fitch and Moody's Investor Service are encountering reluctance from hospitals to give specific details about their Year 2000 preparedness. The fear of lawsuits is the major factor. A lot of hospitals, especially the ones that are just starting to access their vulnerability to Y2K failures, are fearful they'll be sued should any patients die or receive improper treatment.

Computer glitches are already producing panic attacks in Great Britain's hospitals. Some surgeries are being postponed because computers are failing to provide doctors with correct information. According to a report by the *Sunday Times*, a hospital in north London postponed an operation after the computer told surgeons the hospital's supply of critically-needed swabs was depleted. Actually, the hospital had plenty of swabs. The error was caused when the computer read the expiration date on the swabs – the Year 2001. The computer read the use-by date as 1901. (4)

A 1998 survey of U.S. health care facilities by Rx2000 found that 62% have already experienced Year 2000 failures. (5)

Biomedical Devices Are Infected With Y2K Bug

When it comes to embedded microchips, what some hospital administrators are discovering is enough to give them a bad case of heartburn. Embedded microchips are prevalent throughout every health care facility in thousands of biomedical devices. These devices process, analyze, record, display, and transmit medical data about the health of patients.

One such health care professional is Rx2000's Mr. Joel Ackerman, Director of Technology Management for a health care organization in Minneapolis, MN. Mr. Ackerman's IT team examined biomedical devices at his organization's 10 acute care facilities, and numerous other clinics.

"My team is, quite frankly, horrified at the risks within the laboratories," Mr. Ackerman told the Senate Special Y2K Committee. (6) "A few of the manufacturers have told us to not test their product with a date roll-over, for fear that it will experience catastrophic failure."

He then told the Senators about many of the failures.

"We have had significant hard crashes with chemistry analyzers, hematology analyzers and urine analyzers, coagulation profilers, and immuno-assay analyzers," Mr. Ackerman said. He also said they have found considerable Y2K risk in blood gas analyzers – a device used in operating rooms while the patient is anesthetized.

Mr. Ackerman says every piece of equipment must be checked – regardless of what the manufacturer says. "Manufacturer's model and serial numbers may be alike, but the chips and boards inside test with different responses. Some work and some fail. Also, the manufacturers know about this."

One medical device checked by Mr. Ackerman's team had been certified by the manufacturer as Y2K compliant. It was. It failed the test, however, for Leap Year on February 29, 2000.

Embedded microprocessors are the greatest Y2K risks to hospitals. Health care facilities are just beginning to understand the threat. St. Francis Healthcare Services in Honolulu, HI, has 5,000 pieces of biomedical equipment. The Mayo Foundation in Rochester, MN, has 30,000 pieces of equipment. Mayo's Y2K manager, Mr. Patrick Davitt, estimates that between 10% and 20% of the hospital's medical devices may not be Y2K compliant. (7)

Y2K has the potential to affect every piece of medical equipment that contains a date-sensitive microchip. Take ambulances, for example. A vital piece of equipment is the external defibrillator, used to keep a patient's heart from beating too fast. Each time the device sends an electrical shock to the patient, it prints a date and time stamp on paper. A defibrillator with a noncompliant microchip will print incorrect dates and times, thereby requiring medical technicians to manually record the correct information.

Embedded microchips are everywhere in any modern hospital. As the cost of microchips has decreased, the number of medical devices containing embedded systems has risen. Consequently, almost all bio-medical devices contain microchips today. The ventilators that keep premature infants breathing. Heart monitors, CAT scanners, MRI systems, and infusion pumps too. Just because the device has an embedded chip, however, doesn't mean it will fail. Only devices that use microchips that are date-dependent or time-dependent are at risk of failing. Experts believe the number could be as high as 30% of all biomedical devices in a typical hospital.

The monumental task is to examine every device to determine whether it is at risk of a Y2K failure. The stakes are high. When a device is hooked to a patient's body, there can be no mistakes. Dr. Kenneth Kizer, Undersecretary for Health for the VA, explained to the Senate Special Y2K Committee the dangers of what he calls the "Millennium Bug Syndrome" – or MBS. Dr. Kizer said, "For example, an incorrect date or time sequence in the output of a blood gas analyzer could cause confusion when interpreting the sequential results, causing errors in diagnosis and treatment. Likewise, an incorrect age calculation which is stamped on an automated chest X-ray could prompt unnecessary further testing or even cause a misdiagnosis." (8)

Y2K errors in medical devices could also endanger patients' lives by transmitting data about the wrong patient. "Similarly, if a Year 2000-induced error causes a piece of laboratory equipment to skip a function, or perform a function twice, a patient could get the lab results of the patient who preceded or succeeded him or her, with potentially adverse consequences," Dr. Kizer explained to the Senate committee during his testimony.

With human lives at stake, hospitals have two choices: Repair or replace. Neither option is easy. Finding out the Year 2000 status of bio-medical equipment has been frustrating for the health care industry. Manufacturers are keeping their mouths shut. At the Senate hearing in July 1998, a group of heavy hitters in the health field blasted the medical equipment manufacturers for stonewalling. Among those displaying their ire were the American Medical Association, the U.S. Department of Veteran Affairs, the American Hospital Association, and the American Nurses Association.

The groups charged that many manufacturers of computerized bio-medical devices have not – or will not – tell hospitals whether their products will function after January 2000. The most damaging testimony came from Dr. Kizer who told the Senate Special Y2K Committee that the VA Department has requested data from manufacturers – as many as four times – and still does not have replies from a substantial portion.

So far, the Department of Veteran Affairs have received certification from 694 manufacturers that their products are Y2K compliant. Thirty-four manufacturers have reported that 182 models of devices are not Y2K compliant and are no longer serviced by the manufacturer. Even though many of the devices are commonly used in numerous hospitals, the manufacturers consider them obsolete. A total of 673 models produced by 102 manufacturers are not Y2K compliant, but the companies intend to fix the devices, although the manufacturers have not said how the devices will be repaired and who will pay the bill. Fifty-three manufacturers are still conducting tests on their products. "Return to Sender" was marked on letters sent to 201 manufacturers. Ninety-six companies have gone out of business. The remaining 233 manufacturers have not responded to multiple inquiries.

The overall response of the biomedical equipment industry is appalling. From the VA's inquiries, we know that 855 models of biomedical devices are not Y2K compliant, and the manufacturers will not fix 20% of those items. Even after four inquiries from a federal agency, 30% of manufacturers have refused to respond.

Medicare's Prognosis: Doctors May Feel the Pain

America's hospitals and health care facilities receive approximately half of their revenues from Medicare, Medicaid, and other taxpayer-funded programs. A sudden loss of so much money would financially cripple almost every hospital.

Medicare is administered by the Health Care Financing Administration (HCFA), an agency under the U.S. Department of Health and Human Services (HHS). Electronic data exchange is a vital part of the operations of the Medicare program. The Medicare and Medicaid programs utilize 183 computer systems, with 98 considered "mission critical."

According to Nancy-Ann DeParle, HCFA's administrator, "Medicare is the most automated health claims payer in the country." (9) Ninety-eight percent of inpatient hospital and other Medicare Part A claims are processed electronically. Eighty-five percent of Part B claims to physicians are processed electronically too. Medicare's one billion claims each year – 17 million transactions each week - are processed by 60 outside contractors. Medicare has informed the outside contractors that it is their responsibility to become Y2K compliant.

When it comes to being ready for the Year 2000, Medicare is sick.

Very sick.

The giant government benefits agency thought it had to review 20 million lines of computer code.

Think again.

Medicare officials recently discovered, after bringing in a consultant, that it really has 50 million lines of code to review and fix.

Right now, Medicare doesn't look good. Few experts have confidence the agency can meet the December 1999 deadline. With so much money coming from Medicare, failure to become Y2K compliant will be equivalent to an earthquake in the health care industry. "If we do not fix all information systems that might have Year 2000 problems, enrollment systems might not function, beneficiaries could be denied services because providers may not be able to confirm eligibility, and providers could have cash flow problems because of delayed payments," stated Nancy-Ann DeParle. (10)

Cash flow problems, indeed!

So, what happens if Medicare doesn't make it?

Paper. Lots of paper.

"Processing paper claims by hand is one contingency if we fail," said HCFA's administrator. "Given the nearly one billion Medicare claims we process each year, it is a possibility that strongly motivates us to succeed."

24 Government Services: The Time Is Now 2000. Do You Know Where Your Government Is?

"We just don't know the status of the federal government...Our entire way of life, in essence, is at risk, we are so dependent on digital equipment. We won't be able to conduct national security, collect taxes, distribute benefits, manufacture products, or manage commerce."

> *Rona B. Stillman — Chief Scientist for Computers and Technology*
> *United States General Accounting Office*
> *Remarks before the Year 2000 National Security and Global Economy Conference, U.S. Army War College*
> *June 29, 1998*

If the federal government were a high school student, it would bring home a report card with a big "F."

That's the grade a congressional subcommittee gave the federal government's state of readiness for the Year 2000 as of June 1998.

"There is no doubt that the year 2000 problem is real. It isn't a figment of someone's imagination. There is no doubt that all systems will not be compliant in time," warns Mr. Stephen Horn, a California congressman and chairman of the House Subcommittee on Government, Management, Information and Technology. (1)

Congressman Horn has been closely watching the progress - or lack of progress - by federal government agencies in preparation for the Year 2000. He doesn't like what he sees. Federal agencies are falling behind schedule, not catching up. "Now overall, the federal government earned an F, and they really had to work at it, because they had a D or so the last time," Congressman Horn said. (2) "Underlying this dismal grade is a disturbing slowdown of the government's rate of progress."

Each quarter, Congressman Horn's subcommittee grades the federal government's 24 largest departments and agencies. The grading is based on each department's current standing based on four main criteria: Do they have a contingency plan in the event of system failures? Are they dealing with embedded microchips? Will the agency's telecommunication system work? Will the agency be able to electronically exchange data with other organizations? The grades were based on self-reporting from the departments and agencies. The information, however, was scrutinized by the subcommittee, and verified by the General Accounting Office.

The analysis by Congressman Horn's subcommittee is alarming. Crucial systems are at risk. Social Security checks could be delayed or lost. National defense could fail. Air traffic safety could be dangerous.

Despite his dismal grading, Congressman Horn said, "We must not panic."

Sadly, there is absolutely no coordination among federal government agencies. "No one is responsible for establishing common test criteria or assuring that a master schedule (for the entire government) exists," said Rona Stillman, the GAO's chief scientist. (3) And that is precisely the problem! Mrs. Stillman hit it on the head when she told an audience at the U.S. Army War College that "no one is in charge." (4)

The departmental grades were:

F– State Department, Energy Department, Transportation Department, Health and Human Services, Environmental Protection Agency, and Agency for International Development.

D– Department of Defense, Agriculture Department, Justice Department, and Department of Education.

C– Department of Housing and Urban Development, Treasury Department, Labor Department, Department of Veteran Affairs, Office of Personnel Management, Interior Department.

B– NASA, Department of Commerce, Small Business Administration, Nuclear Regulatory Commission.

A– Social Security Administration, Federal Emergency Management Agency, General Services Administration, National Science Foundation.

What troubles Congressman Horn so much is that grades for nine federal agencies actually declined from the previous report card. The VA Department dropped from an A issued in March 1998 to a C three months later. Health and Human Resources fell from a D to an F. And the EPA fell dramatically from a B to an F during the three-month interval. (5)

At the rate federal agencies are repairing their mission-critical systems, many of the departments will not be finished until 2004, or later. "A reduction in productivity is deeply troubling," said Congressman Horn. "This trend must be reversed." (6)

The General Accounting Office released a report in May 1998

warning that the Year 2000 problem is a "high risk" threat to government services. The report states that "serious vulnerabilities remain" and "much more action is needed to ensure that federal agencies satisfactorily mitigate year 2000 risks to avoid debilitating consequences." (7)

According to the GAO, less than half of the 42 agencies it surveyed had finished the initial phases of completing an inventory and assessing data exchanges. The report said "little progress has yet been made in completing key steps such as reaching agreements with partners on data formats, developing and testing bridges and filters, and developing contingency plans for cases in which year 2000 readiness will not be achieved." (8)

The GAO says federal agencies are falling further behind, that is too late to fix all government computers, and that it is inevitable some crucial government computers will fail on January 1, 2000.

It is estimated that federal agencies will spend a combined total of $50 billion to get ready for the Year 2000.

Social Security: The Check is not In the Mail!

The Social Security Administration stands out among all federal agencies as an agency that takes the Year 2000 seriously. Unlike other government (or business) organizations, the Social Security Administration got an early start on Y2K problems. To its credit, the agency recognized the Year 2000 threat almost a decade ago. The Social Security Administration initiated an early awareness program among its departments and partners. Because of the knowledge gained through its early start, the agency has become a source for other federal agencies seeking Y2K information.

Despite its early start and leadership, the Social Security Administration still faces major hurdles in its effort to assure that America's retired citizens will receive their Social Security checks on time after January 2000. For a while, officials at SSA thought they were right on schedule to review and repair its 34 million lines of computer code.

That was in late 1996.

Independent computer consultants, however, were brought onboard to study 42 of the agency's 54 state disability determination services. To everybody's shock, the consultants discovered an additional 33 million lines of computer code that SSA had overlooked. The SSA failed to include the state disability determination services in its initial assessments. With government leaders looking to the SSA as a model of Y2K preparations, the discovery of 33 million more lines of code sent shivers down the spines of Washington bureaucrats. If SSA missed so much code in its assessment, what surprises are in store at agencies that are far behind?

In addition to the 42 state disability determination systems, the GAO warns that SSA faces two more major threats.

Corrupted data is the second big risk at SSA. The giant government benefits agency has over 2,000 data exchanges with other federal and state agencies, and numerous third parties. The General Accounting Office pointed out the problem in a 1997 report. "Because SSA must rely on the hundreds of federal and state agencies and the thousands of businesses with which it exchanges files to make their system compliant, SSA faces a definite risk that inaccurate data will be introduced into its databases," the GAO wrote. (9)

Millions of disability checks could be delayed. The GAO report said that "given the potential magnitude of this undertaking, SSA could face major disruptions in its ability to process initial disability claims for millions of individuals throughout the country if these systems are not addressed in time for corrective action to be completed before the change of century." (10)

A complete lack of a contingency plan is the SSA's third major threat. The disclosure of additional lines of code prompted U.S. Senator Charles Grassley (R-Iowa) to ask to see the SSA's contingency plans. Senator Grassley charged in a December 1998 (11) letter to Mr. Kenneth Apfel, Social Security Administration Commissioner that some SSA officials refused to cooperate with the GAO's auditors. SSA officials told the GAO auditors that a back-up plan was being developed. When the auditors asked for a copy of the contingency plan, the Social Security bureaucrats balked at the request. The bottom line is that the Social Security Administration doesn't have a back-up plan if its systems fail in January 2000.

Even if SSA miraculously repairs its 67 million lines of code, state disability determination systems, and thousands of electronic data exchanges with third parties, the Social Security checks still may not get mailed.

Why?

Because the Social Security Administration does not mail the Social Security checks!

In 1997, nearly 40 million Americans received Social Security retirement checks. Another 6.6 million people received SSI benefit checks, while 6.1 million received disability insurance benefits. In total, nearly 53 million people received Social Security benefit checks in 1997.

Not one check, however, was mailed by the Social Security Administration.

The Financial Management Service, a division of the Treasury Department, issues Social Security checks.

Guess what?

The Financial Management Service is in trouble.

Congressman Stephen Horn described the Financial Management Service's Y2K preparations as a "dismal performance." (12) It was the major reason the Treasury Department was given a "C" grade.

Congressman Horn said that all of the work by the SSA "may be naught" if the FMS doesn't "get with it."

"Despite the urgent calls for progress in March (1998), FMS accomplishments over the last three months have been far from reassuring, and a lot of urgent action is needed if we are going to remedy that situation," warned Congressman Horn.

IRS Finds Y2K Very Taxing

Don't get too excited, but the Internal Revenue Service could collapse in January 2000. It is one of the federal agencies least prepared to deal with the millennial bug.

Even before Y2K came along, the IRS has never had much luck with computer systems. In fact, they've been a big headache at the Internal Revenue Service. The same IRS that must quickly prepare for the Year 2000 is the same IRS that wasted over $3 billion on a computer upgrade that everybody agrees was a disaster.

Confronting the friendly folks at the IRS are 80 outdated mainframe computers, fourteen thousand minicomputers, and several hundred thousand PCs and desktop computers at workstations throughout the nation. The agency also has 250,000 commercial software programs.

Failure to meet the January 2000 deadline could cause the IRS computers to freeze, thus shuts down. Major errors in taxpayers' returns could also be another serious problem. For example, confused computers could fail to credit employees for taxes withheld by employers, or miscalculate interest owed on back taxes.

The IRS has 750 computer programmers and 250 outside contractors working on the huge mountain of computer code and systems. Aggressive corporations, however, are robbing the IRS and other government agencies of their talent. The loss of computer programmers forced the IRS to give a 10% pay increase in 1998 to programmer to hold on the job. The agency's employee attrition rate has doubled in the last two years as programmers have defected to private employers.

Mr. Charles Rossotti, IRS Commissioner, calls his agency's Y2K problem a "dangerous and risky situation." (13) Mr. Rossotti told a Congressional committee that failure by the IRS to fix its computers before the year 2000 "would create a genuine risk of a catastrophic failure of the nation's tax collection system in the Year 2000."

Taxpayers won't be getting refunds either.

"Frankly, there is no way to issue refunds without a computer system," Mr. Rossotti explained to the Congressional members. (14)

State Governments Face Millennial Meltdown

If the situation at the federal level is bleak, then state and local governments are even further behind. The dismal lack of alarm by state and local governments will unleash havoc in communities throughout the nation when vital services collapse.

While some state officials such as Pennsylvania's Governor Tom

Ridge have been calling attention to Y2K problems, most states are just waking up to the Y2K threat. Denial is everywhere. When North Carolina's State Controller said it would take $300 million to fix the state's computers, the legislature responded by giving him $7 million to spend.

In the land of Lincoln, the state of Illinois is far behind other major states. State officials estimate the Y2K repair bill will top $100 million. As of March 31, 1998, only 31% of the state's mission-critical computer systems were Y2K compliant. These systems control programs for health, welfare, public safety, and tax collection.

A Virginia legislative committee – the Joint Commission on Technology and Science – issued a gloomy assessment of the readiness of state agencies. The report, issued in May 1998, listed 11 agencies that pose a "high risk" because of tardiness in fixing mission-critical computer systems. Among the agencies listed were the Department of Corrections, Department of Medical Assistance, Department of Environmental Quality, Department of Social Services, Virginia Workers Compensation Commission, and the Virginia Retirement System. The commission also cited 10 universities and colleges such as the College of William and Mary, Virginia Military Institute, and James Madison University. Two state departments didn't even file Y2K progress reports: the Department of Fire Programs, and the Department of Health.

Wisconsin's Governor Tommy Thompson told a news conference in Madison, "I am very fearful." (15) The governor said at the July 28, 1998, news conference that the state government had been taking the Year 2000 seriously for months. His late discovery of Y2K seriousness may explain his fear.

Time is running out.

The State of New York finally got around to filling 300 vacant computer programmer jobs in 1998 when the state's hiring freeze was thawed and pay raises were granted to programmers. The shortage of programmers was so acute that state personnel managers asked hundreds of retired state employees to come back to work.

Ohio's Y2K team is reviewing and fixing the state's approximately 70 million lines of computer code. Although the state government has been working on it for three years, by mid-1998 state agencies had completed less than 45% of needed repairs. The Ohio Lottery, Department of Youth Services, Department of Education, and Department of Human Services lag even further behind.

State officials know time is running out. Mr. John Scaggs, director of the Y2K project for the Department of Human Services, was quoted in Cleveland's *Plain Dealer* newspaper bluntly describing the consequences of failure. "There would be no welfare checks issued. That's probably one of our biggest concerns," said Mr. Scaggs. "There would be no Medicaid providers being paid. It could be a very ugly scene.

Believe me, we're doing everything we can to make sure we meet the deadlines." (16)

Yes, it will be an ugly scene.

Too many state governments are ignoring embedded microchips.

Soon they'll discover the chips.

High security prison systems are certainly places they may want to look. Electronic gates and doors that mistakenly open or fail to shut will put correctional employees in serious danger. At Folsom Prison in Sacramento, CA, corrections officials were surprised to learn that Folsom's electronic doors would automatically default to "open" on January 1, 2000.

Government facilities will face Y2K problems caused by malfunctioning embedded microprocessors. Telephone systems, heating and air conditioning units, emergency radio equipment, medical equipment, and fire trucks are just a few examples of potential Y2K headaches for government officials. Airports, harbors, toll roads, prisons, universities, courthouses, office buildings, and state hospitals must be checked for the presence of embedded chips.

With so little time remaining, the only alternative state governments will have in 1999 will emergency contingency plans.

County and City Governments: On the Front lines in 2000

It has been said often "all politics are local." When something goes wrong, citizens call their nearest government official.

That will never be truer in 2000.

Mayors, city council members, county commissioners, police chiefs, and fire marshals are in for a tough time.

Mr. John Koskinen, President Clinton's Y2K czar, says local governments are ignoring the coming crisis. He says "a lot of counties and cities are paying no attention to this, as if it doesn't affect them." (17)

Y2k will, however, affect them - and effect them in big ways.

The Year 2000 computer virus will make its presence felt in city halls and county courthouses from Maine to Oregon. Highway toll booths, police Breathalyzers, mass transit systems, county jails, 911 emergency call centers, hospitals, public schools, water and sanitation facilities, landfills, driver's license and motor vehicle permit offices, pensions, tax collection, and traffic lights are just a few of the multitude of local government services and vital functions that will be stung by the Millennial bug.

Because local government is "where the rubber meets the road," it will be local government officials who feel the most severe brunt of local outrage from citizens. There simply isn't a function of local government that will not be affected by Y2K problems and the costs involved in solving the glitches.

Consider America's thousands of local public school districts. Computers are the heartbeat of modern school administration systems.

Student enrollments, attendance, report cards, class scheduling, and test scores are managed by computer technology. Computers also handle administration and school building management. Personnel, payroll, pensions, substitute teacher records, maintenance, supplies, lunch cafeterias, bus schedules, athletic programs, teacher contracts, and accounting are managed by computers in thousands of offices at local boards of education.

Public safety is another local government function that will be adversely affected by Y2K problems. From the time a police officer is dispatched, to when the criminal is incarcerated, computers track and record criminal and judicial activity. In numerous cities, computer systems that handle 911 emergency dispatching will need repairs or replacement. Embedded microchips are prevalent in many pieces of modern fire fighting equipment. Police department and courthouse computers that handle criminal records will need repairs. So will police telecommunication systems and radio systems. Jails and detention centers must be checked for embedded microchips in electronic security systems.

Communities, large and small, are coming to grips with the quickly approaching Year 2000 deadline. Some are faring better than others are. The City of Albuquerque, NM, needs immediate help with its old mainframe computers. According to a Y2K status report dated July 13, 1998, the City Hall had only found one computer programmer willing to work for a mere $75 per hour!

Albuquerque is discovering what many more cities and towns will discover soon. The pool of available talent is shrinking fast. Labor costs are exploding. Time is running out.

Y2K Will Cripple the Welfare State

Some local governments are learning another hard lesson. In some communities, local officials have been given rosy Y2K progress reports by bureaucrats, only to discover that little work was actually done.

One such community is McHenry County, Illinois. Elected county officials thought they had the jump on Y2K problems. The county's Information Services Director had been diligently leading the effort to upgrade the local government's computers, so they were told. The director resigned in May 1998. To their disbelief, the County Board discovered the next month that hardly anything had been done on Y2K. The interim Information Services Director informed the County Board members that the sheriff's department alone would take 1,875 business days to reprogram the computers. That was more than three times as many days as remaining before January 2000.

City officials in the nation's capital are bracing for the worst too. In a city government that doesn't function smoothly in normal times, the Year 2000 will bring enormous trouble to Washington, D.C.

Led by Mayor Marion Barry, it appears city bureaucrats forgot to save copies of the original source code that run the numerous software programs. IBM representatives estimate the city's source code was written in as many as five different computer languages.

This is a city where citizens normally expect to spend a day waiting in line at the Motor Vehicles department for driver license renewals and motor vehicle registration. This is the city that takes weeks to remove snowdrifts. This is the city where murder occurs daily on the streets. This is the city where a substantial portion of its population receives welfare and government benefits.

This is the city that will be in a state of anarchy.

Y2K problems abound in Washington, DC As late as September 1998, the Washington Metropolitan Area Transit Authority was attempting to assess the extent of its exposure to Y2K problems. With nearly one million people riding its buses and subway trains every weekday, the Transit Authority already knows every *Farecard* vending machine in the subway terminals and every fare box on every bus is not Y2K compliant. The Authority is also worried about embedded microchips in the subway's nearly 750 escalators and elevators, plus the high-speed subway trains.

Congressman Thomas Davis III, chairman of the House committee that watches over the District of Columbia's affairs, says Washington is "at the crisis stage" in its lack of preparation for the Year 2000. (18)

"Are we talking computer Armageddon here?," asked City Councilman Ed Thomas at a Denver Mayor and City Council meeting in August 1998. (19)

Officials in Denver, CO, are getting more and more bad news about the city's infrastructure. After spending $13 million to replace some outdated computers, city council members were informed they needed to spend another $43 million to fight the Y2K bug at City Hall. Another $2.5 million is needed to buy new equipment for the city's 911 emergency call center.

In the ensuing days prior to January 2000, politicians will wake up to their worst nightmare. Big government is coming to an end. Y2K will cripple the welfare state.

America has come a long way from the admonishment of President Thomas Jefferson that the best government is the one that governs the least. Unlike the hearty pioneers who founded and built this great nation, today's citizens have come to believe their existence depends on government.

Their dependency on government services and programs will be badly jolted.

A seven-year global depression, public utilities crippled by embedded microchip failures, civil unrest, high unemployment, and greatly reduced tax revenues will bring the government dragon to its knees.

Citizens who go months without electricity, water, and sanitary services will be in a bad mood. If rioting and looting become so bad that police officers stay home to protect their families and property, the stage will be set for marshal law. When banks won't lend more money - and unemployed taxpayers are demanding relief - governments will go on a literal "crash diet."

Those who worship at the altar of big government are in for a big shock. As a nation, we'll be facing a fork in the road. One road will lead back to the land of freedom, responsibility, and self-reliance as envisions by our founding fathers. The other road will lead to a benevolent dictator who will promise to solve the nation's problems.

Which way will America go?

25 New World Disorder: Country Boys Can Survive!

"…it is preferred that participation by owners and operators in a national infrastructure protection system be voluntary."

Presidential Decision Directive 63
Signed by President William Jefferson Clinton
May 1998

Descending from the night sky, 12 Black Hawk helicopters swooped down upon an unsuspecting neighborhood in Charlotte, NC. Frightened residents, aroused from their sleep by the sound of whirling helicopter blades and gunfire, were stunned at what they saw.

Terrified citizens grabbed their guns. Others hid.

The 911-telephone line was jammed with frantic callers.

Many frightened residents called Mayor Pat McCrory's home. The background noise from the helicopters and gunfire was so loud the mayor could barely hear the pleas by his citizens for help.

The lights on the helicopter were blacked out, except for one red taillight on each aircraft. The fleet of military helicopters was only several hundred feet above homes and apartment buildings. Dangling from ropes, dark-suited infantry soldiers repelled down onto the streets. As they stormed an abandoned warehouse, the sound of rapid gunfire from assault weapons ricocheted off surrounding buildings.

The sound of simulated grenades exploded.

Real explosives blasted open the warehouse doors.

Terrified residents demanded to know what was going on. The mayor and police chief didn't know.

It was Exercise Cauldron Chariot, the code name for an urban anti-terrorism training program by the secretive U.S. Army Special Operations Command.

Before the Charlotte simulated raid, the Army Special Operations Command conducted similar surprise nighttime raids in 21 American cities, including Atlanta, Dallas, Chicago, Houston, Detroit, Los Angeles, Miami, Pittsburgh, New Orleans, and Seattle.

Frightened folks haven't liked the program.

The troops were ordered to leave Pittsburgh. In Houston, two soldiers were hospitalized when their helicopter rolled over after a hard landing.

Currently, the United States Marine Corps are involved in urban warfare training. Called *Urban Warrior*, the experiment is designed to develop methods and equipment to fight wars in foreign cities. Military leaders say such exercises are necessary to train American troops to prepare for the "wars of the future." Because terrorism is changing the nature of warfare, U.S. military leaders expect future battles will take place inside heavily populated areas.

They insist the skills they're developing in urban warfare training will never be used on American citizens.

Unlike the Army "invasions" that terrified sleeping citizens and puzzled local police, *Urban Warrior* doesn't have camouflaged troops repelling from helicopters with guns firing. Instead, the Marines are armed only with clipboards and pens. They refer to it as a "tactical exercise without troops."

They're mapping the infrastructure of major U.S. cities.

Because urban environments favor the defenders, the Marines are learning how to seize control of cities. *Urban Warrior's* strategy is to seize key infrastructure in a city to isolate the enemy, without unnecessarily killing residents.

Urban Warrior is sending teams of Marines into major American cities to "learn how a city operates so that we will be better at fighting in any city of the world," Lt. Col. Jenny Holbert told the Chicago Tribune newspaper. (1)   When the 80 Marines arrived in the Windy City in May 1998, Lt. Col. Holbert said it was "the first time we've actually gone into a city and looked to see what's involved in the infrastructure and terrain."

What are they looking for?

Local police and fireman are walking the Marines through their cities, pointing out critical infrastructure such as sewers and underground tunnels. Skyscrapers, stadiums, and other tall buildings that can interfere with military communications. Mechanized bridges over rivers that must be secured. The best way to take control of a city without endangering public utilities such as electricity, water and sanitation facilities.

In other words, everything you need to know to maintain military control of a city.

New weapons and gear are being developed for the Pentagon's urban warfare program.

During the New York City visit, Marines learned how to cross from the 20th floor of a skyscraper to the 10th floor of another building. Marines shot grappling hooks between buildings so troops and supplies could be transported across the Big Apple's concrete canyon.

American soldiers will have rifles with mirrors, permitting troops to peer around the corners of buildings. Slippery foam will be deployed on streets that make is impossible for people to stand. Heat sensors will allow troops to "see" people through building walls. Foam barriers erected quickly to block streets will help maintain crowd control. Uniforms will include flak jackets that include handles on the back, which permit soldiers to lift one another through windows, and pads for elbows and knees. At Camp Lejeune in North Carolina, Marines are being trained to use laser-guided guns for future urban battles.

The Army has developed a fixed-winged unmanned aerial vehicle equipped with cameras, to perform reconnaissance, drop pamphlets, or carry nonlethal weapons. U.S. military units will also rely on satellite surveillance to track enemy troops moving through city streets and alleys.

Military snipers are also being trained in the Marine's new Urban Sniper Course conducted by the Special Operations Training Group. The two-week course focuses on marksmanship skills for close-proximity sniping exercises. The course emphasizes precision firing, minimizing damage to building, and avoiding the killing of friendly citizens. In addition to rapid bolt manipulation and precision shot placement, the course teaches Marines how to snipe from helicopters hovering above a city's skyline.

Using new M-40A1 carbines, a short-barreled rife that fires the same ammunition as M16 rifles, the Marines are being trained to shoot people at close range, from 300 yard and up to the target. The short-range precision drills involve firing five rounds in less than 15 seconds at a three-inch circle.

The Pentagon is conducting a series of tests under the Military Operation in Urban Terrain Advanced Concept and Technology Demonstration (MOUNT). Among the technologies being tested is a breaching round designed to be shot from short range to knock a door off its hinges. Booby trap detection and disarming equipment, nonlethal grenades, night vision equipment, and precision mortars are some of the urban warfare weapons and equipment being tested.

One new urban warfare weapon is the Minimum Signature Envelope Recoilless Gun (MISER), a shoulder-fired launcher designed to shoot down doors. The 81mm weapon traps the propulsion gases that are emitted by big guns, thus lessening the blast. With no fire flash and little noise, the weapon will not give away the soldier's position.

So far, _Urban Warrior_ has mapped out the infrastructure of Chicago, Jacksonville, FL, and Charleston, SC. More major American cities will be mapped too.

Launched with a model city at Camp Lejeune, _Urban Warrior_ is a two-year training program in urban fighting.

It will end with a mock battle in a still-undisclosed West Coast city in late 1999.

Martial Law: Land of the Free? Home of the Brave?

For those knowledgeable about the Y2K threat, the thought of martial law is on their minds.

Too many troubling preparations such as the *Urban Warrior* program are causing even the most levelheaded citizens to wonder whether federal officials are quietly preparing for anarchy in 2000.

Gold Sword IV is another military project that is raising eyebrows.

Held at Fort A.P. Hill in Virginia, four-day field exercise was intended to help military police units to set up and manage large prisoner-of-war camps. The June 1998 event brought together over 2,500 soldiers. With two years of advance planning, *Gold Sword IV* greeted the incoming "POWs" with guard towers and razor-sharp perimeter wire. The mock POW internees were issued uniforms, photo identification cards, and a bag of toiletries.

Directed by the 800th Military Police Brigade, *Gold Sword IV* trained 68 Army Reserve, National Guard, and active duty units from all 50 states.

Why is the U.S. Army swooping down on unsuspecting cities in helicopters at night?

Why are the Marines mapping out the infrastructure – streets, sewer tunnels, bridges, utilities, and bridges – of America's major cities?

Why are MPs from the 800th Military Police Brigade training Army Reserve and National Guard units from all 50 states techniques in rounding up and incarcerating prisoners-of-war?

Is the federal government aware of plans by foreign and domestic terrorists to unite in 2000 against the USA?

The Year 2000 is not just a technology problem. It may be rooted in a simple two-digit software error, but its impact will shake the foundations of our society. Currently, the general populace is in denial. With few exceptions, the media is soothing the public with reassuring reports that most Y2K problems will be fixed in time. Washington politicians don't want to tell the truth, lest they rock the economy. Wall Street certainly isn't interested in spooking the general population. Corporate America will not talk frankly about the coming computer meltdown.

Responsible leaders, however, see the potential for social chaos. Fear will be the greatest threat.

Mr. Edward Yourdon, a respected computer programmer and author of *Time Bomb 2000*, predicts that New York City will look like war-torn Beirut, Lebanon.

The closer we get to the January 2000 deadline, more people will wake up to quickly approaching crash. By summer 1999, awareness and concern will be high among informed citizens. A series of high-profile computer crashes in major corporations and government agencies will attract extensive media attention. General panic will hit the nation in fall 1999. Most likely, the panic will explode after September 9, 1999 – the "end of file" code in many software programs. Nervous investors will flee Wall Street's inflated stocks. Massive cash withdraws will drain billions of dollars from banks, mutual funds, and insurance cash value policies.

Hoarding will be rampant in late 1999. Rioting, looting, and civil unrest will rock every large American city. Taking advantage of the confusion, militant Muslims could ignite pandemonium throughout the USA through a coordinated campaign of terror.

Is martial law a real possibility in America?

A growing chorus of respected leaders is raising the issue.

At a Senate Armed Services Committee hearing on June 4, 1998, Senator Robert Bennett openly discussed martial law. Senator Bennett asked Defense Deputy Secretary John Hamre whether the Pentagon is making contingency plans for martial law. Citing how the riots after the assassination of Dr. Martin Luther King ripped apart the nation's social fabric, the Utah senator recalled seeing GIs in battle dress at every intersection in the nation's capital.

Senator Bennett then commented that the Canadian government is talking "about emergency plans to provide emergency services to communities in the event of Y2K failures that produce some kind of social unrest, whether it's either interruption in the power grid or water services or communication services or something." (2)

He then asked the Big Question.

"Do you have any plans in place, as apparently they do in Canada, to provide emergency services to communities in the event of a Y2K-induced breakdown of community services that might call for martial law on a regional-specific basis?"

Deputy Defense Secretary Hamre replied that Canada's constitution allows domestic military operations, similar to America's Federal Emergency Management Agency. Mr. Hamre said he didn't want to be "melodramatic," but "it gets to a larger issue." He said the next decade would be a "decade of homeland defense," citing "year 2000 problems and the social disruption that comes with it" and the "astounding ramifications" of a terrorist attack inside America's borders. Mr. Hamre also raised the specter of a cyber-attack by a foreign nation against America's infrastructure such as the electric power grid.

Although U.S. military forces are barred from domestic operations, Mr. Hamre said that's "an artificial distinction in the world of cyberspace." He said we have "fundamental issues to deal with that go beyond the Year 2000 contingency planning."

The Deputy Defense Secretary said the Pentagon is "not anxious to get more missions." He left the door open, however, to possible military involvement.

"But we see ourselves being pulled into a national security issue in this decade of home line defense that's in front of us."

It won't take much pulling.

Few Americans know that the legal framework for martial law already exists in the United States. The process began with presidential executive orders signed by John F. Kennedy during the Cuban missile crisis in 1962. Since then, both civilian and military federal officials have added layer upon layer of executive orders granting the President broad emergency powers during a disaster.

Among the many Executive Orders signed by Presidents from John Kennedy to Bill Clinton are:

Executive Order 11002 empowers the Postmaster General to "assist in the development of a national emergency registration system." The Post Office is responsible for the "procurement, transportation, storage, and distribution of safety notification and emergency change of address cards..."

Executive Order 11003 empowers the Federal Aviation Administration to prepare emergency plans "covering the emergency management of the Nation's civil airports, civil aviation operating facilities, civil aviation services, and civil aircraft other than air carrier aircraft."

Executive Order 10997 empowers the Secretary of the Interior to prepare an emergency plan covering "electric power; petroleum and gas; solid fuels; and minerals."

Executive Order 10998 empowers the Secretary of Agriculture to seize control of all "food resources" during a national emergency including "biological warfare, chemical warfare...including attack upon the United States." The order gives the Department of Agriculture control over farms, ranches, farm equipment, fertilizer plants, and all food products.

Executive Order 10999 empowers the Secretary of Commerce to prepare a national emergency plan for "highways, roads, streets, bridges, tunnels, and appurtenances; highway traffic regulation; allocation of air carrier aircraft for essential military and civilian operations; ships in coastal and intercoastal use and ocean shipping, ports and ports facilities; and the Saint Lawrence Seaway; except those elements of each normally operated or controlled by the Department of Defense."

National Driver's License ID Coming in October 2000

With Y2K civil unrest lurking over the horizon, it is no surprise that the Clinton Administration is preparing to install a national Driver's License Identification Number to track every citizen. Entitled "Driver's License/SSN/National Identification Document," the Department of Transportation rule will compel all states to comply by October 1, 2000.

Under the Clinton Administration rule, all state driver's licenses must be linked to the individual's Social Security number. State identification cards must also be linked to the individual's Social Security number. State ID numbers will be issued to minors too.

Each citizen must submit a "biometric identification" such as fingerprints, retinal scans, and DNA samples. Embedded in each card will be a computer chip containing the individual's Social Security number.

All citizens will be required to carry the card. States that do not participate will cause their citizens to be denied government benefits, travel rights, and employment.

All citizens will be required to present the new federal ID card upon applying for a job. Employers will be required to check on ID against a national database. Clinton Administration officials are justifying the federal ID program as a way to combat illegal immigration, infiltration by terrorists, and drug smuggling.

Citizens without the new federal ID card will be denied government services such as welfare, Medicare, and school enrollment. Passports will be issued only to citizens possessing the ID card. Gun purchases will be monitored since the card will link into a national database. Because children will eventually be required to have an ID card too, the national database will maintain medical records, behavioral problems, school records, and juvenile criminal history.

Do you still think martial law is impossible in the United States?

Why is the Clinton Administration forcing states to adhere to its federal mandate for a Driver's License/SSN/National Identification system by October 1, 2000?

Ask your state legislator if this is true.

World Governments Brace For Disaster

Don't call it a bunker.

The mayor says it is an *emergency management center*.

Whatever you call it, New York City Mayor Rudolph Giuliani is building a $15 million bulletproof, bomb-resistant command center.

Officially, the high-tech facility will house the New York City Office of Emergency Management. On the street, it's called "Rudy's bunker." Located on the 23rd floor of Number 7 World Trade Center, the command center will keep the city running in the event of a disaster.

City officials say the facility will be able to withstand a nuclear blast. The command center – with its own food, water, power, communications, and air ventilation system – will permit 30 individuals to direct the city's response to a nuclear attack, hurricane, electrical blackout, civil unrest, deadly germs, or a chemical attack.

It is not just Mayor Giuliani who is preparing for disaster. Around the world, governments and corporations are bracing for a Y2K storm.

Never before in human history has the entire world been forced to deal with a single problem with a fixed deadline.

A federal commission appointed by the Canadian government warned the nation's emergency response system to plan for disasters such as a prolonged electrical power blackout. Bell Canada's CEO, Jean Monty, says health and safety in Canada may be threatened by Y2K trouble. "We are now urging all firms to develop effective contingency plans to prepare for possible failures and to protect themselves from unprepared partners." (3)

Australia's chairman of the Australian Stock Exchange, Mr. Maurice Newman, warns that the Year 2000 computer bug could drop Australia into a deep recession, with thousands of companies pushed into insolvency and hundreds of thousands of lost jobs. In New Zealand, government officials says contingency plans must be developed to write two million welfare and pension checks each month by hand if the computers aren't Y2K compliant by June 1999.

Mr. Alan Simpson, a retired officer with the UK's Royal Air Force Intelligence Service, is a highly respected business executive in the satellite industry. He openly warns about a possible famine in the United States if Y2K disrupts the global food chain.

Dr. Edward Yardeni worries about the interconnections between nations in today's global economy, saying "we basically have glued this global computer network together over a 40-year period." (4). He is especially concerned about Asia's denial of Year 2000 problems. "Today, Asia is toast," he said at a Y2K conference on June 2, 1998. "In the year 2000, Asia will be burnt toast." Mr. Yardeni has good reasons to be concerned about Asia. Japan is the world's second largest economy. If Japan's banks crash and burn, we'll all have smoke in our eyes.

Thailand's scientists are warning their government that failure to take urgent action to repair computers for the Year 2000 will result in widespread financial chaos. The Bangkok Post newspaper quoted the deputy director of the National Electronics and Computer Technology Center as saying the government should have started on the problem when computer programmers first warned about it in 1995.

In Belgium, a major European computer company estimates that more than 70% of the nation's large computer systems are based on outdated 1970s technology. Most of Belgium's software is written in obsolete COBOL language. Few programmers are left in Belgium who understand the language.

England's Controller of the Audit Commission, the UK's equivalent of America's GAO, issued a serious warning in June 1998 about the dangers of Y2K failures in vital public services. Mr. Andrew Foster, the Commission's Controller, told the BBC News that "drivers could find the roads snarled up, patients could be barred from operating theaters (rooms), and homes could go up in flames as the equipment controlling traffic lights, sophisticated medical devices and fire brigade response centres started malfunctioning." (5)

Y2K denial is so pervasive in Germany that a major European computer technology consulting company, SRI International, charges that three-fourths of German companies don't expect to complete their Y2K repairs before December 31, 1999.

In May 1998, delegates to a summit of European Union member states gathered in London to hear frank reports from computer experts.

The public was not allowed to attend. Mr. Robin Guenier, England's foremost spokesman on preparing for the Year 2000, said "not nearly enough is being done – unless this threat is tackled far more urgently, the well being of hundreds of millions of people throughout Europe could be seriously threatened." (6)

Y2K Preparations: Americans Prepare for Worse Case Scenario

Business is brisk at Lehman's Hardware store in Kidron, Ohio.

Primarily catering to the Amish farming families in Wayne and Holmes counties, Lehman's bills itself as the world's largest retail distributor of nonelectric appliances and gadgets. Apple-peelers, juicers, wood burning stoves, and a vast array of garden tools fill the store's walls, shelves, and floor space.

People are driving long distances to load up.

Preparing for Y2K, they say.

It is happening all over the nation. Twenty-year veterans of computer programming are quietly purchasing farmland in Western states, far from large urban populations. Church pastors are advising parishioners to stock up on food, water, and basic necessities. Independent businessmen are selling their expensive homes – some even selling their capital-intensive businesses - and moving to rural communities to prepare for the coming storm.

We're not talking about fanatics and survivalists. No, the people taking the most drastic preparatory actions often are college educated individuals with management-level jobs and above-average incomes who "see the hand-writing on the wall."

As the deadline approaches, every citizen will have to come to grips with the meaning of the Year 2000 computer crisis. Countless families will have to mentally and emotionally deal with some very intense gut wrenching questions.

Is Y2K a lot of hype? Hot air by greedy computer consultants making a fast buck?

If it is a real threat, will they solve it in time?

Do you believe the government?

If they don't solve it in time, how bad will it be?

If electric power goes out for a month or more, how will I provide heat for my family? How will we cook?

What about food supplies? Will the food supply chain break? Will food supplies be rationed? What if a drought comes upon America? How long will it last?

What about my job? Will my company survive? Do I have skills that will be needed in a new post-Y2K economy? How will I make a living?

Should I withdraw my savings? What about my retirement nest egg? Will it be safe? If I withdraw my funds, will I help start a nationwide bank panic? Will U.S. money be worth anything? Should I buy gold?

How will I pay my debts?

Will real estate values drop by 50% or more?

Should I stay where I live now? Or should I move to a safer community?

How much food should I store? Am I responsible to feed neighbors and relatives who didn't take precautions?

Will my family be safe? If government welfare checks stop and public services fail, will civil unrest and rioting threaten my family's safety? How long will the local police be able to hold off the looters? Will it be like the Wild West?

Should I own weapons? Will there be a federal ban on ammunition sales in late 1999? Will guns be confiscated by federal troops in 2000? Would I shoot a human being to protect my family?

What will happen to churches? Are they prepared to minister to millions of terrified and destitute individuals? Will pastors remain on the job? Will debt-laden churches close their doors, unable to pay for multi-million dollar building programs started in 1999?

If embedded microchips fail in vital industries such as oil production, how will I get fuel to travel to work? Will there be any work? Will fuel supplies be rationed by the federal government?

How will they fix the computers after January 2000? Will there be a military draft of computer programmers? Will essential services and vital industries be given priority over other organizations for available programmers?

Do I have a reliable supply of drinking water? What if the city's water purification plant is inoperable because of embedded microchips? Will I be standing in line each day for a year waiting for my daily ration of water delivered by military troops?

Will the President declare martial law? Am I prepared to surrender my God-given freedoms and rights as an American in order to bring law and order back to the nation? Will the Constitution ever be restored?

Will our children despise us for losing the American dream?

Will foreign enemies and terrorist take advantage of America's weakened state? Could we be invaded? Could United Nations peacekeeping troops be dispatched from Europe to quell civil war in America? Would the President surrender the United States to the United Nations?

What about American troops stationed overseas at military bases? Will they be cut off from the United States? Will they be vulnerable to attacks by nationals? How will we protect them?

What are the possibilities of an accidental nuclear launch by Russia or China?

Where will I be on December 31, 1999? At a wild New Year's Eve party? On my knees praying to God?

What sins have I personally committed that has helped to bring Divine Judgment on our nation?

How long will God's chastisement last?

These are just a few of many tough questions we will all be forced to answer in the days ahead. Some citizens are dealing with the issues now. Others know about Y2K, but are in denial. And, yet, there are still millions of citizens who are simply uninformed about current events.

For them, the storm will catch them totally unprepared in late fall 1999.

There are no right and wrong answers. Quite frankly, nobody knows what will happen. There are, however, too many informed and educated people who are sufficiently troubled by the Y2K menace. Too many voices are sounding the alarm.

The danger is too great to ignore or flippantly brush off as meaningless.

Young or old, rich or poor – nobody will escape Y2K.

Everyday life will soon change. It will never be the same.

God will soon shatter our greedy, selfish, violent, sin-filled world.

This is not the end of the world. It is the end of the world as we know it.

These are the last days of the End Times.

Are you ready?

26 The Dead Hand: Russia Prepares for Nuclear War

"I'm saying that more than 100 weapons out of the supposed number of 250 are not under the control of the armed forces of Russia. I don't know their location. I don't know whether they have been destroyed or whether they are stored or whether they've been sold or stolen. I don't know."

> General Alexander Lebed — Commander of Russia's
>   14th Army
> *Comments on CBS 60 Minutes*
> *Regarding missing nuclear suitcase bombs.*
> *September 7, 1997*

An elite group of Russian military troops has secretly infiltrated the United States. Their mission is to prepare for war with the United States - a war they believe is inevitable.

Using fake passports, the special forces - Russia's top secret *Spetznatz* military intelligence unit - have been entering the U.S. for years falsely posing as tourists.

The *Spetznatz* troops inside America include an assassination "hit squad." Sensitive information about American political leaders has been gathered by the GRU (Glavnoye Razvedyvatelnoe Upravlenie), Russia's military counterpart to the KGB - now known as the SVR. The list includes the President, Vice President, Speaker of the House, Congressional leaders, Cabinet secretaries, top Pentagon officials - plus their wives and children.

The information is gathered for one purpose: assassination of America's political and military leadership. Under control of the GRU, the elite forces penetrate countries shortly before a war. They are the "Rambos" of Russia. Trained to kill quickly, even without weapons. Highly skilled with weapons and explosives. Able to drive all types of military vehicles, including helicopters. Highly fluent in the English lan-guish.

At a predetermined time, they will try to kill as many American government leaders as possible, including their wives and children. Top

U.S. military generals will be targeted for death. Critical infrastructure in the U.S. will be destroyed - such as dams, bridges, telephone switching systems, and electric power utilities. In all, nearly 100 strategic sites in the United States are targeted for destruction.

Spetznatz Special Forces know the secret landing strips for Air Force One. The President of the United States will be onboard the aircraft continuously during a war. When Air Force One lands for servicing, *Spetznatz* troops will be waiting at the secret runways to kill the President, including his family and staff.

Even more terrifying, the *Spetznatz* troops operating inside America today, have at their disposal miniature nuclear "suitcase bombs." The tactical nuclear weapons have been smuggled into America through a variety of methods, including stealth missiles flying undetected by American radar. Weighing under 60 pounds, the "suitcase bombs" are hidden outside Washington in Virginia's Shenandoah Valley, at secret locations along the Skyline Drive. Bombs are also hidden in the Hudson Valley outside of New York City.

Since it is Russia's military doctrine to poison water supplies to large cities, the *Spetznatz* have hidden biological and chemical poison supplies near the tributaries to major U.S. reservoirs. When the war starts, America's water supply will be poisoned.

Preposterous?

The plot for a new Tom Clancey novel?

No, just information recently given to the CIA and FBI by Stanislav Lunev, a former military intelligence colonel in Russia's GRU.

His bone-chilling accusations against his former homeland are documented in his book, *Through the Eyes of the Enemy.* (1)

America Faces Gangsters with Nuclear Bombs

Col. Lunev is dying from cancer. He knows his time is short.

His conscience bothers him.

Before he dies, he feels an obligation to "warn America of the dirty tricks that can be played against her." (2)   He says his message is this: "The new cold war is between the Russian Mafia and the United States." Col. Lunev says in his book, "America is facing a nation led by gangsters - gangsters who have nuclear weapons. And some of those weapons are actually on American soil..." (3)

He charges that after the fall of Communism, the leadership vacuum was filled by an odd coalition of Russian Mafia leaders, former KGB spies, and former communist politicians. The result today is a ruling class of criminals - criminals with nuclear weapons.

According to Mr. Lunev, "Russia remains terrified of the power of America, and Russian military intelligence does everything it can to prepare for a war that it considers inevitable." (4)

Mr. Lunev first came to America posing as a news reporter for TASS, the former George Bush and other important federal government agencies.

Getting sensitive information was easy.

"I was amazed - and Moscow was very appreciative - at how many times I found very sensitive information in American newspapers," Mr. Lunev says. (5) He said American reporters care more about getting the next big news scoop than about national security. Finding so much sensitive information in the American news "made my job easier," says Mr. Lunev.

American military and intelligence agencies have extensively debriefed Mr. Lunev. He is now under the FBI witness protection program. By moving him frequently throughout America, the FBI conceals his identity and whereabouts.

He insists that Russia is preparing for an attack against the United States. "Russian pilots are training for action against NATO and the U.S. military. Russia still considers the United States and NATO the main potential military adversaries." (6)

Col. Lunev says Americans are complacent because the ravages of war have never been fought on our soil. He says Russians understand war.

"The only way you get an enemy to submit is by bringing the war to his people." (7)

Russia Develops New Weapons For World War III

In his book, Colonel Lunev describes new weapons of war being tested by the Russian military.

One such terrifying weapon is a seismic explosive device. Planted at a fault line, the device is capable of triggering earthquakes. He says Russia military units, experimenting with the device, almost destroyed several towns in the Transcaucasus Mountains. The seismic weapon device, Mr. Lunev says, would be used on the West Coast of America and other areas prone to earthquakes.

HERF guns are another high-tech weapon developed by Russian military and intelligence agencies. HERF guns are also known as "electromagnetic pulse" weapons, or EMPs. Using high-energy pulses to destroy electronic circuitry, HERF guns could overload electrical power grids and shut down computers in a large city.

Russia is also a leader in laser technology. In April 1997, a Canadian military pilot and an American Navy liaison sustained eye damage from a laser fired from a Russian freighter off the coast of Tacoma, WA. Col. Lunev says Russia is developing laser weapons capable of blinding entire cities.

Colonel Lunev says the "most troubling" new weapons the Russians are building employs very low frequency radio signals. Russian scientific research reveals that the very, very low frequency radio signals can cause brain damage in human beings. He says the Russian military is seeking to construct a "delivery mechanism" powerful enough to broadcast the radio signals. The Russians believe they could kill millions of people using such a weapon from a long distance.

Russia Plans to Launch Giant Space Mirror

It was one of the most bizarre news articles ever reported.

The *Sunday Times* in London reported on June 14, 1998, that Russian scientists were planning to launch a fleet of giant mirrors into space. (8)

An experimental 75 foot-diameter mirror was set for an August 15, 1998, launch onboard the unmanned spacecraft Progress M40, owned by the Space Regatta Consortium project.

Originally, the mirror was set to reflect a powerful beam of sunlight back to Earth on November 9, 1998. Called Znamya 2.5, the giant mirror would appear as a second moon. For several minutes, the mirror would reflect back to earth a light beam 10 times brighter than a full moon. The light will be bright enough to read a newspaper by.

The beam would light up cities across the Northern Hemisphere – from Russia to London, then to Quebec and all the way to Seattle, Washington.

Using a huge aluminized screen that unfolds after reaching orbit, the space mirror is intended to bring sunlight to Russia's Arctic regions where endless nighttime enshrouds villagers in perpetual darkness.

Hoping to create artificial daylight, the Russian scientists plan to launch an entire fleet of space mirrors, circling the globe with the enough mirrors capable of illuminating whole cities for hours. Besides providing sunlight to Arctic residents, the scientists speculated that the mirrors could also be used during natural disasters – such as earthquakes – to provide sunlight to rescue teams searching for survivors.

While Russian scientists said the mirror is meant to help mankind, other scientists around the world immediately greeted the news with alarm.

Many see the bizarre plan as a front for a sinister weapon.

While the plan is to reflect sunlight to the dark side of the Earth, what happens if the mirrors are used to reflect sunlight to the sunlit side of the Earth?

During a sunny day, would millions of people in a city be suddenly blinded if a burning beam of pure sunlight were to be directed down from space into their eyes?

After the news broke about the August 1998 launch, Russia announced that the experimental mirror would not be aboard the spacecraft.

Budgetary cutbacks were cited as the reason for canceling the experiment.

General Lebed: 100 Suitcase Bombs are Missing

Russia has a problem with loose nukes.

"The nuclear horse is out of the Russian barn," said Mr. Arnaud DeBorchgrave, director of the Global Organized Crime Task Force. (9)

Following the collapse of communism in the former Soviet Union, the upheaval unleashed tremendous political, social, and economic instability in the nation. With its communist financial system in ruins, the new Russian Federation was broke. A proud nation with 150 million people and 20,000 nuclear warheads – but still very broke.

Rocket scientists formerly employed by the Soviet Union have been reduced to poverty. Military officers – including high-ranking generals - sometimes go months without paychecks. Food and clothing for the Army is scarce even today. There is no money for maintenance of military weapons and facilities.

Organized crime – the Russian Mafia – moved in to seize the opportunity. President Boris Yeltsin told the upper house of the Russian Duma in September 1997 that "Criminals have today brazenly entered the political arena and are dictating its laws, helped by corrupt officials. They can penetrate everywhere unless the whole of society from top to bottom joins in this effort to eradicate this scourge." (10)

The German BND intelligence service, however, claims Russian spies are in the hip pockets of Mafia bosses. (11) The German intelligence agency says large numbers of Russia's spies "belong" to criminal gangs. The German report says the Russian spies are cooperating with the Russian Mafia "with the support" of President Boris Yeltsin's government.

In recent years, over 500 Russian business executives have been murdered. "Not a single widely publicized murder has been successfully investigated in Russia over the last five years," charged a leader of a Russian political party. (12)

According to a report on global organized crime by former FBI director William Webster, the Russian Mafia has formed alliances with criminal counterparts in 50 nations, 200 large organizations, and 26 cities in the United States.

Some of their global partners are narco-terrorists: criminals who finance their terrorism through international drug cartels.

Organized crime has taken advantage of Russia's desperate financial condition. Russia's nuclear arsenal is poorly maintained for lack of funds. Military officers and rank and file soldiers are broke, hungry, and very dispirited.

Russia's financial crunch forced many of her most capable fighting men – including decorated generals – to leave the armed forces. They were given no pensions or housing. To survive in the New World, many of Russia's premier fighting men turned to the Russian Mafia for income.

Many brilliant Russian scientists with extensive experience in rocket science, and nuclear, biological, and chemical weapons have turned to the Mafia too.

The Mafia, rocket scientists, Muslim terrorists, and nuclear weapons are a lethal combination.

Many nuclear arsenals went unguarded for years following the collapse of the Soviet Union. Unguarded sites in Kazakstan and Georgia gave U.S. intelligence agencies great distress. At a closed Russian air base outside the Latvian city of Riga, dozens of unprotected nuclear warheads were lying in an abandoned bunker for years. The radioactivity is so great that Geiger counters jump off the top scale 30 feet away from the bunker's steel doors. Only crude warning signs on wooden posts on the perimeter of the former top security Red Air Force base alert visitors to the danger.

The radioactivity inside the bunker means certain death to any intruder. Would a Muslim fanatic, however, dare to retrieve warheads from inside in order to please Allah? Would a desperate, poverty-stricken father risk his life by removing nuclear warheads to sell to the Russian Mafia if it was the only way to help his family escape the region's poverty?

When 17 Russian generals and admirals visited the United States in 1994, they were asked to rate, on a scale of 1 to 10, the possibility of Russian nuclear weapons being sold or given to Middle East terrorists and rogue nations such as Iraq. With one being highly unlikely, and ten being highly likely, all 17 generals and admirals rated it as a ten.

While America wallows in unbridled sin and financial prosperity, her enemies are busy preparing for America's downfall.

Consider the mysterious price quote found in the notebook of the leader of the Japanese Supreme Truth Cult, the terrorist group that released deadly chemical warfare agents inside a Japanese subway. At the trial of the group, which had accumulated assets over $1 billion, the leader's notebook was presented to the courtroom. It noted a $200 million price tag for a tactical nuclear weapon – commonly known as a nuclear "suitcase bomb."

General Alexander Lebed, former Commander of the 14th Russian Army, startled the world in 1997 when he said his inventory of Russia's nuclear arsenal revealed that many nuclear suitcase bombs are missing and their whereabouts are unaccounted. General Lebed is also a former national security advisor to President Yeltsin. At first, the Russian government denied the existence of "suitcase bombs." Alexei Yablokov, a respected Russian scientist, however, stepped forward to confirm the existence of the bombs.

Officially, the miniature nuclear bombs are called tactical atomic demolition munitions. Mr. Yablokov, a member of the Russian Academy of Sciences, said on television in Moscow on September 22, 1997, that he personally talked with scientists who made the bombs.

Mr. Yablokov and General Lebed both said the devices were secretly produced and maintained by the KGB and never included in any official inventory of nuclear weapons. Thus, many high level Russian leaders are not even aware of their existence. Consequently, nobody knows exactly how many were manufactured, where the weapons are stored, or how many are outside the hands of the Russian government. To the best of his ability, General Lebed estimates approximately 250 nuclear suitcase bombs were built. He estimates that 100 suitcase nukes are missing.

Dr. Yablokov believes the Russian Ministry of Atomic Energy produced 700 suitcase-size nuclear bombs for the KGB and Spetznaz secret intelligence unit. He said the one-kiloton bombs, equal to one thousand tons of TNT, were designed to be used by special commando units during wartime to blow up dams, power plants, and other strategic sites inside the enemy's borders.

The very same devices and strategy as told by Col. Stanislav Lunev!

General Lebed says the suitcase bombs are capable of killing up to 100,000 people if detonated in an urban area.

Dr. Yablokov says the Palestine Liberation Organization has declared twice that it illegally purchased suitcase bombs in Russia. In 1995, rumors swirled around Moscow that Vilnius, Lithuania, and Chechen rebels purchased suitcase bombs. Zavtra, a Russian newspaper, reported the story. Later, the reporter who wrote the article was abducted and threatened with death if he did not retract the story. The newspaper withdrew the article.

In the book *One Point Safe*, authors Leslie and Andrew Cockburn, wrote that Chechen rebels threatened the United States with nuclear blackmail. The rebels said they would sell a suitcase bomb to Libyan dictator Gaddafi if Washington didn't diplomatically recognize the Chechen state.

Russia Building Huge Underground City

Deep inside Yamantau Mountain located in the southern Urals, near the town of Beloretsk, the Russian government is busily constructing a mammoth underground city.

Started in the 1970s by Soviet Premier Leonid Brezhnev, the underground military complex in Siberia has cost billions of dollars to construct. Twenty thousand workers are employed in the construction. A railroad and a major highway serve the complex.

The manmade cavern contains two cities. The underground facility's size is incomprehensible. U.S. military officials estimate it is larger than metropolitan Washington, DC inside the Beltway.

A 1997 top-secret CIA report, obtained by the *Washington Times*, states that the "underground construction appears larger than previously assessed." (13) The twin underground cities are capable of housing 60,000 people, with access by a railroad.

The CIA describes the bunker as a "nuclear-survivable, strategic command post" which appears to "provide the Russians with the means to retaliate against a nuclear attack."

Russia is building more underground facilities than the one at Yamantau Mountain. The country is feverishly constructing underground bunkers, secret subway tunnels, and underground command posts to help Russian leaders escape Moscow and survive a nuclear war.

The CIA report says Russia is building four complexes within Moscow to house senior Russian leaders during a nuclear war. The facilities include a bunker at Voronovo, 46 miles south of Moscow. Another bunker at Sharapovo is 34 miles outside of Moscow. The bunker has a secret subway train. It is also reported that another secret subway has been constructed from the residence of President Boris Yeltsin. His dacha is 13 miles west of the Kremlin.

According to the CIA report, the subway trains will allow for "rapid evacuation of leaders during wartime from Moscow."

The *Washington Times* reported that the CIA is closely monitoring Russia's preoccupation with surviving a nuclear war. "Three decrees last year on emergency planning authority under Yeltsin with oversight of underground facility construction suggest that the purpose of the Moscow-area projects is to maintain continuity of leadership during nuclear war." (14)

So far, the Russian government doesn't want to talk about the underground city. At times, the Russians have said it is a mine, a safe repository for valuable Russian artifacts, a food warehouse, nuclear waste dump, and an ore-processing plant.

They just won't call it a nuclear bunker.

When the *New York Times* asked, the Russian Defense Ministry tersely replied that "The practice does not exist in the Defense Ministry of Russia of informing foreign media about facilities, whatever they are, that are under construction in the interests of strengthening the security of Russia." (15)

That's OK with the Clinton Administration.

Under President Clinton, the United States has closed most of its underground bunkers such as facilities at Virginia's Greenbriar and Mount Weather locations.

Despite the mystery, the Clinton Administration is not worried. *USA Today* quoted Defense Department spokesman Kenneth Bacon as saying, "We do not regard the program as a threat." (15)

Interestingly, another Clinton Administration spokesman became visibly agitated when the *Washington Times* first broke the news story. When U.S. State Department spokesman Nick Burns was asked about the article at an April 1997 press briefing, Mr. Burns blew up. He then launched into a personal attack on the *Washington Times* reporter who uncovered the story. The *Asian Times* reported that Mr. Burns angrily stated, "I find Mr. Gertz spends most of his time collecting alleged intelligence reports and then regurgitating them on the pages of his newspaper...Clearly there must be another way of reporting on the US-Russian relationship...so I don't think I'll give it (the question) the time of day." (16)

While the Clinton Administration shows no alarm, some people in

Washington are very concerned. Congressman Curt Weldon (R-PA) has been pointing at the underground bunker for several years, trying to get Americans to pay attention. He's concerned that Russia continues to pour hundreds of millions of dollars into Yamantau Mountain while the country's economy is in ruins.

Congressman Weldon also raises the issue of American financial aid to Russia. Uncle Sam is sending hundreds of millions of American dollars to Russia to help dismantle its nuclear arsenal. Russia has also received billions in International Monetary Fund loans.

U.S. Strategic Command chief General Eugene Habiger is worried too. He was quoted in *USA Today* (March 31, 1998) saying he is concerned "because I don't know what is going on there."

How can the Russian government justify spending so much on a huge underground bunker when it is broke and needing American dollars to stay afloat?

Doesn't Russia's construction at Yamantau contradict their statements that they have no funds to comply with international nuclear arms control treaties?

If the Russians are so preoccupied with nuclear war, what assurances do we have they are truly dismantling their nuclear missiles?

If Russia is willing to spend billions of dollars on this massive underground city, how important is it strategically to Russian leaders?

What is the purpose of a top-secret underground military command center capable of withstanding a direct nuclear hit?

How can the United States be so gullible?

Perhaps the answer can be found in knowing the meaning of Yamantau Mountain.

In Russia, it is known as the Evil Mountain.

The Dead Hand: Russia's Doomsday Machine

The Russians conducted an unusual nuclear weapons test in July 1996. Ordinarily, command and control exercises are "wars" conducted on maps.

This time, however, Russian military leaders launched ballistic missiles from nuclear submarines assigned to its Pacific Fleet.

BBC News reported that the "headquarters were moved to underground bunkers. A telemetrics ship was at sea. Nuclear submarines took their positions and ballistic missiles were launched from three places in the ocean depths." (18)

Because of deep budget cutbacks since the fall of communism, the Pacific Fleet had barely fired its main weapons since 1993. The test commemorated the 300th anniversary of the Russian Navy. The BBC reported that, after the test, it appeared that pride had returned to the Russian officers and rank and file Navy members.

Is Russia committed, as claimed by Col. Stanislav Lunev, to an inevitable nuclear war with the United States?

Is it still official Russian policy that they can not only survive a nuclear war, but can actually win a nuclear war?

On November 13, 1984, the Soviet Union fired two long-range missiles 40 minutes apart. American intelligence agents tracked the trajectory of the missiles. It was not an ordinary missile test.

The Soviet Union was testing the **Dead Hand**.

It is a Doomsday Machine that will automatically launch a nuclear strike against the United States without any input by human beings.

The Dead Hand is a computer.

When the computer believes that Russia's military commanders are dead, it is programmed to automatically launch the nuclear arsenal. The system was designed to be a deterrent to the U.S., believing the Americans would hesitate to launch a first strike against Russia if they feared the Dead Hand would launch a retaliatory attack on the U.S.

Dr. Bruce Blair, Senior Fellow at the Brookings Institution in Washington, first disclosed the existence of the Dead Hand in 1993. Dr. Blair said the system is fully intact and on full alert.

During an interview on National Public Radio (October 8, 1993), Dr. Blair described the Dead Hand as "a highly computerized technical gadget." He expressed his concern in 1993 that the "early warning system that would activate the machinery is no longer as reliable as it was before the breakup" of the Soviet Union.

The system is composed of an assortment of command bunkers, radio transmitters, underground antennas, and communications rockets. When the Kremlin believes the U.S. has launched a nuclear attack, Russian military officials will activate the device from Moscow's underground war room.

A network of electronic sensors rings Moscow. When the sensors detect a nuclear attack – and when the Dead Hand determines that communications has broken down – the computer will transmit a "fail deadly" message from the Russian general's staff to a special radio bunker 40 miles south at Cheklov.

The radio message will contain the "unlock codes" held by Russia's top military officials designed to keep missiles from being launched without authorization. The transmission of the "unlock codes" activates the radio station, enabling it to transmit by an underground radio antenna "launch orders" to a fleet of communications rockets.

Upon electronically registering a break in communications above ground, the Dead Hand will transmit launch orders into emergency communications rockets hidden in SS-17 silos. After automatically launching themselves, the communications rockets would fire themselves on trajectories that cover all the nuclear fields in Russia. During their 30-minute flight into outer space, the communications rockets electronically relay automatic launch orders to nuclear-armed intercontinental missiles in silos and on mobile railroad cars.

With no further intervention by human beings, the Dead Hand will automatically fire a horrifying salvo of deadly nuclear warheads.

It is believed that the Dead Hand is now housed deep inside the massive underground bunker at the _Evil Mountain._

The existence of the Dead Hand is a sobering thought about the types of misfortunes the Year 2000 could unleash upon the Earth. Russia's deployment of a doomsday machine is further evidence of the nation's paranoia with surviving an all-out nuclear holocaust.

There are three features in the Dead Hand that should heighten everybody's concern for the Year 2000. First, the Dead Hand is a completely computerized system. Any nuclear-launch system that is 100% computer-based is frightening. Second, it bypasses human beings. Once it is activated, the system automatically sets in sequence the firing instructions to Russia's nuclear arsenal. Third, the firing signals are transmitted when there is a break in electronic communications.

If computer screens go dark at military command center in both the United States and Russia on January 1, 2000, will frightened Russian military officials believe that the U.S. has launched a military strike?

What happens if telecommunications between the two nations are down too?

What if Russia's aging computer systems fail? Will the Dead Hand receive erroneous data?

What if the Dead Hand loses communication with the sensors above ground? Will it assume everybody above ground is dead? Will it proceed to launch the rockets?

A Nuclear Holocaust is a Real Possibility in 2000

Whether intentional or accidental, a nuclear war is a real threat in 2000.

An accidental launch of nuclear weapons in 2000 is not a far-fetched possibility. In 1995, President Yeltsin came within six minutes of launching nuclear missiles against the United States. The Russians mistakenly identified a Norwegian weather research rocket as an approaching American Trident ballistic missile.

President Yeltsin activated his "nuclear briefcase" which contains the secret codes to unlock the Russian nuclear launch sequence. Moscow reportedly began the 10-minute countdown to launching a retaliatory strike. With six minutes to spare, Moscow switched on the communications system, which connected President Yeltsin with the missiles in silos, onboard trains, and submarines.

The fact that the United States came within six minutes of an accidental nuclear war should make everybody ponder the uncertainty the Year 2000 computer crisis will bring to the world.

What kind of crisis in America would precipitate a sudden attack by a foreign nation to sabotage our core national infrastructure?

Strategically, the best time would be when our technology-dependent national defense system has crashed. During a national emergency, with the electrical power supply and the telecommunication systems shut down throughout the U.S., chaos could rapidly overtake American society.

Could there be such a time ahead?

Are foreign enemies planning to use the Year 2000 computer crisis to unleash, without warning, a calculated plan of terrorism and sabotage against the United States of America?

Will America' enemies take advantage of Y2K confusion and chaos?

How many nuclear suitcase bombs are circulating in the world? How many are already secretly hidden inside the United States?

Do militant Muslim terrorists, rogue Arab nations, Russian Mafia, and former KGB agents see the Year 2000 as their window of opportunity to bring down the great USA?

Do remnants of the old Soviet Union, and their counterparts in the ruthless Communist Chinese government, see the Year 2000 as their only chance to destroy America, and restore the brutal rule of communism?

Will the world's violent and criminal malcontents – Jew-hating terrorists, drug cartel lords, Arab dictators, Mafia criminals, and former communist KGB agents - unite in 1999 to launch World War III? Following President Clinton's bombing of Afghanistan and Sudan, the Vice President of Chechnya, Vakha Arsanov, said the American missile attacks were the start of "undeclared World War III." (19)

These are serious questions that must be asked. Many will laugh at even the mention of such concerns. We live, however, in a dangerous and violent world. There are many nations and individuals that hate the United States of America with a burning passion. Our naiveté must not blind us to the possibility of a coordinated attack against us - employing nuclear suitcase bombs, HERF guns, seismic explosive devices, computer hackers, and chemical and biological weapons - to unleash terror and pandemonium in the American public.

Remember, Col. Lunev says Russian military leaders believe the only way to take control of a people is to bring war to their land.

Has America's morals sunk so low that we're willing to be led by a liar in the White House? Has a "lying spirit" come over America, lulling her into complacency?

Is America rotting inside? Does the stench of our immorality, wickedness, and violence repulse God?

Is America still a Christian nation?

Do you confidently believe God's hand is still over this land?

27 America the Beautiful: We Forgot Who Gave Us All This Stuff

"All these curses shall pursue and overtake you until you are destroyed – all because you refuse to listen to the Lord your God. These horrors shall befall you and your descendants as a warning: You will become slaves to your enemies because of your failure to praise God for all that he has given you. The Lord will send your enemies against you, and you will be hungry, thirsty, naked, and in want of everything. A yoke of iron shall be placed around your neck until you are destroyed."

Deuteronomy 28:45-48
The Living Bible

America was born in prayer and thanksgiving.

By the close of the fifteenth century, Islam had spread to much of the known world. Muslims, who regard Islam as a universal religion, zealously sought to advance Islam to every nation.

After the armies of King Ferdinand and Queen Isabella wrestled control of Spain from the Muslims, Christianity was locked in a fierce competition with Islam for the souls of the world's people.

It was Queen Isabella, a convert to Christianity, who offered to pawn her crown jewels to finance the daring voyage of a sailor whose parents named him in honor of Jesus Christ.

Today's sanitized, politically correct history books omit that Christopher Columbus set sail for the New World because he deeply believed God had divinely inspired him.

God's hand was on America from the beginning.

When the Plymouth colonists gathered their first harvest in 1621, Governor William Bradford humbly proclaimed a day of thanksgiving and prayer. Colonists and Native Americans celebrated the harvest together.

In 1623, however, a severe drought threatened the survival of the beleaguered colonists. Once again, they gathered. This time, it was a day of prayer and fasting. They beseeched God to end the drought. Without food, the struggling colonists would starve. The dream would end.

It rained.

That day became our Thanksgiving Day.

One hundred and sixty-six years after the first Thanksgiving Day, a ragtag colonial army had won independence from the King of England, but the new nation was deep in debt to wealthy individuals who financed the Revolutionary War. When the war for independence ended, the colonies had their freedom – but the new nation was broke. Money issued by the Continental Congress had depreciated to one-fortieth of its face value. The brave frontiersmen, who courageously faced the Red Coats and bitter winters, returned home to see their farms sold at debtor auctions. Many were cast into debtor prisons.

In 1786, a desperate band of 2,000 farmers and veterans led the new nation's first armed uprising. Shays Rebellion was smashed when the Massachusetts militia killed three "Shaysites" at a violent confrontation in Springfield.

Events did not bode well for the new nation.

General George Washington despaired over the tragic ending to Shays Rebellion. The Father of America wrote to General Knox, "I feel infinitely more than I can express to you, for the disorders which have arisen...Good God! Who besides a Tory, could have foreseen, or a Briton predicted them?"

The Americans had won their freedom, but could they keep it?

A system of government had to be formed, a system that would hold together the new nation's dream of freedom and liberty.

Following the war, the new independent states were held together by the Articles of Confederation, a temporary agreement that granted only limited authority and power to the Continental Congress. The fragile compromise between the sovereign states could not last forever. Economic and political pressure was building to establish a federal government.

Amid the turmoil in the new Confederation of States, 55 of America's most prominent men gathered in Philadelphia on May 25, 1787, for the purpose of hammering out a new federal constitution. Bitter disagreements over the powers of the new government --and a chief executive – deeply divided the delegates. James Madison presented his "Virginia Plan" that proposed a three-part federal government. Alexander Hamilton, a Federalist who passionately advocated a strong federal government, called the Virginia Plan a "shilly-shally thing of milk and water, which could not last."

Political divisions threatened to sink the new nation.

Could the 13 states ever agree to a document that would bind them and their descendants to a single nation?

Once again, the American dream was imperiled.

By the end of June, the Convention was on the verge of collapse. Controversy over the shape and powers of the new federal government was too great. No compromise could be found.

All seemed lost.

Then Benjamin Franklin rose to his feet.

Because all the sparring factions respected the elder statesman, their attention was turned toward the great patriot from Pennsylvania. If George Washington was the Father of the Nation, then Benjamin Franklin was the beloved Grandfather. Mr. Franklin addressed the hushed gathering of patriots, commenting that for "four or five weeks" the men had vainly searched for the perfect form of government. Their searching, Mr. Franklin reasoned, led only to "a melancholy proof of the imperfection of the human understanding."

Mr. Franklin told the delegates they had been "groping as it were in the dark to find political truth," but had never once thought about humbly asking the "Father of lights to illuminate our understanding." He reminded the distinguished delegates that "In the beginning of the contest with Great Britain, when we were sensible of danger, we had daily prayer in this room for the divine protection."

"Our prayers, Sir, were heard, and they were graciously answered," Benjamin Franklin stated.

He also reminded them that they all witnessed God's favor to the colonists during the war with England.

Oh, then he asked two questions that pierced the hearts of every patriot in the assembly.

"And have we now forgotten that powerful friend?"

"Or do we imagine that we no longer need his assistance?"

His eyes penetrated their souls. The gracious statesman shared the wisdom of his years. "I have lived, Sir, a long time, and the longer I live, the more convincing proofs I see of this truth – that _God governs in the affairs of men._ And if a sparrow cannot fall to the ground without his notice, is it probable that an empire can rise without his aid?"

Mr. Franklin quoted the Scriptures, reminding the men that "except the Lord build the house they labor in vain that build it." He said that without God's help, they would "succeed in this political building no better than the builders of Babel." If they did not receive God's blessings, the new nation would "become a reproach and by-word down to future ages."

What did Mr. Franklin want them to do?

"I therefore beg leave to move – that henceforth prayers imploring the assistance of Heaven, and its blessings on our deliberations, be held in this Assembly every morning before we proceed to business, and that one or more of the clergy of this city be requested to officiate in that service."

Yes, Mr. Franklin called a prayer meeting.

Two and a half months later, the Constitution of the United States was adopted by the assembled delegates.

America's Greatest Sin

The loving and generous hand of God has been upon America since Christopher Columbus' inspiration to sail to a new land.

Above all other reasons and motivations, colonists came to America to freely worship God.

Despite the odds, the American frontiersmen won the war against the King of England.

God held us together through the bloody civil war.

He watched over us throughout the First World War.

His hand divinely protected America during World War II, shielding us from the tyranny of demon-possessed Adolf Hitler.

When the godless system of communism rose up in Russia, God guarded us from nuclear war.

He blessed the farms of our heartland.

He blessed the work of our hands.

He blessed our factories, schools, and cities.

In an earlier, more innocent time of our nation, children said prayers each morning at the start of the school day. They bowed their heads at lunch. "God Bless America" was proudly sung in public schools across the land.

We sent men to the moon.

And our farms sent surplus food around the world to feed the world's starving masses.

Yes, America became the greatest, richest, most powerful nation ever to exist in the history of the world!

That was then. This is now.

Something went wrong.

Today, schoolboys gun down other children. The most shameful pornography is abundantly available on cable television, video rental stores, and the Internet.

In Alabama, the governor risked his political career by threatening to send in National Guard troops to protect the Ten Commandments on the wall of a local courthouse.

The President of the United States has been accused of a multitude of sins and crimes - including possible treason with Communist China - yet with each revelation of wrongdoing, his public support only soared higher.

Vulgar language is the norm on television and movies.

Murderers and violent criminals rule America's streets.

The most popular talk show parades society's most emotionally sick members across the studio, provoking them to violence and vulgarity on the air.

The federal government funds "artists" who defile images of Jesus Christ in urine.

Militant Muslim leaders inside the United States openly label the

Jewish people as "bloodsuckers" and call for their extermination. Black Muslim Khalid Muhammad extorts his followers to kill American police officers with their own revolvers and nightsticks.

Haters of God and righteousness proudly denounce religious beliefs in the media.

Any mention in public of God, the Holy Bible, or righteousness is treated like a toxic waste that must be delicately removed with rubber gloves, lest anybody be contaminated with religion.

Much is wrong in America. Our sins are many.

Violence, greed, political corruption, dishonesty, and sexual perversion – certainly grievous to God's heart – are not America's greatest sin.

If we would heed Benjamin Franklin's advice to search the Holy Scriptures, we would see, as Mr. Franklin observed, that God truly does "govern in the affairs of men." The greatest sin a nation can commit is found in the Holy Bible's Book of Deuteronomy.

God warned the Israelites about this deadly sin.

"When the Lord your God has brought you into the land he promised your ancestors, Abraham, Isaac, and Jacob, and when he has given you great cities full of good things – cities you didn't build, wells you didn't dig, and vineyards and olive trees you didn't plant – and when you have eaten until you can hold no more, then beware lest you forget the Lord who brought you out of the land of Egypt, the land of slavery. When you are full, don't forget to be reverent to him and to serve him and to use his name alone to endorse your promises." Deuteronomy 6:10-12 (TLB)

America has committed the greatest sin.

America has forgotten God.

28 Father Knows Best: America Gets A Spanking

"America is great because its people are good. And if the American people ever lose their goodness, America will cease to be great."

Alexis de Tocqueville
Circa 1830

Bad things happen to blessed nations that become wicked.
God gets their attention.
He has a pattern.
Drought, famine, pestilence, and war.
Judgment is at America's door.
"If you won't listen to the Lord your God and won't obey these laws I am giving you today, then all these curses shall come upon you:
Curses in the city.
Curses in the field.
Curses on your fruit and bread.
The curse of barren wombs.
Curses on your crops.
Curses upon the fertility of your cattle and flocks.
Curses when you come in.
Curses when you go out.
For the Lord God himself will send his personal curse upon you. You will be confused and a failure in everything you do, until at last you are destroyed because of your sin of forsaking him. He will send disease among you until you are destroyed...He will send tuberculosis, fever, infections, plague, and war. He will blight your crops, covering them with mildew. All these devastations shall pursue you until you perish." (Deuteronomy 28:15-22. The Living Bible. Tyndale House)
Will America always be the richest and most powerful nation on Earth?
That is up to us.
God reserves the right to lift up or tear down nations.
We are nothing but clay and God is the potter. He can do with

the clay anything he desires. If the clay doesn't turn out to be pleasing, the potter can break it and begin again.

"Whenever I announce that a certain nation or kingdom is to be taken up and destroyed, then if that nation renounces its evil ways, I will not destroy it as I had planned. And if I announce that I will make a certain nation strong and great, but then that nation changes it mind and turns to evil and refuses to obey me, then I too will change my mind and not bless that nation as I had said I would. Therefore, go and warn all of Judah and Jerusalem, saying: 'Hear the word of the Lord, I am planning evil against you now instead of good; turn back from your evil paths and do what is right" (Jeremiah 18:7-11. The Living Bible. Tyndale House.)

Drought and Famine Coming to America in 2000

A rebellious nation - like a rebellious child - must be disciplined. God can not ignore America's rebellion forever, lest he be rendered impotent by the arrogance of modern men and women.

Americans - including many church attending Christians - have lost their fear of God. They don't believe God will ever do anything about our nation's wickedness and rampant sins.

Therefore, the Most High will put the fear of God back into us.

The Year 2000 computer crash will be the vehicle God uses to chastise the United States of America.

Our idols will fall.

We don't think we need God's help anymore. Certainly, we don't want his laws anymore. That is obvious. Just mention the Bible in public and the God-haters froth.

Because we don't want God's help anymore, he will stop giving it. He will let us go on our own. Let's see how well we do without the blessings of God!

Therefore, he will send drought and famine to America.

"The Lord shall make the rain of your land powder and dust: from heaven shall it come down upon you, until you are destroyed." (Deuteronomy 28: 24)

"You will sow much but reap little, for the locusts will eat your crops. You will plant vineyards and care for them, but you won't eat the grapes or drink the wine, for worms will destroy the vines." (Deuteronomy 28:38-39)

Just as the brazen image of Baal fell and shattered upon the ground, our technology will fall too.

God feeds us - not technology.

Americans trust in technology. The booming economy is our idol. That explains why an overwhelming majority of Americans told pollsters they didn't care about the adultery and lying of their president as long as the economy continued to be good!

But God says to be careful that your heart doesn't turn from him.

"Take heed to yourselves, that your heart be not deceived, and ye turn aside, and serve other gods, and worship them. And the Lord's wrath be kindled against you, and he shut up the heaven, that there be no rain, and that the land yield not her fruit; and lest ye perish quickly from off the good land which the Lord giveth you." (Deuteronomy 11:16-17)

Y2K-related computer failures will strike hard. There will be no mercy. Like the people of Noah's time who were surprised by the storm's ferocity, people in 2000 will be stunned by fierce destruction brought to the world's computer systems and technology.

Oil production will cease.

Fuel supplies will disappear.

Rail transportation will halt.

Electric utilities will go dark.

Looters and rioters will ransack every store.

Grocery shelves will be bare.

Who will be your God then? To whom will you run to for safety?

The skies will refuse to yield its rain. "And I called for a drought upon the land, and upon the mountains, and upon the corn, and upon the new wine, and upon the oil, and upon that which the ground bringeth forth, and upon men, and upon cattle, and upon all the labor of the hands." (Haggai 1:11)

Embedded microprocessors that control public water purification plants will freeze. Terrorists will poison city reservoirs. Drinking water will be rationed. Your drinking water will be distributed by federal troops. "A drought is upon her waters, and they shall be dried up: for it is the land of graven images, and they are mad upon their idols." (Jeremiah 50:38)

Why will God bring famine and drought upon America?

After all God has done for us, we refuse to say, "thank you."

We are proud and ungrateful. Spoiled brats.

How do you make spoiled brats appreciate what has been given them?

Take it away.

In our overwhelming abundance, America has forsaken God. Imagine a loving, kind, generous father who bestows his wealth and favor upon his sons and daughters. It is his pleasure to bless them with abundance and good success. All he asks for in return is their love, respect, obedience, and gratitude.

During their early years, these children are humble, grateful, and, for the most part, obedient.

The father increases his blessings.

He keeps bullies away, sheltering them from heartbreak, pain, and injuries.

Something, however, goes wrong. His children turn from him. He woos them with love. He blesses them even more. He pours out unprecedented prosperity upon them. Despite his kindness, they turn against him.

His sons and daughters rebel.

They mock his ways. They ridicule his commandments. They taunt him to do something about their wicked and vile behavior.

The father weeps.

The father pleads.

The father sends messengers to warn them.

His children scream, "Get out of our lives! We don't need you anymore! We have no intention of ever going back to following your ways!"

Their rejection is unbearable.

Finally, the father acts. His patience is gone. Heartbroken that he must severely discipline the children he loves, he abruptly cancels their allowances, breaks their expensive toys, and locks them in their rooms.

His children curse him.

The father is heartsick. He knows their rebellion will destroy them.

He sees the bully coming down the street. The bully the Father has always kept away from his precious children.

The father walks away.

Foreign Enemies Will Destroy American Cities

God says abundant prosperity is the time to be careful.

He says when you live in a good land - "a land of brooks of water, of fountains and depths that spring out of valleys and hills" - that is when you must guard your heart! God promises his obedient children to give them a "good land" where you "eat bread without scarceness, and shalt not lack any thing in it." That is the time you must beware that your heart doesn't become proud and puffed up!

"But that is the time to be careful! Beware that in your plenty you don't forget the Lord your God and begin to disobey him. For when you have become full and prosperous and have built fine homes to live in, and when your flocks and herds have become very large, and your silver and gold have multiplied, that is the time to watch out that you don't become proud, and forget the Lord your God who brought you out of your slavery in the land of Egypt...Always remember, that it is the Lord your God who gives you power to become rich, and he does it to fulfill his promise to your ancestors." (Deuteronomy 8: 11-18. The Living Bible. Tyndale House)

God will send war against the United States of America.

He will use foreign nations to punish his wayward children in America.

"Hear, O earth: behold, I will bring evil upon this people, even the fruit of their thoughts, because they have not hearkened unto my words, nor to my law, but rejected it." (Jeremiah 6:19)

America's enemies will take advantage of the chaos caused by Y2K.

This very moment, they are plotting their schemes against the USA. They have nuclear suitcase bombs. Chemical and biological weapons too. Missiles that will reach Hawaii, Alaska, and America's East and West coasts.

God has set watchmen in America to blow the trumpet and sound the alarm.

Is anybody listening?

"The Lord God says, See the armies marching from the north - a great nation is rising against you. They are a cruel, merciless people, fully armed, mounted for war. The noise of their army is like a roaring sea." (Jeremiah 6:22-23. The Living Bible. Tyndale House.)

In the Year 2000, the American people will witness something they've never seen. War in our land. Terror will reign. Strong men will faint like women. Brave men will hide from the terror in the night.

"We have heard the fame of their armies and we are weak with fright. Fright and pain have gripped us like that of women in travail. Don't go out to the fields! Don't travel the roads! For the enemy is everywhere, ready to kill; we are terrorized at every turn." (Jeremiah 6:24)

Impossible?

Could never happen in the USA, you say?

We are a Christian nation! We support missionaries! God depends on the American church to do his work! Judgment will never come to America!

Really?

"You think that because the Temple is here, you will never suffer? Don't fool yourselves! Do you really think that you can steal, murder, commit adultery, lie, and worship Baal and all of those new gods of yours, and then come here and stand before me in my Temple and chant, 'We are saved!' - only to go right back to all these evil things again?" (Jeremiah 7: 8-10)

Americans are deceiving themselves if they think war could never strike American cities. We live in perilous times. Terrorists have weapons of mass destruction. Communist China now has 13 rockets with nuclear warheads pointed at American cities! Russia's economy has collapsed. Nuclear weapons have been sold for quick cash to rogue nations!

And you think America's cities will never burn?

You think America can openly allow sin and God will not respond?

Fools!

"For the people...are full of treachery against me, says the Lord. They have lied and said, "He won't bother us! No evil will come upon us! There will be neither famine nor war! God's prophets', they say, 'are windbags full of words with no divine authority. Their claims of doom will fall upon themselves, not us!" (Jeremiah 5: 11-13. The Living

Bible. Tyndale House.)

God warns that people who mock his warnings of war will see destruction come upon them swiftly.

"Because of talk like this, I'll take your words...and turn them into raging fire...See, I will bring a distant nation against you...a mighty nation, an ancient nation whose language you don't understand. Their weapons are deadly; the men are all mighty. And they shall eat your harvest and your children's bread, and your flocks of sheep and herds of cattle, yes, and your grapes and figs; and they shall sack your walled cities that you think are safe." (Jeremiah 5:14-17. The Living Bible. Tyndale House.)

Osama bin Laden, the radical Muslim fundamentalist who has masterminded a spate of bloody bombings around the world, has called for a jihad. His goal is to foment a worldwide religious war that unites the planet's 1 billion Muslims. Osama bin Laden exhorts Muslims to kill Americans wherever they find them. All for the glory of Allah.

This bloodthirsty killer runs training camps for terrorists. He and his Muslim cohorts were involved in the truck bomb attack on the apartment building that housed American soldiers in Saudi Arabia in 1996, killing 19 U.S. servicemen. Bin Laden's associates organized the bloody bombings of American embassies in Kenya and Tanzania on August 7, 1998.

"In our religion, there is a special place in the hereafter for those who participate in jihad," bin Laden stated in London's *The Independent* newspaper on July 10, 1996.

We are entering an age of horrible violence.

In the days ahead, Muslim terrorists will unleash weapons of mass destruction on innocent people in urban areas that will both shock and terrorize the world. The focal point is Israel. At a gathering of Palestinian terrorists in Gaza on July 11, 1998, the leader of the Islamic Jihad called for new suicide attacks against Israel. Hundreds chanted "Death to Israel and America." The radical Muslims see America as Israel's only protector. Therefore, they must cripple America. With the United States out of the way, Israel will be naked and vulnerable.

America, are you prepared for the horror and bloodshed your enemies plan to unleash upon you soon?

Many violent men long for your destruction!

Count them!

Radical Islamic terrorists in the Middle East such as Hamas, Hizbollah, the World Islamic Front, and the Jihad Movement of Egypt. Their extensive network of counterparts in the United States who are training on American soil for the inevitable bloody jihad against America. Osama bin Laden, the wealthy Saudi terrorist, who has declared war on the United States. Ali Fallahian, leader of the Iranian government, who is building a network of militant Muslims inside the United States.

Ramadan Abdallah Shallah, formerly associated with the University of South Florida in Tampa, and now the leader of the Israel-hating group called Islamic Jihad. Red China, the communist regime that now has 13 nuclear missiles pointed at American cities. Include North Korea too, the nation that fired two missiles over Japan in September 1998 – capable of reaching the West Coast of the United States. The twins of terror: Iraq's Saddam Hussein and Libya's Moammar Ghadafy. Nation of Islam leader Louis Farrakhan, who received $1 billion from Ghadafy to unite America's six million Muslims. The vicious Khalid Muhammad, the hate-driven Black Muslim who openly advocates the killing of all Jews and white people. And the list goes on!

Separately, they can not bring down the United States. Working together, they will bring the greatest horror America has ever witnessed. This ragtag collection of political misfits shares one common goal: the complete destruction of our beloved America.

Who will protect us?

Who will shield us from the war they seek to bring to America's streets?

Why should God protect us?

You do not want to be a Christian nation anymore, right?

You do not want the Ten Commandments on your public buildings! You will not allow public school teachers to pray and read the Holy Scriptures to your children! At Christmas, your children can not sing songs about the birth of God's Son! You will not allow nativity scenes to be displayed on public property!

Oh yes, you insist that there must be a separation of church and state.

Fine!

God now separates himself from you!

Who will protect you now?

You angrily proclaim that American women have the right to kill their children in the womb. Millions of your little sons and daughters are murdered each year as a bloody sacrifice to your gods of pleasure and convenience. Even the brains of the infants are sucked out during birth, yet your government will not outlaw such gruesome torture! Your sin is so great, this merciless slaughter does not bother your conscience. What will you do when your enemies kill your children in the streets?

Do you know how far you have strayed from God's protection?

You will soon discover how far you've drifted from God when the sound of the enemy's weapons abruptly shatters the nighttime peace. "The noise of war resounds from the northern border. The whole land trembles at the approach of the terrible army, for the enemy is coming, and is devouring the land and everything in it – the cities and people alike. For I will send enemy troops among you like poisonous snakes which you cannot charm. No matter what you do, they will bite you and you shall die." (Jeremiah 8:16-17. The Living Bible. Tyndale House)

"All the strength of (America) vanishes beneath his wrath. He has withdrawn his protection as the enemy attacks. God burns across the land of (America) like a raging fire." (Lamentation 2:3. The Living Bible. Tyndale House. Parenthesis added.)

The sound of war will be heard throughout the land.

A well-organized army of terrorists will rise up without warning. They are amongst you now. They wait for the war cry.

At the appointed time, this army of vengeance will strike. The horror will be unimaginable. Like a heart attack, there will be no warning.

Your enemies will show no mercy. A campaign of terror will threaten every man, woman, and child. Bombs will destroy America's sacred national shrines. Biological weapons, released in sports arenas and shopping malls, will strike down multitudes. Poisons emptied in rivers and reservoirs will instantly kill thousands. Their missiles will explode in the night sky.

"My grief is beyond healing; my heart is broken. Listen to the weeping of my people all across the land."

"Where is the Lord?" they ask. "Has God deserted us?"

"Oh, why have they angered me with their carved idols and strange evil rites?" the Lord replied.

(Jeremiah 8: 18-19. The Living Bible. Tyndale House.)

The People Will Blame America's Shepherds

Where are America's preachers? Why don't they see what is coming?

"The shepherds of my people have lost their senses; they no longer follow God nor ask his will. Therefore they perish and their flocks are scattered. Listen! Hear the terrible sound of great armies coming from the north."

(Jeremiah 10: 21-22. The Living Bible. Tyndale House.)

Where will the American people hear that sin will lead to destruction? Will America's preachers warn them?

"Then I said, O Lord God, their prophets are telling them all is well – that no war or famine will come. They tell the people you will surely send them peace, that you will bless them."

"Then the Lord said: The prophets are telling lies in my name. I didn't send them or tell them to speak or give them any message. They prophesy of visions and revelations they have never heard; they speak foolishness concocted out of their own lying hearts. Therefore, the Lord says, I will punish these lying prophets who have spoken in my name though I did not send them, who say no war shall come nor famine. By war and famine they themselves shall die!"

(Jeremiah 14: 14-15. The Living Bible. Tyndale House.)

Judgment is at America's door, yet so few preachers hear the sounds of the enemy's army. The American church is deceived by prosperity! Life is too good! The booming American economy is keeping the money flowing into the churches. Why mess up a good thing? Preaching about sin will offend people! Why expose the wretchedness of the typical American lifestyle of materialism, indulgence, and selfishness?

The nation is adrift in a sea of immorality, yet hardly a sound is uttered publicly from the nation's pulpits! Why? Because church members are indulging in the same sins as the public!

The American church is like the church in Laodicea. God told them, "I know you well – you are neither hot or cold; I wish you were one or the other! But since you are merely lukewarm, I will spit you out of my mouth! You say, 'I am rich, with everything I want; I don't need a thing!' And you don't realize that spiritually you are wretched and miserable and poor and blind and naked." (The Revelation 3:15-17. The Living Bible. Tyndale House.)

And did God warn the indifferent Christians in Laodicea?

"I continually discipline and punish everyone I love; so I must punish you, unless you turn from your indifference and become enthusiastic about the things of God." (The Revelation 3:19. The Living Bible. Tyndale House.)

Too many pastors and evangelists are too busy raising money to enlarge their empires. They have no time to call people to repentance. Bigger buildings must be constructed! More money must be raised! More members must be recruited! And what is the driving motivation? Is it to denounce sin and proclaim holiness? Is it to feed the poor and clothe the naked? No! It is so the preacher can have a bigger ministry than his rivals! There's more competition in the church world than the business world. How ironic! Soon, divine judgment will pierce our nation's soul, yet many members of the clergy will be the most surprised!

"Therefore, tell them this: Night and day my eyes shall overflow with tears; I cannot stop my crying, for my people have been run through with a sword and lie mortally wounded on the ground. If I go out in the fields, there lie the bodies of those the sword has killed; and if I walk in the streets, there lie those dead from the starvation and disease. And yet the prophets and priests alike have made it their business to travel through the whole country, reassuring everyone that all is well, speaking of things they know nothing about." (Jeremiah 14:17-18. The Living Bible. Tyndale House.)

When the judgment comes, the people will curse the preachers for not warning them. How can you blame them? Many will say, "I have attended church for five years and I have never heard a sermon about Hell or judgment! I've only been taught that God wants to make me rich and happy. Why didn't my pastor tell me about sin?"

310 • Judgment Day 2000!

"Your 'prophets' have said so many foolish things, false to the core. They have not tried to hold you back from slavery by pointing out your sins. They lied and said that all was well." (Lamentations 2:14. The Living Bible. Tyndale House.)

God told ancient Israel that judgment would strike their nation because of the shallow preaching of their prophets and priests. He told Ezekiel to prophesy against the "foolish prophets" who made up dreams and visions to please the people.

"O (America), these 'prophets' of yours are as useless as foxes for rebuilding your walls! O evil prophets, what have you ever done to strengthen the walls of (America) against her enemies - by strengthening (America) in the Lord? Instead, you have lied when you said, 'My message is from God!' God did not send you. And you expect him to fulfill your prophecies. Can you deny that you have claimed to see visions' you never saw, and that you have said, 'This message is from God,' when I never spoke to you at all?" (Ezekiel 13: 4-7. The Living Bible. Tyndale House. Parenthesis added.)

God warns such preachers that his hand will be against those who seduce people to believe there will be peace, not war, even when the nation is defiled in sin. He says the people are building a flimsy wall around their nation destined to collapse, yet the preachers are encouraging them! "For these evil men deceive my people by saying, 'God will send peace,' when that is not my plan at all! My people build a flimsy wall and these prophets praise them for it - and cover it with white-wash!" (Ezekiel 13:10. The Living Bible. Tyndale House.)

America was, at one time, a righteous nation. We were proud to be called a Christian nation. The Christian wall of righteousness, however, has been replaced by a flimsy wall of humanism and self-gratification. We deceive ourselves into thinking America is safe from outside attacks. We go to sleep at night thinking we're safe, not realizing how naked and vulnerable we are to our enemies.

Our flimsy wall will soon collapse.

"Tell these evil builders that their wall will fall. A heavy rainstorm will undermine it: great hailstones and mighty winds will knock it down. And when the wall falls, the people will cry out, 'Why didn't you tell us that it wasn't good enough? Why did you whitewash it and cover up its faults?' Yes, it will surely fall. The Lord God says: I will sweep it away with a storm of indignation and with a great flood of anger and with hailstones of wrath. I will break down your whitewashed wall, and it will fall on you and crush you, and you shall know I am the Lord. Then at last my wrath against the wall will be completed; and concerning those who praised it, I will say: The wall and its builders both are gone. For they were lying prophets, claiming (America) will have peace when there is no peace, says the Lord God." (Ezekiel 13: 11-16. The Living Bible. Tyndale House. Parenthesis added.)

In too many American pulpits, shepherds are too timid to warn their congregation that judgment is imminent. Their high-income members may depart, seeking a church that doesn't make them feel uncomfortable. If they depart, who will pay for the expensive gymnasium and fancy building projects? Even worse, they may be ridiculed. How could they play golf at the country club if the city's elite is snickering about their "fire and brimstone" sermons?

Plain and simple, they fear men more than God.

Telling people that war and famine are coming will not make you popular. It is not a good way to build a ministry. Americans want to feel good. They want to hear happy sermons about wealth.

Yes, Americans want to hear about the good life. The church is now obsessed with prosperity, not righteousness. We have our priorities backward. God says righteousness comes first, then prosperity. Too many Americans Christians, however, don't want to hear anything in the Word of God that doesn't pertain to money, wealth, and the good life. They fail to understand that the reason for God's prosperity is to meet the needs of others and advance the Gospel around the world – not to squander it on selfish lusts.

Despite the ambivalence of luke-warm Christians, God is sending messengers to sound the trumpet.

"But listen now to the solemn words I speak to you in the presence of all these people. The ancient prophets who preceded you and me spoke against many nations, always warning of war, famine, and plague. So a prophet who foretells peace has the burden of proof on him to prove that God has really sent him. Only when his message comes true can it be known that he really is from God." (Jeremiah 28:7-9. The Living Bible. Tyndale House.)

Pastors of America, are you awake? Are you at your post?

"Someone from among you keeps calling, calling to me: 'Watchman, what of the night? Watchman, what of the night? How much time is left?' The watchman replies, 'Your judgment day is dawning now. Turn again to God, so that I can give you better news. Seek for him, then come and ask again." (Isaiah 21:11-12. The Living Bible. Tyndale House.)

Year 2000: The Nations Will Drink from God's Cup of Wrath

The time of chastisement is here.

Soon, God will shake everything that can be shaken. We will quickly discover who and what is anchored in Christ.

The return of our Lord Jesus Christ is imminent. While nobody knows the day or hour, Jesus did tell us we would know the season. His disciples asked, "Tell us, when shall these things be? And what shall be the sign of your coming, and of the end of the world?" (Matthew 24:3)

Jesus told them, "And you shall hear of wars and rumors of wars:

see that you be not troubled, for all these things must come to pass, but the end is not yet. For nation shall rise up against nation, and kingdom against kingdom: and there shall be famines, and pestilences, and earthquakes in many places. All these things are the beginning of sorrows." (Matthew 24:6-8)

Great woe is about to sweep over the Earth.

The sorrows will soon begin.

God will make the nations drink from his cup of wrath.

In the Book of Jeremiah, God told the prophet he would bring upon the nations all the terrors promised in the Bible. "For the Lord God said to me: 'Take from my hand this wine cup filled to the brim with my fury, and make all the nations to whom I send you drink from it. They shall drink from it and reel, crazed by the death blows I rain upon them." (Jeremiah 25:15-16. The Living Bible. Tyndale House.)

Jeremiah obeyed the Lord and went from nation to nation, making them drink from the cup of God's wrath.

God instructed Jeremiah to tell the nations, "The Lord of heaven's armies, the God of Israel, says, 'Drink from this cup of my wrath until you are drunk and vomit and fall and rise no more, for I am sending terrible wars upon you.' And if they refuse to accept the cup, tell them, 'The Lord of heaven's armies says you must drink it! You cannot escape! I have begun to punish my own people, so should you go free? No, you shall not evade punishment. I will call for war against all the peoples of the earth.'"
(Jeremiah 25: 27-29. The Living Bible. Tyndale House.)

The worldwide crash of computers in the Year 2000 will shake the foundation of mankind's economic and political systems. Nations will reel from the abrupt halt to the global economy. The economies of Japan, China, and Russia will collapse. Panic and fear will grip politicians, scientists, bankers, and financiers. The high and mighty will be unable to contain the events following the breakdown of systems. They won't know how to stop it. A financial tidal wave will crush the economies of Latin America, Africa, and the South Pacific. Governments will topple. Kings will flee their stately palaces. Uprisings will destabilize nations. Militant Muslims will overthrow established thrones in the Middle East, and invade nations in Northern Africa and Southern Europe.

The world will shake violently with turmoil.

The only thing to hold onto will be Jesus Christ.

America, O America, are you ready for the punishment that awaits you?

You will faint in terror when your enemies release deadly biological and chemical agents in your air and water!

"What is happening? Where is everyone going? Why are they running to the rooftops? What are they looking at? The whole city is in terrible uproar. What's the trouble in this busy, happy city? Bodies!

Lying everywhere, slain by the plague and not by the sword. All your leaders flee; they surrender without resistance. The people slip away but they are captured, too. Let me alone to weep. Don't try to comfort me - let me cry for my people as I watch them being destroyed. Oh, what a day of crushing trouble! What a day of confusion and terror from the Lord God of heaven's armies! The walls of (America) are breached and the cry of death echoes from the mountainsides...God has removed his protecting care. You run to the armory for your weapons! You inspect the walls of (America) to see what needs repair! You check over the houses and tear some down for stone for fixing walls. Between the city walls, you build a reservoir for water from the lower pool! But all your feverish plans will not avail, for you never ask for help from God, who lets this come upon you. The Lord God called you to repent, to weep and mourn and shave your heads in sorrow for your sins, and to wear clothes made of sackcloth to show your remorse. But instead, you sing and dance and play, and feast and drink. 'Let us eat, drink, and be merry,' you say: 'What's the difference, for tomorrow we die.' The Lord God has revealed to me that this sin will never be forgiven until the day you die." (Isaiah 22:2-14. The Living Bible. Tyndale House.)

Yes, the Lord God - Commander of Heaven's Armies - will soon shake all the kingdoms of the world. No nation will be spared from his wrath. Grief and terror will be everywhere. Those who mock the Holy One today will hide in utter fear tomorrow. The holocaust will bring unbearable sorrow and grief to the nations.

Many will flee the terror, but have no place to hide.

"But my heart is heavy with grief, for evil still prevails and treachery is everywhere. Terror and the captivity of hell are still your lot, O men of the world. When you flee in terror you will fall into a pit, and if you escape from the pit you will step into a trap, for destruction falls from the heavens upon you; the world is shaken beneath you. The earth has broken down in utter collapse; everything is lost, abandoned and confused. The world staggers like a drunkard: it shakes like a tent in a storm. It falls and will not rise again, for the sins of the earth are very great." (Isaiah 24:16-23. The Living Bible. Tyndale House.)

America, your time is running out!

What will you do?

Will you return to God or will you stubbornly cling to your filthy sins?

29 *God Bless America:* Land That I Love
Personal Words from the Author

"If I shut up heaven that there be no rain, or if I command the locusts to devour the land, or if I send pestilence among my people; If my people, which are called by my name, shall humble themselves, and pray, and seek my face, and turn from their wicked ways; then will I hear from heaven, and will forgive their sin, and will heal their land."

2 Chronicles 7:13-14

For months in early 1998, the Holy Spirit gently nudged me to fast. I ignored his prompting. The quiet, still voice would not depart. Several times each week, I heard inside my heart the voice of the Lord calling me to a time of prayer and fasting.

How could I find the time?

After all, I was the marketing director for the world's largest religious television network. I was too busy working for God to have time for prayer and fasting!

Again and again, the Holy Spirit whispered, "I want you to fast."

Finally, in mid-April 1998, I realized that God was trying to get my attention. Despite pressing deadlines and projects, I had to slow down and listen to the Lord. In the meantime, my son, Jeremy, was completing a presentation for his freshman Public Speaking class in college. His topic: The Year 2000 computer crash.

I had never heard of Y2K.

Because I devour so much news and information everyday, my family has often joked that I must be given intravenous injections of printing ink when I miss the morning newspaper. I've always believed that God wants me to be keenly aware of events in the world – to know the signs of the time – so he could use such knowledge someday in my ministry for Him.

Despite my awareness of world affairs, I had not heard of the Year 2000 computer crash.

Unaware of Jeremy's classroom work, I finally purposed in my heart to shut out the noise of the world and everyday life to be alone with God in prayer and fasting. It did not take long for the Lord to get my attention. Several days into the fast, the Lord spoke to my heart to go to the chapel at my office at Trinity Broadcasting Network's International Production Center in Irving, TX.

My heart immediately broke.

The Lord told me that great trouble is coming to the United States of America.

My mind was flooded with images of chaos, riots, grief, and even war.

"This could not be America," I said to myself.

God told me that I needed to repent of my sins, and prepare my own heart and soul for the difficult times ahead. He said the time of judgment on America would begin soon.

Whenever I believe God is speaking to me, I always ask him to confirm the message with scriptures from the Holy Bible. I cried to God in TBN's chapel, "Lord, what I am seeing is so horrible, you must help me believe this message is from you." I opened my Living Bible and immediately saw Isaiah 24:

"Look! The Lord is overturning the land of Judah and making it a vast wasteland of destruction. See how he is emptying out all its people and scattering them over the face of the earth. Priest and people, servants and masters, slave girls and mistresses, buyers and sellers, lenders and borrowers, bankers and debtors – none will be spared. The land will be completely emptied and looted. The Lord has spoken. The land suffers for the sins of its people. The earth languishes, the crops wither, the skies refuse their rain. The land is defiled by crime; the people have twisted the laws of God and broken his everlasting commands. Therefore the curse of God is upon them; they are left desolate, destroyed by the drought. Few will be left alive."

"All the joys of life will go: the grape harvest will fail, the wine will be gone, the merrymakers will sigh and mourn. The melodious chords of the harp and timbrel are heard no more; the happy days are ended. No more are the joys of wine and song; strong drink turns bitter in the mouth."

"The city lies in chaos; every home and shop is locked up tight to keep out looters. Mobs form in the streets, crying for wine; joy has reached its lowest ebb; gladness has been banished from the land. The city is left in ruins; its gates are battered down. Throughout the land the story is the same – only a remnant is left."

"But all who are left will shout and sing for joy; those in the west will praise the majesty of God, and those in the east will respond in praise. Hear them singing to the Lord from the ends of the earth, singing glory to the Righteous One!"

I began to cry. I love my country very much. America is the

greatest land on earth! Despite our greatness, something is terribly wrong in the land. Our nation's moral fiber has eroded enormously since I was a boy growing up in a rural farming community in Western Maryland. I keep telling my son and daughter, "What you see on television today is not what America was like 30 years ago. We used to be a Christian nation."

The presence of God was so real that April day in TBN's chapel.

Although I didn't want to accept the Lord's message, in my heart I knew I had heard the voice of the Lord. God was showing me the future of the USA. Judgment is coming!

I wiped away tears and said, "Father, if these things are coming to America, then I must tell everybody! I have to tell them in plain language that everybody will understand. I will do whatever you tell me to do."

As I was speaking those words, I opened my Bible again. This time I immediately saw Habakkuk 2:1-2.

"I will climb my watchtower now, and wait to see what answer God will give to my complaint. And the Lord said to me, 'Write my answer on a billboard large and clear, so that anyone can read it at a glance and rush to tell the others.'"

I was shocked at the quick response the Lord gave to my pledge to warn the people. Inside, I knew I had to tell everybody what God was showing me - no matter how unpleasant and troubling the message would be to people.

Even though I promised to obey the Lord and speak the warning, part of me strongly resisted saying such things about America. This is my country. I would gladly die for this land. I don't want to see anything bad happen to this great nation.

The Lord whispered to me, "If you love America, then you'll warn America."

The images of war, destruction, and chaos were so terrifying and real to me that I felt compelled to ask God one more question. "Father, please don't get mad at me for asking this question. I have to know! Will America recover from this judgment? Will life ever be restored? Is there any hope for the United States?"

Once again, I opened my Bible. This time it fell open to Proverbs 20:24.

"Since the Lord is directing our steps, why try to understand everything that happens along the way?"

I knew the conversation was over. God had revealed all that he was going to share with me that day. If God is directing my steps, I don't need to know what is ahead for the United States of America. I just need to be obedient today.

The next day, several unexpected visitors came to my office at TBN. One gentleman was a minister. He told me God was revealing to him that judgment is coming soon to America. I was stunned while listening to his words. He said he preached a sermon the week before based on Isaiah 24.

I had trouble sleeping that night. Without a doubt, I knew my life was about to dramatically change.

The next morning, my 22-year-old daughter, Karissa, told me that Jesus appeared in her sleep the night before. Obviously, such a statement from a family member will get your attention. I asked Karissa what the Lord said to her in the dream.

"He said, 'Daughter, I will speak to you many times in your dreams over the next year.'"

"So, what did he say to you?" I asked her.

"Dad, after Jesus said those words I had a dream, but I don't remember it! It was an important dream. Why can't I remember it?"

I told Karissa not to fret, and that she would remember it when the time is right.

Moments later, I quietly prayed to God about the things he had told me regarding his pending judgment against the United States for our sins. I said, "God, you told me to write down your answer and make it plain so everybody understands. Lord, I promise you right now I will write down everything you want the people to know – and I'll publish it in a book. As long as you help me, I promise to be faithful and diligent. I'll begin today."

Following that prayer, I told Karissa what I had just promised God. When I said God wanted me to write a book so everybody knows that judgment is coming, Karissa's face had a look of astonishment.

"Dad, I just remembered the dream! Oh no! Dad, when you said you would write a book as a warning, the dream flashed in my mind!"

"Karissa, what did you dream?" I asked her.

"I dreamed we were standing in a circle of people. Thousands of people were rotating around us like a carnival carrousel. Their faces were sunken. They looked like skeletons. As they circled us, they stretched out their arms and cried."

"What were they saying in your dream?" I immediately inquired.

"They were crying out, 'If you knew this was going to happen, why didn't you warn us?'"

"Dad, I just remembered a second dream!" Karissa said in surprise.

"It was the Second Coming of the Lord. When he appeared in the sky, I saw millions of souls leap out of their bodies and go up to meet the Lord in the air. I also saw millions of other souls come out of the people's bodies who didn't go up. They reached for Jesus, but their souls collapsed and fell back into each person's body. When they saw Jesus, they wanted to go up, but couldn't!"

"Dad, you have to write that book! Those dreams are too scary!"

A few days later, Jeremy asked me to look at his Y2K slide presentation he made for his college class. I was stunned at the information he had gathered. "Let me see your notes!" I said to him. Electric power plants, medical equipment, government services, banking – Jeremy had outlined the numerous consequences of failing to fix the world's computers before the Year 2000.

Within days, the Lord tied the two things together in my mind: Y2K and judgment.

Over the next several months, my life changed.

There are millions of Americans today where I was at in April 1998 – totally ignorant of Y2K. A date in destiny is around the bend, but most of the nation is oblivious to the coming storm.

People who dismiss the significance of the Year 2000 computer crisis are deceiving themselves. It is about more than computers. Y2K is the global event God will use to bring divine chastisement on all the nations. The Y2K collapse will also permit the restructuring of the world's economic and political systems, making way for those who propose a one-world governmental system.

These things are necessary for the fulfillment of Bible prophecy.

I have tried my best to present in easy-to-understand words the awesome message God has placed inside my spirit. I have not held back any words.

Writing this book has not been easy. Several times I wanted to quit. I didn't want to write these things! I have no choice. I fear God more than I fear the opinions of men.

God told Ezekiel, "I have appointed you as a watchman for the people of Israel; therefore listen to what I say and warn them for me. When I say to the wicked, 'O wicked man, you will die!' and you don't tell him what I say, so that he does not repent – that wicked person will die in his sins, but I will hold you responsible for his death. But if you warn him to repent and he doesn't, he will die in his sin, and you will not be responsible." (Ezekiel 33:7-9. The Living Bible. Tyndale House.)

I have warned you.

I am no longer responsible for what you do.

There is an army coming against the United States of America. It is an army of violent, hate-filled men. They are plotting against the USA this very moment. Unless America repents of her sins and turns back to God, this army of terrorists will launch a bloody jihad in the streets of America's cities. Nuclear weapons will obliterate major urban areas. Horrible race riots, led by violent black Muslims, will erupt across the land. Chemical warfare will poison the air and water. Many, many Americans will die.

I cannot deny what I see.

I cannot refuse to sound the alarm.

I hear the sound of the enemy now!

"My heart, my heart – I writhe in pain; my heart pounds within me. I cannot be still because I have heard, O my soul, the blast of the enemies' trumpets and the enemies' battle cries. Wave upon wave of destruction rolls over the land, until it lies in utter ruin; suddenly, in a moment, every house is crushed. How long must this go on? How long must I see war and death around me?" (Jeremiah 4:19-21. The Living Bible. Tyndale House.)

America, this is your final warning!

This doesn't have to be your fate! Why do you refuse to humble yourself before the Almighty God? Why do you stubbornly cling to your vile sins? What have your idols ever done for you?

"Son of dust, tell your people: When I bring an army against a country, and the people of that land choose a watchman, and when he sees the army coming, and blows the alarm to warn them, then anyone who hears the alarm and refuses to heed it – well, if he dies the fault is his own. For he heard the warning and wouldn't listen; the fault is his. If he had heeded the warning, he would have saved his life. But if the watchman sees the enemy coming and doesn't sound the alarm and warn the people, he is responsible for their deaths. They will die in their sins, but I will charge the watchman with their deaths." (Ezekiel 33:1-6. The Living Bible. Tyndale House.)

America's blood will not be on my hands!

Repent! Turn back to God!

It is not too late!

30

The Sin Amnesty: The Final Call for Repentance

"And the Lord called to the man with the writer's case, and said to him, 'Walk through the streets of (America) and put a mark on the foreheads of the men who weep and sigh because of all the sins they see around them. Then I heard the Lord tell the other men: 'Follow him through the city and kill everyone whose forehead isn't marked. Spare not nor pity them – kill them all – old and young, girls, women, and little children; but don't touch anyone with the mark. And begin right here at the Temple.' And so they began by killing the seventy elders."

Ezekiel 9:4-6
The Living Bible
Tyndale House (Parenthesis added)

For six weeks, I labored 19 to 20 hours each day to write this book. I hardly ever left my office in my home. My spirit was troubled to finish it quickly.

Finally, I completed the manuscript. At last, I could rest. The book was finished.

"There's one more thing I want you to say," the Lord surprised me by saying.

"Tell America I am declaring a Sin Amnesty."

"A what?" I asked.

"A sin amnesty," the Holy Spirit repeated.

Webster's Dictionary says amnesty is to forget. "The act of an authority (such as a government) by which pardon is granted to a large group of individuals."

And what is a pardon?

According to Webster's, a pardon is "divine forgiveness." It is the "excusing of an offense without exacting a penalty." A pardon is a "release from the legal penalties of an offense."

When a government proclaims an amnesty, it gives people a specific time period to turn themselves in to authorities and admit their wrong-doing. As long as the offender turns himself or herself in during the prescribed time period, no punishment will be given. Sometimes state governments declare tax amnesties. People who owe back taxes are allowed to come forward without fear of prosecution. If you don't come forward, however, the punishment is even more severe if you are caught after the amnesty expires.

Well, God the Father says he is declaring a Sin Amnesty in America!

As the supreme authority in the universe, he is offering divine forgiveness to the American people. He is willing to excuse our offenses without exacting a penalty for our nation's sins.

The Holy Spirit spoke inside me saying, "Tell the people the Father will forgive every person who turns himself or herself in to the Holy Spirit. They must confess their wrongdoing and pledge to turn away from their sins. They will not be punished. All of their sins will be forgiven and forgotten. It doesn't matter what they have done wrong. I will pardon all sins. The coming judgment on the nations will not come upon them. I will mark them. I will protect them. They will be brought through the great distress that is soon coming to the world. If they refuse to surrender now during the Sin Amnesty, then there will be no protection when the judgment of America comes."

God has no desire to punish you.

He only desires to give you his blessings.

"For I know the plans I have for you, says the Lord. They are plans for good and not for evil, to give you a future and a hope. In those days when you pray, I will listen. You will find me when you seek me, if you look for me in earnest." (Jeremiah 29:11-13. The Living Bible. Tyndale House.)

Those who put their trust in God will be preserved through all the troubles ahead.

It is not too late.

Turn yourself in! Confess your sins. Ask God to forgive all your transgressions against him. Ask him to forget about all that you've done wrong. Accept his Son – Jesus Christ – into your life as your Savior.

Accept God's Sin Amnesty while you still have a chance.

Say this prayer:

"Dear God, I am a sinner. I have broken your laws. I have done many wrong things. I need forgiveness. Please take away my sins. Don't ever remember them. Write my name down in the Book of Life. Please send Jesus into my heart to be my Savior. Fill me with your Holy Spirit to be my guide, friend, and comforter. Help me to live the right way to please you. Thank you for saving me. Amen."

Tell somebody now that you have accepted Jesus Christ as your Savior.

If you are a Christian – but you are trapped in sin – now is the time to call to God for deliverance. God is not angry with you. He knows you are made of dust. He is not shocked that you sinned –

even after becoming a Christian! That's why he provided a Savior. Even after becoming a Christian, we are still in need of a savior everyday.

Stop beating yourself down with guilt and shame.

Let go of it.

Come back to God now.

He needs you at this critical hour. There is much work to do before the judgment falls. Turn yourself in to God. Go ahead and confess your sins.

Accept the provisions of his Sin Amnesty.

Let him mark you.

"Watch now,' the Lord Almighty declares, 'the day of judgment is coming, burning like a furnace. The proud and wicked will be burned up like straw; like a tree, they will be consumed – roots and all.'

'But for you who fear my name, the Sun of Righteousness will rise with healing in his wings. And you will go free, leaping with joy like calves let out to pasture. Then you will tread upon the wicked as ashes underfoot,' says the Lord Almighty. "Remember to obey the laws I gave all Israel through Moses my servant on Mount Horeb.'

'See, I will send you another prophet like Elijah before the coming of the great and dreadful judgment day of God. His preaching will bring fathers and children together again, to be of one mind and heart, for they will know that if they do not repent, I will come and utterly destroy their land." (Malachi 4. The Living Bible. Tyndale House.)

Bibliography ───────────────

Introduction

1   Christian Science Monitor, March 18, 1998.
2   Moscow News, May 14, 1998.

Chapter 2

1   Washington Post, May 21, 1998.
2   USA Today, April 15, 1998.
3   New York Times, April 15, 1998.
4   Austin American-Statesman, April 15, 1998.

Chapter 3

1   Federal News Service, May 7, 1998
2   Testimony before Banking Committee, U.S. Senate, April 6, 1998.
3   The Doomsday Date by Sue Mellon, DCI, September 20, 1996.
4   Washington Post, April 24, 1998.
5   Newsbytes, April 29, 1998.
6   Federal News Service, May 7, 1998.
7   BBC News, January 14, 1998.
8   BBC News, January 14, 1998.

Chapter 4

1   The Sunday Times, August 17, 1997.
2   The American Banker, April 29, 1998.
3   Business Wire, March 25, 1998.
4   InfoWorld Electric, January 10, 1998.
5   Millennium Journal, Data Dimensions, November 1997.

Chapter 5

1   ComputerWeekly, February 10, 1997.
2   ComputerWeekly, August 5, 1997.
3   The Age, May 12, 1998.
4   ComputerWeekly, August 5, 1997.
5   Lewis Perdue, TechWeek, March 23, 1998.
6   The Independent Business Weekly, November 28, 1997.
7   Computing Canada, March 23, 1998.
8   World Oil, April 1998.
9   New Jersey Online with The Times, May 3, 1998.
10   Rick Cowles, euy2k.com, May 1998.
11   Roleigh Martin, ourworld.compuserve.com, May 1998.
12   South Western Electricity Web site, www.swebuk.com/docs/millen4.htm
13   Florida Power & Light Web site, www.fpl.com/html/2000.
14   CMP Net, TechWeb News, June 2, 1997.
15   Australian Financial Review, April 29, 1998.
16   National Science Foundation, Office of the Director, Notice #120, June 27, 1997.
17   United States Nuclear Regulatory Commission, Notice # 97-61, August 6, 1997.
18   State of Washington Department of Transportation Web site, www.wa.gov/dis/2000/RFQQ/dot83201.

Chapter 6

1   The Dominion newspaper, Wellington, NZ, April 27, 1998.

Chapter 7

1   BBC News, June 5, 1998.
2   The Business Journal, San Jose, CA, June 1, 1998.
3   Probabilities of Year 2000 Damages, Capers Jones, 1998, www.spr.com.
4   Testimony before U.S. Senate Committee on Commerce, Science, and Transportation, April 28, 1998.
5   The Year 2000 Problem, J.P. Morgan Securities, Inc., May 15, 1997,
     www.jpmorgan.com/marketdataind/research/y2kupdate.

6   InformationWeek, April 13, 1998.
7   Business Insurance, May 4, 1998.

Chapter 8

1   Business Wire, April 29, 1998.
2   Asahi News Service, March 18, 1998.
3   Federal News Service, speech to the Brookings Institution, April 14, 1998.
4   M2 Presswire, April 22, 1998.
5   M2 Presswire, April 22, 1998.
6   M2 Presswire, April 22, 1998.
7   Toronto Star, August 10, 1998.

Chapter 9

1   Opening statement of Congressman Michael Castle at hearing of the House Banking Committee, April 28, 1998.
2   Los Angeles Times, May 3, 1998.
3   Los Angeles Times, May 3, 1998.
4   San Francisco Chronicle, May 9, 1998.
5   Cox News Service, April 24, 1998.
6   Agence France Presse, May 8, 1998.
7   San Francisco Chronicle, May 9, 1998.
8   Scotland on Sunday, July 19, 1998.
9   The Daily Telegraph, June 8, 1998.
10   The Daily Telegraph, June 8, 1998.
11   The Daily Telegraph, June 8, 1998.
12   The Daily Telegraph, June 11, 1998.
13   The San Francisco Chronicle, May 9, 1998.
14   The Irish Times, July 1, 1998.
15   Los Angeles Times, March 28, 1998.
16   Los Angeles Times, March 28, 1998.
17   Defense News, June 7, 1998.
18   Defense News, June 7, 1998.
19   Forbes, June 15, 1998.
20   Financial Times London, April 23, 1998.
21   Financial Times London, April 23, 1998
22   Financial Times London, April 23, 1998.
23   Milwaukee Journal Sentinel, June 28, 1998.
24   The Bulletin's Frontrunner, April 28, 1998.
25   Sydney Morning Herald, May 12, 1998.
26   Telecomworldwire, May 8, 1998.
27   Computer Business Review, February 1, 1998.
28   Sydney Morning Herald, June 9, 1998.
29   Computing Canada, March 9, 1998.
30   Canada News Wire, April 7, 1998.
31   The Sentinel, Orlando, FL, April 22, 1998.
32   Washington Post, May 5, 1998.
33   Reuters, June 29, 1998.
34   InfoWorld Electric, October 27, 1997.
35   The Times (London), May 20, 1998.
36   Scripps Howard, May 29, 1998.
37   Scripps Howard, May 29, 1998.
38   M2 Presswire, February 19, 1998.

Chapter 10

1   The Hartford Courant, May 27, 1998.
2   USA Today, May 11, 1998.
3   TechWeb News, May 24, 1998.
4   CNNfn, May 5, 1998.
5   The Hartford Courant, May 27, 1998.
6   CNNfn, May 5, 1998.

Chapter 11
1   Sky & Telescope, May 1998.
2   Press Association Newsfile, June 12, 1998.
3   AAP Newsfeed, April 28, 1998.
4   Stuart News/Port St. Lucie News, March 14, 1998.
5   Newsday, May 5, 1998.
6   San Diego Union-Tribune, June 21, 1998.
7   Stuart News/Port St. Lucie News, March 14, 1998.
8   San Diego Union-Tribune, June 21, 1998.
9   San Diego Union-Tribune, April 28, 1998.
10   Deutsche Press-Agentur, June 20, 1998.

Chapter 12
1   Washington Times, May 7, 1998.
2   Washington Post, May 7, 1998.
3   Florida Times-Union, April 1, 1998.
4   NASA Web site: www.science.msfc.nasa.gov, April 13, 1998.
     The Gazette (Montreal), April 11, 1998.
6   Sun-Sentinel (Ft. Lauderdale), March 8, 1998.
7   AAP Newsfeed, June 9, 1998.
8   The Gazette (Montreal), April 11, 1998.
9   The Millennium Sun-Spot Bug, March 1998.
10   Florida Today Space Online, April 10, 1997.

Chapter 13
1   CBS This Morning, May 21, 1998.
2   Rocky Mountain News, May 10, 1998
3   GAO Report to Congress: Year 2000 Computer Problems Threaten
     DOD Operations, April 1998.
4   The Daily Oklahoman, June 26, 1998.
5   GAO Report to Congress: Year 2000 Computer Problems Threaten
     DOD Operations, April 1998.
6   Washington Post, June 12, 1998.
7   Washington Post, June 12, 1998.
8   Washington Post, June 12, 1998.
9   Testimony before Senate Committee on Armed Services, June 4, 1998.
10   Testimony before Senate Committee on Armed Services, June 4, 1998.
11   Testimony before Senate Committee on Armed Services, June 4, 1998.
12   M2 Presswire, July 2, 1998.
13   Boston Globe, June 21, 1998.
14   Sunday Times (London), March 22, 1998.
15   Sunday Times (London), March 22, 1998.
16   Sunday Times (London), March 22, 1998.
17   Federal Document Clearing House, Inc., July 6, 1998.
18   Rocky Mountain News, May 10, 1998.
19   Rocky Mountain News, May 10, 1998.
20   Rocky Mountain News, May 10, 1998.
21   Rocky Mountain News, May 10, 1998.
22   National Journal, June 22, 1998.
23   Reuters, July 14, 1998.
24   Testimony before Senate Armed Services Committee, June 4, 1998.
25   Testimony before Senate Armed Services Committee, June 4, 1998.
26   Testimony before Senate Armed Services Committee, June 23, 1998.
27   Russia Today, June 29, 1998.
28   Reuters, August 12, 1998.
29   Armed Services Newswire, May 18, 1998.
30   Reuters, June 17, 1998.
31   CNN, June 14, 1998.
32   AAP Newsfeed, April 30, 1998.

33   AAP Newsfeed, April 30, 1998.
34   Chicago Tribune, June 25, 1998.
35   Defense Week, June 29, 1998.
36   Network World, March 9, 1998.
37   Testimony before Senate Armed Services Committee, June 23, 1998.
38   Federal Computer Week, August 24, 1998.
39   Memorandum For Secretaries of the Military Departments, Office of the Secretary of Defense, August 1998.
40   Reuters, June 5, 1998.
41   Reuters, June 5, 1998.

Chapter 14
1   Associated Press, February 25, 1998.
2   Waikato Times (Hamilton, New Zealand), March 7, 1998.
3   CNET NEWS.com, June 12, 1998.
4   MSNBC, June 12, 1998.
5   ComputerWorld, May 15, 1998.
6   San Jose Mercury News, August 1, 1998.
7   Orlando Sentinel, May 25, 1998.
8   ITAA Year 2000 Outlook, January 23, 1998.
9   ITAA Year 2000 Outlook, January 23, 1998.
10   Electrical World, March 1998.
11   CBN News, June 9, 1998.
12   Testimony before Senate Special Committee on the Year 2000 Technology Problem, June 12, 1998.
13   CBN News, June 9, 1998.
14   Orlando Sentinel, May 25, 1998.
15   MSNBC, June 12, 1998.
16   Orlando Sentinel, May 25, 1998.
17   San Jose Mercury News, August 1, 1998.
18   The Australian, March 2, 1998.
19   Netly News, May 13, 1998.
20   Testimony by John Laakso before House of Representatives Subcommittee on Technology, May 14, 1998.
21   ComputerWorld, May 25, 1998.
22   Statement before House of Representatives Subcommittee on Technology, May 14, 1998.
23   State before House of Representatives Subcommittee on Technology, May 14, 1998.
24   Statement before House of Representatives Subcommittee on Technology, May 14, 1998.
25   Statement before House of Representatives Subcommittee on Technology, May 14, 1998.
26   Computergram International, July 28, 1998.
27   New York Times, July 9, 1998.
28   New York Times, August 22, 1998.
29   Earth in Space, Vol. 9, No. 7, American Geophysical Union, March 1997.
30   Earth in Space, Vol. 9, No. 7, American Geophysical Union, March 1997.
31   News World Communications, December 8, 1997.
32   Earth in Space, Vol. 9, No. 7, American Geophysical Union, March 1997.
33   News World Communications, December 8, 1997.
34   The Australian, August 6, 1998.
35   Sunday Times (London), February 15, 1998.
36   MSNBC, June 12, 1998.

Chapter 15
1   Deseret News, June 16, 1998.
2   ComputerWeekly, November 6, 1998.
3   ComputerWeekly, March 5, 1998.
4   M2 Newswire, July 8, 1998.
5   Computingnet News Desk, August 13, 1998.
6   The Ottawa Citizen, July 7, 1998.

Chapter 16
1   Testimony before House of Representatives Subcommittee on Oversight of the House Ways and Means Committee, June 16, 1998.
2   Statement before Senate Special Committee on the Year 2000 Technology Problem, July 31, 1998.

3   Statement by Gerard Roth before House of Representatives Ways and Means Subcommittee on Oversight, June 16, 1998.
4   MSNBC, June 16, 1998.
5   Statement by Gerard Roth before House Ways and Means Subcommittee on Oversight, June 16, 1998.
6   TechWeb News, April 28, 1998.
7   Statement by Gary Beach before Senate Special Committee on the Year 2000 Technology Problem, July 31, 1998.
8   Statement by Gary Beach before Senate Special Committee on the Year 2000 Technology Problem, July 31, 1998.
9   Federal News Service, April 28, 1998.
10   AFR Net Services Financial Review, June 29, 1998.

Chapter 17
1   Biography, Dr. Ed Yardeni's Economic Network, www.yardeni.com
2   The Ottawa Citizen, May 14, 1998.
3   Dr. Yardeni's Y2K Net Book, www.yardeni.com.
4   The Ottawa Citizen, May 14, 1998.
5   The Ottawa Citizen, May 14, 1998.
6   Internet forum hosted by Peter de Jager, Ed Yardeni on Merrill Lynch Y2K study, July 11, 1998.
7   Harvard Business Review, July-August 1998.
8   The American Banker, February 18, 1998.
9   CNET NEWS.COM, July 7, 1998.
10   Federal Reserve System Web site, www.bog.frb.fed.us/y2k.
11   Bloomberg News, August 8, 1998.
12   Testimony by Peter Miller before U.S. Senate Special Committee on the Year 2000 Technology Problem, July 6, 1998.
13   Washington Times, July 7, 1998.
14   AFX News, April 6, 1998.
15   Newsbytes, April 8, 1998.
16   Newsbytes, April 8, 1998.
17   News release from Bank for International Settlements, www.bis.org/wnew.
18   News release from Bank for International Settlements, www.bis.org/wnew.
19   Speech to Bank for International Settlements, www.webcom.com/~yardeni/public/y_19980407.pdf.
20   Testimony before House of Representatives Committee on Banking and Financial Services, March 24, 1998.
21   Testimony before House of Representatives Committee on Banking and Financial Services, June 23, 1998.
22   Speech to Bank for International Settelements, www.webcom.com/~yardeni/public/y_19980407.pdf.
23   Reuters, January 16, 1998.
24   Associated Press Worldstream, August 11, 1998.
25   Boston Business Journal, July 27, 1998.
26   Washington Times, July 22, 1998.
27   Washington Times, July 12, 1998.

Chapter 18
1   Mealey's Year 2000 Report, June 1998.
2   Reuter's, August 7, 1998.
3   National Underwriter, June 15, 1998.
4   TechWeb News, August 5, 1998.
5   BusinessToday.com, May 17, 1998.
6   The Times (London), July 25, 1998.
7   Business Insurance (Crain Communications), June 29, 1998.
8   USA Today, August 12, 1998.

Chapter 19
1   Washington Post, June 6, 1998.
2   New York Times, June 6, 1998.
3   Statement before House of Representatives Subcommittee on Government Reform, February 4, 1998.
4   Statement before House of Representatives Subcommittee on Government Reform, February 4, 1998.
5   New York Times, January 29, 1998.
6   Traffic World, January 12, 1998.
7   Traffic World, February 16, 1998.
8   Statement before House of Representatives Subcommittee on Aviation, March 5, 1998.
9   Statement before House of Representatives Subcommittee on Aviation, March 5, 1998.

10   Statement before House of Representatives Appropriations Subcommitee on Transportation, February 3, 1998.
11   Statement before House of Representatives Subcommittee on Aviation, March 5, 1998.
12   ComputerWorld, January 19, 1998.
13   Statement before House of Representatives Subcommittee on Aviation, March 5, 1998.
14   Washington Post, August 7, 1998.
15   ComputerWorld Today, August 3, 1998.
16   Air Safety Week, February 2, 1998.

Chapter 20
1   Fortune, April 27, 1998.
2   ComputerWorld, June 22, 1998.
3   InternetWeek, August 17, 1998.
4   Computer Weekly, January 29, 1998.
5   TechWeb (CMPnet), August 9, 1998.
6   TechWeb (CMPnet), August 9, 1998.

Chapter 21
1   ABCNews.com, "Community Farms Take Root," 1998.
2   Statement before U.S. Senate Committee on Agriculture, Nutrition, and Forestry, July 22, 1998.
3   Statement before U.S. Senate Committee on Agriculture, Nutrition, and Forestry, July 22, 1998.

Chapter 22
1   The Sunday Times (London), May 31, 1998.
2   CNET News.com, June 17, 1998.
3   Reuters, May 21, 1998.
4   Shipping Times (Singapore), June 17, 1998.
5   Journal of Commerce, June 22, 1998.
6   ComputerWeekly, May 28, 1998.
7   Speech before Sixth North Sea Conference, The Petroleum Economist, April 21, 1998.
8   World Oil, April 1998.
9   Speech before Sixth North Sea Conference, The Petroleum Economist, April 21, 1998.
10   Octane Week, July 20, 1998.

Chapter 23
1   Opening statement before Special Senate Committee on the Year 2000 Technology Problem, July 23, 1998.
2   PR Newswire, July 23, 1998.
3   The Bond Buyer, May 27, 1998.
4   The Sunday Times, May 3, 1998.
5   Statement before Senate Special Committee on the Year 2000 Technology Problem, July 23, 1998.
6   Statement before Senate Special Committee on the Year 2000 Technology Problem, July 23, 1998.
7   ComputerWorld, August 17, 1998.
8   Statement before Senate Special Committee on the Year 2000 Technology Problem, July 23, 1998.
9   Statement before Senate Special Committee on the Year 2000 Technology Problem, July 23, 1998.
10   Statement before Senate Special Committee on the Year 2000 Technology Problem, July 23, 1998.

Chapter 24
1   Statement before House of Representatives Subcommittee on Government Management, Information and Technology, June 22, 1998.
2   Federal News Service, June 2, 1998.
3   PC World, July 8, 1998.
4   TechWeb News, June 29, 1998.
5   Federal News Service, June 2, 1998.
6   MSNBC, June 2, 1998.
7   Associated Press, May 8, 1998.
8   ComputerWorld, August 6, 1998.
9   GAO letter report: GAO/AIMD-98-6, October 22, 1997.
10   GAO letter report: GAO/AIMD-98-6, October 22, 1997.
11   Letter from Senator Charles Grassley, December 18, 1997.
12   Federal News Service, June 2, 1998.
13   CNET NEWS.com, May 8, 1998.

14   New York Times, May 8, 1998.
15   Milwaukee Journal Sentinel News, July 28, 1998.
16   The Plain Dealer, July 7, 1998
17   CIO Magazine, August 1, 1998.
18   Washington Post, August 4, 1998.
19   Rocky Mountain News, August 19, 1998.

Chapter 25
1   Christian Science Monitor, May 7, 1998.
2   WorldNet Daily, June 18, 1998.
3   Montrealgazette.com, July 7, 1998.
4   Center for Strategic and International Studies conference, June 2, 1998.
5   BBC News, June 16, 1998.
6   BBC News, May 8, 1998.

Chapter 26

A   Through the Eyes of the Enemy, Regnery Publishing, Inc., 1998.
B   The Sunday Times (London), June 14, 1998.
C   Testimony before House of Representatives Subcommittee on Military Research and Development, October 1, 1997.
D   Testimony before House of Representatives Subcommittee on Military Research and Development, October 1, 1997.
E   Scottish Daily Record & Sunday Mail, October 5, 1997.
F   Testimony before House of Representatives Subcommittee on Military Research and Development, October 1, 1997.
G   Washington Times, April 1, 1997.
H   Washington Times, April 1, 1997.
I   New York Times, April 16, 1996.
J   Gannett News Service, March 31, 1998.
K   Asia Times, April 3, 1997.
L   BBC News, July 16, 1996.